THE UNDISCOVERED
PAUL ROBESON

THE UNDISCOVERED PAUL ROBESON

Quest for Freedom, 1939–1976

Paul Robeson Jr.

John Wiley & Sons, Inc.

Published by John Wiley & Sons, Inc., Hoboken, New Jersey
Published simultaneously in Canada

For general information about our other products and services, please contact our Customer Care Department within the United States at (800) 762-2974, outside the United States at (317) 572-3993 or fax (317) 572-4002.

Wiley also publishes its books in a variety of electronic formats. Some content that appears in print may not be available in electronic books. For more information about Wiley products, visit our web site at www.wiley.com.

ISBN: 978-0-471-40973-1

Printed in the United States of America

10 9 8 7 6 5 4 3 2 1

To my late son, David, who possessed vision beyond his years, gave of himself to many, and bore burdens which were too heavy.

To my daughter, Susan, who deeply understands my father's spirit.

To my wife, Marilyn, whose dedicated and loving support made it possible for me to finish this book.

The artist must take sides. He must elect to fight for freedom or slavery. I have made my choice. I had no alternative.

—PAUL ROBESON, 1937

CONTENTS

Photo galleries begin on pages 78, 185, and 277.

PREFACE

"I AM LOOKING FOR FREEDOM"

In this second volume of *The Undiscovered Paul Robeson*, which covers the years from 1939 until my father's death in 1976, I have drawn heavily upon the vast collection of family papers, photographs, clippings, and phonograph records that my mother, Eslanda, gathered and preserved over more than four decades. These materials make up the Paul and Eslanda Robeson Collections and are deposited at Howard University's Moorland-Spingarn Research Center in Washington, D.C. However, my personal insights and my feel for the historical context of the latter part of Paul Robeson's story derive primarily from the direct experiences I shared with him over thirty-six years.

My relationship with my father broadened and deepened as I matured and he gradually shared more aspects of his life with me. Like him, I loved music, sports, chess, the Russian language, and reading. He went to considerable lengths to stimulate those interests of mine, and especially to help me develop a growing intellectual curiosity. He was a thinker and a teacher at heart, and derived great pleasure from mind games with ever-changing rules. I found such encounters fascinating and rewarding, because from them I learned as much about his way of thinking as I did about the subjects he illuminated for me.

During my college years, he introduced me to his closest circle of friends, took me along to his rehearsals and performances. We had long conversations about politics, culture, race, and ideology. When I was twenty-one, he accepted me into his inner council of advisers, and I worked closely with him in several different capacities during the next twenty-five years.

While it is true that a son's perspective is inevitably personal, mine is also closely informed by my father's words and eyewitness accounts of his life and times.

In this volume, I tell the dual story of my father's rise to the pinnacle of success and his determined use of this stature to advance the struggle of his people for full U.S. citizenship. By the mid-1940s, he symbolized the best in America and his name was a household word to millions. He had become a superstar, referred to as "America's Number One Negro."[1] Throughout his rise, Paul continually challenged the foundations of American racism. As he put it, "I am looking for freedom—full freedom, not an inferior brand."[2]

Paul's impact as an artist and spokesperson aroused the opposition of the U.S. government and compelled him to face critical personal, political, and artistic choices. This is the story of the choices he made and their consequences.

My first volume of *The Undiscovered Paul Robeson*, which covered the years 1898–1939, explored the path Paul Robeson traversed as a child of destiny—from motherless child to scholar and athlete, to titan of the theater, concert stage, and film, and then to leading spokesperson for the causes of antiracism, antifascism, and anticolonialism. The vast arc of development encompassed by those forty-one years was anchored to his value system—the cultural traditions of southern field slaves that had been transmitted to him by his father, an escaped field slave who became a minister.

Against the backdrop of the emerging Harlem Renaissance, he established the foundation of his subsequent career. He became an honor student and All-America football star at Rutgers College and financed his studies at Columbia Law School by playing professional football. In 1921, he married Eslanda Cardozo Goode, a Columbia University graduate student two years his senior from a prominent black Washington, D.C., family. Then, with Eslanda's encouragement and support, he redirected his talents to the performing arts. Six years later, he was being hailed as America's foremost black actor, a leading recording artist, and a bright new singing star of the concert stage.

To escape the stifling racial environment in the United States, Paul departed to London in 1927 and chose to live there for twelve years, returning home only for concert tours, to make films, and to perform in the theater. In London he found a far more diverse world than the one he had lived in at home. He studied African cultures at London University and met leaders of the anticolonial freedom movements throughout Africa and Asia. His search for folk songs of many lands launched him into the continuous study of a variety of languages, including two African languages, German, Italian, French, Spanish, and especially Russian.

From 1930 through 1932, Paul took the time to reflect upon the personal and public aspects of his burgeoning career. The more he reflected, the more clearly he understood that he had to make some basic personal decisions. He chafed under what he viewed as Eslanda's excessive control of all aspects of his artistic career, whereas Eslanda felt she had earned the right to an unlimited partnership. She wanted a closed marriage in which she could count on his fidelity, but he insisted that she agree to a discreetly open one. After a stormy two-year separation, Paul ended his vacillation. He resolved to reconcile permanently with Eslanda despite their differences. The skein of their complex relationship remains a central aspect of my narrative in this volume.

In 1934, Paul, who was fluent in Russian, accepted an invitation from the famous Soviet filmmaker Sergei Eisenstein to visit the Soviet Union. En route to Moscow, he had to change trains in Hitler's Berlin. After being menaced by a ring of Nazi storm troopers on the station platform just before boarding the Moscow train, he likened the city's racial climate to that of Mississippi and vowed to "fight fascism wherever I find it from now on."

His warm and respectful reception in Russia stood in dramatic contrast with the racist Nazi hostility. Everywhere he went, ordinary Russians and high Soviet officials welcomed him as an honored guest. At the end of the visit he said, "Here for the first time in my life I walk in full human dignity."[3]

Upon his return to London, he concentrated heavily on his work in commercial film. However, he found that no major studio would permit him to cross the boundary between a tragic black hero who is a victim and an epic black hero who triumphs over all odds. His response was to turn his back on the commercial film industry at the peak of his career. By the mid-1930s, Paul was speaking his mind freely about both cultural and political issues, flouting the custom that constrained artists from taking political positions. Despite his left-wing political views, his popularity as a concert favorite, recording artist, stage actor, and film star continued unabated as he sang concerts across England at low prices that working people could afford.

In 1939, as World War II began, Paul decided to end his twelve-year stay in England and return permanently to the United States.

ACKNOWLEDGMENTS

I could not have written this book without my parents' letters, notes, and manuscripts so carefully preserved by my mother and have relied greatly on the numerous conversations and interactions with my parents, which took place over many years. I have also drawn upon conversations, over the years, with many of their friends and acquaintances.

My wife, Marilyn, typed the manuscript and editorial corrections, in addition to providing vital assistance in making editorial decisions. My daughter, Susan, read through two versions of the manuscript and made valuable comments and suggestions.

I deeply appreciate the efforts of two acquaintances who provided me with my father's medical records from the Priory Hospital in London and Gracie Square Hospital in New York, respectively. These records, which were denied to me, proved to be invaluable in evaluating my father's medical treatment.

My thanks go to all those—both activists and elected officials—who were responsible for the enactment of the Freedom of Information Act. The materials I was able to obtain under this legislation reveal the vast scope of the repressive actions of the U.S. government against my father.

My appreciation to Carole Hall, who was my Wiley editor for the first part of this book. I am especially grateful to Hana Lane, my new editor at Wiley, for guiding and encouraging me during the most difficult phase of my endeavors. My thanks to the entire dedicated team at Wiley that has produced the book.

My literary agent and longtime friend Lawrence Jordan helped me to conceive the idea of writing this book in two volumes and then with characteristic dedication and patience saw the idea through to fruition.

I
"AMERICA'S NUMBER ONE NEGRO"

(1939–1945)

Paul with his Othello beard at the Enfield
house in Connecticut, 1945. *Photo by Eslanda
Robeson. From the personal collection of Paul Robeson Jr.*

Paul speaking at a meeting in New York, 1939.
*Photo by Eslanda Robeson. From the personal collection of
Paul Robeson Jr.*

I

THE CALLING

(1939–1940)

On October 23, 1939, my father, Paul Robeson, the American singer, actor, and movie star, strode off the gangplank of the USS *Washington* in New York Harbor. He had come home from England with my mother, Eslanda (Essie), myself, and his longtime accompanist Lawrence "Larry" Brown one month after the start of World War II in Europe. In the wake of Hitler's invasion of Poland and the subsequent declaration of war against Germany by Britain and France, Paul, after twelve glorious years in London, had decided he must return to his native Harlem to be with his people during a time of international crisis.

Essie, gracefully regal in her manner, remained beautiful at forty-four. Although a wide streak of gray ran through her hair, her light olive complexion remained as smooth as ever, and her vivacious personality had the same irresistible charm. Her five-foot-two-inch frame was beginning to thicken, but she countered with a fashionable wardrobe, an ever-expanding intellect, and undiminished energy. Larry, forty-eight, handsome, elegantly dressed, moved with an athletic grace that reflected his young days as one of Florida's top amateur boxers. Paul, even in the swirl of passengers debarking at the Port of New York, was the center of attention. He had sailed out of that same harbor twelve years earlier as the "King of Harlem," and now he returned as an international celebrity.

He cut a striking figure. At forty-one years of age, with no trace of gray hair, standing six feet three inches tall with broad shoulders, a barrel chest, and a still narrow waist, he towered over most of the crowd. The engaging smile flashing in his dark brown face, the large, wide-set, expressive eyes, and his huge, athletic body gliding forward made him instantly recognizable. Admirers called to him from all sides. Gripping his music briefcase in his left hand, he saluted them with his right, tipping his fashionable Stetson hat. Two customs officials, one white and one black, who had hurried out to meet our party as if we were visiting royalty, led the way.

Grandma Goode, Essie's mother, and a small group of friends greeted us as we emerged from the customs area. Ramrod straight, with her iron gray hair, high-top shoes protruding from under a long black dress, a cane, and a piercing gaze, Grandma was a disciplinarian. She had been my primary caregiver until my father liberated me a few years earlier to live with him and my mother, and I hoped that this arrangement would continue. The exchange of greetings was soon interrupted by the approach of a large group of reporters who bombarded Paul with questions, most of them controversial. Why had he returned from "exile in London"? What was his "current attitude on the race issue"?

In step with the rising black resistance to segregation, Paul was determined to make U.S. racism the main issue. He replied, "My roots are here, and I always expected to come back. In England I considered problems from the point of view of Africa; in this country I look at everything from the point of view of the Negro worker in Mississippi. I wanted success not for money, but so that I could say what I wanted."

"Are you a communist, Mr. Robeson?" a reporter from the Hearst press yelled in response.

"I am not a communist, and I am not a fellow traveler; I'm an antifascist," Paul shot back.

"What about the Stalin-Hitler nonaggression pact?" another reporter challenged.

"No matter what other countries do, including Russia," Paul answered, "I think America should play a key role in building a worldwide antifascist coalition. You don't negotiate with fascists—you fight them."

"But why won't you criticize Stalin?" the reporter persisted.

"Because in Russia I didn't find any race prejudice," Paul answered curtly.[1]

For the third time, Essie, who didn't think Paul should deliberately antagonize the press, tried to terminate the impromptu press conference. The first time, Paul had ignored her. The second time, he had waved her off peremptorily. Now he shrugged good-naturedly, waved, turned abruptly on his heels, and glided off with huge, rapid strides. Essie quickly organized us to fall in behind him, effectively blocking off the press. Over the next several days, Paul arranged multiple interviews with the black press to make certain that his message was disseminated accurately to a nationwide black audience. His subtext conveyed the view that white racists were the main enemies of blacks and that Hitler's Nazis were just like the racists. The Soviet people, who were strongly antiracist and anticolonialist, were the allies of blacks.

For the next few weeks, we lived with Hattie and Buddy Bolling in their comfortable Harlem home, a huge apartment occupying most of the top floor at 188 West 135th Street in Harlem. To my great relief, I stayed there with my parents instead of being shunted off to live with Grandma in her Greenwich Village apartment. Hattie, a heavyset "earth mother" figure in her late forties with a smooth brown complexion and an outgoing disposition, had played the role of older sister to Essie for many years. Buddy, a thin, smallish man ten years older than she, worked at a service job in a major downtown office building. He smoked cigars, told wonderful stories, and had a dry sense of humor. The foursome shared a love for bid whist and spent long evenings at the card table.

Paul rehearsed regularly with Larry, who lived on the floor below. Partners since 1925, the two men had become one of the world's best-known musical teams. Larry was a brilliant arranger and sensitive accompanist. He had helped Paul construct a vast repertoire of the world's folk songs and provided a tenor counterpoint to Paul's bass baritone. Essie prodded Paul to accept any appropriate offer and make a quick reentry onto the American cultural scene. After his long absence abroad, procrastinating even a short while might jeopardize the impending lucrative fall-winter concert season. Paul rebuffed her good-naturedly, believing that an ideal offer would come his way. It soon did.

• • •

The *Pursuit of Happiness Hour* was one of the most popular prime-time entertainments, radio being the principal mass medium of the day. The show's producer, Norman Corwin, was a progressive activist with a keen ear for patriotic songs, and the left-wing composer Earl Robinson had written an eleven-minute-long populist cantata titled "Ballad of Uncle Sam." Corwin had a hunch that Robinson's tribute to democracy would appeal to a sorely divided nation, where conservatives were fiercely attacking liberals over Roosevelt's New Deal and the new labor unions battled management to organize industrial plants. After hearing Robinson perform the cantata, Corwin renamed it "Ballad for Americans" and, with Robinson's enthusiastic agreement, called Bob Rockmore, Paul's combined attorney, agent, financial manager, and friend, with an offer for Paul to sing it on his radio program.

Bob and his Russian-born musician wife, Clara, were both dear to Paul. Short, chain-smoking, balding, and about Paul's age, with piercing eyes and a businesslike manner, Bob had earned Paul's abiding trust. From a working-class Lower East Side Jewish background, he was a partner in the distinguished law firm Barron, Rice and Rockmore, and as one of the East Coast's most accomplished entertainment lawyers, he stayed keenly aware of Paul's professional and financial needs. Bob promptly forwarded Corwin's offer to Paul, along with the music for "Ballad for Americans" and an attached personal note from Corwin.

With Larry at the piano, Paul bit into the cantata like a ripe peach, savoring its everyday language and folk-inspired structure. From the outset of his singing career, Paul had rejected the classical operatic style. Instead, he had adapted his singing technique to his physical attributes. His vocal cords were not particularly strong, but his enormous fifty-one-inch chest expansion, wide throat, large palate, and broad nasal cavity were a sublime match for folk music.

Paul also realized that John LaTouche's simple lyrics were ideally suited to the delivery of a progressive message in song. Throughout the piece, soloist and chorus relate America's struggle for democracy. They tell about George Washington, Thomas Jefferson, and "Old Abe Lincoln, thin and long":

> His heart was high and his faith was strong;
> But he hated oppression, he hated wrong.

And he went down to his grave to free the slaves.
Man in white skin can never be free
While his black brother is in slavery.

However, the CBS three-minute time limit required pieces of the seamless eleven-minute cantata to be cut. Paul, with Essie's encouragement, decided he should preserve the artistic integrity of the piece and made Corwin a counteroffer. He proposed that the entire eleven minutes be broadcast and requested a fee of a thousand dollars. That sum was unheard of, especially for a black performer, and the three-minute maximum for a song was one of radio's most rigid standards. Corwin's boss at CBS refused to pay Paul's fee or program the full eleven minutes, but Corwin, not to be discouraged, asked Robinson to perform "Ballad" for a group of top CBS executives.

They were bowled over. "Wouldn't Robeson knock the hell out of this!" Vice President Bill Lewis exclaimed. CBS was ready to bet that the combination of the message and the messenger would be irresistible, and Lewis accepted Paul's terms. The agreement was signed and Paul plunged into intensive rehearsals with Robinson.[2]

At four-thirty on Sunday afternoon, November 5, 1939, six hundred people assembled in the main CBS studio, along with the CBS orchestra and chorus. For the next forty-five minutes, millions across the nation sat by their radios tuned to the *Pursuit of Happiness Hour* until finally the host, actor Burgess Meredith, announced, "What we have to say can be simply said. Democracy is a good thing. It works. Life, liberty, and the pursuit of happiness—of these we sing. 'Ballad for Americans'—and the singer, Paul Robeson."

Backed by orchestra and chorus, Paul's majestic voice rolled out over the airwaves, singing in praise of all the ordinary people who made the country great and kept it strong. The compelling, unifying message was that America could overcome any crisis because it put its hope in its people in all their diversity. The ending held out great hope for the future:

Out of the cheating, out of the shouting,
Out of the murders and lynching,
Out of the windbags, the patriotic spouting,
Out of uncertainty and doubting,
It will come again—our marching song will come again,

Simple as a hit tune, deep as our valleys,
High as our mountains, strong as the people who made it.
For I have always believed it,
And I believe it now,
And you know who I am—
AMERICAAAAA!

The ovation from the studio audience lasted for two minutes while the show was still on the air and continued for fifteen minutes thereafter. Hundreds of phone calls jammed CBS's Manhattan and Hollywood switchboards. Thousands of letters poured in requesting words, music, and recordings. "Ballad for Americans" became an instant hit. By popular demand, the radio broadcast was repeated with equal success on New Year's Day. Performances spread across the country among school choruses and choirs. The universally popular recording was issued a few months later. Paul Robeson was now the voice of America.[3]

Fresh from the success of "Ballad," Paul and Essie settled into living quarters of their own. It was a relief. For all of his sociability and energetic engagement with public affairs, Paul was an intensely private person. He thrived on study and solitude. The release of his creative powers required a quiet, comfortable, hospitable retreat from which he could venture forth at will from isolation to engagement. And, notwithstanding his nomadic spirit, he also craved a stable home base with a warm family hearth. Essie had provided this anchorage throughout the nineteen years of their marriage despite the emotional conflicts between them.

Since Paul wanted to live in Harlem, the center of black America's cultural and political influence, Essie found an ideal spot on Sugar Hill, the fabled enclave of the Harlem elite. Located at 555 Edgecombe Avenue, it was a spacious five-room apartment on the fourteenth floor with extensive views south and west. The apartment lent itself to studious work habits as well as to gracious entertaining. Above, on the penthouse floor, was a three-room apartment with a terrace where Grandma Goode and I would live.[4]

I was glad to be in Harlem despite being parked, once again, under Grandma Goode's authority. I accepted my exile to the penthouse with as much grace as a twelve-year-old could muster, but I spent as much time as I could with my parents downstairs. Seeking the closeness I had experienced with my father in London, I carefully observed his usual daily schedule. A late riser, he ordinarily ate a leisurely brunch while reading the morning papers. A spurt of work or study would follow. Currently, he was studying Chinese using his collection of books and records on the Chinese language. By late afternoon, he was ready to relax for a couple of hours before dinner.

After school one day, I found Grandma gone from the penthouse—an unusual occurrence. Spared of her organizing efforts, I dumped my books and headed downstairs in the hope that I might catch my father in a good mood for a chess game. My arrival interrupted a highly contentious family discussion taking place in the guest room. Grandma Goode was sitting on the bed, her jaw tight. My father, clearly in command, stood in the middle of the room wearing a calm but determined expression. My mother had taken up a position near the foot of the bed. She looked distraught and subdued.

I stopped just inside the room, taking everything in. After a brief silence, Paul looked at Essie and said, in a quiet but commanding voice, "Are you going to tell him?" Essie snapped back, "Well, since you've decided this, *you* should tell him." My father turned to me without hesitation. "I've decided you'll move in with Mama and me down here. We're going to be a regular family. This room is yours. You can bring your things down anytime you like."

I was both surprised and elated, but I took my cue from his matter-of-fact demeanor. "Okay," I said. "I'll go get them now."

It did not take long for Paul to feel at home again in Harlem. Strolling in its heartland around 135th Street and Seventh Avenue, he recalled his days as a local football hero. The Harlem YMCA down the street from Larry's apartment was a familiar landmark. His older brother Ben's church, Mother A.M.E. Zion (the second largest church in Harlem), on 137th Street between Seventh and Lenox avenues, was another.

Uncle Ben, a gentle dark-skinned father figure graying at the temples, was not as tall or broad as Paul but radiated a commanding presence. He welcomed Paul's visits, as did the parishioners when Paul occasionally came to Sunday services and sang with the senior choir. Essie, who had relinquished neither her long-standing remoteness from Ben nor her quasi-atheism, gave the church a wide berth.

Top celebrities now, Paul and Essie appeared together at important Harlem events and cultivated an influential social crowd. More often, Essie organized intimate parties or quiet evenings with friends. This group included educator Ira Reid and his wife, Gladys, Harlem lawyer Hubert Delany, and Dr. Louis Wright, the first black fire department surgeon, and his wife, Corinne. The couple I remember best, Walter White and his wife, Gladys, lived just a few blocks down Edgecombe Avenue and were important acquaintances. They had known my parents since the early 1920s. Walter, the longtime general secretary of the NAACP, was treated as the most important black leader by President Franklin D. Roosevelt.

Because Essie and Paul's white friends and acquaintances rarely came to Harlem in the evening, they would travel downtown to see them. Paul renewed his long-standing affair with designer Freda Diamond, whose husband, Alfred "Barry" Baruch, maintained a cordial relationship with Paul. Essie, despite her resentment, established a friendship with Freda. Both Paul and Essie revived their contacts with friends from the 1920s and added new ones from left-wing and liberal cultural circles.

Paul decided to keep a strict separation between his artistic performances and his political activity. Rockmore ably took care of his professional career but had neither the time nor the inclination to become involved in his political life. Consequently, Paul turned to Max Yergan to serve as his political aide and speechwriter. Max, the stocky, light-brown-skinned, erudite executive secretary of the Council on African Affairs, of which Paul was the chairman, had met the Robesons in the 1930s and found common ground with them. With the aid of scholar-researcher Alphaeus Hunton, he had made the council the leading U.S. organization concerned with African affairs. Its mission was to promote the independence of all African colonies and to support the full freedom of colored peoples throughout the world. Aside from his post as executive director of the council, Max was president of the National Negro Congress, which had strong roots in the black South. In his dual capacities, he maintained close ties with both the black elite and the communist-led left.

The council, funded through private contributions and public benefits, sponsored conferences and forums on current events and lobbied government officials. A permanent headquarters with a research library was maintained at 23 West 26th Street in Manhattan, and the membership of twenty to twenty-five, which included Essie, had ultimate decision-making power. Paul's political statements were often issued as press releases.

Paul established a link with the Communist Party USA through his close personal friend Benjamin J. Davis Jr. A top black communist leader, Davis was a well-known and popular Harlem figure. Almost as big as Paul, jovial Ben was a Harvard-trained lawyer who played the violin and had a passion for tennis.

Paul's connection with the Soviet Union was continued through his friendship with the Soviet ambassador to the United States, Konstantin Umansky. In his early forties, urbane, brilliant, witty, and gregarious, Umansky spoke perfect unaccented English and was highly knowledgeable about American politics and culture. He was also a canny judge of Soviet politics and shared some of his insights with Paul.

As the popularity of "Ballad for Americans" grew, Bob Rockmore sought a network radio slot for Paul. All attempts resulted in quick failures—American radio had no room for a regular black presence, no matter how great the talent. The networks were not ready to override the deep-seated racial bias of their affiliates throughout the South. Denied consistent radio work, Paul readily accepted an offer to narrate and sing in an independent documentary film on U.S. civil rights and labor struggles. *Native Land*, codirected by Leo Hurwitz and Paul Strand, with a score written by Marc Blitzstein, achieved the status of a classic in its genre. The film was not released until 1942 due to financial difficulties that Paul helped to resolve by personally raising funds. But substantive projects of this kind were unusual. Both Paul's color and his controversial political views kept the radio, film, and theater worlds at a distance. Undiscouraged, Paul sought a suitable Broadway play he could star in. One possibility was already on the table: the lead role producer Sam Byrd had offered him in the musical *John Henry*. The dramatic adaptation of the novel by white author Roark Bradford told an epic folktale about a legendary black railroad worker. It was consistent with Paul's beliefs, revealed some stirring truths about his people, and showcased his strengths as a performer. He thought it merited a gamble.

Essie, however, had her doubts. She had rejected an earlier version of the script on the grounds that it was poorly written and lacked a strong central character. As she put it:

> John Henry is always physically magnificent, but is in the end a dumb beast. I don't think you could do him. I think you could do a dumb, humorous, mischievous ne'er do well, but I don't think you could do a serious no-count character. You are now too aware, too definite-minded, too militant yourself, and you haven't the technical equipment to go against your set personality and quality.[5]

Two rewrites failed to change Essie's mind. Paul, however, calculated that even if the play failed, he would still be viewed as a marketable theatrical star. He felt it was worth the risk. Essie, highly skeptical, reluctantly agreed the project was worth a try.

In late November 1939, Paul began rehearsals for the pre-Broadway run of *John Henry*. The music by innovative New Orleans composer Jacques Wolfe proved true to the southern black folk idiom and comfortable to sing. The diffuse dramatic structure was tightened through painstaking trial and error. On December 11, 1939, a capacity audience at Philadelphia's Erlanger Theater gave Paul and the entire cast a rousing ovation. The most important critics divided three to two against the play but were unanimous in applauding its star. The drama editor in the December 12 issue of the *Philadelphia Daily News* summed up the prevailing view: "*John Henry* was a case of presenting one iridescent bubble as though it were an entire soap factory. Paul Robeson's bass-baritone voice lent an air of importance to the proceedings, despite their general unimportance. For his performance there is even higher praise." The play also fared badly with the Philadelphia public, and its reception in Boston was similar—a short run with fine performances, weak drama, mixed reviews, sparse audiences, but a personal triumph for Paul.

Two weeks later, *John Henry* opened at New York's Forty-fourth Street Theater to a fanfare of positive publicity. Byrd had hired a new director; there was less music and more of a story. The premiere performance drew an enthusiastic packed house that was about evenly divided between blacks and whites. The hundreds of Harlemites who had marched down to the theater created this highly unusual mix. Soon after the ovation from the first-nighters faded away, however, the play suffered the same fate that had befallen it in Philadelphia and Boston. All six of the major reviews hailed Paul's singing and acting, but five dismissed the play.[6]

With the show deeply in the red, Paul and Essie agreed with Bob's recommendation to close it down after only a week's run. The commercial failure was more precipitous than Paul expected, but he had managed to deliver a performance that achieved at least the minimum results he needed: excellent publicity and much acclaim. Brooks Atkinson's *New York Times* review said it all: "It serves chiefly to renew acquaintance with a man of magnificence who ought to be on the stage frequently in plays that suit him. For there is something heroic about this huge man with a deep voice and great personal dignity. Count as one of the theater's extravagances the fact that Paul Robeson is not an active figure in it."

Equally important, the play about a working-class hero had enhanced Paul's image as a man of his people. At the reception following the New York opening of the play, the artist Frank Herring approached him with the remark, "I'm painting your entire race from the lower crust up, until now I want to paint you." Paul replied, "Sir, you must excuse me, but I recognize no such distinction."[7]

When the exclusive Dutch Treat Club, a lily-white luncheon club whose membership comprised many of New York's outstanding writers and journalists, invited him to sing, Paul failed to honor the invitation and notified no one. The January 20, 1940, issue of the *New York World-Telegram* noted that the club had never suffered "such a complete and embarrassing stand-up," adding that one of the members subsequently recalled an incident in 1925 when the club had invited Paul to be the guest star and left him to eat by himself in another room.

After his back-to-back successes with "Ballad for Americans" and *John Henry*, lucrative professional offers came to him from all directions. However, few, if any, were even remotely consistent with the artistic and personal standards he required as a symbol of black male dignity. Among the offers he declined was a $5,000-a-week contract from Herman Stark, owner of the legendary Cotton Club, to head the club's lavish revue. Cordial as Paul was to the entertainment world at large, he had long since turned his back on entertaining in nightclubs.

While waiting for a suitable offer, Paul joined efforts to create opportunities for black actors uptown by supporting the organizers of the Negro Playwrights' Theater. His ongoing sponsorship of the theater culminated later that year in a prominent appearance with bandleader Cab Calloway, writer Richard Wright, and other Harlem celebrities at the opening of the play *Native Son* based on Wright's novel.[8] Paul also joined Essie and Bob Rockmore in lobbying theatrical producers to take on a Broadway production of Shakespeare's *Othello*. British actress Peggy Ashcroft, who had been Paul's Desdemona in the 1930 London production, agreed to undertake the role again, and Margaret Webster, one of England's leading Shakespearean directors, consented to direct, play the role of Emilia, and fulfill the role of coproducer.[9]

Although the press gave these efforts positive coverage, the leaders of the Broadway theater establishment, along with all of the major white producers and actors, gave the project a wide berth, fearing racial controversy. They assumed America was not yet ready for a black Othello who married a white Desdemona and strangled her onstage. Even Bob and Essie were not convinced that a Broadway production of *Othello* could be mounted at this time. They urged Paul to forget about it and take another crack at the movie industry. Paul would have none of this; he was determined to perform Othello on Broadway in a production over which he exerted control.

Little had changed on the international front between Paul's arrival in the United States in October 1939 and the closing of *John Henry* in January 1940. In the aftermath of the August 1939 Treaty of Nonaggression between Germany and the Soviet Union, the invasion of Poland by Nazi Germany from the west on September 1, and the immediately following annexation of the eastern half of Poland by the Soviet Union, World War II remained in its shadowboxing stage. There were no significant military clashes as the world waited to see whether Hitler's army would march east or west.

Against this backdrop, the Soviet Union's 1939–1940 "Winter War" against Finland greatly increased the American public's hostility toward Stalin's Russia. But Paul refused to criticize the Russians, maintaining steadfastly that their foreign policy was essentially defensive rather than aggressive. At the same time, he openly contradicted the Soviet Union's line, which was also the line of the U.S. Communist Party, that British and French imperialism on the one hand, and Nazi imperialism on the other hand, were *equally* the enemies of progressive humankind. In staking out his own independent position, Paul emphasized his consistent theme that the main enemy was Nazi Germany.

In a series of interviews, he said the goal of the current pro-fascist British and French governments—the "Munich men" who had appeased Hitler with the Munich accord in 1938—was to "save" Nazi Germany from Hitler. If they were successful in this, he said, they hoped to join a de-Hitlerized Germany in a war against communist Russia. Therefore the United States should stay out of the present war.

He added that the absence of significant military clashes between the British-French alliance and the Germans was a sure sign of a "phony war" designed to conceal negotiations between the "Munich men" and the anti-Hitler faction within the Nazi Party. The purpose of the negotiations was to establish "a Western civilization that would not include the Negro, just as it would also exclude Russia, Asia, Africa, China, Japan and India." Based on this analysis, Paul called for an all-out war against fascism led by a coalition of Britain, France, Russia, and the United States.[10]

Bob Rockmore warned Paul that radio network executives were complaining bitterly about his provocative pro-Russian statements, and his apparent immunity from punishment by the entertainment industry was vanishing. But to Bob's chagrin, Paul not only refused to participate in the widely popular theatrical benefits to raise money for "brave little Finland" but also publicly continued to support the Soviet Union's "defensive war" against "reactionary Finland." He shrugged off the resulting wave of criticism, replying that the anti-Soviet crusaders would soon "find themselves in the pro-fascist, pro-Hitler, pro-Mussolini camp."[11]

Despite these interviews, Paul's general popularity continued. At Hamilton College in upstate New York, where he received an honorary degree of doctor of humane letters on January 21, 1940, he gave his audience a glimpse of the broad cultural context that was the source of his political stands. He sang several songs, and then reflected briefly on the universality of diverse cultures. "In the future reorganization of the world," he said, "it is necessary to think of hundreds of millions of colored peoples belonging to other cultures. [At the same time], one can think of a synthesis of all cultures into one human culture."[12]

In April and May, the German army carried out its "lightning war" against Western Europe, occupying Norway and Denmark and sweeping across Holland and Belgium to outflank the French fortified zone from the north. France fell quickly, and the Germans soon reached the shores of the English Channel, where they began to prepare for an invasion of Great Britain. Winston Churchill came to power as prime minister on May 10, 1940, as the Nazis began their air war against Britain as the first stage of a full-scale invasion. Churchill's first official pronouncement pledged that his nation would never surrender to the Nazis and would fight them to the finish. He inspired his people to close ranks and crush Hitler's air assault.

As a result, Paul reversed his opposition to U.S. aid to Britain. However, this did not placate his critics, who demanded that he denounce the Soviet Union's foreign policy. Faced with lack of opportunity in radio, film, and theater, Paul concentrated on preparing for his first major U.S. concert tour in over five years. In view of his political vulnerability, he decided to stop making political statements until he completed the tour. In the interim, Rockmore scheduled him to appear at major special events during the spring and summer.

On May 13, 1940, Paul opened the Los Angeles Civic Light Opera Festival at the Philharmonic Auditorium with a week's run of the musical *Show Boat*. An all-star cast had been assembled, including several actors from the original 1927 production. Hattie McDaniel, who had played opposite Paul in the popular 1935 film and was a star in her own right, wrote to him regretting that she would miss the opening and hoping that she might be able to play her *Show Boat* role again. She added "an extra wish that 'Joe' will bring down the house with 'Old Man River' (as usual)." The press reported after opening night that Paul had "become an institution as 'Joe,' and when he entered the stage with a bale on his back the audience acted like a football cheering crowd, and almost forgot . . . the operetta."[13]

As he prepared for the concert season, Paul refined his interpretation of "Ballad for Americans," working out a solo version with

Earl Robinson and Larry. Robinson recalled Paul as being extremely cooperative: "He continually checked with me how I wanted a phrase sung, a line read." On June 25, in New York's Lewisohn Stadium, the capacity audience of fourteen thousand applauded for twenty minutes at the close of the concert, and the management was forced to douse the lights. On July 23, Paul was scheduled to sing a concert featuring "Ballad for Americans" in the Hollywood Bowl in Los Angeles. But his agent couldn't find him a hotel after two hours of trying. Paul told him to try again. Finally, a deluxe suite was found at the Beverly Wilshire for $100 a night (about $1,000 in today's currency), which Paul could have if he registered under a different name and agreed to take meals in his room. He took it.

Having arrived at the hotel a couple of days before the concert for rehearsals and publicity, Paul made it a point to spend a few hours every afternoon sitting conspicuously in the lobby. His purpose was to open the way for Marian Anderson, Roland Hayes, and anyone else to have a place to rest their heads when they next came to Los Angeles. And he succeeded, partially. The hotels were open to selected black guests after that.

The ingrained habits of racism ran deep in the concert world, but they came as a shock to Earl Robinson. On the morning of Paul's performance, the composer of "Ballad for Americans" got a taste of Jim Crow, Southern California style:

> As composer of the piece, I attended a breakfast given by the Hollywood Bowl Association on the morning of the concert. Paul didn't show up, but I didn't think much of it, figuring he was busy or sleeping late. That afternoon I asked him, "Where were you this morning?"
>
> "Where was I what?" he answered. Turned out, he had not been invited—the star of the show, the only person aside from soprano Lily Pons who could guarantee to fill the Bowl.

That evening, a record crowd of twenty-five thousand filled the Hollywood Bowl and gave Paul a great ovation, calling him back to the stage eight times.[14]

On July 28, Paul attracted 165,000 people, as black and white Chicagoans filled Grant Park and overflowed onto the surrounding lawns. This was a highly unusual show of racial unity in a city known for race riots. Chicago's black newspaper, the *Chicago Defender*, hailed Paul under the headline "Robeson 'Recaptures' Chicago":

> It is easy to understand why Paul Robeson is the most beloved and the greatest of [the] artists we have produced. Robeson is an artist-fighter for Negro America. Robeson is more than an ambassador for his people. He sings for freedom.
>
> Robeson the singer has learned the relation of art to politics and politics to art. He saw how some Negro artists are used to make a caricature of their own people, to play the Uncle Tom and buffoon. Robeson refused to be [either].
>
> The Negro artist must learn to be a spokesman for Negro freedom. This is what adds greatness to our art. It has made Robeson the greatest of our living artists, the spokesman in art for complete equality for us in all walks of life.

In August, Paul sang at Philadelphia's prestigious Robin Hood Dell before a capacity audience of six thousand, which accorded him "limitless cheers" for a program ranging from a group of spirituals and a Hebrew prayer, through English and Russian folk songs, to a solo arrangement of "Ballad for Americans." The inevitable encore, "Ol' Man River," capped the evening. The critics were no less appreciative than the audience.[15]

A few days later, Paul appeared in a summer theater production of *The Emperor Jones*. Written by Eugene O'Neill more than two decades earlier as a breakthrough in the portrayal of the black male with a measure of human dignity, the play was encumbered by stereotypes. Nevertheless, the erstwhile Pullman porter Brutus Jones had become a signature of Paul's to a degree almost matching the song "Ol' Man River."

Paul cut the word "nigger" from the script. He also asked director James Light and composer Colin McPhee to add new elements and construct innovative scenery. The weeklong August run of *Emperor* at the Country Playhouse in Westport, Connecticut, broke all records for that theater, and a second one-week run followed with equal success at the McCarter Theatre in Princeton, New Jersey.[16]

Paul accepted a major offer in October. John Hammond, of the Columbia Recording Corporation, talked him into doing a blues tribute to Joe Louis—"King Joe"—with Count Basie's jazz band.

Novelist Richard Wright had written the lyrics, and Basie himself had composed the song. With Paul singing, Hammond was convinced the recording would be a classic. Paul tried his best at the studio session, but it became obvious that the blues were not his forte. After the session, Basie and Paul joked about it, with Paul laughing good-naturedly at Basie's admonition: "You should stick to what you know." Ironically, the record, released on the Okey label, became an immediate best-seller—a tribute to the marketing power of four famous names.[17]

Bob Rockmore negotiated a pathbreaking concert tour contract for Paul. In addition to top fees, it included the highly unusual stipulation that he would not appear before segregated audiences. Paul shunned political appearances throughout the summer of 1940. Ironically, "Ballad for Americans" was featured at the nominating conventions of the Democratic Party, the Republican Party, and the Communist Party, but he refused to perform it at any of those venues.

Paul prepared for his tour systematically, remembering his past vocal difficulties under the stress of such grueling marathons lasting seven months or more. Working with Professor Harold Burris-Meyer of Stevens Institute of Technology, he participated in the development of an electronic sound system for the concert stage. The mechanism provided a sound envelope around Paul so he could easily hear himself while performing, allowing him to sing in a relaxed manner in large halls without forcing his voice. The equipment was simple and compact: a small microphone in front of the footlights fed the sound to an amplifier, and a small highly directional speaker at the side of the stage threw back significant harmonics to the performer without affecting the sound heard by the audience. He became so used to this device that whenever he sang without it on informal occasions he took to cupping his right hand to his ear to hear himself. They dubbed this pioneering system "Synthea."[18]

Paul invited Clara Rockmore, Bob's wife, to join him on the tour as the associate artist. Diminutive and charming, Clara was a brilliant musician and retired concert violinist. She cut a striking figure—large dark eyes, a flashing smile, and jet black hair framing a beautiful face with an alabaster complexion. Having emigrated from Russia in the 1920s, she remained steeped in Russian culture, and her fluent English was tinged with a piquant accent. She and Paul delighted in their long talks in Russian about music and Russian poetry.

Clara had mastered the theremin, the world's first electronic instrument, which she played almost magically by moving her hands in the air through electromagnetic and electrostatic fields. She was arguably the only person able to achieve the artistry and muscle control required to produce classical music on this instrument. Paul admired its violinlike, ethereal sound and asked her to play as a regular part of his concert program. Clara's keen intellect, broad range of interests, and vast musical knowledge belied her almost childlike manner. But at the beginning of the tour, Paul had to educate her in the grim realities of American race relations. One day she gave him a playful hug in public and he instantly detached himself from her, remonstrating, "Do you want to get me killed?"[19]

On tour, both Paul and Clara were in rare form. The headline in the October 2, 1940, issue of the *Manchester Union* of New Hampshire read, "Robeson Thrills Throng of 1,700; Clara Rockmore on Mysterious Theremin Shares Acclaim." The article hailed Paul's "flawless singing," which inspired demands for "encore after encore." On October 4, the *Troy Record* of upstate New York reported on a "performance that was an unforgettable event for Troy music lovers." Paul sang "with the fierce energy of groundswell emotion, or smoothly and sweetly with the lightness of an errant breeze."

On university campuses, in small cities, and in large urban centers, Paul's performances had to appeal to a wide variety of audiences. His populist repertoire of Negro spirituals and folk songs of many lands enthralled them all. A typical program consisted of an opening set of spirituals, a group of classical Russian songs, the patriotic favorite "Ballad for Americans," and a closing mix of traditional folk songs. Songs with more social significance were saved for the encores.

A few music critics questioned this emphasis. For example, an October 24 review in the *Minneapolis Star Journal* complained that Paul's program should have offered "greater [musical] tasks and more significant songs." Paul brushed aside these criticisms, noting with satisfaction the praise of the Mussorgsky songs he regularly included. He added several more classical songs with a folk base, including two main arias from Mussorgsky's opera *Boris Godunov*.

Despite the immense popularity of Paul's concerts, he was not universally welcomed. An ugly racial incident occurred at one of San Francisco's most famous restaurants, Vanessi's. When Paul's party went to eat there, they were refused service, and a scuffle nearly erupted between the owner and Paul. A lawsuit against the restaurant was brought by Paul along with eight black and white friends, but it never came to trial.[20]

By December 1940, Paul had established himself as arguably the most popular concert singer in the United States. His appeal lay not only in his singing but also in his stage persona. The lithe grace of his huge strides as he glided onto the stage, the relaxed and informal introductions of his songs, the stillness of his towering frame as he sang, and the range of emotions infusing his delivery combined to produce a compelling effect. As a Buffalo, New York, critic put it, "For Mr. Robeson the song he is singing—be it art-song, simple folk-tune or popular song of the day—is the most important thing. Unconventional, yes, and perhaps for the chance musical cultists or Brahmins who may have been present, uncomfortable; but for those who love beautiful and sincere singing, completely delightful."[21]

Clara toured for three seasons with Paul, growing to respect him as a musician. She never ceased to be amazed at the contrast between his calm dismissal of racial slights directed at him personally and his frightening anger at insults or violence directed at his people as a whole. In 1946, during a particularly vicious spate of violence against returning black war veterans in the South, she remembered him pacing the floor of her living room in such a rage that she felt compelled to calm him down.

Paul and Clara shared a unique relationship as intimate friends but not as lovers. I met Clara during those years, and we maintained a friendship until her death in 1999. Over several decades, we spent many hours talking about my father. She felt Paul made far too much of his inability to sight-read. While he could not spontaneously sing a musical composition at first sight, she knew him to read music, including orchestrations and choral arrangements, more than adequately for his performance needs. As to the issue of whether Paul should have studied opera, Clara, contrary to some critics, thought that singing opera and other classics such as German lieder would not have made him a greater singer and might well have diminished the unique quality of his voice.

The triumph of Paul's return to the American concert stage after an extended absence freed him to ignore the minority of music critics who continued to carp about his lack of "classical" repertoire and style. By creating an endearing populist image of himself in the mind of the public, he had become the singer who belonged to the people.

Writing to Paul on December 29, Brooks Atkinson, the theater critic of the *New York Times*, reverently expressed this phenomenon: "A few days ago I bought a copy of your 'Ballad for Americans.' I feel thankful for your voice . . . and for the fortitude and honesty of your character. They fill this extraordinary ballad with the sort of humanity I respect and love."[22]

2

THE QUEST

(1941)

On January 2, 1941, Paul sent a greeting of solidarity to the British People's Convention in London, an inclusive labor-based organization, identifying himself with their war against Nazi Germany: "All my warmest greetings. Feels strange not being there to do my bit. From here we eagerly follow your courageous struggle for the freedom and well-being not only of the English but of all peoples. Magnificent." His support of the British war effort and his urgent calls for the destruction of German fascism distinguished him from those on the left who supported the Soviet line equating British imperialism and Hitler's fascism. The recent Soviet replacement of Ambassador Umansky with Maxim Litvinov gave Paul the feeling that Stalin's policy was changing, since Litvinov favored an alliance with the United States and Britain against Hitler. Paul renewed the friendly acquaintance he had made with Litvinov during his 1934 visit to the Soviet Union.[1]

Conservatives in the U.S. government, greatly alarmed at the prospect of collaboration between the United States and the Soviet Union, intensified their investigation of anyone friendly toward Russia. On January 13, 1941, the first memorandum appeared in an FBI Robeson file that would grow to thousands of documents. The inspector of the U.S. Immigration and Naturalization Service office in Vancouver, Canada, wrote the following letter to his district director in Seattle:

> Robeson appeared early this winter in Vancouver under the auspices of Hilker Attractions. [blacked out] and [blacked out] told me that

23

the first person to telephone Robeson after his arrival was [blacked out], and that later he was visited in his room by two representatives of the Civil Liberties League, and by representatives of the local "Housewives League," which organization is known to include in its membership the wives of well known communists and which is rapidly becoming communistically controlled.

A note at the bottom indicated that the inspector had searched the Immigration Index as far back as 1923, the Naturalization Index back to 1929, as well as the Statistical Records from 1929 to 1941. But no useful additional information on Paul was uncovered.

A month later, the special agent in charge at the FBI's Seattle office forwarded the letter to FBI director J. Edgar Hoover with the comment that it referred to "PAUL ROBESON, prominent American vocalist and alleged member of the Communist Party." Hoover, who had become director of the Bureau in 1924, at the young age of twenty-nine, was a national icon on the strength of his crime-busting campaigns of the 1920s and 1930s. He had developed a passion for quelling political dissent during the rise of the industrial labor movement and was obsessively anticommunist. Hoover personally oversaw an open-ended investigation of Paul's activities, recruiting other government agencies in the process.

A July 29, 1941, memorandum appeared in Paul's file in the Division of Foreign Activity Correlation of the U.S. Department of State. It noted that a "Mr. Allan" of the Internal Revenue Service had reviewed Paul's file in a search for illegal political contributions. Included with the State Department memorandum was a note from Hoover requesting that the IRS review take its lead from two enclosed telephone logs. These logs, obtained from phone taps secretly installed on Hoover's orders without legal restraint or accountability, consisted of several conversations Paul had conducted with Bob Rockmore and Max Yergan concerning a proposed contribution by Paul to the Council on African Affairs.

The Roosevelt administration, however, considered Paul an important political asset in the effort to secure American public support for U.S. participation in a worldwide crusade against fascism. In January, Paul was invited to appear on a series of CBS radio broadcasts to the U.S. armed forces and the nation under the sponsorship of the

Council of National Defense and the War Department. The programs created by leading playwrights, performers, and producers dramatized key social problems whose "proper solution," according to an official of the Department of State, "will either make us or break us as a democracy under pressure." These popular nationwide broadcasts were well suited to Paul's compelling radio personality. After the programs were aired, Secretary of War Henry L. Stimson sent a letter of appreciation to Paul for "your contribution to the highly successful radio program 'Salute to the Champions.'"[2]

During the January–April 1941 phase of Paul's tour, he sang mostly in small and moderate-size towns where his reception was even more enthusiastic than in the larger, more sophisticated earlier venues. He also sang concerts at colleges and universities where the prices were far lower than in local concert halls and working people could afford to attend. Having successfully completed his first formal concert tour, Paul was in an excellent position to advance his career in theater, film, radio, and recording. Both Essie and Bob Rockmore urged him to move in this direction immediately. But to their chagrin, he chose to concentrate on the politics that he had been compelled to forgo while he was on tour.

Paul's immediate priority was support for the desperate Chinese resistance to Japanese occupation. He had begun to study Chinese songs of resistance to the Japanese invasion. Liu Liang-mo, secretary of the Shanghai YMCA and originator of the patriotic mass-singing movement in China, had met Paul in New York in December 1940. Soon after, Liu had written to Paul, offering to coach him both in Chinese and in the musical style required for the songs. The Chinese, he added, were "very anxious" to hear Paul sing patriotic and revolutionary songs of China, and that his doing so would "help China's struggle for liberation to an unimaginable extent." Paul had readily accepted Liu's suggestion, and by the spring he was singing several of the songs at benefits sponsored by the China Aid Council and United China Relief, national umbrella organizations.[3]

In late April, the Washington Committee for Aid to China booked Paul for a benefit at Constitution Hall. The news hit Washington like a bomb. The Daughters of the American Revolution, who had barred Marian Anderson from singing in Constitution Hall in 1939, denied access to Paul solely because he was black.

The sponsors asked Mrs. Cornelia Bryce Pinchot, wife of Pennsylvania's former governor and a close friend of Eleanor Roosevelt's, for urgent help. Mrs. Pinchot agreed to chair the benefit and organized a prestigious group of honorary sponsors headed by Mrs. Roosevelt, the Chinese ambassador to the United States, Hu Shih, Mrs. Francis Biddle (wife of the attorney general), and Mrs. Hugo Black (wife of the Supreme Court justice). Then she secured the seven-thousand-seat Uline Arena for April 25, only to learn that the arena had a policy of segregated seating.

Under pressure from Mrs. Pinchot, the arena management agreed to suspend this policy for the China benefit *only*. However, the controversy did not end there. With Paul's appearance as a powerful attraction, the Washington Committee for Aid to China turned to the large Washington, D.C., black community to help fill the Uline Arena. The China Aid Council struck an agreement with the local chapter of the National Negro Congress, which had an extensive black base. In return for selling 10 percent of the tickets in advance and working toward a black attendance of at least three thousand, the congress was offered 50 percent of the net ticket sales.

When Mrs. Pinchot learned of the organizers' agreement with the National Negro Congress, she precipitated yet another crisis. Angered by the communist connections of the congress and worried by the prospect of an audience including thousands of working-class blacks, Mrs. Pinchot decided to abort the event.

In a letter to Paul, she attempted to dissuade him from appearing. She began by asserting that "a number of complaints have been heard emanating from organizations and individual members of your race to the effect that the hall engaged for your concert discriminates against negroes [*sic*]." Then, mentioning that there were "a number of other reasons which it is unnecessary to burden you with," she announced that she, Mrs. Roosevelt, and the other honorary sponsors had decided to resign "because we are unwilling to ask a great negro [*sic*] artist to appear in any place which is believed to discriminate against members of his race."

In her draft of a proposed press release, which, along with her letter to Paul, she cleared with Mrs. Roosevelt, Mrs. Pinchot acknowledged that "even if the conditions set by the Negro Congress for withdrawal could have been met, the ramifications from the original errors have spread too far to be corrected."

Paul ignored Mrs. Pinchot's letter and press release. On the strength of his name, the Uline Arena was sold out to a mixed audience. No one missed the departed sponsors. The newspaper headlines declared, "Robeson Stirs Audience to Shouts," "Paul Robeson Sings to a Grateful Race," and "Audience in Storm of Applause."[4]

In the waning days of April, Paul costarred with jazz artist Benny Goodman in a concert of Russian music presented at New York's Carnegie Hall by the American Russian Institute. The program featured the music of Shostakovich, Prokofiev, Scriabin, and Mussorgsky, and included several renowned pianists, a string quartet, a quintet, Goodman's sextet, and Paul singing a variety of Russian songs.

Carnegie Hall was packed to capacity, with standing room filled. The house went wild when Paul made his entry. According to Howard Taubman, the *New York Times* music critic, "Paul Robeson stole the show. Singing songs in Russian—contemporary works as well as songs by masters of another day like Mussorgsky—he scored a stunning triumph."[5]

In May, Paul was still singing at major cultural events or benefit appearances for causes that were closest to his heart, despite his recent completion of a grueling seven-month concert tour. He appeared in Detroit on the heels of a United Auto Workers (UAW) strike at the Ford Rouge plant—the world's largest industrial unit. The strike had ended when Ford agreed to a union certification election between the Congress of Industrial Organization's (CIO) UAW and the American Federation of Labor's (AFL) union at all of the Ford plants. Black workers would be the decisive factor in the vote.

Back in December 1940, when Paul was in Detroit for a concert, he had made a strong statement supporting the CIO, which had established nonsegregated unions in contrast to the AFL's segregated local chapters. Leaflets with Paul's appeal had been distributed throughout the black community urging black workers to join the CIO's UAW. Now he arrived to campaign for the union in the last days before the May 21 vote on union certification.

On May 19, Paul sang and spoke to a crowd of a hundred thousand auto workers at a UAW rally in Detroit's Cadillac Square. Later that day and throughout the next two days until the close of voting, he campaigned at the shop gates of the Rouge and Lincoln plants, shaking hands and talking to the workers. In the evenings, he spoke and sang to the union organizers at union headquarters and appeared in the major black churches to sing and urge black workers to back the union.

His efforts made an impact on the election results. The UAW won a resounding victory: 70 to 27 percent in the Rouge plant, and 73 to 21 percent in the Lincoln plant.[6]

Paul enjoyed his political appearances, but Essie felt he made far too many and was missing a golden opportunity to capitalize on the momentum of his tour. Years later, he told me how one evening at dinner with Walter and Gladys White, Essie had spoken her mind: "Paul should just give up his Moses complex; he could be a Hollywood star. Our folks wouldn't follow him anyway. He's a singer, not a preacher." Paul's reply had been, "Well, Moses sure beats Uncle Tom." Gladys, catching the acerbic tinge in his tone, had quickly moved everyone to the living room for coffee and dessert.[7]

Bob Rockmore was more philosophical about Paul's political activity, although he shared Essie's opinions in this matter. He would shrug: "That's just Paul. Nobody's going to change him. He'll never be just an artist; he's more than that." Bob was often sorely tried. He found many performance opportunities for Paul, most of which Paul ended up rejecting. On the other hand, those few he accepted usually led to spectacular successes.[8]

Paul still managed to find time for many Harlem social functions, occasionally attending with Essie but most often showing up unaccompanied. He went to balls and benefits, sang at friends' weddings, gave free recitals for local institutions, and graced the position of leading example for black youth. The largest black newspaper, the *Baltimore Afro-American*, chose Paul as the top black performing artist of the year.

Paul and Essie continued to enjoy each other's company, especially when they spent quiet evenings with close friends like the McGhees and the Bollings, went to the theater, or met interesting celebrities. During Paul's long absences on tour, Essie kept busy with her writing and lecturing and spent time in her own wide circle of New York friends. As usual, she devoted a lot of time to me, attending my school functions, overseeing my homework, and keeping track of my social life.

However, Essie was not thriving in the big-city environment. Her persistent efforts to establish a writing career had borne meager fruit, and she realized there was little chance of achieving a significant presence in New York's highly competitive literary world. With her role in Paul's career management largely taken over by Rockmore, she sought status in her own right.

A country home within driving distance of New York, Essie thought, would fulfill one of her cherished dreams. With Paul poised to become the highest-paid concert singer in the country, the family could afford it, and establishing their primary residence in nearby Connecticut would reduce Paul's income tax dramatically. Essie also found a small apartment in the Harlem building where the Bollings and Larry lived that could serve as an ideal place when they visited New York together or when Paul spent extended periods there.

Paul initially resisted this idea, since home for him was New York City. Moreover, Essie's plan to have her mother live with us did not appeal to him. But in the end he felt that he could not deny Essie her dream. Rockmore agreed, somewhat reluctantly. This was enough encouragement for Essie. She bought a new car and soon unearthed a country estate in the small, all-white, semirural, middle-class community of Enfield in north-central Connecticut. About three hours from New York City and only eight miles from the culturally vibrant and ethnically diverse city of Springfield, Massachusetts, the spacious colonial house, tennis court, and recreation house situated on two and a half acres of land offered both Essie and Paul a near-perfect country retreat.

Although the house was in considerable disrepair and the grounds needed a lot of work, the $10,000 purchase price was strikingly low. "The Beeches," with four large columns bracketing the front door, offered twelve rooms, three baths, two sun porches on the ground floor, and several decks on the second floor. The third floor, in addition to guest rooms, provided a comfortable apartment for Cecelia Whitner, our part-time New York housekeeper and cook.

With monumental effort, careful thought, and considerable expense, Essie designed the renovation of the house and grounds to serve the entire family's needs admirably. We moved to Enfield in June 1941. Essie had already charmed the entire neighborhood into welcoming all the Robesons with open arms. And Paul did his part to win over our new neighbors when he showed up unannounced for the annual "Class Night" at Enfield High School, where I was enrolled, and sang four songs. Essie was deeply satisfied with the fruits of her labors.

In the Enfield house, my father was his usual affable self, accessible and full of good humor. He loved games and wasn't overly concerned with winning. For him they were primarily a source of enjoyment and education, rather than a means to prove one's manhood. From his example, I learned to appreciate sports, not just to excel in them. I learned how to analyze a game or sport—to take apart its components, examine them separately, and then reassemble them. In the course of actual play, he would show me how to make the most of my strengths and to improve my weaknesses. It didn't matter whether it was chess, billiards, football, basketball, or body control for any active sport; he could make it fun to learn while you played.

But the most vivid memories I have of those days are the ones associated with the intellectual stimulation my father provided. A consummate teacher when he was relaxed and took the time, he devised an endless variety of mind games. He led me on exciting tours of history, literature, language, films, poetry, plays. With Essie's assistance, he familiarized me with the immense and varied library they had accumulated—authors ranging from Shakespeare and Sherwood Anderson to Aesop and African proverbs, from Confucius and Cicero to Frederick Douglass and W. E. B. DuBois, from Charles Dumas and Victor Hugo to Charles Dickens and James Joyce.

Essie seemed happy. The Enfield home provided her with a base that eased the pressures of the "open marriage" to which she and Paul had agreed in the early 1930s after their two-year separation. Now she could develop a satisfying independent life with secure status as Mrs. Robeson. And when Paul was home, each of them had a comfortable environment, privacy, and ample space.[9]

• • •

On June 22, the Nazis invaded the Soviet Union. Stalin's monumental policy errors over the preceding five years—his unwarranted 1937 purge of tens of thousands of military commanders, his misguided implementation of the 1939 Treaty of Non-aggression between Germany and the Soviet Union, and his persistent failure to heed reliable warnings of the impending onslaught by four million German troops—caused a near-fatal Soviet military disaster. Most U.S. military analysts were predicting that the Soviet Union would not last out the year.

Paul remained optimistic despite the consistently grim news from the Russian front, confidently expressing the view that the Russians would survive their initial defeats and ultimately crush the German armies. He also discerned the increased likelihood that President Roosevelt would soon find a way to join Britain and Russia in the war against Germany.[10]

Paul resolved to use his 1941–1942 fall-winter concert tour to mobilize pro-war sentiment. Bob Rockmore negotiated an ambitious contract for the tour—seventy-one concerts at the top fee of $2,500 each. In addition, Paul scheduled several concerts at southern black colleges in order to reach the majority of the black population that still lived in the South. His strategy was to connect the war against fascism with the black freedom struggle.

Once again, Paul tried to get his *Othello* project off the ground. Having abandoned any hope of convincing top Broadway actors or actresses to take the risk of joining him in the cast, he took matters into his own hands and engaged a young, talented, but relatively inexperienced married couple who had never played Shakespeare—José Ferrer and Uta Hagen—for the critical roles of Iago and Desdemona. Margaret Webster agreed to Paul's casting, since there was no other choice.

In her memoirs she wrote, "Everyone gave different reasons, but they were all plain scared [of the racial issue]." Refused by every Broadway management they approached, Paul and Webster arranged to test their production in a summer theater the following year. Paul offered to pay all freight charges plus the cost of assembling the cast. But summer gave way to fall without any success. Most summer theater companies were as frightened of the racial implications of the play as were Broadway managements. In August, Paul left Webster to continue the search while he explored the possibilities of film on the West Coast.[11]

The Nazi invasion of the Soviet Union, coupled with the rise of the industrial union movement in the United States, markedly increased the already significant influence of left-wing and progressive writers and producers in Hollywood. Having noted this trend, and after careful thought and extensive discussion with Essie, Paul developed a proposal to make a realistic film about black sharecroppers in the South.

He approached film producer Boris Morros, who had solid Hollywood connections. Morros, well known for distributing Soviet films in the United States, was closely associated with the U.S. Communist Party and had been strongly recommended to Paul by Max Yergan. He liked Paul's proposal and promised him a true people's film that was independently produced, with the script written by a left-wing writer, participation by politically progressive Hollywood stars such as Edward G. Robinson, Charles Boyer and Henry Fonda, and distribution by 20th Century-Fox studios. The proposal seemed ideal; the political time was ripe, and Morros appeared to be sincere.

In an uncharacteristic departure from his innate caution, Paul agreed to do the film on Morros's terms, failing to consult either Bob Rockmore or Essie. While neither one of them would have tried to dissuade him—they had been urging him to give Hollywood another try—they undoubtedly would have helped him gain better leverage over the script. Paul signed a rather loose contract with Morros to star in the film that became *Tales of Manhattan*, and shooting at 20th Century-Fox was scheduled for late December.

A week later, he wrote Essie an enthusiastic letter from San Francisco:

Hello Darling:

Thanks for your letter in L.A., and don't collapse at receiving an answer. But I miss you terribly and would so like to nestle and be patted and called Sweetie Pie and oh so many things.

I've had a wonderful time. The concert [at the Hollywood Bowl] was a great success, and I've got the film [signed the contract]. I had dinner with the producer Boris Morros, and he liked both Larry and myself enormously and is dying to meet you.

I went to the [Hollywood] Bowl to hear [Vladimir] Horowitz. He was great and had tremendous success. Incidentally, Mrs. Toscanini and Mrs. Horowitz were at my concert and couldn't get over the quality of the reception, warmth, affection, etc.

How's my boy? Everyone, everywhere asks about him, and I tell them how sweet, intelligent and thoughtful he is, what an athlete— and a few other things. They conclude that I like him enormously and am very proud of him. I think they are perhaps right about that.

I love you very, very much and miss you until it hurts. I do like my place so much, both in Conn. and in your heart—and I feel I'm camping out until I get back to both. Lots of love to all,

Sweetie Pie

During the rest of August and into September, Paul spoke and sang at many political rallies—Russian War Relief, British War Relief, industrial union meetings, and left-wing gatherings. His messages and songs addressed to freedom fighters all over the world via frequent government radio broadcasts elicited many responses. On August 2, a letter came from Jawaharlal Pandit Nehru, with whom Paul and Essie had become friends when Nehru visited London in 1938, and who was now imprisoned in India:

My dear Essie,

Just over a year ago, I think, I wrote you from Kashmir. Meanwhile, as you know, much had happened and I had changed my habitation. I could not answer your letter or even acknowledge it, for the life we live in prison is hedged and circumscribed in innumerable ways.

What a Year! I have now been a little more than nine months in prison and I have gazed at this very extraordinary and very mad world of ours from this solitary corner, trying to tear the veil of the future and make out what all this is leading to. Not an easy job. Yet being denied action, one takes refuge in adventures of the mind.

Ever since the war began the flow of books from abroad to India has largely dried up, and it is difficult to get anything worthwhile. It is not easy to know even what is appearing. Still, I am mentioning some titles below, mostly new or moderately new books, [and] some old ones.

It seems cruel to ask you to send books when your own beloved books, so carefully selected for years, have been destroyed by the bombing of London. How much more will go this same way before this destruction ends! Whatever the future may hold, it is clear that there has been something radically wrong about this vaunted civilization of ours.

All good wishes

Yours
Jawaharlal Nehru

A few months later, with most of the world uniting against fascism, Nehru, Patel, and hundreds of other prominent fighters for Indian independence were freed from detention. Indian politics then took an antifascist turn when the political leadership of the independence movement followed Nehru in his advocacy of a two-front struggle for independence and against fascism instead of following those, like Gandhi, who wanted to struggle for independence only.

Paul began his 1941–1942 concert tour in the South with recitals at Hampton Institute, a black college in Virginia, and at North Carolina College for Negroes in Durham. People came from all over the state to hear Paul's Durham concert. They ranged from black and white workers and farmers to bankers, mill owners, and the racist governor of the state, Clyde R. Hoey. Whites defied local segregation laws to attend. Paul stayed at the college to learn and teach for three days, during which he gave a radio interview and led a discussion at a Southern Negro Youth Congress meeting where he urged the students to play a greater role in the freedom struggle. His stay ended with a concert for the senior citizens at the county home.[12]

At intervals during Paul's tour, he recorded worldwide government radio broadcasts that inspired international antifascist resistance. He sang to Red Army troops in Russian, to the Chinese troops and guerrillas in Chinese, to the Maquis resistance fighters of France in French, and to the underground movement of the Nazi heartland in German. He even found time to learn a Norwegian song for the resistance in Nazi-occupied Norway.

As enthusiastic as Paul was about these radio broadcasts, he felt an increasing desire to address his black constituency via the radio. However, there were no radio programs aimed at a black audience, and commercial radio networks had no interest in creating any. Consequently, Paul welcomed the opportunity to play the leading role in the *Freedom's People* series.

Conceived and organized by Ambrose Caliver, a black educator and federal employee at the U.S. Office of Education, *Freedom's People* was the first federally sponsored radio series on black history. As "Senior Specialist in the Education of Negroes," Caliver was intensively lobbying the Roosevelt administration for funding when he invited Paul to anchor the first program. The program was played at the White House for the president and the First Lady, and Caliver noted that both "expressed great interest and commendation. They were very generous in their approval of the presentation. Others in the party who listened to the program were Lord and Lady Mountbatten and Secretary [of the Treasury] and Mrs. Morgenthau." Caliver was successful in convincing NBC to run the full series.[13]

Paul's tour extended to Canada, where he was met with great acclaim. The *Ottawa Evening Citizen* headlined, "Paul Robeson's Dramatic Power Stirs Huge Crowd." The governor-general and Princess Alice were in the audience as Paul delivered a "superb" and "well arranged" concert. Clara Rockmore's theremin playing was described as "a delightful novelty." In Winnipeg, Paul's rendition of the "Prayer and Death" from *Boris Godunov* was hailed as "an overwhelmingly dramatic experience." At Nanaimo military camp near Vancouver, he sang an entire program comprised of requests to eighteen hundred Canadian soldiers from a boxing ring in the timber-vaulted drill hall under glaring ring lights. In Seattle, the students at the University of Washington called him back for twelve encores.[14]

As he traveled, Paul called for all-out support of beleaguered Russia's war effort. Addressing a packed auditorium in Vancouver on November 22, he said, "There seems to be some hesitation in Canada about Russia, a feeling that one mustn't mention the name of the Soviet Union. That's not only nonsensical, it's suicidal." At that very moment, the battered Red Army, supported by tens of thousands of poorly trained, poorly armed but courageous civilian volunteers, held the Germans at the gates of Moscow and Leningrad until the first deep winter snows sapped the German army's awesome offensive capability. In the face of the compelling nobility of Russia's epic resistance despite staggering losses, public opinion began to turn decisively toward support of the Russian people.[15]

On December 7, 1941, the Japanese bombed Pearl Harbor, and the United States declared war on Japan, Germany, and Italy. There was an immediate seismic shift in the U.S. political landscape. Conservative and right-wing groups who opposed U.S. entry into the war against Germany were rendered politically irrelevant. President Roosevelt was finally free to pour massive military aid into Britain and the Soviet Union. By declaring war against Germany and Italy as well as Japan, Roosevelt united the entire nation under his banner, neutralized any potential opposition from the left by including it in his pro-war united front, and assumed virtually unlimited executive power under the War Powers Act.

In this new political configuration, Paul became one of the Roosevelt administration's most important allies in rallying blacks to support the war against fascism. Paul responded by campaigning for victory in two wars—the war against fascism abroad and, equally, the war against racial segregation at home. By adopting this position, he broke ranks with the administration, the black civil rights leadership, and the Communist Party, all of whom assigned first priority to the destruction of fascism. Paul also found himself in direct opposition to A. Philip Randolph and the Black nationalists who refused to support the war unless Jim Crow was abolished first. However, the black masses responded by flocking to recruiting stations while simultaneously escalating their resistance to racial discrimination throughout U.S. society, including within the armed forces.

Paul added appearances at war bond rallies and military bases to his regular concert schedule. His voice thrived on the activity. After his appearance with the San Francisco Symphony Orchestra before a capacity audience of six thousand, the music critics went out of their way to praise his vocal gifts. One stated flatly that "Paul Robeson still has the greatest bass voice in the world." Others wrote of "the splendor of his tone," "the mellow richness and expressiveness of his voice," and "his instinctive feeling for phrase and melodic line and rhythm." By the end of December 1941, halfway through his second national concert tour since returning from London, many considered him to rank with Chaliapin and Caruso as one of the three greatest male vocal artists of the twentieth century.[16]

Christmas was in the air when Paul went out to Los Angeles to film *Tales of Manhattan* at 20th Century-Fox studios. With a big budget, ten writers, and a huge cast of major stars, the set was buzzing. Eddie (Rochester) Anderson, Charles Boyer, Henry Fonda, Rita Hayworth, Elsa Lanchester, Charles Laughton, Thomas Mitchell, Clarence Muse, J. Carroll Naish, Edward G. Robinson, Ginger Rogers, Cesar Romero, George Sanders, Ethel Waters, and Roland Young were already in the lineup. Paul was to play opposite Ethel Waters in the role of a poor southern sharecropper.

A rude surprise awaited Paul upon his arrival. He read the script, which was far less than satisfactory, and suggested numerous changes to the director. His producer friend Boris Morros appeared in place of the director. Morros, in his characteristically ebullient manner and without apology, explained that in order to get 20th Century-Fox to distribute the film, he had been compelled to give Fox ultimate script control. Of course he added, the director was a dedicated and sensitive left-winger, and Paul would have no problem finding common ground with him regarding the script.

Deeply angered by what he considered to be a calculated betrayal, Paul nevertheless held his fire and did the best he could in difficult negotiations with the director. At one point he even considered buying back the rights, but the price was beyond his reach. Finally a compromise was reached that Paul felt approximated his minimum requirements. He shot the film, approved the takes, and put any lingering doubts out of his mind. Knowing he could no longer influence the outcome significantly, he didn't bother to view the edited rough cut.

Paul stayed on for a couple of days at 20th Century-Fox to do Essie a favor. He had received a cable from her asking him to help her arrange a screen test for the role of Pilar in the epic film *For Whom the Bell Tolls*, based on Ernest Hemingway's novel about the Spanish civil war. Paul convinced Boris Morros to schedule Essie's screen test at 20th Century-Fox, arranged to pay expenses connected with the test, and flew her out to Hollywood to make the detailed arrangements herself. Nothing came of these efforts, but Essie was gratified that Paul had gone to such trouble on her behalf.[17]

Before heading home, he made a stop to sing to three thousand inmates packed into the mess hall at the California State Prison at San Quentin. The newspaper of that racially segregated institution reported, "Out of his great chest and through his cultured voice rolled the traditional simple beauty and joy of all the Negro people. His was the voice of his race."[18]

Paul, the first major concert artist to sing to prison inmates, was gratified when he read that review. It confirmed the rightness of his chosen quest. Now white America recognized him as the voice of black America.

3

HERO AND ENEMY

(1942–1943)

On New Year's Day 1942, as Paul was relaxing in Enfield during a tour break, Essie wrote in her diary, "Paul has been home most of the week, and we have had great fun." However, *Othello* was on his mind. One evening at dinner, he talked with us about his plan to launch a trial production of the play in the summer. Addie Williams, the Theatre Guild's live-wire publicity director, and Freda Diamond, a good friend of guild president Lawrence Langner, had finally convinced Langner to enter into negotiations with Paul and Rockmore. No doubt, Paul's continually growing popularity was a factor, but apparently Langner had come to appreciate the historic nature of a Robeson *Othello* in an America fighting a war for democracy against fascism.

When Paul met with Rockmore and Langner, his eloquent presentation convinced Langner to mount a Theatre Guild Broadway production in the 1943–1944 season, provided a 1942 summer tryout was successful. Paul would own a major share of the enterprise and have approval of all major production decisions, including casting. Essie did not participate in the meeting, nor did Paul consult her about it. To her chagrin, this signaled a departure from their previous partnership in his theatrical ventures.[1]

Back on tour, Paul constantly confronted racial segregation. While singing for the armed forces was top priority, he was often compelled to sing to segregated audiences in order to reach both black and white troops.

In an effort to offset this discriminatory practice, Paul visited servicemen in the black social halls and chapels while avoiding "white only" gathering places. Those white servicemen who wanted to meet him had to come to the areas designated for blacks. He followed the same policy at factories where the workers had separate social facilities. The news photographs of Paul smiling broadly during his appearances at military bases and defense plants mask his anger at the indignities and brutalities his people were compelled to endure. His friendly, empathetic manner, in public and in private, remained unaffected. A picture of Paul greeting Eleanor Roosevelt warmly at a "Salute to Negro Troops" offers no hint that he deeply resented the president's failure to end racial discrimination in the armed forces.

Just a few days into the New Year, a black man named Cleo Wright was arrested in Sikeston, Missouri, on suspicion of attempting to rape a white woman. A white lynch mob hauled him from jail, tied him to the back of a car, dragged him through the black section of town, and set his body on fire in full view of black churchgoers, including Wright's wife. Black outrage across the nation was so great that, after 3,842 recorded lynchings without a single federal indictment, a federal grand jury was convened for the first time since 1889 by the Roosevelt administration. Although it denounced the lynching and the behavior of the local police, the grand jury found no violation of federal law.[2]

By early 1942 the effective prosecution of the war was threatened by the escalating racial conflict. A poll of New York blacks revealed that 38 percent placed spreading democracy at home above defeating fascism, and 50 percent believed they would be treated better by the Japanese than by white Americans. The survey also showed that in games, black children preferred to play the roles of Japanese, since they could identify with getting revenge against whites. On the other hand, government pressure, driven by wartime necessity, was gradually eroding the color line as blacks gained an economic foothold in the defense industries. This development evoked a wave of antiblack violence. A majority of whites throughout the nation fought successfully to keep public schools, restaurants, hospitals, and neighborhoods segregated. At the request of the Treasury Department, Paul interrupted his concert tour to make a series of Midwestern appearances aimed at reducing white-black and labor-management conflicts.[3]

Immediately after resuming his tour, Paul refused to sing a concert scheduled for Santa Fe, New Mexico, because a local hotel had canceled his reservation when guests objected to the presence of a black man. In Kansas City, having sung the first half of his concert to a segregated audience in violation of his performance contract, Paul expressed regret at having to interrupt the concert as the second half began: "I have made it a lifelong habit to refuse to sing in southern states or anywhere that audiences are segregated. I accepted this engagement under guarantee that there would be no segregation. Since many leaders of my own race have urged me to fill this engagement, I shall finish the concert, but I am doing so under protest."

Some whites in the audience got up and left; a few went and sat in the black section, and a significant number of blacks moved to the white section. Paul went on to sing "Jim Crow" with its unmistakable racial-protest lyrics. A few more whites left, and after that the concert went on normally. The Kansas City black newspaper, the *Call*, wrote Paul to thank him for his protest, which "has spurred the Negro citizens here to wage a campaign against discrimination in our tax-supported buildings."[4]

On April 5, 1942, Earl Robinson excitedly wrote Essie, "Big news unless you have heard by wire already. Paul and I have been invited by Eleanor Roosevelt to sing [my] new Roosevelt number for her and the President. I imagine Paul told you about it. I wired back that I could come and that Paul would undoubtedly want to come." A cable from Eleanor Roosevelt to Paul arrived at Enfield the next day. It read, "Mr. Earl Robinson will come on Wednesday evening April eighth to play his new musical piece. It will give me great pleasure if you can arrange to come here that evening at ten forty five and sing for the President and me." Paul, despite having spent several days with Robinson rehearsing the newly composed thirteen-minute tribute to the president, "Battle Hymn," decided not to go. He was determined to avoid direct personal association with a president who failed to use his vast executive powers to end racial segregation in public life. Instead, he appeared that evening as the main speaker at a mass meeting in New York sponsored by the Council on African Affairs. The event, hailed by a cable from Indian leader Jawaharlal Nehru, called for the United States to back the immediate freedom of the colonial peoples of Asia and Africa. This issue was an embarrassment to the Roosevelt administration because of the president's wartime appeasement of British and French colonialism. Paul sounded the theme of the meeting: "We face in Africa a whole continent that is the [gateway] to control of the world. We are dealing with a people who must have their freedom if they are to fight [against fascism]. Their freedom is tied up very clearly with the freedom of fifteen million Colored Americans."

A few weeks later, Paul sang Earl Robinson's "Battle Hymn" on CBS radio, and Mrs. Roosevelt wrote Robinson that "the President heard the whole program. We both think it was magnificent."[5]

In April, Paul toured the Deep South for the first time. At Tuskegee Institute in Alabama, he sang to the Fifth All-Southern Negro Youth Congress. Four thousand people, black and white, poured onto the Tuskegee campus where the first black fighter pilots were training. According to the special May issue of the conference's newspaper, "the rafters shook with applause" from the packed audience of delegates, soldiers, students, and townspeople in response to a concert program that concluded with the "The Bill of Rights," a song written by Langston Hughes. In a brief speech, Paul called for solidarity with the people of the Soviet Union, China, and Africa and predicted full freedom for the colonial peoples and black Americans.[6]

Although it was common knowledge that the Southern Negro Youth Congress, the sponsor of the congress, was closely allied with the U.S. Communist Party, President Roosevelt sent a warm greeting to the delegates. In it he coupled his endorsement of the congress's "expressed purpose [to] dream, organize and build for Freedom, equality, opportunity" with his commitment to a victory that guaranteed "peace and universal freedom such as men have not yet known," and a reminder that "every American, without regard for his race or his creed, has an irrevocable interest in the outcome of this struggle for victory."[7]

Paul went on to Nashville, Tennessee, where he sang and spoke at a meeting of the Southern Conference on Human Welfare, sharing the spotlight with Eleanor Roosevelt, who presented the Thomas Jefferson Awards. Paul sang two groups of songs in addition to performing "Ballad for Americans" with the Fisk University Choir. Mrs. Roosevelt described the performance as "a thrilling experience," and the *Nashville Tennessean* called it "one of the musical high spots of the season."

Paul spoke, demanding that postwar freedom be extended to blacks, who had "suffered the hardships of modern serfdom though Constitutionally free." He warned against those who "sow disunity, create race wars, crucify labor," accusing such forces of "having fascism in mind." He also included a direct appeal for the freedom of Earl Browder, the imprisoned leader of the Communist Party.[8]

On July 9, looking distinguished with a beard and mustache, Paul met with director Margaret Webster in her Greenwich Village apartment to review the final arrangements for a two-week run of *Othello*—one week at the Brattle Theatre in Cambridge, Massachusetts, followed by a week at the McCarter Theatre in Princeton, New Jersey. Paul left no doubt in Webster's mind that he would have the ultimate say in the production. Realizing that a unique historic opportunity beckoned her as well as Paul, Webster agreed, but she never shed her deep resentment of Paul's authority. To her, he would always remain an amateur in the theater.[9]

After one week of rehearsal in New York and another in Cambridge, the play opened on the stiflingly hot evening of August 10, 1942, at Cambridge's Brattle Theatre to a packed and sweating audience. Paul's costumes were so drenched that they had to be wrung out between scenes. Despite the oppressive heat, the tiny stage, and an insufficient number of rehearsals, the performance was a triumph for the entire company, and especially for Paul. The ovation from the entire house was overwhelming. And the reviews the next day matched the enthusiasm of the audience. They all agreed on three points: the performance had proven that a black Othello with a white supporting cast would be accepted by a white audience; Paul was a fine Othello; and Margaret Webster's direction had given the play a convincing structure and coherence.

Elliot Norton, the *Boston Post* critic, wrote, "Despite certain imperfections, this is the first great Othello some of us have ever seen." But he felt Paul could do better: "The performances of Miss Uta Hagen as Desdemona and of her husband, Jose Ferrer, as Iago, are much nearer present perfection than is Mr. Robeson's."

However, according to Louis Kronenberger in the August 13 issue of the New York newspaper *PM*, Ferrer was not up to maintaining "the Othello-Iago balance"; he was always dominated by Othello. But Kronenberger added that Ferrer "showed more skill than I am giving him credit for and that what his Iago needs most of all is time to mature and deepen." Hagen's Desdemona "was sweet and fragile and pathetic, a trifle too much child rather than woman, though effectively so and capable at times of real strength."

Paul's performance, Kronenberger continued, "was uneven and in places unsatisfactory, and it perhaps owed more to personality than to art, but as a whole it had great force and at its best it was towering and tremendous. Robeson—in look, in voice, in bearing, and in something from within—plays the Moor always (if here and there a little too much) in the real grand manner." Kronenberger's main criticism was that Paul "was least effective as the tortured, almost animal victim wracked with violence. The violence was perhaps not too much for the character, but it *was* too much for the stage. Yet if sometimes clumsy and sometimes overdone, Robeson's performance as a whole was extremely powerful—something that, though it failed of great art, was almost as satisfying as great art."

During the remainder of the Cambridge run, Paul, mindful of Kronenberger's criticisms, worked successfully with both Hagen and Ferrer to achieve a better balance between his role and theirs. He helped Hagen to become more woman than child, embodying a Desdemona whose air of sweetness and fragility coexisted with intelligence, strength, and even a touch of defiance. With Ferrer he developed an instinctive rapport that allowed Ferrer to inhabit an Iago who, while becoming a monumental villain to the audience, is impeccably honest and loyal in Othello's eyes. Paul also revealed that he had attended medical school classes to research his portrayal of Othello's epileptic fit.[10]

Rudolph Elie Jr., less of a traditionalist than Kronenberger, noted in *Variety* that Paul's performance was a "revelation." The "transition to the terrible rage of a betrayed husband" was accomplished with "devastating power of expression." He added that "[Robeson's] voice is capable of the utmost nuances, from the ineffable tenderness of his troth with Desdemona to the dreadful gibberish of an epileptic in the throes of insane jealousy. Beyond that, however, is his terrific capacity for changing pace, and every tortured thought finds its logical expression." In Elie's view, Paul's performance was of such a stature that "no white man should ever dare presume to play it again."[11]

The *New York Times* reviewer summed up the universal view when he noted that Robeson "makes this Othello a man to command and to command respect. You believe in him first as a great soldier." Now Paul's main preoccupation became the refinement of the portrayal of Othello's jealous rage. The *Time* magazine critic had complained, "Robeson unwisely tried to reproduce Othello's violence—which on the stage becomes grotesque—instead of finding a way to suggest it." Paul experimented with the effect of controlled fury rather than violent anger.[12]

Paul's experimentation unsettled Webster. To her, Othello believed himself a member of a race not considered equal to whites; therefore he was unsure of himself and became easy prey for Iago. In contrast, Paul's Othello loomed as a heroic figure whose vulnerability stemmed from his overconfidence rather than from insecurity. Webster became so upset that she wrote Essie a note requesting a talk with her about Paul's performance. Essie politely declined. Since Paul had not invited her, she had not attended any of the New York rehearsals or performances in Cambridge. Paul updated her routinely on how he was doing but did not ask for advice. Outwardly, Essie expressed no resentment at being left on the sideline.[13]

Webster took the production to Princeton feeling that her lead actor was unpredictable and unreliable. Nevertheless, the Princeton run proved as successful as the week in Cambridge, and the reviews were comparably enthusiastic. Albert Einstein came to see the play and afterward went backstage to congratulate Paul on the profound impact of his performance. He urged him to take the play on a national tour after its Broadway run.[14]

The black community expressed great pride at Paul's historic success. The *Boston Chronicle* hailed him for bringing "great glory to his people." The *Chicago Defender* declared that "a milestone in the history of the American theater" had been reached. The drama critic of the *Baltimore Afro-American* hailed the power of Paul's performance. An editorial in the *Pittsburgh Courier* proclaimed, "In one leap, Negro artistry has gone from the bottom to the highest

pinnacle of this profession. Although the day of our redemption
has not yet dawned, the darkest part of the night has passed." The
Worker struck a political note: "Robeson's Othello is a defiant plea
for equal rights."[15]

A Broadway opening of the play had become a certainty by the
end of the run, although it would be delayed a year to accommodate
Paul's extended concert tour scheduled for the 1942–1943 season.
The August 31, 1942, issue of *Life* magazine featured a piece titled,
"*Life* Goes to a Performance of Othello: Paul Robeson is the first
U.S. Negro to play the Passionate Moor." The text begins, "Most
distinguished event of the theater's summer season was an unusual
and electrifying presentation of *Othello*."

At this heady moment, the film *Tales of Manhattan* opened in Los
Angeles and instantly became a flashpoint in black cultural circles.
Its outdated but familiar stereotypes were all the more objectionable
because of their banality. Deep down, Paul had known that despite
the positive changes he negotiated, the film fell far short of his
minimum standards. Now he would have to face the consequences
of his carelessness.

The movie was a modest box-office success, and Bosley Crowther's
New York Times review was typical of the benevolent, if lukewarm,
response of the mainstream press:

> *Tales of Manhattan* is one of those rare films which, in spite of its
> five-ring-circus nature, achieves an impressive effect. Neither pro-
> found nor very searching, it nevertheless manages to convey a
> gentle, detached comprehension of the irony and pity of life. [In]
> the epilogue, the coat, with a wad of greenbacks in it, is dropped
> by a fugitive bandit in the South, and is found by a group of poor
> Negroes who turn out, conveniently, to be Paul Robeson, Ethel
> Waters, and most of the Hall Johnson Choir. After a bit of ante-
> bellum hallelujahing, they split the swag righteously and turn the
> coat into a scarecrow.

The *New York Daily News*, representing the conservative Hearst
press, complained about the "hefty piece of Communist propaganda"
lurking in one of Paul's lines about sharing the land in common.[16]

It was a minor consolation to Paul that the left-wing press was critical of the film but not of him. *PM* reviewer John T. McManus wrote, "The final incident missed a chance to be great through utter failure to visualize Negroes in any realer terms than as a *Green Pastures* flock. . . . The sequence's heart is undoubtedly in the right place, but its feet bog down in that same old Mississippi mud." The Communist Party newspapers, the *Daily Worker* and the *People's World*, waited to report on the film until Paul had commented on it.[17]

The response in the black press was divided but, from Paul's point of view, dismal overall. One headline read, "Paul Robeson, Ethel Waters Let Us Down." The body of the article warned, "We have a battle to fight, and it's not solely with the producers. It's with our Ethel Waters [*sic*] and Paul Robesons who, we believe, can lead the way by refusing roles like the 'Luke' and 'Esther' of *Tales of Manhattan*." Two West Coast black newspapers, the *Los Angeles Tribune* and the *Los Angeles Sentinel*, organized a large group to picket the opening.

The black establishment's attitude was reflected in Walter White's positive comments in which he hailed a new departure in Hollywood. The film, he noted, did not show blacks interacting with whites in the usual servile or clownish manner. Instead, they were realistically portrayed at the bottom of the economic scale, and their real aspirations for land, machinery, schools, and hospitals were depicted. In a long article published in the *Pittsburgh Courier*, Clarence Muse came to Paul's defense. Robeson, Muse said truthfully, "has refused more roles than any other artist in America when they failed to measure up to his ideals." He also hurled a challenge at black critics. "What do you find that will warrant production? *Native Son*, the greatest book of the day on a subject that most of the NAACP members would object to on the screen?" And Dan Burley's column in the *Amsterdam New York Star-News* called *Tales* "a powerful indictment of the absentee-landlord and sharecropping system in the South."[18]

These arguments replicated those Paul had made in the 1920s and 1930s to justify his appearance in plays and films with antiblack stereotypes. They also coincided with his actual reasons for approving the obviously flawed script of *Tales of Manhattan*. Given the deep division in black ranks concerning the film, it would have been easy for him to ride out the criticism and make an honorable peace with both Hollywood and black America.

For years Paul had refused virtually every major black male part in American film—from *Hallelujah* and *Green Pastures* to *Gone with the Wind* and *Uncle Tom's Cabin.* Currently he was being offered leading parts in *Porgy and Bess* and *Moby Dick*, and an excellent singing part in *The Life of Rimsky-Korsakov.* Despite the furor over *Tales of Manhattan*, there was little doubt that he could pioneer a new, greatly improved black male image in American film. Yet Paul chose an entirely different course.

He began by admitting his error immediately. In interviews with the black press, he declared that "the criticism being leveled at me for my part in 'Tales of Manhattan' is justified, and the film does reflect on my race." However, his explanation that he hadn't recognized the derogatory nature of the offending scenes until the shooting was untrue, since he had objected to them unsuccessfully at the script stage. Consequently, he disowned the film entirely, even going so far as to say that if the picture were to be picketed in New York, he would join the picket line himself. Paul sensed that the rank-and-file black public was sick of compromises and half-measures. They wanted to see full-blown black heroes and heroines who conceded nothing whatsoever to white people's preferences. And in light of their response to his *Othello*, Paul felt a responsibility to lead the fight for that goal regardless of the impact on his future in Hollywood.[19]

Having made up his mind to meet this responsibility, he proceeded to denounce Hollywood's "plantation" attitude toward blacks. Declaring that the movie magnates were determined to appease the South by continuing to portray African Americans exclusively as "hallelujah shouters," he vowed he would "never make another picture in a major studio." He called for low-budget independent films on new black themes, and demanded that the federal government tell Hollywood, "You can't make this objectionable type of picture any more."[20]

Having endeared himself to the black public and burned his bridges to Hollywood, Paul went to see the completed version of *Tales of Manhattan* for the first time.

In September, Paul, city councilman Adam Clayton Powell Jr., and other notables appeared at a "Free India" rally in New York's Madison Square Garden. Paul urged the audience to "overcome the imperialists denying freedom to India," and to pressure President Roosevelt to support Indian independence publicly. A few days later, he sang

"Ballad for Americans" to a hundred thousand New Yorkers gathered in Central Park at a CIO-USO Salute to the Armed Forces rally.

Then Paul flew to California and visited Moore Shipyards in Oakland. "I know what this is; I worked in a shipyard in the last war," he said to the workers. The *Oakland Tribune* described the meeting:

> Introduced by the Negro chairman of the yard's committee against discrimination, Robeson met with the workers at their lunch period. He spoke only briefly and sang for them as they squatted on piles of steel plate and ate their lunches.
>
> They put down their sandwiches and thermos bottles as Robeson sang "Water Boy." They stopped chewing and listened silently as he introduced his "Ballad for Americans:" "This will never be a real America until my Colored brothers are working by your side. We too are real Americans. We all have to be here together. That's what democracy really means."
>
> As the sun climbed over a steel shop, Robeson cupped his ear with his right hand to shut out the noise of a plane overhead, took off his hat and broke into the "Star Spangled Banner." Off came the shiny helmets, the goggles and the greasy hats, and three thousand men and women shouldered in beside the big Negro to sing the National Anthem.

The next day, Paul was in Los Angeles, singing and speaking at a Win the War rally in the Philharmonic Auditorium. "Today we fight for a world of common men," he declared. "We stand at a threshold of history with the opportunity of seeing to it that the common people everywhere have a decent life."[21]

Occasionally, when Paul's travels took him briefly to the New York or Boston areas, Essie would drive from Enfield to spend time with him. Despite her seeming acceptance of Paul's long absences, her letters to him sometimes had a plaintive tone. In one of them she wrote:

> So I'm a widder. A pure widow. Not pure by preference. Pure because there is nothing interesting about, and I am too occupied with my lovely house, my really sweet family—mainly Pauli, and my own affairs, to go out on the prowl. So I don't take any credit for purity, and you needn't either.

> Anyway, I love you, and I think you're swell. Why I don't know, but I do. I miss you. Maybe we will have a little time before your October 5 start??[22]

Paul did spend some time at Enfield as the leaves on the trees turned gold and red—time enough to give me some heavy-duty football coaching. "Don't try to be elusive when you run with the ball," he advised. "Make one move and then drive forward. Use your speed and power to run off tacklers' shoulders rather than around them." He also taught me how to set in a comfortable position so I could get an explosive start. Then he headed off to work with Larry in preparation for seventy scheduled concert appearances. On the eve of his departure from New York, he wrote Essie a note: "Hello Honey—Be sure to write if you can. If I don't hear soon, will telephone. Heard from Pauli. Start on Sunday. Will let you know how everything moves. Love to everyone there. Take it easy. Love, Paul"[23]

With acquaintances and friends spread out across the country, Paul enjoyed a varied and stimulating social life separate from Enfield. His 1942 appointment book, with a list of addresses in the back, tells of varied social encounters. A typical set of entries for January 1942 included the following New York City highlights: "took Mother Diamond [Freda's mother], to the theater; lunched with Lil Landau [a close associate of left-wing American Labor Party congressman Vito Marcantonio] and visited with [blues singer and guitarist] Josh White." The addresses and phone numbers of Paul's close friends included trade unionist Revels Cayton in Seattle, philanthropist Louise Bransten in San Francisco, actor Clarence Muse in Hollywood, Dr. Lucien and "Spider" Brown in the Bronx, novelist Theodore Dreiser and his wife in Los Angeles, and Paul's college sweetheart Gerry Neale Bledsoe. Although Gerry had been married for over twenty years, they still saw each other when Paul came to Detroit, where she had settled after her marriage.

The new concert season opened in October in New Orleans. An interracial audience gathered in the heart of the black community, filling the Booker T. Washington High School auditorium. Standees lined the rear of the orchestra and the balcony. The strains of Mendelssohn's "Elijah" and Mussorgsky's "Prayer and Death" came together with spirituals, the "Hasidic Chant," a French art song, and "Ballad for Americans" with a sixty-voice choir from Southern

University to create a musical world of spiritual grandeur. The Chinese freedom cry "Chee-Lai," the Russian marching song "From Border unto Border," "Water Boy," and "Ol' Man River" added a contemporary, topical edge. The solemn beauty of Paul's voice, his effortless delivery, and his delicate phrasing stimulated a contagious enthusiasm in the audience. Deeply moved by this introduction to New Orleans, he expressed his feelings before singing his encores:

> I had never put a correct evaluation on the dignity of my people in the deep South until I began to come south myself. Deep down, I think, I had imagined Negroes of the South beaten, subservient, cowed.
>
> But I see them now courageous, and possessors of a profound and instinctive dignity; a race that has come through its trials unbroken, a race of such magnificence of spirit that there exists no power on earth that could crush them. They will bend, but they will never break. Nothing the future brings can defeat a people who have come through three hundred years of slavery and humiliation and privation with heads high and eyes clear and straight. I must continue to come to the South. I must do so to be with my people and to refresh my soul with their strength.[24]

At the Wheat Street Baptist Church in Atlanta's black district, music lovers from all over the city came to hear a combined chorus from Spelman, Morehouse, and Clark, the historically black colleges in the area, sing "Ballad for Americans" with Paul. The next morning, sixteen hundred students and faculty at Spelman College listened as he recounted his international experiences. The message he left them with was that "no matter how fortunate any of us can be, our destiny lies with the destiny of our people." Then he sang "Ballad for Americans."[25]

In November, with Russia still desperately fighting for its life, Paul appeared at two tributes to the Soviet Union on the twenty-fifth anniversary of the October Revolution—one in the afternoon at the Soviet embassy in Washington, D.C., followed by an evening at Madison Square Garden in New York City. With the public image of the Soviet Union having been transformed from communist pariah to brave Russian ally, twelve hundred guests, including Secretary of State Cordell Hull and other leading members of President Roosevelt's cabinet, crowded into the embassy. In Madison Square Garden, Vice President Henry

Wallace and a parade of mainstream celebrities joined Paul in hailing the Soviet Union.

Two weeks later, having stopped the advance of the German army in the epic battle of Stalingrad, the Red Army struck at dawn on November 19, 1942, with overwhelming force. Russian armies under the command of Marshal Georgi Zhukov trapped and annihilated a Nazi army of 250,000 in a twenty-five-by-thirteen-mile area around Stalingrad. This Russian offensive broke the spine of the German military colossus. The tide of war swung in favor of the antifascist alliance.

Knowing Stalin well, Maxim Litvinov, Paul's friend and the current Soviet ambassador to the United States, sensed the onset of a change in Stalin's foreign policy immediately after the Soviet victory at Stalingrad was sealed. For Stalin, the war for Russia's survival had been transformed into a war to determine the distribution of world power after the military defeat of the fascist Axis. Now he would want a tougher voice in Washington than Litvinov's.

With this in mind, Litvinov prepared for the coming change by readying his young deputy, Andrei Gromyko, to step confidently into the position of ambassador. Gromyko, despite his youth and relative inexperience, proved to be an adept and imaginative pupil underneath his dour exterior. Litvinov's premonitions soon proved correct. During 1943, Stalin replaced both Litvinov in the United States and Ivan Maisky in Britain. Gromyko became the Soviet ambassador to Washington and remained in this post for three years until he became the Permanent Russian Representative to the United Nations.[26]

Throughout 1942, the FBI kept Paul under surveillance, tapping his telephone, as well as those of Bob Rockmore and Max Yergan, among others. FBI informants reported regularly on Paul's public activities and private conversations, and agents frequently followed him. By 1942, Paul had become one of Hoover's prime targets. The FBI director was determined to prove Paul was engaged in espionage for the Soviet Union and was a member of the U.S. Communist Party.

When Paul accidentally left a notebook containing Chinese characters in a taxicab, an eager special agent in Los Angeles retrieved it and sent it to FBI headquarters. He attached a memorandum suggesting that Paul might be a Soviet spy transmitting U.S. secrets using a Chinese code. Hoover's reply, dated May 27, 1942, commented dryly that the material in the notebook was "clearly of no significance to anyone other than its owner." The Translation Section of the FBI noted that Paul's writing featured "a vocabulary list of 858 words, for each of which are given the Chinese pronunciation, the English meaning, and an improvised description of how the character is written in Chinese." It appears that this episode ended Hoover's quest to pin the spy label on Paul, but his efforts to brand him a member of the Communist Party redoubled.[27]

A fourteen-page FBI report from the New York City Field Office to Bureau headquarters summarized information obtained from an array of confidential informants in left-wing organizations, including the Communist Party. Dated December 8, 1942, the report was "predicated on the fact that it appears that Paul Robeson is a member of a number of Communist front organizations." Fourteen such organizations were listed in which Paul was said to be a member, beginning with the American Peace Mobilization and ending with the Joint Anti-Fascist Refugee Committee. The report also noted various issues of the Communist Party newspaper, the *Daily Worker*, in which there appeared commentary on Paul Robeson. In all, eight confidential informants were quoted.

While Paul was on tour, Hoover devoted considerable personal attention to the Robeson file. On January 12, 1943, he sent a letter concerning Paul Robeson to Lawrence M. C. Smith, chief of the Special War Policies Unit of the War Division. The letter was accompanied by a December 8, 1942, FBI report and requested that Paul "be considered for custodial detention in view of the existing emergency."

Although Hoover had not been able to find any solid evidence that Paul was a Communist Party member or that he had engaged in subversive activity, he convinced Smith to authorize Paul's indefinite detention in the event of a national emergency. On April 30, 1943, Hoover wrote to the special agent in charge at the FBI's New York Field Office that a custodial detention card had been prepared at the Bureau, captioned as follows: "ROBESON, PAUL; Native Born; Communist." From this point on, the FBI treated Paul as a dangerous subversive and assigned him to a category similar to that of suspected spies and saboteurs. His surveillance was intensified accordingly.

In contrast, Paul was a popular hero to most Americans. A broad spectrum of liberals, including many in the Roosevelt administration, identified with him and called upon him frequently to support their cultural projects. Writer Pearl Buck joined with Paul to circulate a strong statement advocating an anticolonialist U.S. foreign policy. The Hollywood Writers' Mobilization requested his participation in a national radio series, *The Free World Theatre*. Even though many of America's most popular film actors and sports stars, including world heavyweight boxing champion Joe Louis, were being drafted into the armed forces, Paul was exempted from the military draft with a 3A classification as essential to the war effort in his civilian capacity.[28]

On January 10, 1943, six hundred people braved the bitter cold and snowdrifts as they struck out for the concert hall in Mountain Lakes, New Jersey, to hear Paul sing. A blizzard had left the side roads impassable to cars, forcing most people to take the train and walk the mile and a half from the station using pocket flashlights to light their way. A group of seventy-five walked three miles, and others trudged as far as five. One man skated a mile and a half across Mountain Lake. Despite their travails, 80 percent of the audience signed up for their next season's subscription at the end of the concert.[29]

Paul's tour closed on March 10 in a junior high school auditorium in Eureka, California, to "an outpouring" of the greatest applause accorded to a performer in their concert series. At the end, he "motioned the audience to stand, and the strains of the Star Spangled Banner filled the auditorium in patriotic fervor with the great singer leading."[30]

4

THE ROBESON *OTHELLO*

(1943–1945)

At the close of his concert tour in April 1943, Paul came to Enfield to rest, to spend some time with Essie and me, and to escape his public. He was in excellent spirits, and my parents appeared to be comfortable and affectionate with each other. However, the heart of Paul's active life remained in New York City. At regular intervals, he worked out at the Harlem YMCA to condition himself for the taxing Othello role. He subjected himself to brutal two-a-day sessions with a trainer who had helped condition boxing champions Joe Louis and Henry Armstrong, ran laps, and played full-court basketball. By September, having lost twenty pounds, Paul was trim. He worked on his Othello role, often conferring with Margaret Webster. When he was in New York, he stayed with the McGhees on East 89th Street, on the top floor of Freda's East 37th Street brownstone, or occasionally with Uta and Joe Ferrer at their East 58th Street town house.[1]

My father drew me closer during that spring and summer. As usual, we played. Ping-Pong proved to be his game, as well as mine, and he was deceptively quick. We also played a lot of chess and worked out with a football.

More important, my father was interested in what I thought and felt. And he shared more stories about his past than ever before. Five months short of sixteen, I was to begin my senior year in high school that fall, so we talked about colleges. He had appeared on a great many campuses across the country, and offered a wealth of information. He agreed with my decision not to go to Rutgers, where

I would inevitably find myself in his shadow. When I expressed interest in Cornell University, he promised to make inquiries through his sources.[2]

We talked about politics. I had joined a left-wing youth group and was thinking about ultimately joining the Communist Party. When I asked his advice about the party, he suggested I talk with Ben Davis. I asked him why he had never joined the party. After thinking a moment, he replied that he wasn't willing to submit himself to party discipline. "I come and go. I do what I want to, say what I want to, sing what I want to. I listen to what others say, but I make my own decisions." I wanted to know what was most important to him, his politics or being Negro. He replied that he put the interests of the Negro people ahead of any political ideology. "I'm a human being first," he said, "a Negro second, and a Marxist third. But all three of those levels are inseparably connected."

We talked a lot about race in America. Although I had learned to cope with racial prejudice in the North, I was shocked by his description of the vicious racism in the South and parts of the Midwest. The North, too, he said, held plenty of dangers for me as a black male teenager—dangers from which his name couldn't protect me. On my upcoming sixteenth birthday, I would be eligible to get my driver's license. "You'll be a target of the state police, especially after dark," my father said, and offered me detailed advice on what to do in order to minimize my risk. He also urged me to stay alert whenever I found myself in an unfamiliar white neighborhood: "Always be conscious of where you are, what is going on, and who is around you," he counseled.

I asked him what his attitude would be if I dated a white girl—a theoretical question, since I had not done so and at that time didn't plan to. After a moment's pause, he replied that such an idea would have seemed unattractive, not to say wholly unrealistic, when he was my age. Now it would be "a tough row to hoe," but possible if I felt that way. It would certainly be all right with him.

On June 1, 1943, the 76th Commencement Day at Morehouse College in Atlanta, Paul was awarded the honorary degree of doctor of humane letters during an eloquent address by Dr. Benjamin E. Mays, Morehouse's president:

> You, perhaps more than any other person, have made Negro music accepted as first rate art by the world at large. You have rendered the Negro race and the world a great service in "Othello" by demonstrating that Negroes are capable of great and enduring interpretations in the realm of the theater. You have had the courage to dignify and popularize the folk-songs composed by the oppressed peoples of the earth. You embody in your person the sufferings of mankind. Your singing is a declaration of faith. You sing as if God Almighty sent you into the world to advocate the cause of the common man in song. You are truly the people's artist.

After thanking Dr. Mays, Paul's address focused on winning the war against fascism:

> In our country a powerful minority wages unrelenting battle with the [Roosevelt] Administration and the "Win the War" forces. The most reactionary forces in our nation have no more respect for "The Dignity and Manhood of the Free Man" than do their likes in other lands. For this principle presumes the respect of others' cultures, contributions and potentialities. I firmly believe, however, that with Fascism destroyed the conditions for progress are assured—for us as well as for millions of others.[3]

Three weeks later, on June 20, the Detroit race riot erupted. In the first half of 1943 there had been 242 incidents of racial violence in forty-seven cities, in addition to clashes on military bases. So the potential for violence was high at the Packard Motors plant when twenty-five thousand white workers walked out in protest against the advancement of three blacks. One white worker declared that he would "rather see Hitler and Hirohito win than work next to a nigger."

A series of small racial clashes followed, culminating in a rampage by ten thousand whites against Detroit's blacks. In some black communities, gangsters, off-duty black policemen, and security guards joined ordinary citizens to repulse the invaders. Elsewhere, white members of the United Auto Workers union rescued trapped blacks from white lynch mobs. By the time federal troops restored order, twenty-five blacks and ten whites had been killed and hundreds injured.[4]

However, the racial rift was bridged at the large summer concerts where Paul was the main attraction. His June 28 open-air concert at the Watergate, in otherwise racially segregated Washington, D.C., attracted a record mixed crowd of twenty-two thousand blacks and whites. Others lined up on the stone bridges overlooking the impro-vised stadium, sat on the grass in neighboring areas, and perched on the steps of the Lincoln Memorial several blocks away. "Ballad for Americans" filled the night air while lights from the bridges glimmered in the Potomac River. On July 1, an integrated audience of twenty thousand New Yorkers filled Lewisohn Stadium in West Harlem for a Robeson concert. For thirty minutes of encores, roars rose from every section of the amphitheater as people shouted their requests.

In the Midwest, at the Great Lakes Training Station on July 22, two thousand sailors applauded, cheered, screamed, and whistled as one, although a photograph documents that there was a sea of white faces on the left and another sea of black faces on the right. On July 24, in Chicago's Comiskey Park, Paul sang and spoke to a mixed audience of thirty-five thousand people at the American Negro Music Festival.[5]

In August, Paul tackled his compelling priority. He wrote to Essie:

Darling Sweet—

We're just outside Chicago, riding fast. Ready to change trains and get down to Othello. We had a couple [of] swell rehearsals—Webster and I. She's going to be wonderful, exactly what I had hoped. You might ring her and tell her so. She's going to get me to do plenty—and she'll fill in the gaps. I'm really excited and encouraged.

I miss you terribly. I wanted so much to come up Monday, if only for a few hours; but I had to rehearse, and the costumes had to be attended to. They're swell—I think you'll love them. Fine lines and make me feel easy.

I'll write you from the Coast. Wish you'd be there. Lots of love. Write me—Love me—Hug me often. I adore you—Love you.

Paul[6]

Essie called Margaret Webster to express Paul's appreciation of Webster's support and guidance. Webster had a different view. She felt that Paul was "difficult to direct." She tried, as she had before, to discuss this with Essie, who once again politely declined to get involved. A series of preview performances starting in New Haven would tell the tale.[7]

Paul invited the entire family to the opening performance in New Haven on September 11, 1943. Essie drove down with Grandma Goode, our housekeeper Cecelia, and me. His brother Ben drove up from Harlem with his wife, Frances, and their three daughters, Marian, Vivian, and Bennie. Aunt Marian's husband, Dr. William Forsythe, drove Marian and their daughter Paulina up from Philadelphia. Paul made all the arrangements. The performance was a hit with both audience and critics.

In a typical review, Elinor Hughes of the *Boston Herald* wrote, "[Robeson's] very presence on the stage heightens the power of the drama and makes the final tragedy wholly inevitable and deeply moving. Where most Othellos fail, Paul Robeson succeeds, fully and completely. You accept his leadership, his magnetism, his lack of guile and, above all, the agony of the mental and physical torture that drives him to destroy the thing he loves. His performance has deepened and simplified since last summer and is a memorable and exciting event in our theater." On the other hand, Elliot Norton wrote in the *Boston Sunday Post* that Paul's "ascent from uneasy doubt to maniacal jealousy was utterly unconvincing. There was no trace of the iron self-discipline and great qualities of self command which distinguished the earlier Othello." This review served as a reminder to Paul that he had not yet mastered the nuances of Othello's rage.

A few days later, Essie wrote to him:

I had a wonderful time with you in New Haven. Pauli had the time of his life. He thought your performance was so interesting and exciting. The family loved the play, and were seething with pride over your performance.

I love you, Mr. Robeson. I think you're nice, too. I like you, too. You were especially sweet in New Haven. I came home very happy, and determined to streamline myself so that I could match your beautiful good looks, so that we will "go well together." What with the premiere [Broadway opening] coming on, I want to look my best.

I'm giving you my plans, so that if and when you want me to come to Boston, you can suggest the time that will be best for you, and still won't interfere with my schedule.

Love and kisses, Affectionately,
Sweet[8]

Paul hurt Essie deeply by not inviting her to Boston. He didn't even reply to her letter.

By opening night at Boston's Colonial Theatre, the play had acquired the aura of commercial success. Every performance was a sell-out. Mayor Maurice Tobin gave Paul a key to the city, Massachusetts governor Leverett Saltonstall wrote him a congratulatory letter, and the reviews were full of praise for the entire company. The production moved on to a weeklong run at Philadelphia's Locust Theatre, where it scored a similar triumph.

Webster was credited with "marvels in directing" and with "making Shakespeare fit the modern stage" by reducing five acts and fifteen scenes to two acts of four scenes each. In doing so, she created an ideal acting environment for Paul who was singled out for his voice—"deep, resonant and capable of infinite inflection." His overall performance was hailed for raising "what might be common jealousy to supreme tragedy."[9]

Paul and Margaret Webster maintained a public show of unity, but backstage there had been repeated clashes. At the start of rehearsals, the Theatre Guild, producers of the play, had decided to replace the husband-wife team of José Ferrer and Uta Hagen in the supporting roles of Iago and Desdemona. Webster had agreed, but Paul had vetoed the decision, announcing that he would leave the show if it was carried out and issuing an ultimatum that the Ferrers would have to get costar billing with him above Webster's name.

Webster complained bitterly about Paul in letters to her mother, Dame May Whitty, expressing deep resentment about being compelled to "get a show out of that big black jellyfish and those two conceited little asses." But her hands were tied, and she was left to straighten out the contractual problems.[10]

Othello opened on Broadway on October 19, 1943, with great fanfare and even greater expectations. The Shubert Theatre was buzzing. Margaret Webster, who also appeared in the play, long remembered the excitement and suspense:

> I have never been so paralytic with fright. I didn't listen to the opening scenes. Jauntily, I landed with Uta at Cyprus. I hadn't been on the stage two minutes before I knew for certain that it was going

to be all right. That night "the spirit gave us utterance": it was the most exciting evening I have ever experienced in the theatre. When, as Emilia, I finally "died," I lay on the floor (back to the audience, of course) helpless to move a muscle, with the tears running down my face.

There followed an ovation worthy of one of today's pop singers, lasting twenty minutes. [And then] the next morning's adjectives: "unbelievably magnificent," "terrific," "consummate genius," "one of the great events of theatre history," and a line at the box office as soon as it opened.[11]

The cast gathered at Freda Diamond's house to celebrate, along with close family and friends. Marian and Ben, accompanied by his family, were there. But just as in Boston, Essie was not. Her absence, overlooked by the press in the general excitement surrounding the event, stood out in bold relief at the party. It was also obvious that Paul was having an affair with Uta Hagen. Ferrer did not seem to object, but Freda was jealous.

The theater critics fell mainly into two categories—the traditionalists who acknowledged the greatness of Paul's performance but expressed significant reservations about it, and the modernists who were essentially unstinting in their praise.

The traditionalists were best represented by Louis Kronenberger of *PM*:

> This is an *Othello* both rich in blessings and spotted with weaknesses. Margaret Webster has directed Shakespeare with vigor and lucidity, making it always intelligible, always dynamic, and very often highly dramatic. If it is not abundantly and splendidly Shakespearean in spirit and effect, the difficulties of *Othello* ever being so on stage are obvious.
>
> All of Othello's presence and some of his power and nobility were expressed by Mr. Robeson, and a good share of Iago's suppleness and dexterity was expressed by Mr. Ferrer. The combination was harmonious, and it was often exciting. Physically, and not in look alone, but in bearing, in voice, in grandeur of manner Paul Robeson is all that Othello could hope to be. Here stood revealed Shakespeare's most passionate and noble hero, though not—as Othello is—his most poetic one. There is a tendency at times to confuse solemnity with grandeur, and to assert his power by force of will rather than force of character. But where shall we find an Othello to equal him?

Kronenberger added that Paul brought "great dignity" to the role but had "not yet mastered the art of reading Shakespearean verse."[12]

Howard Barnes of the *New York Herald Tribune*, the modernist, wrote:

> The production is the first I have seen in which a Negro played a role obviously designed for him, and it takes on more meaning and grandeur than I could have believed possible. It is Robeson's color as much as his fine acting skill which brings a rather tricky melodrama into sharp and memorable focus. Lines which meant nothing when a white man played the part of the Moorish soldier of fortune who became a great Venetian general loom impressively, giving a motivation for murder which has been obscure to most of us in the past.
>
> There are those who have found the Robeson performance less than satisfactory, objecting to his deliberate delivery of lines in the early scenes, and his gestures of hapless anger as he is caught up in a web of jealousy. For my money it is exactly these accents which illuminate the tragedy for the first time on a stage and give it melo-dramatic force, without which the eloquence is for the library rather than the theater.[13]

Paul felt confirmed in his rejection of the traditionalist approach when he studied Barnes's review. Despite her modernistic direction, Webster, to the contrary, felt vindicated by Kronenberger's confirmation of her underlying traditionalism.[14]

Among all the substantive reviews, only one was predominantly negative—Margaret Marshall wrote in the *Nation* that "Paul Robeson . . . performs passably well, but he creates no illusion. . . . He is not the Moor as Shakespeare conceived him." Marshall believed the premises of a black Othello and a racial subtext to be "false and foolish."[15]

Four days after the Othello opening, Essie wrote Paul:

> Baby Darling:
>
> I saw the ad in the Tribune of Thursday. It was very handsome indeed. I love you VERY much, and am very proud of you. This is certainly a milestone. More power to you.
>
> Always affectionately,
> Sweet

Essie, realizing that *Othello* would probably run for months, intensified her independent activities. She worked on the manuscript of a book about her 1936 trip to Africa, and became a sought-after lecturer on race relations and on Africa. Her front streak of gray hair imparted an air of elegance. Her ready smile and the bounce in her step were again evident.

Essie's increasing vitality and independence kept the FBI busy. On October 16, 1943, Roger F. Gleason, special agent in charge at the FBI's New Haven Field Office, wrote to Hoover asking "whether or not the Bureau has any information regarding the activities of MRS. PAUL ROBESON as regards Communism." On November 1, 1943, Hoover replied that "Bureau files contain no information relative to the Communistic activities of Mrs. Robeson." Nevertheless, Hoover ordered a continuation of the FBI's intensive surveillance, and in a June 10, 1944, letter to the special agent in charge in New Haven he wrote, "Please be advised that a security index card has been prepared at the Bureau, captioned as follows, ROBESON, ESLANDA GOODE (with aliases: Mrs. Paul Leroy Robeson, Essie Robeson); Native Born; Communist."

After his opening success, Paul focused on how he would sustain the dramatic impact of his portrayal throughout a long run. He could strive to make his performance as repeatable as possible—the approach that Webster insisted upon. Or he could follow his intuition and adjust each performance to the way he felt and to the audience he faced, thus creating a unique experience. He chose this latter approach—one that he had honed to a fine art during his many concert tours. The result proved highly successful but drove Webster to distraction. To her, Paul's behavior demonstrated that he was undependable and could not understand the acting craft. He made no attempt to convince her otherwise. Instead, he relied upon continued work with Ferrer and Hagen to refine their mutual performances.[16]

The black press headlined Paul's success and compared his Othello to the classic portrayal by the nineteenth-century black theater icon Ira Aldridge, expressing the view that Paul had struck a "big blow against intolerance" and calling the play "a great social document." Mary McLeod Bethune wrote Paul, "It gives me a thrill to know you are a part of us. We thank God for you; for your great ability and your marvelous manner." William L. Dawson, a black congressman from Chicago, wrote, "I read every available word which comes to my attention about you as 'Othello.' I take pride in your reflected glory."[17]

In addition to his seven shows a week, Paul made many public appearances. In October, he played a leading role in the successful campaign to elect Ben Davis to the New York City Council. On one November day, he sang at Harlem's Savoy Ballroom to a packed audience of black servicemen and their dates after a matinee performance in *Othello*, and then went back downtown to appear at a war bond rally in Madison Square Garden.

On November 16, 1943, Paul spoke on "American Negroes in the War" at the Twelfth Herald Tribune Forum. He noted that Negroes, like the direct victims of fascist aggression, had "a genuine awareness of the democratic significance of the present conflict"—an awareness "born of their yearning for freedom from an oppression which has predated fascism." He declared that "the disseminators and supporters of racial discrimination and antagonism are to the Negro, and are, *in fact*, first cousins if not the brothers of the Nazis. They speak the same language of the 'Master Race' and practice, or attempt to practice, the same tyranny over minority peoples."

On December 3, Paul was asked to be the spokesman for a delegation of black publishers who met in New York with high commissioner of baseball Kenesaw Mountain Landis and the owners of the sixteen major-league baseball franchises. They had assembled to discuss breaking the Jim Crow barrier in organized baseball. Commissioner Landis introduced Paul with the comment, "Everybody knows him or what he's done as an athlete and an artist. I want to introduce him as a man of great common sense." Paul's comments were pointed and personal:

This is an excellent time to bring about an entry of Negro players into organized baseball. The time has come that you must change your attitude toward Negroes. To me, the most indicative thing that has happened in the fight against racial discrimination is the reception I've been given in *Othello*. I was told before the play was produced that America was not ready to accept me or such a delicate theme, but I've never appeared before friendlier audiences.

When I played football at Rutgers, we met Southern teams that threatened to cancel games if I was in the lineup. The games were played and nothing happened. I was almost killed the first year, but I was accepted after I had proved my ability.

I can understand the owners' fears that there would be trouble if Negroes were to play in the big leagues, but my football experience showed me such fears are groundless. Because baseball is a national game, it is up to baseball to see that discrimination does not become the American pattern.

I come here as an American and former athlete. I urge you to decide favorably on this request, and that action be taken this very season. The American people will commend you for this action which reflects the best in the American spirit.

Paul's speech drew vigorous applause from the owners. After the meeting, Commissioner Landis announced that they had unanimously agreed to remove all barriers to the participation of blacks in organized baseball. Although a far cry from hiring a black player "this very season," the decision did plant a seed that bore fruit two years later. On October 23, 1945, Jackie Robinson was signed by Branch Rickey, president of the Brooklyn Dodgers, to play on the leading Dodgers farm team, the Montreal Royals of the International League.[18]

Month after month Paul's *Othello*, the leading Broadway show, was sold out. However, his many appearances for left-wing causes aroused conservative opposition. In January of 1944, the New York State AFL (American Federation of Labor) union leadership attempted to interfere with Paul's performances. Since he was a member of Actors' Equity, an AFL affiliate, they demanded that he rescind his honorary membership in three CIO unions (which were left-wing) or lose his right to perform on stage, screen, or radio. He openly defied the ultimatum, saying that the CIO treated blacks far better than the AFL did. Finally the Actors' Equity council met and decided to take no action against Paul. The parent AFL body was stymied, since Actors' Equity was an autonomous affiliate.[19]

On April 16, 1944, the Council on African Affairs honored Paul at a grand party celebrating his forty-sixth birthday at New York City's 17th Regiment Armory. Eight thousand people attended and four thousand were turned away. The three-and-a-half-hour program featured Duke Ellington, Zero Mostel, Lionel Hampton, Hazel Scott, Jimmy Durante, Ray Lev, Count Basie, Howard Da Silva, Mary Lou Williams, Josh White, Pearl Primus, Teddy Wilson, and Uta Hagen. José Ferrer served as master of ceremonies; the speakers included

Mary McLeod Bethune, Joseph Curran, Ben Davis, Donald Ogden Stewart, and Max Yergan.

Personal messages to Paul poured in by the hundreds—from Babe Ruth to Rabbi Stephen Wise, and from Theodore Dreiser to Vice President Henry A. Wallace. Best-selling writer Fannie Hurst rejoiced because his "fine talent and fine spirit" had passed her way. Football immortal Lou Little wrote that there had never been a greater player in the history of football than Paul. Helen Hayes called him "a pride to your country and to the theater of the world." Hazel Scott wrote, "What can anyone say to someone such as you? I will sing my message." In Moscow, the elite of the Soviet theatrical and musical world toasted Paul. A few days later, Mary McLeod Bethune wrote him, "What a lovely birthday party! I would not have missed it for anything. Keep on being our brave and courageous 'Paul.' All Negro America is proud of you."[20]

In his response at the close of the program, Paul chose to emphasize the themes of unity among the world's progressives to win the war, and freedom for the colonial peoples of Africa and Asia. Then he sang "Joe Hill." The absence of virtually the entire black leadership—Walter White, A. Philip Randolph, Adam Clayton Powell Jr., and others—was conspicuous. They stayed away because of the left-wing sponsorship.[21]

I saw *Othello* more than a half-dozen times during the spring and early summer of 1944. Each performance was slightly different and left me plying my father with questions about how he elicited Othello's varying emotions. His most difficult task, he replied, was the portrayal of intimidating rage. To achieve this, he summoned up a mix of explosive anger and menacing stillness. For his rage in the epileptic scene he transported himself psychologically to a place where he could be vulnerable. And in the final scene where Othello strangles Desdemona his rage was rooted in a deep sense of betrayal, not merely jealousy. Thus for Othello the killing of Desdemona was partly an agonized execution punishing her betrayal rather than a passionate murder stemming from jealousy. Apparently, Webster did not agree with this interpretation. Paul failed to communicate "the agony of the final scene," she wrote in her memoir. "He worked hard at feeling it, but it never rose and engulfed him."[22]

After the theater, my father and I would go to Cafe Society, either uptown or downtown. The uptown venue was more spacious and elegant, and served far better food (Paul usually was ravenous after an evening performance). Hazel Scott, a wondrous jazz pianist who sang beautifully, often performed there. She and Paul were close friends, and she often joined us at our table. I remember her as a sweet and sensitive person with a lively personality and an infectious sense of humor. Another close friend of Paul's who played Cafe Society uptown was bandleader-pianist Teddy Wilson. Among others who came by were Lena Horne and Zero Mostel.

One night a slightly tipsy white man about Paul's age came over to our table and asked him for an autograph. Trying to make a polite personal connection but feeling awkward, the man said something about being from North Carolina and having a similar name— "Roberson." Then he blurted, "My grandfather gave your family his name." For a fleeting moment, Paul's body stiffened; his eyes narrowed, and his face clouded over. Then he looked up with a broad smile. He wrote out a personalized autograph and handed it to him with the comment, "Let's just say my father worked for your grandfather." The man left with his prize.

In response to my quizzical look, my father said, "History lesson—grandson of slaveowner asks son of slave for an autograph." Somewhat indignantly, I asked him why he hadn't vented any anger. "It is far better to educate than to humiliate," he responded. "Save your anger for the real enemy."

Downtown Cafe Society was less sophisticated, offering a smaller below-street-level space and catering to a folk music and blues audience. One night a shy, thin, dark-skinned teenager came to the microphone, clutched it for dear life, and began singing tentatively through the clatter of people eating, drinking, and talking. Suddenly Paul's deep voice boomed out from beside me. "Excuse me! I'd like to hear the young lady sing!"

An immediate hush fell over the room. The singer closed her eyes, threw her head back, and out of her mouth came an unforgettably sweet sound. After that, the audience wouldn't let her go; she sang song after song. This was my introduction to the magic of Sarah Vaughan. When I met her forty years later, she recalled that incident.

During the rest of the *Othello* run, I would usually find my father at the McGhees' apartment or at the spacious Bronx home of the Brown family. He had moved out of Freda's house because he was having an affair with Uta Hagen and Freda had become jealous. Dr. Lucien Brown, a highly successful West Indian physician, had been a close friend of Paul's for years. A tall, stately, brown-skinned man with a lively intellect and a dry sense of humor, he and his family adopted Paul, who played a combined role of brother, brother-in-law, and uncle. His wife was a strong-willed but compassionate "earth mother" whom everyone called "Spider." The three teenage daughters, Barbara, Constance, and Jacqueline, referred to "Uncle Paul" and soon became like cousins to me. I had never seen my father more comfortable than he was at the Browns'.

Paul's performances continued to attract attention. *Othello* still had over two months to run when the May 1944 issue of *American Magazine* named Paul "America's Number One Negro." On May 19 he received the Gold Medal for Good Diction on the Stage from the National Academy of Arts and Letters—an honor awarded for only the ninth time in the twenty-one years since its inauguration. Popular columnist Ed Sullivan summed up his awed, if somewhat ambivalent, feelings about Paul when he wrote:

> What other worlds now are left for Rutgers' Robeson to conquer? The only big role is as spokesman for his race. But in this, Paul Robeson must beware of the Iagos who murmur innuendos that inflame the Negro and arouse the whites. Such a man as Robeson, revered by his own race and admired by the white race, can here achieve the most important triumph that has ever distinguished him.

Paul read Sullivan's gratuitous and patronizing admonition about "the Iagos who murmur innuendos" as a public demand by the liberal cultural establishment that he curb his advocacy of uncompromising opposition to racial segregation. His response was to intensify his efforts.[23]

Speaking to a nationwide audience on an NBC radio program celebrating the eightieth anniversary of the Emancipation Proclamation,

Paul demanded the formal end to segregation, attacked the supporters of states' rights, and called for presidential enforcement of fair employment practices. He declared that "the struggle of the Negro" had become part of the worldwide struggle against fascism. In a pointed warning against U.S. anticommunist and pro-colonialist trends, he urged blacks not to be used against "our natural allies and friends, the oppressed here and everywhere."[24]

Audiences were still packing the Shubert Theatre with standing-room only when *Othello* finally closed on July 1, 1944. A half million people had paid to see it, and the run of 296 performances almost doubled the previous record for a Shakespearean play on Broadway. A nine-month national tour of the play was scheduled to begin in the fall. *Billboard* awarded Paul its first annual Donaldson Award for the best male performance of the 1943–1944 theater season on July 4, 1944, with José Ferrer the runner-up and Elliott Nugent third. The September 24, 1944, issue of the *New York Times Magazine* included him among eleven people in its "Gallery of American Leaders."[25]

Paul spent time at Enfield after *Othello* closed. During July and August, he rested, studied his languages—Chinese, Norwegian, Polish, French, Swahili—avoided public appearances, and enjoyed the visits of close friends. He also kept track of the rapidly changing political climate.

The war in Europe and the Pacific had turned into an almost uninterrupted victory march for the Allies. American air and sea power had eviscerated the Japanese air force and navy; at enormous human cost, the Soviet Union had already demolished much of the Nazi military juggernaut as the Red Army swept westward across Eastern Europe; U.S. and British forces landed in Italy and were closing in on Rome. On June 6, 1944, Allied troops landed on the beaches of Normandy to begin the liberation of Western Europe. The goal of unconditional surrender by both Germany and Japan was now achievable.

The left, including the Communist Party, having opted to place national unity in the war effort at the top of its agenda, continued to relegate the issue of racial segregation to secondary status. Oppression of blacks throughout the South continued unabated; the U.S. armed forces remained segregated, with blacks constantly subjected to humiliating treatment; the North maintained its unofficial racist practices; and the larger section of the labor movement—the American Federation of Labor—adamantly refused to rescind its policy of racially segregated locals.

Paul made certain that his performance contract for the upcoming *Othello* tour excluded appearances in venues that practiced racial segregation, publicizing the cancellation of the Jim Crow cities of Baltimore and Washington, D.C., from the tour list. Moreover, since President Roosevelt had not agreed to end segregation in the nation's capital, Paul vetoed a performance at the White House sought by the First Lady. To moderate the sting of his refusal, he spent a day at the Wiltwyck School for Boys, founded by Eleanor Roosevelt, and agreed to sing a benefit concert for the school.[26]

In August, Paul, the Ferrers, and the tour cast recorded the complete version of the play for Columbia Masterworks. Paul had not informed either Margaret Webster or the Theatre Guild. Webster resented her exclusion from the recording project, and in her memoir she revealed that "the Guild and I decided it would be wisest to acquiesce rather than imperil the tour by a fight with Paul. The records were not good and I was sorry that they should be considered a fair representation of the production." Uta agreed with Webster, but Paul and Joe felt the records were fine. Their purpose was to make the play come alive to a listening audience rather than to a theater audience. Thus, in the eyes of theater traditionalists, they were guilty of "overacting."

The result—seventeen double-face twelve-inch 78 rpm records issued in three volumes—broke new ground in the history of the recording industry. The albums, which successfully conveyed the excitement and drama of the play, won an enthusiastic audience reception and excellent reviews, especially in small-town newspapers. A typical review by Victor Prahl in a Springfield, Massachusetts, paper praised the "perfect enunciation, down to the softest whisper," the "remarkable" extent to which the drama was projected, and the "technical excellence" of the recording. What Prahl called a "monumental achievement" has endured to this day.[27]

The *Othello* tour opened the 1944–1945 theater season on September 2, 1944, in Trenton, New Jersey, embarking on a 14,300-mile journey covering forty-five cities in seventeen states and playing to sellout audiences. Paul, Joe, and Uta had by now refined their performances to consistently mesh and reinforce one another, driving the story forward at a rapidly increasing pace. Webster's direction was highly effective, adapting the action to various constraints on makeshift stages in giant movie houses and large community centers. She changed scenery, altered lines, and even modified some scenes in order to adapt the performance to the environment, and the audience loved it.[28]

Responses were generally excellent. A Hartford, Connecticut, critic felt that Othello was "most admirably portrayed" by Paul's "whole stage figure, his walk, gestures, his voice that has no comparison." Iago was "cleverly unfolded by Jose Ferrer," who played "a magnificent villain." Uta Hagen was "a beautiful Desdemona, and attained the most subtle nuance of expression." Overall, "comparing the performance last night with the first presentation over a year ago, in a crowded summer theater in Cambridge, Mass., the production has taken on a tremendous shape and meaning." A Boston reviewer, under the headline "*Othello* Still Grips Audience," wrote, "There is no doubt that Mr. Robeson's portrayal of the brooding Moorish general has attained distinguished heights."[29]

These reviews reflected the manner in which Paul, Joe, and Uta had modified the interpretations of their roles to make them more understandable. Joe put new emphasis on Iago as a superb soldier feeding on his seething resentment of the Moorish general who has passed him over to promote a wealthy but unproven nobleman. Iago's evil deeds stem more from a warped sense of justice than from the classically portrayed monstrous and unmotivated innate evil. Uta's Desdemona became more "modernistic." No longer merely a beautiful and compliant decoration, she exhibited flashes of feistiness and intelligent assertiveness. Othello's suspicion of her became more credible.

It took immense effort to maintain the high quality of the performances during the exhausting tour schedule. Throughout some of the fall Saturday matinees, Paul, Joe, and Uta resorted to an ingenious device to maintain their concentration. Paul had a radio in his dressing room, and he used it to keep up with my Saturday games as a varsity player on the Cornell University football team. According to the prescribed routine for Othello, Iago, and Desdemona, whoever arrived freshly onstage was obligated to update the other two concerning the score of the game and my accomplishments.

On one occasion, Paul was "strangling" Uta as she gasped, "But while I say one prayer!" He rumbled, "It is too late." Then, under his breath: "Cornell won 14–13. The kid set up the tying touchdown and kicked the winning point." A startled Uta started to laugh uncontrollably but forced herself to remain silent, and a frightened audience thought she might be having a seizure.

At other times there was little thought of humor and no lack of concentration. In Cincinnati, then an openly racist city, a high level of tension hung over the entire first half of the performance. Paul was very careful about how close he got to Uta. Not until midway through the second act did the audience relax.[30]

The reviews demonstrated wide acceptance of a black Othello. A Seattle critic proclaimed Paul to be "probably the greatest Othello of all time." The critic of the *Sacramento Bee* wrote that "it is hard to think of any other actor than this famous Negro in the role. He is actually Othello. Robeson plays the role with disarming simplicity, as if he were not acting at all. From this time on, theater history will be dated as before and after [his] Othello."[31]

The black press provided proof that most African Americans appreciated Paul's thoughtful and independent attitude. In the November 18, 1944, issue of the *Pittsburgh Courier*, columnist P. L. Pratis described him as "a great intellect" because he could "see so much further than other men" and had the "facility of revealing to them" what he saw. And on December 30, 1944, the *Chicago Defender* called him "possibly now the foremost political leader of the Negro people."

Throughout the fall, Paul supported President Roosevelt's reelection and campaigned for the Democratic Party at virtually every stop on the tour—a highly unusual activity for a star in a major touring play. In a November 5, 1944, radio broadcast on station WHK, Paul emphasized the "all-important question of jobs for all." He accused the Republicans of wanting to return to "a system of unbridled private profit," whereas Roosevelt was a proven friend of labor. "It is Roosevelt who rightly believes the rights of man [to be] more important than the rights of private property," he added.

But then he warned that "while our attention is concentrated on the war against Fascism abroad, we must not overlook the presence of similar forces here at home. We cannot sacrifice lives to crush Nazi brutality and condone basic inequalities in our own country."

Paul's all-out endorsement of Roosevelt had proved to be a valuable asset in the Democratic campaign, especially among African Americans. Yet both the president and the First Lady refrained from acknowledging Paul's influence directly. Instead, Eleanor Roosevelt wrote Essie, who had also been campaigning for Roosevelt, that "the President and I appreciate the tribute you pay to us and the valiant work you are doing in his behalf. I am sure you have helped greatly." The lack of recognition did not disturb Paul.[32]

The last stop before returning to New York was Chicago, where Paul's opening night performance was, uncharacteristically, below par. Two days later, on April 12, 1945, President Roosevelt died, and the nation mourned. The cast was in Chicago that day and dedicated their performance to his memory. Paul turned in one of his best performances of the tour. At the end of the curtain calls, he delivered a moving tribute to Roosevelt.[33]

In the meantime, a distraction clouded the horizon. Paul had resumed his affair with Uta Hagen, and Bob Rockmore had heard rumors that Freda Diamond planned to attend the Chicago opening. He asked Paul's permission to enlist Essie's help in protecting Paul from public embarrassment. In Essie's presence, he believed that Freda and Uta would act appropriately. Paul, though relatively unconcerned about the matter and determined not to allow his professional concentration to be broken, agreed.

Essie came; Freda did not, and Uta was charming and respectful. The Ferrers got along so well with Essie that she invited them to visit her at Enfield. Several months later, they accepted the invitation and, judging from an appreciative letter from Uta to Essie, greatly enjoyed their stay.[34]

The tour ended with a special two-week engagement at New York's City Center Theater in June 1945. When the final curtain dropped to a standing ovation from the capacity audience, the *Othello* company had created a landmark in the American theater. On top of its record-breaking Broadway run that had played to half a million people, the tour reached another half million theatergoers and achieved a record gross. Tour audiences included many who did not regularly attend the theater—union members, blacks, and many who knew of Paul only through his concerts, recordings, radio broadcasts, and films.

The day after the farewell cast party, Margaret Webster wrote Paul a letter that reflected her ambivalence about working with him. Citing a reluctance "to say goodbye properly" in the presence of so many people the previous night, she reflected on the many "ups and downs—way ups and way downs" that she had gone through. She summed up with the thought that the play "certainly achieved, beyond our wildest dreams, the purposes with which we set out." She felt they had both "learned a great deal" and would "put it to good use." In signing off, "Ever yours, Peggy," she expressed the hope that "perhaps, after all, it's not the end."[35]

Later that summer, Paul wrote an essay for the autumn 1945 issue of the *American Scholar* titled "Some Reflections on *Othello* and the Nature of Our Time." In it he commented on how "strikingly contemporary" and "painfully immediate" audiences across America had found the play. "In actual fact," Paul wrote, "Othello's world was breaking asunder. Medievalism was ending, and the new world of the Renaissance beginning. Now we stand at the end of one period in human history and before the entrance of a new. All our tenets and tried beliefs are challenged."

> We have been engaged in a war in which the capacity of our productive processes and techniques have clearly presaged the realization of new productive relationships in our society—new conceptions of and assumptions of political power, with all sections of the people claiming a place in the social order. And what a vista lies before us!
>
> We must have faith in the whole people, in their potential and realized abilities. This faith must include the complete acceptance of the assumption of positions of great power by the true representatives of the whole people, the vision of no high and no low, no superior and inferior—but equals, assigned to different tasks in the building of a new and richer human society.

Paul rejected the idea of a Hollywood film of the play, saying to a Canadian interviewer that he hoped to make the film in England, "because they would and could do a good job of it there, and I don't think I would be allowed to do the role properly in Hollywood." He effectively rejected Hollywood offers by demanding the right to approve the final edited version of the film.[36]

Before heading home to Enfield, Paul participated in a flurry of public events. His appearance at a Madison Square Garden Negro Freedom Rally as one of the main speakers gave support to the fight for a bill to eliminate the poll tax in the South and to establish a permanent Fair Employment Practices Committee. Howard University in Washington, D.C., the nation's premier black university, conferred the honorary degree of doctor of letters upon him at commencement, where he was mobbed by autograph-seeking students.[37]

Meanwhile, international events were developing rapidly. On April 25, 1945, U.S. and Russian soldiers linked up at the Elbe River in the heart of Germany. The next day, the Russians stormed into Berlin from the east, and by May 1 the Soviet flag was flying over the Reichstag. On May 7, the Nazi generals, fleeing from the Russians, surrendered unconditionally to U.S. general Dwight D. Eisenhower in western Germany, and Japan's defeat in the Pacific was imminent. The United States and Soviet Russia emerged as the world's two most powerful nations.

Roosevelt's successor, Harry S. Truman of Missouri, signaled a determination to reverse foreign policy, choosing confrontation rather than collaboration with the Soviet Union. Additionally, Truman's swift appointment of several conservative southern Democrats to his cabinet convinced Paul that he intended to dismantle FDR's domestic policies in the service of a shift to the right. Pondering how he could make a significant political impact before the start of his scheduled fall-winter concert tour, Paul accepted an invitation from the War Department to make a USO concert tour of American military bases in Europe.[38]

After the *Othello* tour, my father spent almost two months in Enfield. He was in especially good humor, entertaining us on a number of occasions with impersonations—an art in which he excelled but practiced only in private. He felt that his firmly established public image as the personification of black male dignity precluded him from playing either comical roles or villains. However, for the family, he impersonated a hilarious slow-motion version of the black comic Stepin Fetchit.

Political discussions around our dinner table were especially lively when Ben Davis visited us. The U.S. Communist Party was in turmoil over its postwar identity. A letter to the U.S. party leadership from French communist leader Jaques Duclos, published in the April 1945 issue of his party's theoretical journal *Cahiers du Communisme*, had brought to the surface a yearlong conflict within the U.S. party over differing views of postwar America. His letter sharply criticized the fundamental premises of the position held by Earl Browder, who, along with a majority of the leadership, believed that the national unity and anti-imperialist trend nurtured by the Roosevelt administration would continue after the war ended. A significant minority led by William Z. Foster thought that such a view was overly optimistic, and was convinced Roosevelt's progressive policies at home and abroad would not survive in the war's aftermath. Truman's move to the right in both foreign and domestic policy tended to confirm the Foster view.

At this sensitive moment, the media publicity accompanying the publication of the Duclos letter dramatically shifted the U.S. Communist Party's inner debate into the public arena. The Foster group won an overwhelming victory over Browder at the emergency National Convention of the Communist Political Association on July 26–28, 1945. Although Paul avoided taking a position on the party debate, his public statements on issues signaled his sympathy with Foster's political outlook. This attitude was reinforced by Browder's inclination to subordinate the desegregation issue to the need for national unity.[39]

On July 25, 1945, the New York office of the FBI sent headquarters a report on Paul Robeson that began, "The title of this case is being changed in order to reflect the additional alias of the subject, JOHN THOMAS, inasmuch as Confidential Informant [name deleted], whose name is known to the Bureau, advised Special Agent [name deleted] on April 27, 1944 that subject's Political Association name was JOHN THOMAS."

The "Confidential Informant" was Manning Johnson, a paid FBI informer who later testified publicly that as a member of the U.S. Communist Party National Committee prior to 1940 he had "frequently met Paul Robeson at Party headquarters, going to or coming from meetings with top Communist leaders." Since Paul had been in Europe prior to 1940, Johnson obviously lied under oath. Moreover, the absurdity of Paul Robeson, the most recognizable black man in the world, slipping unrecognized in and out of Communist Party headquarters transcended rational bounds. Nevertheless, the report continued, "While his Communist Party membership book number is not known, his actions, connections and statements definitely classify him as a Communist."

By this time, FBI logs of Paul's telephone conversations covered every facet of his life. The homes, offices, and apartments of many of his closest friends and associates were bugged. Virtually every one of his public appearances was covered by an FBI agent or informer, and Essie was subject to similarly pervasive surveillance. However, Paul's popularity remained undimmed, especially among blacks. The black press carried stories with headlines such as "Robeson, Citizen of the World" and referred to his "astounding grasp of international trends," noting that "more than any other American, unless it be Roosevelt himself, [Robeson's] world outlook contains a sympathetic understanding of the common men of every nation, race and clime."[40]

Portrait (1941). *From the personal collection of Paul Robeson Jr.*

Essie at the Enfield house, Connecticut, 1945. *From the personal collection of Paul Robeson Jr.*

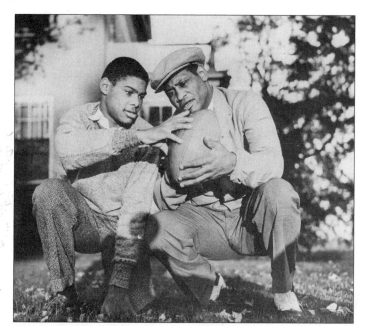

Sharing football tips with me, Enfield, Connecticut, 1941. *Photo by Frank Bauman/* Look *magazine. From the personal collection of Paul Robeson Jr.*

With conductor Dean Dixon and the American People's Chorus rehearsing "Ballad for Americans" for the International Workers Organization (IWO) pageant, New York City, February 1941. *Courtesy CPUSA Photographs Collection, Tamiment Library, New York University.*

Live premiere broadcast of "Ballad for Americans,"
conducted by André Kostelanetz at CBS studio, New
York City, 1939. *From the personal collection of Paul Robeson Jr.*

Paul, before a performance,
circa 1942. *From the personal collection
of Paul Robeson Jr.*

Singing at San Quentin prison,
California, 1941. Paul was the first major
concert artist to perform for prison
inmates. *Photo by Taylor Davis. From the
personal collection of Paul Robeson Jr.*

Speaking over HOL radio, circa 1941. *From the personal collection of Paul Robeson Jr.*

With American veterans of the Spanish civil war who fought as volunteers on the Loyalist side: Milton Wolfe (center), David McKelvie White (right), New York City, 1939. *Daily Worker photo. Courtesy of the Paul Robeson Foundation.*

At the headquarters of the Ford Organizing Committee, United Auto Workers conference, Detroit, 1941. *Photo by Mike Martin. From the personal collection of Paul Robeson Jr.*

Paul (center) at the Broadway opening of *Native Son* with Cab Calloway (left) and Richard Wright (second from left), New York City, 1941. *Photo by Morgan Smith. From the personal collection of Paul Robeson Jr.*

Paul (front row, center) with the Cee Pee Johnson Band at the Rhumboogie Club. (Clockwise from Paul) C. P. Johnson, Buddy Collette, Alton Redd, Johnny Miller, Raymond Tate, Loyal Walker, Dudley Brooks (partial view), Buddy Banks, and Kirk Bradford. Hollywood, 1941. *From the personal collection of Paul Robeson Jr.*

At the "Stars for China," War Relief benefit, Philadelphia, 1941. *From the personal collection of Paul Robeson Jr.*

With Gertrude Lawrence at a British War Relief benefit, Dennis, Massachusetts, 1941. *From the personal collection of Paul Robeson Jr.*

Letter from Eleanor Roosevelt thanking Paul for agreeing to perform at Wiltwyck School for Boys benefit, 1944. *From the personal collection of Paul Robeson Jr.*

First Lady Eleanor Roosevelt (center) and actress Helen Hayes listen to Paul's address, "Salute to Negro Troops," at the Cosmopolitan Opera House, New York City, January 12, 1942. *Photo by Morgan Smith. Courtesy of the Paul Robeson Foundation.*

THE WHITE HOUSE
WASHINGTON

September 23, 1944.

Dear Mr. Robeson:

I am delighted to hear that you have so generously offered to give a benefit for the Wiltwyck School. It will mean a great deal more to the boys and the people working there than just the financial help. It will be a tremendous encouragement.

The boys are still talking about the day you were there and how thrilled they were.

Best wishes for a very successful tour.

Very sincerely yours,

Eleanor Roosevelt

With Benny Goodman, 1941.
Courtesy of the Paul Robeson Foundation.

With Lena Horne in the Christmas Seals campaign, 1942.
From the personal collection of Paul Robeson Jr.

Signing autographs at
the Apex defense plant,
Los Angeles, 1942.
*From the personal collection
of Paul Robeson Jr.*

With Ruby Elzy in *John Henry*, 1940. *From the personal collection of Paul Robeson Jr.*

Paul (right) in
the film *Tales of
Manhattan* with
Eddie "Rochester"
Anderson and Ethel
Waters, 1942. *From
the personal collection of
Paul Robeson Jr.*

With Clarence Muse (second from left) and his wife, Billie Muse (far
right), Hollywood, 1942. *From the personal collection of Paul Robeson Jr.*

With students at Bennett College, Greensboro, North Carolina, 1942. *From the personal collection of Paul Robeson Jr.*

Essie's screen test for Pilar in *For Whom the Bell Tolls*, Los Angeles, 1942. *From the personal collection of Paul Robeson Jr.*

Paul sings to students at Abraham Lincoln High School, Brooklyn, New York, 1942. *From the personal collection of Paul Robeson Jr.*

With the "Ballad for Americans" chorus, Montana University, 1942. *From the personal collection of Paul Robeson Jr.*

Paul (third from right) at the Detroit Racial Harmony Rally after the Detroit race riot, with (l. to r.) Lawrence Brown, Joe Louis, Marian Anderson, Bill Robinson, Lionel Hampton, and Olivia de Havilland, 1943. *Courtesy of the Schomburg Center for Research in Black Culture/NYPL.*

Paul as Othello, Theater Guild production on Broadway at the Shubert Theater, New York City, 1943/1944. *Photo by Ellie Marcus. From the personal collection of Paul Robeson Jr.*

With José Ferrer as Iago in *Othello*, Theater Guild production on Broadway at the Shubert Theater, 1943/1944. *Performance photo by Richard Tucker. From the personal collection of Paul Robeson Jr.*

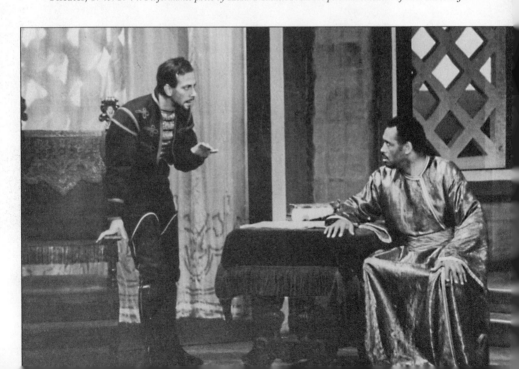

With Uta Hagen as Desdemona in *Othello*, Theater Guild production on Broadway at the Shubert Theater, 1943/1944. *Photo by Vandam Studio. From the personal collection of Paul Robeson Jr.*

Paul at second base in the Broadway Softball League, Central Park, New York City, 1944. *Photo by Abraham Mandlestam. From the personal collection of Paul Robeson Jr.*

Paul at bat in the Broadway Softball league, Central Park, New York City, 1944. *Photo by Abraham Mandlestam. From the personal collection of Paul Robeson Jr.*

Harry Bridges, president of the International Longshore and Warehouse Union (ILWU) presents Paul with honorary membership in the ILWU, Hotel Roosevelt, New York City, circa 1944. Daily Worker *photo. Courtesy of the Paul Robeson Foundation.*

With the leaders of the Furriers Union, 1943. *From the personal collection of Paul Robeson Jr.*

With Congressman Adam Clayton Powell Jr. (left) and Malcolm Ross, chairman of the Federal Fair Employment Practices Committee, at the Third Annual Negro Freedom Rally at Madison Square Garden, New York City, 1945. *From the personal collection of Paul Robeson Jr.*

With New York mayor Fiorello LaGuardia and an unidentified man, New York City, 1943. Daily Worker *photo. Courtesy of the Paul Robeson Foundation.*

Radio program with Raymond Massey and children, 1944. *From the personal collection of Paul Robeson Jr.*

Singing at a union hall, 1944. *From the personal collection of Paul Robeson Jr.*

Paul with Jimmy Durante at Paul's forty-sixth birthday celebration, New York City, 1944. Daily Worker *photo. Courtesy of the Paul Robeson Foundation.*

BABE RUTH
NEW YORK

April 11, 1944.

Dear Paul:

I am delighted to see your many admirers giving a birthday party in your honor, which you richly deserve.

You have contributed much in the world of entertainment.

Along with your many friends, I want to add my congratulations and best wishes on your 46th birthday.

Good luck to you and may you enjoy many, many more.

Sincerely yours,

Geo H Babe Ruth

Birthday greetings from Babe Ruth, 1944. *From the personal collection of Paul Robeson Jr. Babe Ruth's letter used with permission by the Family of Babe Ruth and the Babe Ruth League, Inc., www.BabeRuth.com.*

Me in the Springfield
Technical High School
track and field practice
uniform, Enfield,
Connecticut, 1944. *From
the personal collection of Paul
Robeson Jr.*

Freda Diamond relaxing in the country, 194
From the personal collection of Paul Robeson Jr.

With Soviet sniper Lyudmilla Pavlichenko,
Central Park, New York City, 1942. *From the
personal collection of Paul Robeson, Jr.*

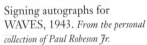
Signing autographs for
WAVES, 1943. *From the personal
collection of Paul Robeson Jr.*

With wounded veterans holding the
Potsdam Peace Pledge, circa 1945.
Daily Worker *photo. Courtesy of the Paul
Robeson Foundation.*

Singing for members of the Armed
Services at a USO canteen, New York
City, 1943. *From the personal collection of
Paul Robeson Jr.*

Essie in her Red Cross uniform, 1945. *From the personal collection of Paul Robeson Jr.*

Leaving for Europe on first integrated USO overseas tour of performing artists for U.S. troops, 1945. *From the personal collection of Paul Robeson Jr.*

At a U.S. Army base in occupied Germany, 1945. *From the personal collection of Paul Robeson Jr.*

Speaking at a meeting of the Council on African Affairs, New York City, 1945. *From the personal collection of Paul Robeson Jr.*

II
AGAINST THE TIDE

(1945–1949)

Paul with Paul Jr. at the Enfield house during
Paul Jr.'s furlough from the Army Air Force,
Connecticut, 1946. *Photo by Eslanda Robeson. From the
personal collection of Paul Robeson Jr.*

Paul on a makeshift stage at a Peekskill concert,
surrounded by the union volunteers who vied
for the privilege of protecting him from snipers,
Peekskill, New York, 1949. Daily Worker *photo by
Max Arons. From the personal collection of Paul Robeson Jr.*

5
CHALLENGING THE MIGHTY

(1945–1946)

In August 1945, Paul and Larry set out on the first interracial USO tour of American military bases in Europe. Two talented young artists, violinist Miriam Solovieff and pianist Eugene List, accompanied them across the Atlantic in a giant C-54 provided by Air Transport Command. Small army planes and staff cars ferried the intrepid company over rugged, washed-out roads through war-torn terrain. Larry, who hated to fly, suffered the most.

For the next two months, during thirty-two appearances in France, Germany, and Czechoslovakia, Paul's group brought their vibrant spirit to the troops. On the bases, a softening of segregation had already begun, and Paul's sought-after appearances accelerated this trend. U.S. commanding generals vied with each other to get him to sing for their divisions.[1]

An exuberant letter home from a white GI in Germany described the experience of a Paul Robeson performance:

> I've just returned from a U.S.O. show given by Paul Robeson's group, and it was so good I feel like writing about it. Tonight he sang "Old Man River" and instead of the last line which goes, "I'se so weary and sick of tryin', I'se tired of livin' and feared of dyin'," he sang: "I'se so weary and almost dyin', but I keeps laffin' *and keeps on tryin'*." And as he sang these words his face lit up in a ferocious fighting grin, and he pounded his fist in his hand and sang directly at the group of colored boys in the audience. And you can bet that I was saying with every atom of me, "More and more power to you."

Later he sang "Ballad for Americans," a song that must have been written for him as I don't believe anyone else could do the number justice. The political hue of his artistry was obvious to me and—I thought a bit *too* bold—but it went over big.

After the program we went to the Red Cross Club here in Augsburg, and by gum if he and his small group weren't in there having coffee and doughnuts! To me it was a strangely affecting experience to see a headliner so close. He is obviously strong as two or three ordinary men but very gentle in carriage. He talked like an average friendly guy—not like a headliner at all, and as far as color consciousness is concerned, there just wasn't any. He is conscious of his human worth and that's something few whites can claim. I would risk a guess that Paul Robeson doesn't hate his enemies.

Perhaps the Army is educating some whites. It's sure helping Negroes to get rid of their racial inferiority complex.[2]

My father's appearances also inspired black soldiers throughout Europe and gave a badly needed boost to their morale. At a base in southern Germany, Paul spoke with soldiers who had liberated the Buchenwald and Dachau concentration camps, and they recounted the horrors they had witnessed. During his subsequent concert at the base, Paul halted the performance, announcing that the German prisoners of war in the back of the hall would have to leave because violinist Miriam Solovieff was Jewish and refused to play in their presence. They were promptly expelled to the cheers of the U.S. soldiers.

One evening near the end of the tour, Paul dined with a group of top U.S. generals as their guest of honor in a castle in southeastern Germany, home ground to Hitler's core constituency. When the conversation turned to politics, two generals from Patton's Third Army and one from General Curtis LeMay's Air Force complained loudly about the "softy" politicians in Washington who refused to let them go on to Moscow from Prague and "take out those damn Russkies while they're still weak." Startled by the ferocity of the comments and the obvious hostility to Supreme Commander Dwight Eisenhower's de-Nazification policy, Paul merely listened and asked noncommittal questions. But when he returned home, Paul mobilized the resources of the Council on African Affairs to expose these attitudes to the U.S. public.[3]

The black community continued its laudatory recognition of Paul. The October 1, 1945, issue of the *Howard University Bulletin* carried a citation by President Mordecai Johnson calling him "one of the

surpassing examples of human genius in the history of our country."
On October 18, 1945, Paul received the NAACP's thirtieth annual
Spingarn Medal, the highest award conferred by the black elite, at a
dinner ceremony in New York's Biltmore Hotel. The award ended
the persistent rumor that political motivations had prompted the
group to pass him over for the previous five years.

Essie, confident and elegant, entered the Biltmore on Paul's arm
to share center stage with him. Her book *African Journey* about her
1936 African odyssey had just been published, winning major recognition, and the National Council of Negro Women was honoring her
as one of the twelve outstanding women of 1945.

To the chagrin of an anxious Walter White, Paul had declined to
submit an advance copy of his remarks for the press, and Max Yergan
had been unsuccessful in his attempts as an intermediary. But Walter's
fears that Paul's acceptance speech would be politically controversial
were somewhat allayed as a buoyant Paul and Essie chatted amiably
with their neighbors on the star-studded dais and greeted a stream
of friends and acquaintances. White served as master of ceremonies,
and Marian Anderson sang.

Marshall Field, publisher of the *Chicago Sun*, presented Paul
with the Spingarn Medal "for his distinguished achievements in the
theater and on the concert stage, as well as his active concern for
the rights of the common man of every race, color, religion, and
nationality." Paul stepped to the podium flashing his engaging smile,
thanked the NAACP and Marshall Field, and paid fulsome tribute to
the NAACP's past contributions to the civil rights struggle. Then,
asserting that artists should speak out on social issues, he urged his
audience to "look again at the world." He proceeded to present a
vivid picture of the current scene:

> We have just finished destroying one of the most powerful forces
> against human freedom. Now we are starting all over again, in a
> struggle against those in our very midst who now in desperation
> seek to destroy millions of people all over the world. The peoples
> of Asia and Africa want to realize the promises made to them. This
> is the world today!

To the dismay of a majority of his audience, many of whom either sub-
scribed to the new anti-Soviet national mood or feared to challenge it,

Paul noted that the Soviet Union had shown what so-called backward peoples could accomplish in "one generation of endeavor." In Russia, full employment was a fact and racial discrimination was nonexistent. Declaring the Soviet Union a nation "in the main stream of change," he condemned U.S. resistance to reform. In closing, he called for the creation of a world where people, whether white, black, red, or brown, could live in peace and harmony:

> If you are for the people, you are for them; if you are against them, you are for fascism. We people in America had better help our allies all over the world. Democracy can take many forms. We must be careful in selecting the proper way of progress, so that the wealth of the world can be used for the advancement of mankind. I hope the NAACP will stand strong beside the people in the struggle for a real peoples' world.[4]

This was a far cry from the message the dinner guests expected to hear. It was greeted with tepid applause. Many sat in stunned silence, while a minority led by W. E. B. DuBois, Essie, and a few others applauded enthusiastically. Walter White and his deputy Roy Wilkins looked grim and sat on their hands. Paul had embarrassed the NAACP leadership by publicly challenging the foreign policy of the Truman administration.[5]

After a two-year absence from the concert stage, Paul and Larry were thriving on an eighty-five-concert 1945–1946 tour that began in September. Music critics found Paul's vocal artistry undiminished, and his audiences received him as eagerly as ever. William Schatzkamer, one of the leading young pianists on the American musical scene, was the assisting artist.

Paul pitched his songs lower than usual, favoring the bass range. The reviews called him a "basso profundo," noting that he "plumbed the vocal depths and accomplished some superior singing." However, they felt his voice sounded "entirely too heavy" when he performed the English art songs and other parts of his program that required a "lightness of touch." As the tour progressed and his voice became conditioned to the concert regimen, Paul reclaimed his entire baritone range with authority. By the fifth week, reviewers were calling his softer, quieter singing "delightful."[6]

Paul kept his voice rested and fresh by spacing his political appearances sparingly. In October, he joined Joe Louis and Duke Ellington to sponsor a reelection rally for Ben Davis, who had retained his Harlem city council seat by a comfortable margin. Speaking to the Central Conference of American Rabbis at the Jewish Institute of Religion in New York City on November 25, Paul said:

> Since the first days of the American Revolution, Jews and Negroes have fought and died together. There were men of Hebrew faith in John Brown's brave company of men who fought to emancipate the slaves in Kansas in 1855. Many Jews contributed money to purchase the freedom of escaped slaves. And many Jews distinguished themselves in the Northern Army during the war to end slavery.
>
> Some time ago, at the time of the disgraceful anti-Semitic outbreak in Boston, I said, "America has a choice—either to fulfill its historic destiny and abolish inequalities, or follow the fascist idea of dog eat dog. The struggle for freedom in which we are presently engaged means the freedom of all individuals."
>
> The unity of the three major powers affirmed by Roosevelt, Stalin and Churchill two years ago at Teheran is being dangerously assailed. The slander and vilification against the Soviet Union stems from the same reactionary quarters as does the slander against the Negro, the Jew, and other minority peoples.[7]

On January 5, 1946, Paul spoke at the "Artist as Citizen" symposium sponsored by the Independent Citizens Committee of the Arts, Sciences and Professions at New York City's Henry Miller's Theatre. When he arrived, "an uproar lasting a full ten minutes went up from the overflow crowd." He brought them to their feet once more when he told them there was but one of two choices to be made: "back to fascism, or on to socialism." The people who had suffered under the yoke of fascism had made their choice, and America had not. "Label this onward movement, left, red, communist or what have you; it is here, and the sooner we get in step with the rest of the world, the sooner will we commence to straighten out our problems, including those of our minorities."[8]

• • •

On March 5, 1946, former British prime minister Winston Churchill spoke at Fulton, Missouri, and changed the national political climate. Speaking at the invitation of President Harry S. Truman, Churchill officially launched the cold war with a thinly veiled call for an Anglo-Saxon alliance against the Soviet Union. Mutual recriminations between the United States and Russia escalated dramatically in the wake of his address, and burgeoning anti-Soviet public opinion presaged a domestic anticommunist crusade.

Max Yergan called Paul to discuss the draft of a letter to President Truman from Paul that criticized Churchill's speech and Truman's endorsement of it. Paul significantly moderated the tone of Max's draft. He decided the letter would come from the Council on African Affairs and be cosigned by him and Max. The sharp attack on Churchill could remain, but Truman would not be criticized directly. Paul was not yet ready to challenge the president personally—especially not in the midst of a concert tour.[9]

Paul's tour remained free of controversy until April, when he went to Ishpeming, a steel town in the Michigan iron ore range. Unknowingly, Paul and Larry arrived in the midst of a bitter steel strike. As Paul told the story:

> I come up from the University of Wisconsin on a Thursday afternoon, and I sing Saturday. I get in, and I'm entertained by Kiwanis and all the big boys—I'm singing for all the steel owners. And I'm sitting down to dinner, and a guy says, "You know, there's a strike up here; these sons of guns, trying to do this and that, and these labor guys in here." I said, "Is that so?"
>
> I listen to all this kind of nonsense, and then somebody tells me there's a telephone call. The Steel International [Union] is on the next floor saying, "Paul, please come up here as soon as you can." I get through dinner, and then I go up. Everybody's very polite; we have a drink, and nobody says anything.
>
> Finally I said, "Do you want me to help out? Why don't you ask me?"
>
> "Well, you've got a concert and everything."
>
> I said, "What do you want me to do? Do you want me to go on the picket line?"
>
> "Oh; well gee, would you do that?"
>
> And they've got a radio program, which they bought. So I find myself next noon on the radio program attacking as fiercely as I could all the guys I'm going to sing for Saturday night.

The next day I went on the picket line. We're singing "Joe Hill," "Talking Union"—all the songs. There was quite a group out there. Then the scabs came out, protected by the sheriff with a gun—about twenty guys who were maintaining the mine. They came by me, and they were all bent over.

I said, "What are these guys bent over for?"

"Oh, they've got guns to shoot if the sheriff tells 'em to."

This wasn't playing! But the union won the raise and beat that mine.

When I came to sing my Saturday night concert, the manager came running over—"I'll lose my contract here; the people will send their tickets back!"

I said, "I've got my fee. If they don't come, you can have your fee back. And you'll just fill it with strikers. Now don't worry."

Well, a couple of tickets were sent back, but the place was packed. So I walk on and start to sing. I assure you, for twenty minutes you will never see such ice to cut. I went into songs you've never heard before. Used all kinds of charm, I thought. Said I was just a little boy from Jersey who had played a little football. I couldn't get away with that.

Finally I broke through with something, and the concert broke open very well. When I finished, I told them not to blame the manager; the New York office was responsible. And I thanked them all and finished with "Joe Hill."[10]

Paul arrived in Enfield on May 19 toward the end of his tour. He planned to take most of the summer off in Enfield bowling, playing billiards, reading, and continuing his language studies. By now—as he would often joke—he could argue in Chinese, French, Spanish, German, Russian, Norwegian, Hebrew, and two African languages. However, Essie was preparing for a challenging trip. Within the week she flew to Central Africa on a three-month anthropological trip to do research and write some feature articles for the *New York Herald Tribune*.[11]

By mid-September, after postponing the start of his concert tour until October 24, Paul was leading a crusade against lynching. When Walter White and most other leaders of the black establishment, such as A. Philip Randolph, Adam Clayton Powell Jr., and Mary McCleod Bethune, refused to back such an initiative, Paul asked W. E. B. DuBois and Albert Einstein to join him in a national call for a mass protest meeting in Washington, D.C. They agreed, and the National Negro Congress provided the organizational base for mobilizing grassroots support. Many black church leaders backed the call despite White's attempts to dissuade them. In these circumstances, Paul decided to confront Truman personally.[12]

On September 12, Paul made an impassioned appeal to the CIO Political Action Committee Meeting at Madison Square Garden:

> This swelling wave of lynch murders and mob assaults against Negro men and women represents the ultimate limit of bestial brutality to which the enemies of democracy, be they German Nazis or American Ku Kluxers, are ready to go in imposing their will. Are we going to give our America over to the Eastlands, Rankins and Bilbos? If not, then *stop the lynchers!*[13]
>
> What about it, President Truman? Why have you failed to speak out against this evil? When will the Federal government take effective action to uphold our constitutional guarantees?
>
> Impatient for action, the people will now go to Washington themselves on Monday, September 23, in a mighty American Crusade to End Lynching.

Nine days later, at the Madison Square Garden antilynching rally that closed the 150th anniversary celebration of the African Methodist Episcopal Zion Church, Paul "drew shouts of approval and applause from the audience of 10,000 as he demanded that the Federal government take the lead in stopping lynchings." And on September 23, he inaugurated a hundred-day Crusade to End Lynching by reading a new Emancipation Proclamation to three thousand black and white delegates who had gathered for a rally at the foot of the Lincoln Memorial. Later that day, he led a delegation of nine to the White House to meet with President Truman. Albert Einstein, co-chairman of the crusade, was not able to attend.[14]

Paul began to read the delegation's statement:

> Mr. President, we are here representing fifteen hundred delegates from various parts of the country, attending a conference to inaugurate an American Crusade to End Lynching. We know that you have received delegations concerned with the rising wave of lynching and mob-violence in the United States, but you have thus far refrained from issuing a formal public statement expressing your views on lynching, and recommending a definite legislative and educational program to end the disgrace of mob violence.

Truman interrupted at this point, stating he was "thinking about it" and it was "being worked on." Mrs. Harper Sibley, president of the Council of Church Women, pointed out the contradiction between U.S prosecution of Nazi war criminals and the refusal to punish lynchers at home. Truman objected to the comparison, noting that all Americans were obliged to support U.S. foreign policy regardless of domestic events.

Paul and other speakers contended that lynch terror had created a national emergency, requiring action similar to his use of federal force to end the railroad strike. Truman replied that political considerations prevented him from acting decisively against lynching. The timing was not yet right. Paul asserted that the temper of the Negro people might change "if some protection is not brought to them." Asked by the president to elaborate, he replied that Negro veterans might "cause a national emergency that called for federal intervention."

The president reddened, stood up, and shook his finger at Paul. "That sounds like a threat!" he said. Expressionless, Paul slowly rose from his chair, looking directly at the president. The two Secret Service guards on either side of the president's desk unbuttoned their jackets and took a step forward. "I meant no offense to the Presidency," Paul said evenly. "I was merely conveying the mood of the Negro people who constitute ten percent of the U.S. population." Then he waited for the president to sit down. Truman sat down and abruptly terminated the meeting.

Outside the White House, Paul was besieged by reporters. To their inquiry as to whether he was a communist, he replied, "I describe myself as violently antifascist." When asked if he thought Negroes should turn the other cheek, he said, "If a lyncher hit me on one cheek, I'd tear his head off before he hit me on the other one."[15]

As his confrontation with Truman resounded in nationwide press reports, Paul toured the West Coast with his friend Revels Cayton, appearing at antilynching rallies organized by the National Negro Congress. During their stay in San Francisco, Paul sang for the striking longshoremen. According to the union newspaper:

> Five thousand workers left the picket lines to come to that mass meeting, and they stood in the hot sun. Suddenly through the crowd a giant figure of a man could be seen heading toward the truck which served as a platform. A murmur of applause and cheers followed him as the men made way. Paul Robeson waved and grinned hello.

He mounted the truck and stood bareheaded, flanked by an American flag blowing gently in the hot wind as five thousand men thundered their welcome. [And then Paul spoke.]

"I'm mighty proud to be here. This last year I've been on picket lines all over the country. And on those lines I've seen Negro and white together, united for the things all men want. Before that I was overseas. And I saw the workers there. They are with us. All over the world we are on the march. What you are doing here today on the waterfront will help to determine what happens all over the world to workers everywhere. They are your allies as you are theirs.

"I met an old friend on the waterfront today. A boy I knew in Spain. He asked if I'd sing "Joe Hill" at this meeting today. I'd like to sing it."

The great rich baritone flooded the Embarcadero with the song of a murdered worker. Windows in the nearby hotels opened, and faces peered out. Men walked out of restaurants and bars and listened quietly to the song.[16]

On October 7, 1946, Paul sat in a witness chair in Los Angeles. The Joint Fact-Finding Committee on Un-American Activities in California had called him to testify under oath about his ties to organizations the committee deemed subversive. State senator Jack B. Tenney, the committee chairman, and committee counsel Richard E. Combs led the questioning.[17]

Combs: The prime purpose, Mr. Robeson, in having you come before the Committee is to ask you concerning the organization of certain groups that the Committee has in the past been interested in, so that the examination will be pretty much limited to that. Have you made several trips to the Soviet Union in connection with your profession?

Robeson: I went to Europe the first time in 1922, to England, and I have been several times to the Soviet Union, both professionally and non-professionally.

Combs: Was your son educated in the Soviet Union?

Robeson: He [had a Soviet education] from the time he was 8 until he was about 12.

Combs: Is he a citizen of the Soviet Union?

Robeson: He is not. He was born in the United States.

Combs: Do you know Revels Cayton?

Robeson: We are working together in the National Negro Congress.

Combs: Now, there are two organizations, comparable organizations, are there not, for the interest and benefit of the colored people: the National Negro Congress, to which you referred; and isn't there also an organization known as the National Association for the Advancement of Colored People, too?

Robeson: It has been long established, and it has done great service.

Combs: Are you affiliated with both of them?

Robeson: Yes, I work for them.

Combs: You know of an organization called the Joint Anti-Fascist Refugee Committee?

Robeson: Yes.

Combs: Are you an officer or were you ever an officer in that committee?

Robeson: No. As a Negro in America who is also heading a Crusade Against Lynching, I know a lot about fascism. I know what it means because I have seen it; I have helped fight it. I might have to participate a great deal more.

Tenney: I may be going far afield here, but are you a member of the Communist Party? I ask it of everybody, so don't feel embarrassed.

Robeson: No. I am not embarrassed. I have heard it so much. Every reporter has asked me that. I will certainly answer it, Mr. Tenney. Only you might ask me if I am a member of the Republican or Democratic Party. As far as I know, the Communist Party is a very legal one in the United States. I sort of characterize myself as an anti-fascist and independent. If I wanted to join any party, I could just as conceivably join the Communist Party, more so today than I could join the Republican or Democratic Party. But I am not a Communist.

Tenney: You are not? I suppose from your statement, would I be proper and correct in concluding that you would be more sympathetic with the Communist Party than the Republican or Democratic Party?

Robeson: I would put it this way: I have no reason to be inferring communism is evil, or that someone should run around the corner when they hear it, as I heard here this morning. Because today Communists are in control or elected by people because of their sacrifice in much of the world. I feel that Americans have got to understand it unless they want to drop off the planet. They have got to get along with a lot of Communists.

Tenney: Let me ask you a question, Mr. Robeson.

Robeson: Yes.

Tenney: Do you make any line of division between the dictatorship, we will say, that is inevitable in the growth of fascism and the dictatorship of communism?

Robeson: I would say the first great difference between Hitler's fascism and Russian communism was a very great distinction, because Hitler said in "Mein Kampf" that he would wipe out all Negroes and all Jewish people, and since he had the Jewish people there he did wipe them out. It would be comparable to say that if there were ten million Negroes in Germany, they would have been wiped out. On the other hand, I visited the Soviet Union where before 1917 there were pogroms. They would lynch a thousand Jewish people at any time they wanted to. There in that country great progress has been made. Take the Russian word "Zhid"—it would be "Yid" in America, like the word "Nigger" is used against the Negro. Say about 1934, if a man used that he was put in jail and he was punished. You will answer, "There are many Negro people in America. There aren't any in Russia. If there were, would there be prejudice?" Well, in Russia there are many Asiatic peoples who are generally very dark—as dark as the Negro people in this room; but they were raised in one generation to complete equality within the framework of their government.

Combs and Robeson then continued discussing the American and Soviet systems:

Robeson: We have the American way of life and they have a dictatorship, and the best way to oppose it is with our democracy. We can oppose it by giving freedom to the people who don't have it in our country. We don't need to go to war to decide which way of life is to be chosen. I believe the Soviet Union wants to build their life within one-sixth of world's surface where they are.

Tenney: You mean we should lead by example?

Robeson: That is right.

Combs: Is it your opinion that in October, 1917, when the revolution had its inception, that it would have been impossible to find a better country to test the principles of Marxism than Russia as it existed under the Czars?

Robeson: No. I would say the best country in the world to test the principles of Marxism might be the America of today, with the wealth and so forth.

Combs: Yes, but I am speaking of 1917.

Robeson: I would say it was not a good test because Russia was too poor, if you would want to test it. So I would say no, that Marxist conditions were evolved where proletarians were strongest. It was Lenin who had to practically restate Marxism in order to explain why it happened in Russia, because far from being the strongest link it was the weakest link.

Tenney: Thank you, Mr. Robeson, for coming before us.

Robeson: Thank you.

Paul had succeeded in converting the Tenney Committee's red-baiting questions into a debate about race and Marxism. The press reported his testimony widely under positive headlines such as "Robeson Suggests U.S. Test Marxism" (*New York Times*) and "'Russia Has Real Equality,' Says Paul Robeson" (Associated Press).

Immediately after testifying, Paul refocused his attention on his 1946–1947 concert tour consisting of eighty-five concerts. Larry Brown recalled that Paul reached his "greatest peak as a singer" during this tour. "But music has never meant to Paul what it means to me," Larry mused. "In other circumstances I doubt if Paul would have been a singer. It's irony that at the peak of his career he was more difficult to work with than during all the years before. He was in a terrible mood. He constantly felt he could not sing another concert."[18]

It distressed Paul to walk onto the concert stage night after night to sing to wealthy white audiences for huge fees while his people were being brutalized and lynched. Yet he transformed his offstage anger into artistic energy. He knew that his ability to make a significant political impact depended primarily on his peerless stature as a concert artist. Exercising his twin strengths of a powerful will and iron discipline, he attracted the largest and most enthusiastic audiences of his career. "Crowds Jam Theatre for Robeson Concert; Thunders of Applause," blared the *Herald* in Montreal after his October 28 concert.

And so the tour went across Canada and the United States—Ottawa, Quebec City, Toronto, Chicago, Minneapolis, Duluth, Cleveland, Erie, Bethlehem, New York, among others—until the Christmas break.

In Washington, D.C., FBI director J. Edgar Hoover stepped up his personal supervision of the Robeson file. On November 25, 1946, he wrote the New York Field Office:

> The Bureau desires that your office prepare a report in summary form in this case setting forth by witnesses only such information of a legally admissible character as will tend to prove, directly or circumstantially, membership in or affiliation with the Communist Party, and knowledge of the revolutionary aims and purposes of that organization. Temporary symbols should be used to protect the identities of those informants who are in a position to testify.

Although Hoover had no "legally admissible" evidence, either direct or circumstantial, that Paul was a communist, he continued to label him a Communist Party member who used the alias "John Thomas." Hoover prodded his media contacts in the Hearst press to vilify Paul at every opportunity, relying especially on columnist Walter Winchell. Soon a constant stream of attacks appeared in conservative newspapers across the nation. Paul shrugged off the media attacks and remained outwardly unconcerned about the ever more obvious FBI surveillance.

Paul spent his holiday in New York relaxing among friends, one of whom was Ellsworth Raymond "Bumpy" Johnson, the head of Harlem's "black Mafia" and a favorite chess partner. Bumpy was a self-described "race man" who put most of his teenage numbers runners through college. Required to read a book from his library every week and give him a brief summary, they couldn't cheat because Bumpy had read every book he loaned.

Bumpy, a mild-mannered, brown-skinned man of medium height, resembled a Howard University English professor rather than Harlem's number one gangster. He was dressed casually but elegantly when he ushered Paul into the expansive second-floor den of his fashionable Harlem brownstone. A vast library of books lined the walls. Ivory chessmen were in place on a carved wood chess table.

As usual, Paul and Bumpy talked about everything from world and local politics to Shakespeare's verse in *Othello*. Bumpy had taken his family to see Paul's *Othello* during its Broadway run. When Paul mentioned that he had studied the role in Shakespeare's original Elizabethan English to get a feel of the poetry, Bumpy went to a library shelf and picked out a volume of Chaucer's *Canterbury Tales* and a translation of *Beowulf* from the ancient Anglo-Saxon. With a mischievous grin, he said, "I keep these two volumes right next to my volume of Shakespeare's works in Elizabethan." Paul smiled and shook his head in silent admiration.

Then the conversation turned to Paul's confrontation with President Truman. Bumpy felt Paul had crossed a line and should be concerned about his personal security. The U.S. government would never let a black man get away with something like that and stay in one piece. Paul tried to laugh off the idea but accepted Bumpy's offer of protection whenever he would need it.

Their chess game was in progress when Paul caught a glimpse of several men with long cases hurrying up the staircase past the open double doors of the den.

"What's going on?"

"Nothing much," Bumpy replied. "There's been a misunder-standing with some business competitors sponsored by some folks downtown who would like to encroach on Harlem. The roof needs to be secured."

"Oh. I see," Paul said in a small voice.

Increasingly anxious about the possibility of being caught in the crossfire of a Mafia hit, Paul approached the chess game with a view toward making a quick exit without offending his friend. But he could not afford to be perceived as "throwing" the game. The strain took its toll, and at one point his knees started to shake so much that he had to hold them down with his left hand.

Paul's uncharacteristic choice of an aggressive, unorthodox open-ing designed to force a quickly resolved contest met with little success. Bumpy elevated his game, producing a prolonged struggle ending in a draw. Paul was so engrossed in the game that he temporarily forgot his fear. But when Bumpy suggested a rematch, he bowed out.

When he exited the front door, Paul realized he still had to traverse half a block to find a taxicab. Somehow maintaining his dignity while resisting the urge to run, he walked "mighty fast" to the nearest corner. As the cab arrived at the McGhees' on 89th Street near Fifth Avenue, the black driver said, "Mr. Robeson, a car has been following us: I think it's the FBI." Once again, it was evident that a continuation of his present political course would invite physical danger.[19]

6

STORM WARNINGS

(1946–1948)

When I came home on my Christmas 1946 army furlough, I noticed that my father spent no time at all in Enfield. The estrangement between my parents had obviously grown. Paul had ended his affair with Uta Hagen and resumed his relationship with Freda Diamond. Essie felt neglected, and rumors that Freda might want to marry Paul stoked her resentment. On December 1, she had written to Paul venting her anger:

Paul Dear:

I want to have one more talk with you about money, and then I don't ever want to trouble you about it again. It is also about Bob [Rockmore], and I want to get it off my chest. I don't want the few times we do meet, to have to discuss these things with you. So. Let's get it over with.

For years, Bobby has kept me down to an allowance which really was never enough to run the house. In consequence, I have had to send him bill after bill, and with each bill I have had an argument, and he has scolded me, and told me I'm extravagant, and then has very generously paid it. I have discovered at this late date that he likes to control everything, and he likes to hand out; that's why it went on this way. But if you look back, I've never had a personal allowance of any kind ever since we've been back in America, and I've never had enough to run the house properly. I've always had to work like mad myself to make ends meet, do half the work, shop for prices and so on.

So now I'm through with all that stuff. I feel at 50, which I will be on the 15th, I'm going to start a new life altogether. I'm going to get myself settled and straightened out, so I'll know where I am, where I'm going, and how. In order to do that, we shall have to have some things clear between us:

1. Am I to continue to be Mrs. Robeson? Yes or No.
2. You definitely want to keep the house here? So do I. I love it, and I think we both could be very happy here, without getting under each other's heels.
3. So long as Bobby continues to pay the general bills as he does, I can manage nicely with the $100 a week household allowance, thank you.
4. I want a personal allowance, permanently, when you work, and when you can afford it.

So now you think it over, and decide for *yourself* what you want to do about it. I feel I am at a turning point in my life, and I don't want to make any mistakes, or have any unnecessary complications. My wings are itching, and I think I'm going to fly. But I want good visibility before I take off.

Love to Bert and Gig [McGhee]. See you.

Affectionately,
Essie

Paul didn't reply to Essie's letter. However, he promptly instructed Bob Rockmore to meet her financial demands. She was left with no response to her query about whether she would continue to be Mrs. Robeson, and this caused her great anxiety. When I asked my mother what was wrong, she became distraught. She collapsed in my arms, shaking with sobs, saying Paul was going to marry Freda. I said I didn't think so and promised that I would ask him.

I went to see Freda. She began our conversation by asking me how I would like having two mothers. I answered that I was satisfied with my parental arrangement and would do everything I could to keep it the way it was. Then I politely excused myself.

I found Paul at the McGhees' apartment. With some hesitation, I came directly to the point: Did he intend to divorce Essie and marry Freda? I felt I had a right to know. To my relief, he appeared neither angry nor resentful. After a pause, during which he seemed to be in deep thought, he answered quietly, seriously, succinctly.

Yes, he said, I had a right to know. No, he would not marry Freda. That idea was hers, not his. The path he had chosen ruled out the possibility of divorcing Essie and marrying a white woman. Moreover, Freda had become too possessive, and he had decided to distance himself from her. With that, he closed the subject. Subsequent events demonstrated that he made his position clear to both Essie and Freda: Essie never returned to the issue, and she remained friends with Freda. Life resumed as before, as if there had been no crisis.

Paul concentrated on his singing during the January–May 1947 segment of his concert tour. Determined to demonstrate once more his mastery on the concert stage, he took vocal risks by adding new art songs, such as Monteverdi's "Lamento D'Arianna" and an aria from Jacopo Peri's "Euridice," to his repertoire. Consistently rapturous reviews appeared under enthusiastic headlines: "Paul Robeson Holds His Grip on Audience"; "Robeson Charms 2,300 at Recital with Versatility"; "Robeson Eloquence Stirs 3,000."[1]

But his concern about the racial climate continued to grow. On January 29, 1947, in St. Louis, the largest city in President Truman's home state of Missouri, Paul joined a picket line with thirty members of the Civil Rights Congress in front of the American Theater to protest its policy of racial segregation. Interviewed as he marched, he announced plans to take two years off from his artistic career to "talk up and down the nation against hatred and prejudice. It seems that I must raise my voice, but not by singing pretty songs."[2]

The danger of this stance materialized immediately after Paul's St. Louis concert. Riding in a right front car seat on a Missouri highway, he narrowly escaped death when the left front wheel came off the car. Fortunately, no one was injured. A newspaper headline read, "Paul Robeson Cheats Death in Missouri." Paul's friends wondered who was behind the attempt on his life. I subsequently learned that Hoover's FBI had both Paul and the driver under twenty-four-hour surveillance. Did the FBI play a role in this event? Paul, outwardly unfazed, continued his concert tour.[3]

On March 5, 1947, Paul sang at the University of Utah in Salt Lake City, where he told the packed concert audience that he was retiring from the formal concert stage for at least two years. "From now on," he said, I shall sing for my trade union and college friends—only at gatherings where I can sing what I please." This strategy would soon be tested in Peoria, Illinois, known statewide as an especially racist town.[4]

On April 13, five days before Paul's scheduled evening concert at the Peoria Shrine Mosque, fierce intimidation inspired by the all-white Post No. 2 of the American Legion forced the Shrine Mosque to cancel his appearance. When Paul's sponsors—the local CIO unions, the Illinois Civil Rights Congress, and several black ministers—applied for the use of the Peoria city hall instead, Mayor Carl Triebel blocked them. He called a meeting of the city council, which unanimously denied their application on the ground that Paul had recently been denounced as a communist sympathizer by the House Committee on Un-American Activities.

But Mayor Triebel had overplayed his hand. Twenty-three members of the Peoria Methodist Ministerial Association quickly passed a carefully worded resolution that "greatly deplored the denial of the use of a public building to Paul Robeson, with whose reported views and affiliations we are not in sympathy." Denying Paul the right to public expression was "a disservice to democracy itself." The ministers invited him to speak under their auspices. Mayor Triebel countered by barring Paul from entering the city, citing a state law allowing him to take steps to avoid "riots and other disturbances."

On the morning of the concert, Paul defiantly announced he would leave for Peoria from Decatur on the afternoon train. Triebel ordered eight plainclothes and six uniformed police officers to intercept him at the Peoria train station. Union members from CIO locals and activists from the Civil Rights Congress joined Paul, William Patterson, and Max Yergan in Decatur to assess the danger. They reached unanimous agreement to challenge the ban by avoiding the train station.

A determined Paul and an anxious Larry were driven to Peoria in a convoy of cars filled with union men armed with rifles, shotguns, and pistols to protect Paul from armed groups of racists. The convoy traveled over back roads into the heart of Peoria's black district, where Paul was safe and welcome. There they were joined by armed black volunteers. When Patterson and Yergan arrived in Peoria to confer with Paul, they faced a new crisis. Facing police opposition and concerned by the potential of violence between the heavily armed groups, the three decided to call off the concert.

A reception was held at the home of a local black union leader. There was no violence, but it was a major defeat for Paul and a clear signal that there was a high price to pay for continuing on his present course.[5]

On April 20, on my way home following my discharge from the army, I joined my parents at the gala Washington, D.C., wedding party of a socialite Cardozo cousin. My mother's relatives of all hues—from extremely dark to a blonde, blue-eyed woman who had been "passing" for white since childhood—had converged under one roof.

I was struck by my mother's transformation in the four months since I had seen her at Enfield. She evoked the time seven years earlier when she and Paul were the toast of Harlem's social scene. Paul appeared proud to have her on his arm. He seemed remarkably relaxed, given that he had just come from an armed confrontation, but I discovered soon enough the coiled tension underneath his calm pose.

As the affair ended, my father took me aside and asked that I accompany him to the Soviet embassy. He needed me as a translator because of my fluency in Russian, and as a witness. He explained no further, but his tone manifested an uncharacteristic wariness. I wondered why he needed me, since his Russian was quite good, but I agreed.

A short while later, we sat in an ornate anteroom of the embassy exchanging pleasantries in Russian with Soviet deputy foreign minister Andrei Vyshinsky and his personal translator. His charming manner belied his reputation. He had been the ruthless prosecutor in all three of Stalin's orchestrated purge trials of 1936, 1937, and 1938. Of medium height, stocky, with receding grayish hair, he could have been mistaken for a New England governor. An occasional steely glance augured otherwise.

Abruptly, Vyshinsky leaned forward in his armchair, fixed Paul with a steady gaze, and bluntly stated his agenda. The gist of what he said concerned the Soviet Union's perception of "Zionism" in the United States as an acute danger that was subverting Soviet Jews. The "Soviet people" felt that "progressive America" in general and Paul in particular "could be helpful" in "counteracting" this threat.

I translated for my father, who responded in English. Progressive America, he said, including himself, believed that anti-Semitism, rather than Zionism, was a danger in the United States. The Soviet Union's support of the creation of the state of Israel contradicted the

idea of an international Zionist threat. Moreover, his understanding
was that the loyalty of Soviet Jews was not in question.

Vyshinsky's jaws tightened as his translator conveyed Paul's words.
After a slight pause, he replied with a thin smile that the loyalty of
Soviet citizens was currently being reassessed according to Soviet
standards. After all, ten years had passed since "the homeland" had
been "cleansed." The essential point, he said, was that progressives
had a responsibility to denounce the attempts of American Zionists
to subvert Soviet Jews.

The "cleansing" ten years earlier was a veiled but chilling
reference to Stalin's "Great Terror"—the purge of 1937. This realization shocked us both. Paul paused before replying that he refused
to make such a statement because he disagreed with its content
and the framework within which it had been posed. The translator
softened "refused" to "couldn't" and "disagreed with" to "critical
of." "Framework" became "possible implications." I glanced at my
father, whose command of Russian was sufficient to understand the
changes, and he nodded. I turned to Vyshinsky and, in Russian,
corrected his translator. As they both reddened, Paul suggested in
Russian that we all join the reception. Vyshinsky took a moment to
gather himself, and then, decorum restored, we all walked out of the
room chatting amiably in Russian.

A bit later, as Paul prepared to sing a few songs from the balcony
to the assembled guests and embassy staff, he turned to me and asked
that I write out the lyrics of "Ol' Man River" for him. I looked at him
in disbelief, but seeing the expression on his face, I did as he asked.
Until then he had manifested no trace of stress. Now I realized how
much he had needed me as an aide and witness. Reassured by the
lyrics he held in his palm, he sang without glancing at them. As our
taxi exited the embassy driveway, my father said, "Not a word of this
to anyone, you understand?"

On April 23, Mayor Erastus Corning III of Albany, New York,
pressured the board of education into canceling Paul's scheduled
May 9 appearance in the Philip Livingstone Junior High School
auditorium. The school board's sole reason was the "controversial"
nature of the concert, but the implied reference to the Peoria incident was obvious. The Carver Cultural Society, representing the
black Methodist sponsors, immediately went to court, denouncing

the cancellation as "an insult to the Negro people and to one of the greatest Americans of this age."

Two days later, Paul defended his rights in a speech at a New York City rally organized by the Council on African Affairs:

> There's no clearer example of fascism than what I saw in Peoria the other night. Nor have I seen a clearer example of the use of certain fascist techniques to confuse the people. The main one, of course, is the use of the red bogey, the communist bogey, to break the back of the whole liberal movement in our country.
>
> If this could happen in Peoria, it may also happen in Albany and in other cities. Whether I am or am not a communist or communist sympathizer is irrelevant. The question is whether American citizens, regardless of their beliefs or sympathies, may enjoy their constitutional rights.
>
> I stand here fighting as an artist against fascism wherever I see it raise its head. And since I have seen it raise its head here in our own land—we fight it, you fight it, I fight it, all of us fight it—to the death!!

On May 5, New York State Supreme Court justice Isadore Bookstein issued an injunction restraining the Albany Board of Education from interfering with Paul's concert but barring Paul from making a speech. The Albany public ignored the American Legion's calls to boycott the concert and Paul sang to a capacity audience of eleven hundred people. While the program contained no spoken comments except those that introduced his songs, Paul's political message was delivered through his choice of encores.[6]

On March 12, 1947, President Truman had proclaimed his anti-communist "Truman Doctrine" to a joint session of Congress, and Paul had decided it was essential to rally vigorous public opposition. Touring as a vice chairman of the Progressive Citizens of America for the remainder of 1947, he helped found chapters, promoted the idea of building a third-party to run former U.S. vice president Henry Wallace for president in 1948, and supported CIO unions in their organizing drives.

On May 25, 1947, Paul traveled to the Panama Canal Zone to help the United Public Workers of America unionize. He sang four concerts with tickets that could have been sold for ten dollars, priced at one dollar so workers could attend. The first concert drew an audience of ten thousand; another, held in Panama City's open-air stadium, was attended by the president of Panama, Don Enrique Jimenez.

Paul also scheduled occasional concerts to assert his right to perform professionally. In late June, he sang to a capacity audience in Boston's Symphony Hall, with many turned away. His July 19 concert filled New York City's Lewisohn Stadium with nineteen thousand fans so enthusiastic they compelled him to add seven encores to the first half of his program. During the second half, he prefaced his rendition of the "Hasidic Chant," which contains the line "Why hast thou so oppressed thy people, O Lord?" with the comment that it spoke for his people also. Then he dedicated the Spanish civil war song "The Four Insurgent Generals" to members of the Joint Anti-Fascist Refugee Committee who had just been sentenced to jail for contempt of the House Committee on Un-American Activities.[7]

Press attacks against Paul increased after a June Gallup poll listed him among forty-eight runners-up to America's ten most popular public figures. Hoover enthusiastically approved a syndicated column by conservative George E. Sokolsky, who wrote, "If Robeson chooses to be both singer and propagandist, that is his risk." Across the bottom of the page on which the column appeared, Hoover wrote, "A good summary on Robeson, so don't let it get lost." FBI documents from 1947 also reveal that Hoover influenced the Department of State to refuse the validation of Paul's passport for travel to Europe. A State Department document dated December 5, 1947, and signed by Ruth B. Shipley, chief of the Passport Office, gave "under investigation by the FBI" as the reason for the refusal.[8]

In June 1947, Truman veered to the left in his domestic policy despite pursuing a right-wing foreign policy. The administration's Civil Rights Committee publication *To Secure These Rights* recommended an antilynching law, abolition of the poll tax, statutes protecting the right to vote, integration of the military, denial of federal funds to institutions that discriminate, and federal laws against discrimination and segregation in employment, interstate commerce, and public accommodations.

By preempting the NAACP's civil rights agenda, Truman ensured that most black leaders would remain loyal to him. At the same time, liberals, white and black alike, became deathly afraid of being labeled "pro-Communist" or "soft on Soviet tyranny." This fear prevented them from mounting any coherent opposition to Truman's increasingly imperial foreign policy. Paul's uncompromising left-wing political stance and his open attacks on Truman isolated him from the black elite, making him more vulnerable to right-wing attacks.[9]

Bolstered by the anticommunist political climate and fed by information from Hoover's FBI, the House Committee on Un-American Activities intensified its crusade against the left. Paul was a principal target, as Hollywood actor Adolphe Menjou demonstrated in his October 21, 1947, testimony under questioning by Richard Nixon, Republican congressman from California. When asked what test he would apply to determine whether someone was a communist, Menjou replied, "Well, I think attending any meetings at which Mr. Paul Robeson appeared, and applauding or listening to his Communist songs in America."[10]

Paul responded by intensifying his political activity. On December 29, 1947, he joined a thousand others in Chicago to meet with Henry Wallace in an effort to convince him to make a run for the presidency as the candidate of the newly created Progressive Party. That afternoon, with the press excluded, Wallace received his supporters for over four hours. Hundreds at a time crowded into a suite at the Knickerbocker Hotel. Workers came directly from their factories at the end of the day shift to listen and express their views.

At one point, Paul "pushed his way to the front of the room and spoke briefly on the need for a Presidential candidate who favored race equality without equivocation. Then he sang some of his most popular songs. There were tears in the eyes of both Robeson and Wallace—and of others too—when he finished." For the next six months Paul traveled around the country, often at Wallace's side, bringing the Progressive Party's message in speech and song.[11]

On January 29, 1948, the formal announcement launching the national Wallace for President Committee listed Paul as a co-chairman. Traveling from New York City to New Orleans, and from Richmond,

Virginia, to Louisville, Kentucky, Paul galvanized Progressive Party rallies, meetings, and fund-raisers. During one eight-week period in April and May, he made twenty appearances at major events in New York, West Virginia, Ohio, Massachusetts, and Connecticut.

A request by the International Longshore and Warehouse Union in March came as a welcome change of pace. The union asked Paul to come to Hawaii for ten days to help with their organizing drive. Larry Brown, who hated to fly, decided not to go. Composer Earl Robinson, who joined Paul as accompanist and assisting artist, recalled the trip in his autobiography:

> We traveled by plane and car on six of the islands, presenting a total of twenty-seven concerts. On the first day, in preparation for a concert in Honolulu, Big Paul learned four new songs—in Chinese, Japanese, Filipino and Hawaiian. I was with him when this Filipino fellow came up with a song for him. Paul listened intently, memorized the tune, wrote down the words, and sang it on his program that night and thereafter.
>
> Paul made such a splash, I think the islands have not been the same since. The leading paper in Honolulu had a full page of letters every day we were there, one writer from the American Legion charging that both Paul and I had been cited as Communists in a 1947 Congressional report. But the letters ran about six to one in favor of Robeson, in spite of his never pulling any punches.
>
> We sang for the Leper Settlement at Kalaupappa, where they joined in the singing better than anywhere else. To hear them sing "Aloha-oe" after we finished our concert moved us both almost to tears.[12]

Paul often said that the audience at the leper settlement at Kalaupapa on Molokai Island was one of the most inspiring he had ever experienced. The legend in the islands is that he sang to the lepers "until the stars faded." It was unique for an artist of Robeson's stature to perform there.

Hoover kept looking, unsuccessfully, for evidence of Paul's alleged treachery. In a March 18, 1948, memorandum to the Honolulu special agent in charge, during Paul's Hawaiian trip, he wrote, "In view of the possibility that the subject [Robeson] may be engaged in intelligence activities in Honolulu, you are directed to closely follow his activities while he is there to determine if he contacts any Communist Party members or representatives of allied organizations."

At the same time, Hoover gloated over his successful recruitment of a "confidential informant" in the leadership of the Council on African Affairs. Ever since November 1947, when Attorney General Tom Clark had placed the council on his list of subversive "Communist Front" organizations, Alphaeus Hunton, the council's deputy leader, and Max Yergan, its executive director, had clashed over the organization's direction. Hunton believed Yergan was bent on removing the pro-communist "taint" from the council by adding a noncommunist clause to its bylaws. Doxey Wilkerson, a third member of the council's top leadership, feared that Yergan was attempting to destroy the council from within. My parents' FBI files subsequently confirmed that Yergan was the FBI informant referred to by Hoover.[13]

Wilkerson and Hunton shared their apprehensions with Ben Davis and Essie. Davis discounted them, but Essie was open to their concerns. When she tried to alert Paul, he brushed aside her arguments because of his eight years of close collaboration with Max. Undaunted, Essie followed her instincts and joined the fray at the council in opposition to Yergan. She finally convinced Paul that he needed to throw his full weight as chairman behind the effort to prevent Yergan from taking over the council.

Paul's return from Honolulu was just in time for him to join Essie, Wilkerson, and Hunton in the last of the battles that narrowly succeeded in ousting Yergan from the council. However, victory came at a high price. The organization was exhausted, permanently weakened by the exodus of many of its most prestigious members, who had been alienated by prolonged internal conflict. Judge Hubert T. Delany, Adam Clayton Powell Jr., Channing Tobias, and Mary McCleod Bethune simply stopped coming to meetings. Only W. E. B. DuBois remained loyal, and he paid a heavy price—the NAACP fired him from his position as "Director of Special Research."

As in the Council on African Affairs, the ranks of the Progressive Party leadership were split between those who wanted to disavow communist support and those, like Paul and Henry Wallace, who were opposed to such a policy and prevailed. Wallace paid dearly among mainstream Democratic voters for this position and also for his insistence that diplomacy should replace military confrontation in relations with the Soviet Union.[14]

The Truman administration exploited this rift in Progressive Party ranks by continuously identifying Wallace and the Progressive Party with the communists. At the same time, the president intensified the anti-Soviet nuances of his foreign policy. As Russia grew to be perceived as America's enemy, Paul's continued pro-Soviet stance eroded his popularity among the general public. With the anti-Robeson drumbeat swelling in the press, Paul began to need heavy security whenever he appeared at Progressive Party meetings outside of predominantly black communities. However, it was staunch anticommunist A. Philip Randolph, rather than Paul, who was the main black leader to oppose Truman's March 17, 1948, request that Congress reinstitute the draft to counter the Russian military capability. Randolph demanded integration of the U.S. armed forces prior to resumption of the draft. At a March 22, 1948, meeting between black leaders and President Truman, Randolph declared, "The mood among Negroes of this country is that they will never bear arms again until all forms of bias and discrimination are abolished." Truman replied, "I wish you hadn't made that statement. I don't like it at all." He ended the meeting, but Randolph, testifying nine days later before the Senate Armed Services Committee, warned:

> This time Negroes will not take a Jim Crow draft lying down. The conscience of the world will be shaken as by nothing else when thousands and thousands of us second-class Americans choose imprisonment in preference to permanent military slavery. I personally will advise Negroes to refuse to fight as slaves for a democracy they cannot possess and cannot enjoy. Many veterans, bitter over Army Jim Crow, have indicated that they will act spontaneously in this fashion, regardless of any organized movement. "Never again," they say with finality. I shall appeal to thousands of white youth in schools and colleges. I shall urge them to demonstrate their solidarity with Negro youth by ignoring the entire registration and induction machinery.[15]

In contrast, Paul, who believed that a segregated military was preferable to an all-white force, opposed Randolph's position. Paul reasoned that a large black presence in the U.S. armed forces would serve as an effective deterrent against the possibility of widespread violence being inflicted upon African Americans, whether by white mobs or by the U.S. government itself.[16]

Although most other black leaders also opposed Randolph publicly, a poll of black draft-age college students by the NAACP's Youth Division showed that 71 percent favored a civil disobedience campaign against the draft. Randolph kept up the pressure on the White House throughout the spring of 1948, while Paul helped Wallace's Progressive Party campaign attract large numbers of black voters. Truman eventually bowed to the pressure and desegregated the armed forces on July 26, 1948.

On May 31, Paul went on the offensive, arriving in Washington, D.C., to testify under oath at his own request before the Judiciary Committee of the U.S. Senate in opposition to the Mundt-Nixon bill. The legislation, sponsored by Senator Karl Mundt of North Dakota and Representative Richard Nixon of California, would require members of the Communist Party and of designated "Communist Front" organizations to register with the government. The Progressive Party, as well as many liberals, opposed the bill as a violation of civil rights. Paul was questioned by Republican senator Homer Ferguson of Michigan:

Robeson: [The bill] says that it's to prevent the establishment of a totalitarian dictatorship which in any country results from the ruthless suppression of all opposition to the party in power. That is what I am interested in—this complete subordination of the rights of individuals to the state; the denial of fundamental rights and liberties, and the resulting maintenance of control over the people through fear, terrorism and brutality. I have been all over the United States speaking and attempting to speak, and I have been experiencing this very thing of control over the people through fear, terrorism and brutality.

Ferguson: Mr. Robeson, are you or are you not—

Robeson: I will answer that in just a moment.

Ferguson: Are you or are you not a member of the Communist Party?

Robeson: Can I go on with my discussion? I will answer that.

Ferguson: Yes.

Robeson: This bill seems to me to have as its basic idea not to help the people of the United States or any other people, but to actually stop the struggle by terrorizing people who get rights for

Negro people, for workers and for other Americans who still haven't full citizenship.

Ferguson: Mr. Robeson, are you an American Communist?

Robeson: Just let me finish the point. I will answer that question.

Ferguson: Now I ask you the question; you said you would answer it. Are you or are you not an American Communist?

Robeson: Today, Senator Ferguson, that question has become the very basis of the struggle for American civil liberties. Nineteen or more of the most brilliant and distinguished Americans are about to go to jail for failure to answer that question, and I am going to join them if necessary. I refuse to answer the question.

Ferguson: All right, you refuse to answer—

Robeson: This is an invasion of my right of secret ballot, Senator Ferguson. If you want to know whether I am, the Communist Party is a legal party like the Democratic Party and the Republican Party. I'm going to vote pretty soon, and if you want to send some government officials to take my ballot away, my constitutional right, you can see just what I mean.

Ferguson: Would you fight for America if we were at war with Russia?

Robeson: That would depend on the conditions of war with Russia, how the war came up, and who is in power at the time, etc.

Two days later, Paul led three thousand picketers at the White House protesting the Mundt-Nixon bill. The committee considered citing Paul for contempt but ultimately refrained.[17]

After a ten-day campaign trip for the Wallace presidential ticket in the Deep South—New Orleans, Atlanta, Greensboro, Winston-Salem, Durham, Raleigh, Chapel Hill, and Richmond—Paul sang at a June 26 "Tribute to Negro Veterans"at the Uline Arena in Washington, D.C. World boxing champion Joe Louis took the stage to extol "my friend Paul Robeson":

Paul Robeson fights for the things that Congress didn't do for me and my people. I want Paul to know that I stand squarely, both feet in his corner, because he is in the corner of the Negro people.

There are some people who don't like the way Paul Robeson fights for my people. Well, I say that Paul is fighting for what all of us want, and that's freedom to be a man. None of us can afford to stand aside from what the fight is for and what the fight's against.

So I say again, a salute to Paul Robeson and to all you GIs. We're with you, Paul, in the fight to the end.[18]

Paul was deeply moved by Louis's words and the outpouring of love from the capacity audience. It helped steel his resolve to continue carrying the fight to the Truman administration.

Throughout July, Paul appeared at huge Progressive Party rallies, culminating in the Wallace nominating convention at Philadelphia's Convention Hall. For two days, beginning July 23, 1948, 12,000 people filled the main floor and galleries—3,240 delegates and alternates, joined by 8,400 visitors—exceeding the most optimistic expectations. Wallace was nominated for president on the second day, along with Idaho senator Glen Taylor for vice president. When they appeared onstage with their families, the throng roared, screamed, shouted, and sang for fifteen minutes. Only the candidates' departure ended the demonstration.

That evening, Wallace and Taylor accepted their nominations before a sellout crowd of thirty-two thousand at the Shibe Park baseball stadium, home of the Philadelphia Athletics. Paul had to speak earlier than called for in the program as the insistent chant "We want Robeson!" threatened to bring the proceedings to a halt. After his speech, he sang, and people refused to stop applauding until he reminded them that radio time required it.

When Wallace, profoundly affected by Paul's remarks, closed the evening with his acceptance speech, he spoke in the tones and cadences of a modern Isaiah:

The American dream is the dream of the prophets of old, the dream of each man living in peace under his own vine and fig tree. We are the generation blessed above all generations, because to us is given for the first time in all history the power to make that dream come true.

To make that dream come true, we shall rise above the pettiness of those who preach hate and factionalism, of those who think of themselves rather than the great cause they serve. All you who are within the sound of my voice tonight have been called to serve and to serve mightily, in fulfilling the dream of the prophets and the founders of the American system.[19]

However, the political climate worsened dramatically for progressives. On July 20, 1948, the FBI raided the Manhattan headquarters of the Communist Party USA and confiscated records. Soon after, Attorney General Thomas Clark announced the indictment of the top twelve Communist Party leaders under the Smith Act for "conspiring to teach and advocate the overthrow of the United States Government by force and violence." The twelve were arrested and put on trial, signaling the beginning of an extended period of severe political repression. The ongoing Soviet blockade of the Western-controlled sectors of Berlin, which had begun on June 24, 1948, was dangerously escalating the cold war. In this political environment, the Progressive Party became the target of ferocious red-baiting because its leadership steadfastly refused to denounce Soviet foreign policy or to expel communists from its ranks.

Far from being intimidated, Paul set out with Larry on an August campaign tour for the Progressive Party in California.

Paul spent most of September in and around New York City, relaxing with friends. When he went to Enfield, it was as a visitor, but Essie appeared satisfied with her secure status as Mrs. Robeson. She did not outwardly resent the time he spent with his many friends, including the Rosens, whom he had recently met.

Helen, the wife of Dr. Samuel Rosen, a celebrated and pioneering ear surgeon at Manhattan's Mount Sinai Hospital, had met Paul in the course of her volunteer work for the Progressive Party. The Rosen family, including children Judith and John, adopted him, and his close ties with them endured for the rest of his life. Helen, a member of the wealthy van Dernoot family, came from a background markedly different from the world Paul chose to champion. Paul's relationship with her did not interfere with her marriage to Sam, and for Paul it provided a safe and comfortable haven in the bosom of a loving family. In time, Essie accepted Helen as she had Freda.[20]

On September 26, Paul and Larry began a two-week tour of the South on behalf of the 1948 Wallace-Taylor presidential ticket. On a journey full of hazards, they visited Texas, Louisiana, Tennessee, Alabama, Florida, Georgia, South Carolina, and West Virginia.

Paul recounted some of their adventures during an October 29 radio broadcast with Henry Wallace:

> We read in the papers about a Negro being shot when he goes to vote in rural Georgia. So, many of us think that Negroes don't vote in the South. But there are 20,000 in Savannah who vote and hold the balance of power. So in Atlanta; so in Charleston, South Carolina. They told us we couldn't come into Memphis, Tennessee. Boss Crump sent out the order. But we came; a Negro minister gave us the biggest auditorium in town. We had over 3,000 people—one of the finest meetings that ever took place in Memphis.
>
> In Savannah, we couldn't get an auditorium. The people were horrified when the police moved in and took Clark Foreman of our Party off the platform—some said this was the end. But we held a meeting the next night in the Negro district—a magnificent mass meeting, over 2,000 turned out. For they understood what Wallace meant: not just a question of a few civil rights—but of the liberation, the complete liberation of the Negro people in our time.
>
> In Columbus, Georgia we had a meeting, and the Klan drove up in cars across the way. Somebody said they didn't know what was about to happen. But 100 Negroes just stood there outside the meeting, between the meeting and the Klan. We invited them to come into the meeting—but they said, "I guess we'll stay here." It was a fine meeting, and the Klan didn't move.[21]

On election night, as Paul sang to several hundred campaign workers and volunteers at the Progressive Party's New York headquarters, spirits were high, but expectations plummeted as the evening progressed. By 2 a.m. Truman had won an upset victory over Republican candidate Thomas Dewey, largely by adopting most of the Progressive Party's domestic program. Wallace suffered a humiliating defeat: his vote total of 1,157,172 was 12,000 less than Strom Thurmond received on the Dixiecrat ticket. The vast majority of black voters inspired by the Progressive Party's intrepid campaign to register and vote were won over by Truman, whom they saw as a potential winner.

Wallace, though deeply disappointed at his abandonment by the unions and black voters, urged continued struggle: "We have had an extraordinary victory because nothing can beat a spirit of this kind. We didn't have a chance, but we are going to have it."[22]

Paul, confident that the Progressive Party campaign had succeeded in turning the country away from reaction, was not discouraged.

Two weeks after the election, he declared that he did not fear the next four years: "I do not foresee the success of American reaction; I see only its attempt and its failure. By 1950 there will be no fascist threat in our land. The fact that many people did not vote for Henry Wallace does not greatly dismay me. It is most important that they saw dilemmas clearly and voted for a promise of solution."[23]

Having done what he could, Paul returned to the professional concert stage after a year and a half's absence. He had been working regularly with Larry during that time, and his voice had never been better. Columbia Artists Management booked eighty-five concerts for him during the 1948–1949 season at top fees. Local agents had needed some convincing that Paul's program would be nonpolitical. They were mollified by his promised return to the conventional format of his 1940 and 1941 tours with Clara Rockmore but remained extremely anxious as the tour began.

The opening concerts put all fears to rest. Not only were the halls sold out; critics praised Paul unreservedly. The October 23, 1948, issue of the *Detroit News* reported that he "sang one of his typical programs genially and effectively," and was "in tip-top vocal condition." The program included a group by Mussorgsky, a group of folk songs from several lands, a set of Negro spirituals, and art songs from England, France, and Italy. To these he added "O Isis and Osiris" from Mozart's *The Magic Flute*. The numerous encores included "Water Boy," "Ol' Man River" and "Joe Hill." The review concluded, "He stirred, as usual, great enthusiasm." Paul was back in business as a major concert artist.

The more Paul sang, the better he performed, and the greater the enthusiasm of the public. Several of his November concerts were in the West Indies, including Montego Bay and Kingston in Jamaica, and Port of Spain in Trinidad. In a spontaneous mass outpouring of adulation for him, over fifty thousand people jammed the Kingston race course for a free concert. In Montego Bay he sang a capella for a huge crowd in the city square.

"I feel now as if I had drawn my first breath of fresh air in many years," he wrote upon his return. "I felt that for the first time I could see what it will be like when Negroes are free in their own land. I felt something like what a Jew must feel when first he goes to Israel, what a Chinese must feel on entering areas of his country that now are free. If I never hear another kind word again, what I received from my people in the West Indies will be enough for me."[24]

As Paul headed back to Enfield for a well-earned rest during the Christmas break, Bob Rockmore called with the news that his remaining concerts were sold out. But just before Christmas, Paul received devastating news. The entire set of January–April 1949 performances had been canceled by the local booking agents. Columbia Artists Management, Paul's agency, told Bob that this time the intimidation had not come from local right-wingers. The FBI had secretly fanned out across the nation to all of Paul's concert venues to coerce the local agents into canceling the concerts. The threat was stark—if the Robeson concert wasn't canceled, the booking agent would be accused of being a pro-communist subversive and put out of business.[25]

Simultaneously, the major syndicated conservative newspaper columnists attacked Paul's artistry as "Communist propaganda," with Walter Winchell leading the pack. In short order, Paul was banned from the entire entertainment industry—the concert stage, radio, recording, film, the theater. Record stores refused to display or sell his recordings, and radio stations refused to play them. An unattributed rumor that the Metropolitan Opera Company might be considering Paul for the role of Boris Godunov in Mussorgsky's opera of the same name evoked the threat of a boycott from right-wing syndicated columnist George Sokolsky.[26]

In less than two months, Paul's comeback season had been destroyed at the instigation of the U.S. government. It remained to be seen if this meant the end of his career.

7

INTO THE EYE OF THE STORM

(1949)

For the first time in his professional life, Paul was without access to his concert audience. Needing a haven where he could gather his thoughts and revive his spirits, he returned to Enfield in late December 1948. And despite the tension and alienation that marred his relationship with Essie, she was supportive in his time of crisis.

The entire landscape changed abruptly a few days after his homecoming. Bob Rockmore arrived from New York with startling good news. He brought an offer from England for a concert tour of the British Isles and Scandinavia lasting from early February well into May. He also had obtained, apparently over the objections of J. Edgar Hoover's FBI, the U.S. State Department's written consent to renew Paul's passport. But there was a catch. Paul would have to sign a waiver certifying that his exclusive travel purpose was to fulfill contractual concert engagements and agreeing not to make any political or charitable appearances. He signed the waiver despite its restrictions. As Paul recalled later, "I'm sitting here, and everybody says, 'Well, your career has ended.' So a guy comes over from England, and he wants the Philadelphia Symphony and me. Now, beat that."[1]

My parents were in high spirits when I arrived home from Cornell for Christmas with my girlfriend, Marilyn Greenberg, also a Cornell student. She was an attractive five-foot-six, dark-haired twenty-year-old with a flashing smile, beautiful eyes, and a witty sense of humor, whose parents were turn-of-the-century immigrants from Romania. We had been dating for more than a year and now decided it was time for her to meet my parents.

Marilyn had grown up in New York City's Queens neighborhoods of Sunnyside and Forest Hills, while I was a world traveler and an Army Air Force veteran. But despite our vastly different backgrounds, we delighted in each other's company and were deeply in love—so much so that we largely ignored the hostility our interracial pairing frequently evoked among whites. This sense of security with each other was reinforced by the friendly acceptance we encountered in most black settings and among our wide circle of friends.

One of our difficulties was the opposition of Marilyn's father, Jack. I was not welcome in his home. We dated in Manhattan, rode the subway to Queens, and parted a block away from her front door. For Marilyn's mother, Rae, the situation was an unfamiliar one, initially arousing her concern for her daughter's future welfare. In these circumstances, my parents' approval meant a great deal.

They greeted Marilyn warmly. Essie liked her right away, and Paul put her at ease. The four of us spent a comfortable few days together. On the day of Marilyn's departure, she and I were deep in conversation in a corner of the living room while Essie and Paul were going over some papers across the room. Absorbed with each other, we were barely aware of them. I was in midsentence when the arresting sound of my father's deep bass intruded suddenly: "Congratulations, you two!" Marilyn, my mother, and I were startled. Paul grinned broadly; Essie looked stunned, and Marilyn exclaimed, "How did you know?" Paul laughed his hearty belly laugh: "It's hard not to sense the love between you. When's the date? I'd like to be there."

After a confirming nod from Marilyn, I turned back to my father: "You're right, Dad; we decided last night to get engaged. We're thinking about a June wedding." My mother, still not recovered from her initial shock, congratulated us a little stiffly. She had hoped I would marry someone from the top ranks of the black elite. However, by the end of Marilyn's visit, Essie was a comfortable prospective mother-in-law.

• • •

Steaming across the Atlantic on the *Queen Mary* in early February 1949, Paul wrote Clara Rockmore a letter:

Darling Clarochka,

You'll never know how I enjoyed your thoughts of me. Have worked at Chinese—Yiddish—French—Hebrew & have gone through one pad. I miss you terribly already. Refused to sing a concert [for the passengers], but will sing for the crew. Will let you know how concerts shape up. I really don't much relish them, but I realize how important they are. Read Bob's cable—will be very, very careful.

This is just a note, and I'll try to do this often. Believe it or not, I love you both very deeply, & here's a good hug and kiss for you.

Love, Pavlik [Russian diminutive for Paul]

On February 24, he wrote again to Clara from London, reporting that he had received "a wonderful reception from press and public." His March 16 and April 7 concerts at Albert Hall, with its eight thousand seating capacity, were already almost sold out. "I miss you terribly," he added. "I just can't pick up here with my friends, tho' I've enjoyed seeing them. But I'm terribly lonely." He asked her to write him and to send him clippings about news at home.

Two concerts at London's ten-thousand-seat Harringay Arena on April 17 and 18 were added to the schedule, along with a concert in late April at Manchester's Bellevue Hall, which also held ten thousand. Paul insisted on adding these concerts at low ticket prices so working people could afford to attend. He sang for a dollar tops and as low as a dime (sixpence). Poor people could manage to pay a dime for round-trip bus fare and a dime to hear the concert. Paul's concert manager was outraged. However, he couldn't complain because the highest-priced concerts were already sold out.

By this time, the cold war between the United States and the Soviet Union had heated up. Tensions had increased to the point where some of President Truman's military advisers proposed a preemptive war against Russia, but Truman had so far rejected such extreme proposals. With public opposition to U.S. foreign policy increasing in Europe and at fever pitch in India, Africa, and Indonesia, Paul was bombarded with invitations to appear on behalf of left-wing political causes. However, mindful of his pledge to remain nonpolitical throughout his professional tour, he turned aside all appeals for both personal appearances and sponsorships.

Paul's caution was well advised. He was under close surveillance by the intelligence apparatus of the U.S. government. February 24 and March 9 Central Intelligence Agency reports from the "Field Operations" division, which had been disseminated to both the FBI and the "Intelligence Division" of the State Department, described his every appearance in detail.

However, Paul was often faced with a dilemma. At his Croydon concert in early March, in south London, people "greeted him not only as a great singer, but as a fighter for peace." After the concert, a group that included representatives of African students presented him with a letter signed by four hundred people. It expressed appreciation for his "magnificent work in the fight against race hatred" and for his "efforts to secure peace." Even though Paul had agreed not to talk about political issues, he responded by speaking of the need for unity between the African peoples, both in the United States and Africa, to combat the big boys of Wall Street who were grabbing the copper and the raw materials of Africa for the benefit of a few.[2]

The many expressions of popular acclaim intensified the growing unease Paul felt about his political abstention in a time of world crisis. At his March 18 Albert Hall concert, he changed the last line of his final encore, "Ol' Man River," from "I'm tired of livin' and scared of dyin'" to "I must keep fightin' until I'm dyin'." By March 25, he decided to return to the political arena in defiance of the high risk such a public step would entail.

On that day, he appeared as the main speaker at a packed meeting of two thousand people in London protesting the racist policies of the South African government. The rally was sponsored by the Coordinating Committee of Colonial Peoples in London and had been organized by Krishna Menon, a close associate of Prime Minister Nehru, and Y. M. Pauloo, Indian leader of the African National Congress in South Africa. An East African student later described the great moment of the evening:

> I had expected eloquence from Robeson, and we got it; I hadn't dared to hope for singing as well—after all, this was a meeting, not a concert. But in his opening words, spoken in that amazingly

deep, thrilling voice, he told us that he would sing to us first; and sing he did—a stirring marching song of German workers, sung in German. It was superb, exciting, inspiring.

And as an orator he was as much an artist as in his singing. At times the great voice was low and soft but with the suggestion of enormous power behind it; and the audience sat intent and still. At other times the voice rose till it filled the hall, and the rushing noise of cheering rose to join it. There was emotion in his voice all right, and in his words and among us in the hall; but all that he said was carefully reasoned, and appealed to our intelligence as well as to our emotions.[3]

As a result of that meeting, the South African radio banned the playing of Paul's records, a move reminiscent of the wartime banning of his recordings by the Nazi gauleiter of Norway. Later, Paul met with leaders of the Coordinating Committee of Colonial Peoples in London, and they asked him to bring a message to the Paris Peace Congress on behalf of the seven hundred million colored people of the colonial world. They did not want war; they wanted independence from colonial domination.[4]

The Paris Peace Congress attracted eighteen hundred delegates from fifty countries—cultural figures, scientists, intellectuals, and trade union leaders. The congress had a pronounced left and anti-U.S. tone. Its prominent attendees included Italian socialist leader Pietro Nenni; French physicist Frédéric Joliot-Curie, an open communist who headed France's Atomic Energy Commission; painter Pablo Picasso; England's "Red" dean of Canterbury, Reverend Hewlett Johnson, and the United States' W. E. B. DuBois. Moreover, despite India's officially neutral stance in the cold war, the Indian delegation was openly opposed to U.S. foreign policy.

On April 20, 1949, in the midst of his European concert tour, Paul strode to the rostrum of the congress and made an extemporaneous speech:

I have come among you in the name of my black brothers and of the American progressives. And I bring you a message from the Coordinating Committee of the Black Peoples of Colonial Countries. These peoples wish to have a better life. They wish to see new programs worked out for human emancipation, programs that will oppose those of the enemies of peace. These black peoples and the other peoples of colonial countries, aspiring to a human standard of living, know that Mr. Truman's so-called bold new program and the invasion of Africa recommended by Mr. Stettinius and the trusts with billions of dollars of capital can lead only to a new slavery against which we shall rise.

We in America do not forget that it was on the backs of the white workers from Europe and on the backs of millions of blacks that the wealth of America was built. And we are resolved to share it equally. We reject any hysterical raving that urges us to make war on anyone. Our will to fight for peace is strong.

We shall not make war on anyone. We shall not make war on the Soviet Union. We oppose those who wish to build up imperialist Germany and to establish fascism in Greece. We wish peace with Franco's Spain despite her fascism. We shall support peace and friendship among all nations, with Soviet Russia and the People's Republics.[5]

Then Paul sang three songs, ending with "Ol' Man River."

An Associated Press dispatch headlining Paul's speech to the congress was on the wires in time for that evening's editions of American newspapers, but it was a fabricated version. It bore little resemblance to what Paul had actually said:

We colonial peoples have contributed to the building of the United States and are determined to share in its wealth. We denounce the policy of the United States government, which is similar to that of Hitler and Goebbels. We want peace and liberty and will combat for them along with the Soviet Union and the Democracies of Eastern Europe, China and Indonesia.

It is unthinkable that American Negroes would go to war on behalf of those who have oppressed us for generations against the Soviet Union which in one generation has raised our people to the full dignity of mankind.

As a result of the dispatch containing the fabricated remarks, a typical banner headline in the U.S. newspapers read, "Robeson Says Negroes Won't Fight Russia." The mainstream media launched a frenzy of vituperation against Paul, creating an image of a disgruntled ingrate who had betrayed his country to an enemy nation. Walter Winchell, a prominent newspaper columnist and the nation's leading radio commentator, attacked Paul almost daily with the personal encouragement of J. Edgar Hoover. Given Paul's absence from the United States and the intensity of the media barrage without a significant rebuttal, his public image became shrouded by an aura of treason. Since the public viewed treason as a crime punishable by death, a political environment extremely hostile to Paul rapidly developed.

Some editorials in the right-wing press demanded Paul's deportation to the Soviet Union. The June 26 issue of the *Boston Sunday Advertiser* called him "an undesirable citizen" and regretted that he was born in the United States. A letter from a reader published in the New Brunswick, New Jersey, *Home News* demanding that "this black Communist" be executed in the electric chair shared the page with a report on the lynching of a black man in Mississippi.

With one notable exception, every U.S. mainstream newspaper of any note denounced Paul as an enemy of America. Only the *New York Times* adopted a critical but curiously restrained tone: "Mr. Robeson has advanced the cause of the American Negro by being an outstanding human being. He can do nothing but harm by making himself a propagandist for a party line. We hope, profoundly, that his passion for a good cause will not lead him permanently into support for a bad one. We want him to sing, and to go on being Paul Robeson." This editorial in the "American newspaper of record" was interpreted by Paul to reflect the view of the dominant liberal faction of the Truman administration, led by Secretary of State Dean Acheson, that a serious effort should be made to buy him off. Only the *Daily Worker* and the progressive *National Guardian* weekly newspaper reported what Paul actually said in Paris and defended him unreservedly.

Because the incessantly repeated distortion of Paul's remarks made it appear that he was speaking for all black Americans, many black leaders either volunteered or were pressured to refute his purported statement and to condemn him personally. Max Yergan, an eager volunteer, denounced Paul in a long letter to the *New York Herald Tribune* published on April 23, 1949, only three days after Paul's Paris speech. In it Yergan claimed that "it is reasonable to conclude that the Robeson statements had as their purpose the vicious and cynical effort the Communists in America have for a long time been putting forth to drive a wedge between American Negroes and their fellow American citizens." Lester Granger, head of the National Urban League, issued a veiled warning to Paul that he should worry about his health: "He is probably the biggest personal asset the Communist Party possesses today. They must assuredly say a special prayer for the continued health and vitality of their current star attraction."

Roy Wilkins, acting executive secretary of the NAACP while Walter White was on leave, went on the radio to say that Negroes loved America first no matter how many of them were lynched or Jim Crowed. The editorial appearing in the May 1949 issue of *Crisis* magazine, the official organ of the NAACP, reflected Wilkins's viewpoint:

> Robeson does not represent any American Negroes. How much has he done to help them in their upward struggle? He has inspired them, but when this inspiration is set down, little is left to chronicle. Mr. Robeson, understandably, concentrated on making some money. An expensive country place, unlisted telephone numbers, and the sifting of all correspondence by a midtown Manhattan lawyer all kept "the people" at a safe distance. So Mr. Robeson has none but sentimental roots among American Negroes. At Paris and elsewhere, Mr. Robeson must have fancied himself a general (or at the very least a colonel) in the Communist-led army of the proletariat.

Most black leaders with close ties to the Truman administration but also accountable to a mass constituency criticized Paul in far more moderate tones. Mary McLeod Bethune, president of the National Council of Negro Women, expressed admiration for him as a great artist and supported his right to express his political and economic views as a U.S. citizen. Then she added, "But when Mr. Robeson presumes to speak for me in expressing disloyalty to our country, then I think he has missed his cue."

Congressman Adam Clayton Powell Jr. issued an even milder statement that failed to rebuke Paul:

> By no stretch of the imagination can Robeson speak for all the Negro people, and neither can I. We are Americans. We are against any type of aggressive war on our part or on the part of any other nation. We Negroes are going to keep on fighting to obtain everything that God and the Bill of Rights ordained we should have. In the hour of crisis we will be loyal to our nation, reserving the right

constructively to criticize. Lastly, in the event of war at anytime, against anyone, we will do our part insofar as it will not conflict with our religious beliefs and consciences.

However, there were some major exceptions. W. E. B. DuBois issued a ringing statement supporting Paul unequivocally: "I agree with Paul Robeson absolutely, that Negroes should never willingly fight in an unjust war. I do not share his honest hope that all will not. A certain sheep-like disposition, inevitably born of slavery, will, I am afraid, lead many of them to join America in any enterprise, provided the whites will grant them equal right to do wrong."

The most interesting responses were those of Walter White, the unofficial dean of black leaders, and Marjorie McKenzie, columnist for the *Pittsburgh Courier.* White, pressured by the Department of State to make an immediate and comprehensive comment on Paul's Paris remarks, began his May 1, 1949, syndicated column by saying that, despite sharp differences in ideology, he had a "personal affection" for Paul and "admiration for him as an artist." He added that in response to questions by whites about Paul's influence on blacks, he challenged the assumption that Paul should be "both grateful to America and uncritical of her shortcomings."

Only after that did White dissociate himself from Paul's misreported Paris statement: "But when Mr. Robeson declares in Paris that American Negroes will not fight against Soviet Russia and sets himself up as the authorized spokesman for 14,000,000 Negroes, he and I part company." He closed by saying that the overwhelming majority of blacks would "respond as other Americans to the call of their country in time of war." But then he warned that "this loyalty must not be taken by white America as evidence that the Negro American is going to accept without question a summons to arms irrespective of the treatment given to him by his own country. White America would be wise to abstain from denunciation of the Paul Robesons for extremist statements until it removes the causes of the lack of faith in the American system of government."

McKenzie's column gave voice to a sharper dissent than White's piece, asserting that Paul's statement "burns along the edges of the American consciousness like sagebrush in a forest fire. It suggests a deeper question. If our situation is truly hopeless at the hands of the Truman administration, revolt against selective service for a war makes sense."[6]

Overall, the attitude of the black press toward Paul was significantly different from that of the mainstream press. The relatively conservative *Chicago Defender* ran an editorial titled "Nuts to Mr. Robeson," but the same issue featured a news story in which its Paris correspondent questioned the accuracy of the Associated Press dispatch on Paul's speech. According to the correspondent, the remarks he had personally heard Paul make were not those reported in the dispatch. The progressive *Baltimore Afro-American* editorialized that "Paul Can't Speak for Us," but then added that "there are thousands of Negroes who believe as Robeson does, and the number increases daily because our Government fiddles with the question of equal rights for all citizens." The *Detroit Tribune* tried to defuse Paul's remarks by trivializing them: "Robeson Is Just Blowing His Top."[7]

As reflected by the black press throughout the latter half of April and the first half of May, most black church and civic leaders declared their loyalty to the United States but refused to comment on Paul's remarks until they had heard from him directly. Many expressed doubt that he had been accurately quoted. The prevailing response among rank-and-file African Americans was admiration for Paul's boldness tempered by discomfort at being put on the spot by the controversy he had stirred up. Anger at Paul was notably absent.

By contrast, the mainstream press chronicled the anger and rage many whites directed at Paul, their erstwhile American hero. Overnight, he had turned into an "ungrateful Negro." The depth of this pervasive racial hatred was manifested by the near-avalanche of hate mail that poured daily into the Enfield post office.

The day after his Paris speech, Paul flew to Stockholm to begin his Scandinavian tour, unaware of the furor his remarks were causing in the United States. After a concert before a capacity audience in Stockholm's main concert hall, Paul was besieged by Swedish and American news correspondents. Unwisely, he allowed himself to be entangled in an impromptu news conference. Subjected to a barrage of hostile questions, he gave a snap answer to a question about whether blacks would fight for the United States in a war against the Soviet Union: "I belong to the American resistance movement which fights against American imperialism just as the resistance movement fought against Hitler and fascism. Why should Negroes ever fight against the only nation in the world where racial discrimination is prohibited and where people live freely? Never!"

Paul had unwittingly stepped into the trap set for him by the manufactured Associated Press dispatch. He had articulated in Stockholm the statement that had been falsely attributed to him in Paris.

Meanwhile, Essie was alarmed by Paul's lack of response to the flood of negative publicity about his Paris remarks. She decided to weigh in on his behalf in her address to a Progressive Party dinner on April 27 at New York City's Hotel Commodore. Titled, "The Negro and Peace," her spirited defense of Paul effectively connected with the mood of most rank-and-file African Americans and was widely disseminated in the black press. Her closing words were, "It may well be that a giant Negro, one Paul Robeson, the son of a slave who caught the ear of the world with his golden voice, is putting into words some of the thoughts of the vast majority of the Negro people of this country. Since he has never asked for anything for himself, they may do well to listen to him."

During the rest of his ten-day Swedish tour, Paul sang to turn-away crowds and made no political remarks at his concert appearances. He also spent time appearing at union and left-wing meetings, pondering over the detailed briefings he received by telephone from Alphaeus Hunton, and studying Russian, Czech, and Polish in anticipation of a trip to Eastern Europe. On May 1, he summed up his feelings in letters to Clara Rockmore and Freda Diamond.

He thanked Clara for sending him a broad sampling of U.S. newspaper reports on his Paris speech, calling them "invaluable." Then he reported that he had spoken to an enthusiastic May Day gathering of thousands in a Stockholm park and speculated about his immediate plans:

> Tell Bobby—expenses are academic. I can sing my way around the world. I will only go to Czechoslovakia, Hungary, etc.—they'll pick

me up in Iceland—they just want their people to say hello to me and me to them. That I must do.

I'm aware of press reports—I'll answer in good time. There was one important distinction—I said that Negroes will fight for peace if given a chance to choose. I say war is out of the question.

Lots and lots of love. Landing now in Copenhagen; then to Oslo. Love, love, love.

Pavlik

His letter to Freda was one of reconciliation and shared additional news of his activities and plans:

My darling Sweet—

This has been such a long, long ache—that I'm numb.

I hope to come home the end of May—but if the trial drags on [the Smith Act trial of the twelve communist leaders at Foley Square, New York City], I'll still go on to the East. Then I could return to, shall I say, a turbulent America.

I believe, from what I have seen, that the struggle is sharp, but that peace is winning. The opposition is just too hysterical. Scandinavia is very worried. I have read much of stuff from home. Distorted, but let it rest. I can understand their using Walter [White], but Max [Yergan]!!! I'm ready enough.

I want you to know that I love you with a deep, deep longing—a constant pain—and a deep, deep joy. I loved your cable. I had waited for days for some word.

Whatever personal life I can steal—much more belongs to you than you'll ever know, for you'll always press too hard to find out. I guess I'll never be driven. Neither will you—you have your pride. The very word becomes important to me, [but] only in a public sense, in relation to my oppressors, not in personal relations.

But I love you—and miss you—your loveliness, your warmth, your love. That I know is mine and I treasure it above all, however it may seem on surface.

Always yours,

Paul

Paul sang two sold-out concerts and appeared at several mass peace rallies in Copenhagen. Before leaving for Oslo, he gave an interview to the Danish press in which he said that his Paris remarks had been misquoted: "What I said in Paris was on the struggle for peace, not on anybody going to war against anybody." He also managed to find time to visit with an old friend, Arctic explorer Peter Freuchen, and his wife, Dagmar.

In Oslo, where many recalled listening illegally to his inspirational radio broadcasts during the Nazi occupation, Paul was greeted as a hero. When Alphaeus Hunton finally caught up with him there by telephone to brief him on what was happening on the home front, Paul was surprised to learn of the enormous controversy his Paris speech had produced in the United States. He told Hunton to use his Copenhagen press interview as the basis for responding to his critics. Any further statement from him would have to await his return home.

From Oslo Paul went to London for the second part of his British concert tour, which would last until the final days of May. Realizing the uncertainties and dangers he would face upon his return home, he decided to travel to Czechoslovakia, Poland, and the Soviet Union while he had the opportunity. Larry chose not to go, so Paul selected Bruno Raikin as his accompanist. Peter Blackman, a left-wing West Indian poet and writer, who was both a friend and aide, joined them. At the end of May they began their Eastern European tour.[8]

Paul received a grand reception in Prague. After he spoke and sang in the main sports stadium, university students carried him off on their shoulders. The artistic community raved about his formal concert. Working people constantly greeted him on the streets, especially after he had spent a day singing in Prague's largest factories. However, he noted that some conservatives among his official hosts were at best lukewarm toward his visit. Yet he ignored these negative signs, carrying himself with his usual sunny demeanor.

In Poland, Paul's reception was even warmer. In Wrocław (formerly Breslau) in western Poland, people from nearby small towns and villages came to his hotel bearing flowers, and to hear him sing from a makeshift platform in a soccer field. Later, he addressed a huge crowd from the balcony of the city hall. When an official recalled that Adolph Hitler had spoken from the same spot immediately after the 1939 Nazi occupation of Poland, Paul quipped, "Well, this is a great improvement."

In Warsaw, Paul sang in the capital's main athletic stadium. His chief host was a bit anxious when he saw that the program included a song in Yiddish and a Russian patriotic song. He turned to Paul and expressed his fear that on top of the Yiddish song, which was problematic, a Russian one risked going beyond the audience's tolerance.

"Poles dislike Russians," he said, "and those folks out there aren't the usual refined intellectuals that attend concerts. They're real workers."

"Don't worry," Paul replied with a chuckle. "I know how to talk to workers. I used to be one." And he quickly scribbled down some notes on the back of his program.

He began by establishing a dialogue with his audience. Greeting his listeners in Polish, he apologized for not having learned enough of their language to explain the deeper meaning of his songs in their native tongue. He promised that on his next trip he would speak Polish fluently. In the meantime, he would speak Russian, a mutually familiar language.

The response was appreciative applause, and the stadium gradually transformed into an intimate outdoor living room. Paul sang everything from Negro spirituals to an aria from Mussorgsky's *Boris Godunov*, with a Spanish civil war song, a lullaby, a Chinese resistance song, a Polish revolutionary song, and a song from the English Chartist Revolution of 1832 in between. Along the way, he inserted commentary and anecdotes about the context of the music and lyrics.

Before singing the Yiddish song, which was about the Warsaw Ghetto Uprising in Yiddish, Paul recounted how he had just learned it from a survivor as they stood together on the rubble that was all that remained of the ghetto. And before launching into a Soviet patriotic song, he spoke of the bond between the American descendants of black slaves emancipated in 1863 and Russians descended from peasants freed from serfdom that same year. The applause punctuating the end of the song evoked a sigh of relief from the nervous party leaders seated on the platform. When Paul ended with "Ol' Man River," the audience stood and cheered.

Near the end of his ten-day visit to Poland, Paul went to the Soviet embassy in Warsaw to pick up the Soviet visas that he and his accompanist Bruno Raikin needed for their scheduled visit to Moscow. He was received routinely by a low-level official who handed him one visa. Raikin's was missing. When Paul asked why, the official replied curtly that Moscow had not sent it. He gave no explanation and made no apology.

Paul suspected that the denial of a visa to his Jewish accompanist was related to his private inquiries in Paris concerning the fate of his Soviet Jewish friends who had disappeared from public view. He did not share these thoughts with Raikin or Blackman, although he apologized profusely to Raikin for the visa "misunderstanding." Paul's suspicions were heightened when he and Blackman arrived in Moscow on June 4. Peter watched in silent outrage as Soviet customs officials all but body-searched Paul, requesting him to empty his pockets and his spectacle cases. They rifled through every piece of his luggage, including his music briefcases. Paul was unperturbed, bantering amiably in Russian throughout the process. Later, however, he advised Blackman to "stay close" and avoid any arguments with their hosts.[9]

But Paul owned the streets of Moscow, where, as usual, he was embraced as a great friend of the Soviet people. Yet a disturbing note intruded. The newspapers were conducting a crusade against "cosmopolitanism and Zionism" with a distinct anti-Jewish undertone. He inquired about one of his closest Jewish friends, Itzik Feffer, an outstanding poet and decorated war veteran.

When his hosts were vague about Feffer's whereabouts, Paul was politely insistent. Since this didn't produce a satisfactory result, he told them pointedly that the fulfillment of his schedule, including a nationally broadcast concert from Moscow's famed Chaikovsky Hall on June 8, three days later, would depend on his ability to meet with Feffer. The officials departed in considerable agitation, assuring him that they would do their best to find Feffer. Paul continued his round of Moscow appearances for the next two days without incident, giving press and radio interviews, speaking and singing at the main auto plant, and addressing the 150th anniversary celebration of the birth of Alexander Pushkin, Russia's greatest poet.

At the Pushkin gala, a presiding cultural official approached Paul shortly before he was scheduled to speak and asked him not to refer to Pushkin as an "Afro-Russian poet," adding that "comrade Stalin has pointed out that Pushkin should be referred to as a *Russian* poet." (Pushkin's maternal great-grandfather was an Abyssinian general serving in the Turkish army and was captured in a war between Turkey and Russia. He subsequently served with distinction at the court of Tsar Peter the Great, rising to become one of Peter's favorites.) Paul complied but interpreted the request as a sign of increasing Russian nationalism. In a subsequent radio interview, he was asked how his Russian had become so good. He answered with a chuckle that he had family in the Soviet Union. When the surprised interviewer asked who that might be, Paul replied solemnly, "Why, Alexander Pushkin of course."[10]

On the morning of his Chaikovsky Hall concert, Paul was officially informed that Feffer had been located and would visit him that afternoon. Feffer, who had "disappeared," was brought to Paul's hotel from his cell in Moscow's Lubyanka prison. On the way, his escorts had taken him home, where he changed his clothes and was fed a meal by his wife. They released him in the hotel lobby with instructions to meet them there directly after his visit. As Paul greeted him warmly, Feffer indicated with gestures that the hotel suite was bugged, and the two proceeded to speak in Russian about uncontroversial matters. But using sign language and notes on scrap paper, they shared an unforgettable communion about the realities of Stalin's 1948 purge of the Soviet Union's leading Jewish intellectuals.

Both Feffer and Paul played their roles masterfully. As Feffer spoke about his recent recovery from pneumonia, he peered through the spread fingers of his hands to indicate he was in prison. When Paul, while recounting his recent visit to Poland and Czechoslovakia, handed Feffer a one-word note: "Mikhoels?" Feffer wrote, "Murdered on Stalin's order." While Feffer told a hilarious joke about himself and a close friend, he drew a finger slowly across his throat.

At another point, while talking about his discoveries of new folk songs, Paul pointed to Feffer and then to himself as he silently conveyed his inquiry about what he could do to help. Feffer urgently put his finger to his closed lips, signaling that Paul should keep silent publicly. Then, as he spoke of the research he was engaged in for his memoirs, he scribbled a request: "Letter from you, [Frédéric Joliot] Curie and [Howard] Fast to Stalin via our Embassy." As Feffer rose to go, the two men embraced in tears, and Paul was left to ponder what he could do on the spot to help his friend.

The letter asked for by Feffer during his meeting with Paul was subsequently written and signed by Robeson, Joliot-Curie, and

Fast and delivered by personal courier. Its effect remains unknown. Feffer and his colleagues were executed three years later, in 1952.[11]

Paul's concert that evening was memorable not merely because he was in magnificent voice but also because of the extraordinary passion he communicated to the audience. In a repertoire spanning seven languages—English, Russian, French, Italian, Spanish, Chinese, and Yiddish—he enthralled his Russian audience by linking them to the world's cultures through songs ranging from Negro spirituals to Monteverdi's "Let Me Die," complete with spoken introductions in Russian. Two of his songs—"Water Boy" and the American labor song "Joe Hill"—were so popular that Paul had to repeat them. The final number on the program was "Ol' Man River" (the Russians called it "Meeseeseepee"), which Paul introduced by saying, "At the end of this song the old words said: 'I'm tired of living and scared of dying.' Today we need new words. These are: 'I keep laughing; I must fight to the death for peace and freedom.'" The applause drowned out the piano introduction.

When Paul finished, the entire hall stood up, applauding, cheering, and yelling "bis, bis!" meaning "more, more!" They wanted him to sing it again. Paul stepped forward to the edge of the stage, smiling and acknowledging the ovation. Following the Soviet custom, he applauded the audience. Finally, he held up his hands, motioning for quiet. Speaking in Russian, he explained he would end his concert with a single encore—a special song he had learned recently and wished to dedicate to his dear friend Solomon Mikhoels, whose "premature" death saddened him deeply.

Complete silence greeted Paul's mention of Mikhoels. He could hear gasps as he went on to speak of his meeting with Feffer, whom he described as well and hard at work on his memoirs. This announcement temporarily "rehabilitated" Feffer. Anyone allowed to visit an honored guest such as Paul Robeson could not at the same time be an "enemy of the people."

Paul concluded his remarks by announcing that his encore would be the song of the Jewish partisans who fought to the death against their fascist oppressors in the Warsaw Ghetto. He explained the Yiddish lyrics in Russian:

> Never say that you have reached the very end
> When leaden skies a bitter future may portend;

For sure the hour for which we yearn will yet arrive,
And our marching steps will thunder: we survive.

There was no sound from the audience. Paul leaned forward and sang "Zog Nit Keynmol" with a passion rarely equaled on a concert stage. His listeners sat transfixed, and when he finished they erupted with sustained waves of ovation.

Although the audience included many of Moscow's Jewish intellectual elite who were waiting for Stalin's axe to fall on them, the majority were non-Jewish party members who were then being decimated by a 1949 purge. Jews and non-Jews alike were either walking in the shadow of death or had lost someone close. Strangers fell into one another's arms, sobbing. Others called out Paul's name and patronymic ("Paul, son of William"), an expression of affection. A few sat silently, tears streaming down their faces. Those in the front seats rushed forward and reached up to touch Paul's hand. For minutes on end, the applause would not stop. Every time it died down, it would swell again.

This extraordinary event was broadcast to 180 million Soviet people and tape-recorded. However, Soviet censors edited out Paul's remarks preceding the song, which he described to me, and they have vanished. Neither Soviet nor Western media made any mention of the concert. An exception was the Polish cultural newspaper *Kurjer Codzienny*, which reported that Paul had sung the Warsaw Ghetto song "to stormy applause."[12]

Paul and Peter Blackman traveled to Stalingrad, the "hero city" that was still rising from the rubble of World War II's greatest battle, in which the Russian army had turned the tide of the war against Hitler's military machine. After singing to an enthusiastic audience at the Stalingrad Tractor Plant, Paul was presented with a ring inscribed in Russian: "to Paul Robeson, Stalingrader." This ring was one of an exclusive set made for the handful of survivors of the legendary Red Army unit that had held a strongpoint throughout the siege of the city. The rings had been fashioned from the casing of the last German shell to fall on the site. In a solemn ceremony, one of the surviving veterans, who had hands as large as Paul's, took off the newly inscribed ring and placed it on Paul's finger.

The next day, Paul was back in Moscow participating in a farewell concert in his honor. Prior to his departure, a high Soviet official came to see him with an offer of asylum in the Soviet Union.

He said that Soviet authorities were aware that Paul faced grave danger, including possible attempts on his life, in the United States. Paul replied that although grateful for the offer, he would never contemplate asylum. His place was at home with his people.[13]

When Paul's plane landed at New York's LaGuardia Airport on June 16, 1949, he entered a boiling political cauldron. Customs went through his luggage meticulously, and he was thoroughly patted down. FBI agents were present at the customs search, and they joined in examining every piece of paper in his bags. When Paul finally emerged, he was met by a large welcoming party headed by Alphaeus Hunton, now executive director of the Council on African Affairs. I was present and Essie had planned to be there, but Paul's revised arrival date had conflicted with her address to the National Conference of Social Workers in Cleveland.

Besieged by the press, Paul made an opening statement that he had been greeted warmly all over Europe by overflow audiences, and that there was no "war hysteria" there. On the contrary, the peoples of both Western and Eastern Europe "expressed tremendous sentiment for peace." When a reporter asked about Paul's Paris statement, he replied that he had no comment and would give his answer at the Welcome Home rally at Harlem's Rockland Palace three days later, adding that "everything I said during my tour of Europe was distorted by the Associated Press and the United Press and other American press agencies." The reporter observed that newspapermen in the United States were not given instructions to distort. Paul shot back, "You don't need them."

Paul departed from the airport in a five-car cavalcade that toured through Harlem, receiving friendly greetings until they reached the Hotel Theresa for a brief reception and a meeting with the black press. Paul established a relaxed conversational atmosphere, and the reporters respectfully asked tough but fair questions. Only one newsman from the pro-Republican *New York Amsterdam News* aggressively pursued the mainstream red-baiting line, but Paul parried it good-naturedly.

From there my father took me along to Ben Davis's nearby apartment. We hadn't seen each other for five months and we enjoyed this opportunity to talk. He was looking forward to being best man at my marriage just three days hence, and we discussed the wedding plans. He was concerned that his Welcome Home rally was scheduled for the afternoon of our wedding. I assured him that Marilyn and I welcomed the opportunity to be there, reminding him that we could all enjoy our evening reception at Freda's home.

We talked about his personal security, but he was more concerned about Essie, Marilyn, and me. He was especially worried about Essie, who was isolated up at Enfield but was adamant about staying there. As for himself, he planned to move around with his usual freedom. However, he agreed when Ben, on the spot, temporarily assigned his own personal bodyguard to accompany him whenever he left the safety of Harlem. I was reassured, but at the same time my realization of the danger threatening my father, and by extension my mother, Marilyn, and me, was unsettling.

My father discussed the aftermath of his Paris speech. He believed that his only chance for political, and perhaps physical, survival depended upon a successful appeal to the black rank and file. This required him to go on the offensive, and he would do so in a press release issued by the Council on African Affairs and in his speech at the Welcome Home rally.

Later, Paul met with top party leaders to discuss his political strategy. Some of them took the view that he should clarify his stand by simply reiterating what he had actually said in Paris and contrasting it with the statement falsely attributed to him. Others believed that Paul's had wrongly focused U.S. public opinion on the issue of patriotism rather than on the struggle for peace. They insisted that he repudiate the distorted version of his remarks.

Paul responded that the propaganda blitz in the wake of his April statement in Paris had by now made it impossible for a denial to make any significant public impact. Therefore he had decided to confirm a variation of the distorted statement attributed to him. He read his draft press release: "It is unthinkable that American Negroes could go to war on behalf of those who have oppressed us for generations against the Soviet Union who in one generation has raised our people to full human dignity."

Several party leaders were so startled that they wanted the party to disassociate itself from the statement. Davis and some others vigorously defended it. Finally, a consensus developed under which the party would not take a position on the statement but would do everything it could to physically protect Paul and his family.[14]

The following day, Paul went to the parsonage of his brother Ben's Harlem church, Mother A.M.E. Zion, to meet with Walter White. White, still on leave from his top post at the NAACP, had urgently requested to see him before the June 19 rally. Walter's warm greeting belied his agitation. Paul reduced the tension with a quip about how their visit might cost Walter his job. Walter cracked a smile, but his somber mood persisted. He went straight to the point, choosing his words carefully.

He had come at the request of Secretary of State Dean Acheson, who, unofficially, spoke for the president on the matter at hand. Acheson was prepared to make Paul a firm offer. If he wrote a private personal letter to Acheson declaring his intention to return exclusively to his artistic career for at least the next year and pledged to refrain from making political speeches or singing at political meetings, he could resume his professional life without government interference. Since the executive branch of government had helped instigate the attacks on Paul and orchestrate the media assault on him, they would be able to assist in his rehabilitation. After a year of semiretirement, the past would be forgotten and Paul could reclaim his position as one of the nation's favorite performing artists.

Paul heard Walter out attentively. Then he asked his opinion about what other options might be available. Walter's face clouded over as he implored Paul to accept the State Department deal. "We need you, Paul," he said earnestly. "The guys who run Intelligence will be given license to kill you if you don't take this deal. The mix of the race issue, the communist issue, and the war issue is just too much for them." Paul thanked Walter for warning him but was noncommittal, adding that he would give a lot of thought to what had been said. They parted amicably, White with a sense of foreboding, Paul in a contemplative mood.[15]

The wedding ceremony on June 19 was small. We were joined by Marilyn's mother, Rae, her brother, Harold, and my parents. Reverend Darr, a young Congregational minister whom we had met as peace activists, performed the private noon ceremony. He and his wife lived in a fourth-floor walk-up apartment in a white working-class Manhattan neighborhood at 200 West 107th Street. Alerted by our wedding license application, the press and police were present in force, ensuring that our wedding would not be the private affair we had planned. By the time we arrived, the police presence and prior press reports had attracted a growing and hostile all-white crowd. After the police escorted us to the building's entrance, press photographers aggressively followed us up the many stairs to the Darrs' apartment. We had to slam the apartment door in their faces to prevent them from entering. My father, who had refused to take a bodyguard to our wedding as suggested, was outraged.

Reverend Darr and his young French wife welcomed us warmly and served tea, providing a needed respite from the hostile environment on their doorstep. The personalized and simple wedding ceremony moved us all. But the afterglow did not last long. We had to face the problem of how to get past the ugly crowd of several hundred assembled in the street below.

Harold went in search of two taxis and brought them around to the door, while Essie organized the rest of us to make our exit. Photographers and reporters lined the stairwells as we descended, and the police, who had collaborated with the press from the outset, brought up the rear instead of clearing a path for us. We ran the gauntlet of camera lenses thrust in our faces. Throughout this turmoil, Marilyn, with a pleasant smile, behaved as if this were a normal occasion, exhibiting no trace of anxiety or discomfort. And since she appeared to be coping, I was fine. When we emerged onto the sidewalk, we heard continuous waves of enraged jeers and we felt the racial hatred emanating from the crowd. Some held handmade signs with racist insults such as, "Jew bitch, you married a gorilla."

A police escort to the taxis awaited us at the front entrance, where Paul stopped to shake his finger at the press as he denounced them for their intrusion into a private wedding. He added that this marriage would not have caused such uproar in the Soviet Union. Then he took his seat between Harold and Rae. A photographer suddenly yanked open the curbside door of Paul's taxi and leaned in to take a photo. Paul lunged forward, his face contorted with anger and his right hand raised. The photographer, in a panic, pulled himself out of the cab so fast that he hit his head on the top of the doorframe, banged his camera on the side, then recovered, only to stumble backward over the curb, fall, and drop his camera. Paul, motionless, watched this Chaplinesque dance with amusement.[16]

Later that afternoon, Harlem's Rockland Palace was jammed with five thousand people. About half were white and black left-wing political, union, and cultural activists, and about half were a cross section of community people. We sat in the front row of the balcony listening to the impressive speakers preceding Paul: Dr. W. E. B. DuBois; Richard B. Moore, secretary of the United Caribbean American Council; Charles P. Howard, head of the Des Moines, Iowa, NAACP branch; Rose Russell, legislative director of the Teachers Union; Mrs. Andrew Simkins, executive committeewoman of the South Carolina Republican Party; and Congressman Vito Marcantonio of the New York American Labor Party. Many greetings were read, along with tributes from playwright Clifford Odets, several left-wing unions, and former vice president Henry Wallace.

Responding to a huge ovation, Paul boomed out his warm "Hello there; it's good to be back," sang five songs, and delivered an hour-long inspirational speech with the audience cheering him on. "The road has been long; the road has been hard," he said. "During the Wallace campaign I stood on the very soil on which my father was a slave, where some of my cousins are sharecroppers and unemployed tobacco workers. I defy any errand boys, Uncle Toms of the Negro people, to challenge my Americanism." He spoke of his love for the Soviet people. Then he addressed his Paris remarks, leaving no doubt about his sentiments:

At the Paris Peace Conference I said it was unthinkable that the Negro people of America or elsewhere in the world could be drawn into war with the Soviet Union. I repeat it with hundred-fold emphasis. THEY WILL NOT.

To fulfill our responsibilities as Americans, we must unite, especially we Negro people. We must know our strength. We are the decisive force. That's why they terrorize us. That's why they fear us. And if we unite in all our might, this world can fast be changed. Let us create that unity now.

If we unite, we'll get our law against lynching, our right to vote and to labor. Let us march on Washington, representing 14,000,000 strong. Let us push aside the sycophants who tell us to be quiet. This is the very time when we can win our struggle.

We do not want to die in vain any more on foreign battlefields for Wall Street and the greedy supporters of domestic fascism. If we must die, let it be in Mississippi or Georgia! Let it be wherever we are lynched and deprived of our rights as human beings![17]

This was Paul's defiant public answer to the U.S. State Department's privately conveyed offer. He was not for sale. The mainstream media fiercely attacked the speech. A typical headline in the white press read, "Loves Soviet Best, Robeson Declares." The Hearst newspapers nationwide published an editorial on their front pages, which was headlined "An Undesirable Citizen" and deplored the fact that Paul Robeson was born in the United States.

On the other hand, the black press praised Paul's "first-class oratory," and summarized the full context of his speech. Although the majority of the columnists, led by Lester Granger in the *New York Amsterdam News*, red-baited Paul, the overall coverage was sympathetic, thus helping to rally the support of the black masses.[18]

The wedding party of extended family and close friends at Freda Diamond's home that evening was complete with champagne and a large wedding cake. At one point during the evening, Paul sat down with Marilyn and me to talk about our immediate future. The headlines and front-page photos in the evening papers confirmed that the media publicity surrounding our wedding would make us the targets of racist and anti-Semitic thugs from coast to coast. Since a typical headline read, "Black Singer's Son Weds White Girl from Forest Hills" (the "Forest Hills" reference signaling that Marilyn was Jewish), and the articles contained red-baiting attacks on him, they served to increase the danger to us. Consequently, we would be at great risk if we appeared together in a white neighborhood. Only in a black community could we be out of danger. For at least several months, we were not to go outside of Harlem together without the bodyguard whom the party would assign to us. We reluctantly agreed. It was fortunate that we did, because in the following days even more vicious stories appeared in the press, and a stream of anonymous hate mail denouncing both our marriage and my father arrived at Enfield.

Paul spent the next several days among Harlem's residents. He accompanied Ben Davis on his campaign rounds in anticipation of the fall municipal elections, strolling along Seventh Avenue meeting and greeting people along the way. During a leisurely haircut, he engaged in a spirited debate with several patrons about his Paris statement, fielding difficult, occasionally hostile questions with a touch of humor and folk wisdom. By the end, he won everybody over except one die-hard who was finally silenced by the others. Evenings were spent in Harlem's most popular nightspots. Paul arranged to stay with Revels Cayton, his wife, Lee, and their baby son Michael at the Riverton Apartments on Fifth Avenue near 137th Street. With a base in Harlem, he became a constant presence in the community.

Revels took Paul to many union meetings in the course of his work as an organizer for District 65 of the Retail, Wholesale and Department Store Union. There Paul met rank-and-file members and shop stewards, gaining a deep understanding of their concerns and bringing them a measure of inspiration. Over a year's period, he developed close connections with the New York City trade union movement.

Paul also worked to solidify his support within the broad left-wing grassroots constituency. He went to East Harlem, usually in the company of the local congressman, Vito Marcantonio, or with Revels, who knew all the East Harlem left-wing labor leaders. Paul's ability to speak and sing in Spanish served him well.

On June 28, Paul spoke to a capacity audience at a Civil Rights Congress rally in New York City's Madison Square Garden, expressing his view of the "so-called defenders of the American way of life." He charged that they "haunt the homes of every decent thinking intellectual. They burn the books; they tell us what to read, what to discover, and they have descended to corrupting every part of our constitutional system." He added that "we are the America that inherits our great traditions. And we must rededicate ourselves in struggle for this America that we so deeply love."[19]

In mid-July, the House Committee on Un-American Activities (HUAC), prodded by Walter Winchell and other leading conservative columnists, as well as FBI director Hoover, announced that the committee would begin immediate hearings in response to "requests from members of [Robeson's] race" to provide them with a forum to rebut Paul's "disloyal and unpatriotic statements." The hearings were formally announced as "Hearings Regarding Communist Infiltration of Minority Groups; July 13–18." They opened with extended testimony from Alvin Stokes, a black investigator for HUAC, and black professional informer Manning Johnson.

Stokes claimed that the Communist Party was plotting to establish a black republic in the Deep South and that Paul's voice was "the voice of the Kremlin." Johnson testified falsely under oath that he had personally witnessed Paul attending Communist Party meetings as a party member using an alias. He also claimed that Paul had "delusions of grandeur" and was "desirous of becoming the Black Stalin." When a reporter subsequently asked Robeson to respond to Johnson's "Black Stalin" remark, Robeson replied with a touch of humor that he did not consider himself to be in any way competent to occupy a political position.[20]

A parade of prominent blacks testified. However, to the committee's chagrin, the majority chose to focus on the fight against racism instead of denouncing Paul. Lester Granger, the Urban League leader who had denounced Paul in the black press, now advised the committee to investigate the Ku Klux Klan in order to demonstrate to blacks that the U.S. government was "helping to fight off racism." Charles S. Johnson, the president of Fisk University, declared that he saw no evidence of communist infiltration of black schools and declined to denounce Paul's statements. A minority representing conservative black opinion called Paul's remarks "a great disservice to his race."

Although the hearings exerted the intended influence on white public opinion, they produced a backlash in the black community. For example, when Paul appeared on June 17 at the Bill of Rights Conference of 1,301 delegates in New York City, he received a standing ovation at the end of his speech in which he repeated his declaration that blacks would not "be drawn into" an imperialist war. Then the conference unanimously passed a resolution backing Paul that had been introduced by the 360 black delegates, who represented a wide range of grassroots black organizations.[21]

On July 18, to great fanfare, baseball star Jackie Robinson testified as HUAC's most celebrated witness. The first black player to make it into the major leagues, he had become a dominant player in his initial season as second baseman for the Brooklyn Dodgers. As the number one black hero in the nation, he had been called upon to deliver the decisive rebuttal to Paul.

However, Robinson, an unenthusiastic witness, expressed reluctance in his opening statement. He spent most of his prepared remarks attacking racial segregation, noting that "Negroes were stirred up long before there was a Communist Party and they'll stay stirred up long after the

Party has disappeared—unless Jim Crow has disappeared by then as well." With regard to Paul's Paris remarks, Robinson's testimony was far short of the denunciation that the committee sought:

> I haven't any comment to make on that statement except that if Mr. Robeson actually made it, it sounds very silly to me. But he has a right to his personal views, and if he wants to sound silly when he expresses them in public, that is his business and not mine. He's still a famous ex-athlete and a great singer and actor.

Robinson's refusal to follow the HUAC script undermined the committee's attempt to isolate Paul from his black base. What had been billed as an all-out attack on Paul by loyal blacks had turned mostly into an indictment of racism. The mainstream press unanimously praised Robinson, but much of the black press was critical. The *Carolina Times* editorial advised Robinson to "keep at baseball and stay out of politics," adding that "Robeson is, beyond any question, in a far better position to interpret the true feelings of the darker races of the world." The editorial's main point was that "there isn't a respectable Negro in the South, whether he will admit it or not, who at some time or another has not had the same feeling as that reported to have been expressed by Paul Robeson."

At a two-hour press conference held at Harlem's Hotel Theresa on July 20, Paul declared that he had "no quarrel" with Robinson, adding that his "main concern" was to "get at this Un-American Activities Committee." Asked about Robinson's statement that blacks didn't need the help of communists, Paul replied that he believed that they needed the help of everyone—communist or noncommunist.[22]

Soon after Robinson's testimony, HUAC ended the hearings without calling Paul, thus conceding defeat. By now a strong majority of the black masses, especially in the South, supported Paul. The left and progressive constituencies backed him solidly, including the entire Communist Party leadership. Paul felt he had consolidated a constituency broad enough to provide a good chance of survival.

8

PEEKSKILL, NEW YORK

(1949)

In early August 1949, an interview with Paul appeared as a five-part serial in Dan Burley's popular column in the *New York Age*, a black newspaper. Paul presented his position on the controversy raging around him. "Everybody is trying to explain Paul Robeson," he said. "That isn't hard. I am asked do I think the salvation of the American Negro lies in complete integration or in a highly developed Negro nationalism. Let me answer it in my way":

> The whole Negro problem has its basis in the South—in the cotton belt where Negroes are in the majority. That is the only thing that explains me completely. The Negro upper class wants to know why I am out here struggling in behalf of the oppressed, exploited Negro of the South when I could isolate myself from them like they do and become wealthy by keeping quiet on such disturbing subjects. This, I have found, would not be true of me.
>
> We must come together as a people, and with our own unity we must try to find the right allies—those whose struggles over the past years have driven us together. Suppose that in the South, where the Negroes are in the majority in the agricultural belt, we had the vote like everyone else? What would happen? Wouldn't Negroes be in Congress, be governors, judges, mayors, sheriffs and so on? Wouldn't they be in control in the South and run things?
>
> Negroes of the South must realize that they are the ones who built that which has been and still is being taken from them. Maybe they should think of someday gaining control through constitutional means of that which should have been theirs all along.[1]

By now, Paul had come to terms with the reality that his commercial concert career in the United States was over, but he was deeply concerned about the careers of other black and progressive artists. In mid-August, he spoke at the Conference on the Negro in the Radio Industry held in New York City. The keynote speech, delivered by Canada Lee, one of America's leading black actors, called for a broad-based, uncompromising assault on discrimination against blacks in radio. Paul, introduced by his old friend and colleague Fredi Washington, lashed out at the exclusion of blacks from radio. "You have a whole people cut out of radio," he said. "We know there are hundreds ready to go on the air." He urged his audience to "take this thing into the struggle, into the radio stations, and let them know that the power of the people is in this country."[2]

At an August 13 conference called by People's Artists, a left-wing cultural organization, Paul discussed the monopoly of the concert business imposed by a handful of big concert agencies:

> I am horrified at the thought, as an artist, as one who comes from the people's struggles, that if I hadn't been on picket lines for workers, if I hadn't been doing the progressive causes, the workers in America would never have heard me. My own people would never have heard me. They couldn't pay the prices. If they wanted to struggle to pay the prices, they couldn't buy the tickets. They're sold out. . . . The same people go and sit there year in and year out. Now that's the basis of what they say is musical culture in America. It has nothing to do with America! It has to do with 2,000 people in certain towns. So there is another audience that we must get.[3]

Paul was greatly encouraged by the enthusiastic responses of his black and progressive audiences, as well as by the support of the party leadership. He began traveling about without a bodyguard and was less vigilant. Meanwhile, the FBI mobilized its far-flung resources in a determined effort to dig up incriminating evidence against him.

Aware that Paul was expected to testify at the Communist Party trial, the FBI requested copies of his passport applications to research possible "discrepancies or info that may be used in cross-examination." On July 8, a memo from the Washington Field Office of the FBI to Director Hoover enclosed certified copies of seven of Paul's passport applications, as well as the transcript from his 1948 testimony before the Senate Judiciary Committee and "information obtained from confidential and restricted papers from State Department officials abroad concerning Robeson's recent trip to Europe." One week later, the Albany Field Office reported to Hoover that the New York State Law Board records and the files of the Law Examiners and Court of Appeals of New York State contained "no derogatory information concerning Robeson." The other investigations likewise could find no trace of any legally actionable evidence against Paul. Meanwhile, Hoover stepped up surveillance of Essie, Marilyn, and me.

In mid-August, People's Artists announced that Paul would give his fourth annual benefit concert for the Harlem chapter of the Civil Rights Congress on the evening of August 27 in the Peekskill area. The three previous concerts had been held there with great success, and this one was to take place at the Lakeland Acres picnic grounds just outside of Peekskill, about forty-five miles north of New York City.

However, during the four days prior to the concert, a series of editorials and news stories appeared in the *Peekskill Evening Star* that were extremely hostile to Paul's appearance. One editorial closed ominously, "The time for tolerant silence that signifies approval is running out." But none of the concert organizers or sponsors assigned much significance to these press attacks, since they were judged to appeal mostly to cranks and far-out extremists. Two fairly large communities of Robeson supporters lived nearby, and advance ticket sales were going well.

Before Paul and Larry boarded the train to Peekskill on that balmy Saturday, Paul called Helen Rosen at her summer home in Katonah, fifteen miles from Peekskill, to ask about rumors of a hostile demonstration at the concert. Helen's husband, Sam, turned on the radio and heard that the American Legion, Veterans of Foreign Wars, and several conservative Catholic lay organizations had mobilized a massive protest demonstration at the concert site. Carloads of young men were reported to be blocking the entrance, shouting anti-Robeson, anticommunist, antiblack, and anti-Semitic slogans and obscenities.

At the concert site, the preparations crew, volunteers, and early concert arrivals were trapped in a hollow at the end of the short dirt road leading down from the main highway. The two-hundred-strong hostile mob at the entrance prepared to storm the hollow to attack its occupants, while groups of Legionnaires searched the line of blocked cars on the highway looking for Paul and other blacks. No uniformed police were in sight, and local sheriffs' deputies talked and joked with the members of the mob, making no effort to interfere. Several FBI agents present were taking notes.

In the meantime, Paul and Larry were on the train to Peekskill, intending to take a taxi to the concert site. Sam was housebound with a fractured leg, so Helen Rosen and her fourteen-year-old son, John, intercepted them at the train station. Helen had also asked Sidney Danis, a friend and veteran of the Spanish civil war and World War II, to meet her at the station with two reliable friends to provide security. They described the situation at the concert site to Paul and Larry. Paul insisted on trying to reach the concert grounds, arguing that a principle was at stake—if mob violence succeeded in stopping the concert, it meant that he couldn't make a public appearance anywhere outside of a black community. A compromise was reached; Helen would lead the way in her station wagon, and Danis and his two friends would follow with Paul and Larry.

When they arrived at the bottom of the hill leading up to the concert grounds, an enormous traffic jam was visible ahead. Gangs of men were working their way along the line of cars, checking occupants and pulling them over to cries of "dirty Commie and racist epithets. Helen spotted a cross burning on a nearby hill, ran back to Danis's car, and told him to get Paul out of there. Paul started to argue, but when he saw the burning cross he agreed to leave.

Danis drove Paul to the Rockmores' summer home at Ossining, about twenty miles away. Deeply agitated, Paul spent most of the night talking to Bob and Clara about the nightmarish events. His greatest concern was for those placed in danger and injured because of their support for him.[4]

Back at the entrance, Paul's burning effigy hung from a tree as a throaty cry rose from the mob: "Lynch Robeson!" Down in the hollow, the left-wing writer Howard Fast, a World War II veteran, organized a defense force of forty men to protect the early concertgoers, including a number of women and children. Since the narrow dirt road was flanked by high barbed-wire fences and dense wooden underbrush, the defenders could hold off a far larger force. As darkness began to fall, a mob of about two hundred attacked and an epic battle ensued. Finally the outnumbered defenders were pushed back into the hollow, where they ringed the women and children and prepared for a last stand. But the mob did not continue the attack; instead it burned the chairs and the equipment in a huge bonfire and then dispersed. A mass lynching had probably been averted by the bravery of the forty men, twelve of whom required hospital treatment. The state police, showing callous disregard for the victims of the attack, arrived hours after they had been notified.[5]

The following day fifteen hundred residents of the Peekskill area, profoundly alarmed by the mob violence that had prevented the Robeson concert, assembled on the grounds of the Rosens' country home to form the Westchester Committee for Law and Order. They decided to sponsor a second Robeson concert and subsequently secured the extensive grounds of the Hollow Brook Country Club as the site. Several left-wing unions, led by the Fur Workers, volunteered to provide massive security.

Over the next few days, controversy about the riot raged in the press and in Peekskill, where Robeson supporters were subjected to torrents of intimidating phone calls. The tabloid press trumpeted that Paul had "Asked for It" and that the concertgoers were communist provocateurs. Conservatives echoed these sentiments, and the Peekskill veterans' groups, while disclaiming responsibility for the violence, boasted that they had successively prevented the Robeson concert. Progressives and liberals alike, including Henry Wallace, the American Civil Liberties Union, and the New York chapter of the NAACP, were outraged by the violence and came to Paul's support. Protests demanding an investigation pressured New York governor Dewey into requesting a report from District Attorney George Fanelli. Paul held a press conference at Harlem's Hotel Theresa to demand a Justice Department investigation.

Paul's overriding concern about the rescheduled concert was for the safety of the audience. The party had a sharp debate about what its reaction should be to the Peekskill riot, with some leaders opposing a second concert as a response that was too aggressive. Ultimately, it was unanimously decided that an all-out effort would be made to guarantee the security of an anticipated audience of at least twenty thousand. Thus reassured, Paul agreed to return on Sunday, September 4, for the repeat concert.

On the evening of August 30, three days after the aborted concert, three thousand people packed the Golden Gate Ballroom on Lenox Avenue at 140th Street, and an equal number on the streets listened to loudspeakers. They had gathered to protest the attempt to kill Paul Robeson at Peekskill. They were angry but orderly. The police were out in large force, and so were Bumpy Johnson's men. It was very hot inside the packed hall, but no one made a move to leave. Paul sang three songs—"No More Auction Block," "Scandalize My Name," and "Ol' Man River." Then he spoke:

> They've got their answer here tonight. I don't notice any Legion around *here*. We are part of a historic departure. This means that from now on *we* take the offensive. We're going to have our concerts across this land, and we'll see that our women and children are not harmed again! We understand that here tonight; the surest way to get that police protection is to have it very clear that we'll protect ourselves, and good! No more pint of salt for me; no more driver's lash for me! That's all I'm saying—to the Klan, to the Legionnaires, to big business, even to the chief executive of these United States! The Negro People say, "Give us some freedom! Give us some democracy."
>
> I will be loyal to the America of the true traditions; to the America of the Abolition, of Harriet Tubman, of Thaddeus Stevens, of those who fought for my people's freedom, not of those who tried to enslave them.
>
> I want to thank you. I'm here, and this is the base in the struggle for the freedom of my people in my time, not some hundreds of years hence. Any, any time, that you want to call on me, I'm in there fighting for my people. Because you're with me; because we're all fighting together, for the freedom not only of the Negro People, but of an America which, years hence, our children can be proud of. We'll be proud we helped create an America where they could walk this earth with their shoulders back, full of the dignity of humankind.[6] (Emphasis in the original.)

As Paul came out and was whisked away in a car convoyed by several of Bumpy's Cadillacs, the thousands in the audience joined the massed thousands outside. The huge crowd spontaneously and quietly spilled out into the street, formed ranks, and marched down Lenox Avenue—a broad stream of humanity extending from curb to curb. Nobody organized the march; there were no slogans, no shouting. There was just a quiet murmur and the sound of thousands of marching feet. A police inspector agitatedly ran up to the front ranks, shouting, "Break it up! You have no permit for this march! Who's in charge here?" Someone up front said, "Ain't nobody in charge." And the crowd flowed around the dumbfounded inspector as they kept on marching. It took him a while just to reach the sidewalk.

Although large numbers of police were present, they were helpless as the crowd poured around them and squeezed them up onto the sidewalks. This mass of humanity had an unspoken discipline. It moved at a leisurely pace. There was no pushing. Everyone looked out for older people and children. There was no violence. Not a single policeman was injured or molested in any way, nor were any epithets directed at them. One grandmotherly lady walked past a young white policeman with his back up against a wall and his eyes filled with fear. She paused, patted him gently on the arm and said, "It's all right son, nobody's going to hurt you. Just you-all make sure nothin' happens to Paul Robeson."

By 6 a.m. on September 4, the advance guard of a security force that would grow to four thousand union members, most of them war veterans, had already begun the preparations for the 2 p.m. Robeson concert. They continued to arrive at the Hollow Brook Country Club, a twelve-acre area near the former concert site, in a constant stream of buses. They radiated competence, dedication, and discipline.

The only weapons present were softball bats that were stored at several sites near the command post; walkie-talkies provided radio communication between the various sectors, and the platform and sound system were being put in place. Parking areas for cars and buses were assigned inside the grounds to guarantee their security. A first aid tent and portable toilets were set up; water and food supplies were positioned, and a child care center was organized. Patrols continuously scoured the surrounding terrain, including a hill overlooking the platform.

State officials had announced that the state police would be in charge of maintaining order at the concert, but the intense efforts of the sponsoring Westchester Committee for Law and Order to negotiate police protection had elicited no positive response. The state police command post was set up near the entrance to the concert site, and throughout the morning hundreds of state policemen arrived to patrol the entire area, including the concert grounds.

Suddenly there was a flurry of activity at the edge of the woods behind the open concert area: groups of the union guards carrying softball bats and wearing hard hats ran into the woods. Some local young toughs had infiltrated and been discovered by a patrol of union guards. The intruders were quickly routed. Patrols were intensified. They discovered a sniper's nest in the hills overlooking the concert area and disarmed its occupants. The police not only ignored these incidents, but attempted to restrict the activity of the guards. Leon Straus, the commander of the guards, refused and demanded that the state police leave the concert grounds. The police complied but warned that they would not be responsible for what transpired inside the grounds.

Paul and Larry arrived with a six-car convoy. They entered from a narrow access road without incident and drove to the platform area where there was a solid perimeter of union guards. Paul was advised to stay in his car until the union guards completed another security check. Larry, in another car, was terrified but determined to do his job. Paul conferred with Howard Fast, the master of ceremonies, and Pete Seeger. It was agreed there would be no speeches and Paul would sing two groups of five songs each.

Straus and his head of security told Paul about the sniper's nest. They suggested he consider singing through the loudspeaker system from a secure location where he would not be an exposed target. Otherwise, they could not guarantee his safety. Paul immediately rejected the suggestion. "I came here to sing a concert, and I'll sing it like I always do," he replied. A call went out for fifteen volunteers to form a human barrier between Paul and the hills behind him and a large group of union men almost came to blows scrambling to be chosen. The head of security convinced them to draw straws.[7] A protest parade of eight thousand people, far less than the thirty thousand called for, marched to the concert site under police escort and crowded around the entrance to jeer the concert arrivals. Posters and handmade signs reminiscent of Nazi Germany appeared: "Wake Up America; Peekskill Did." They shouted, "Go back to Russia, you white niggers"; "You got in, but you'll never get out alive"; "Niggers, Jews, commies—Hitler didn't finish the job, but we will."

A steady stream of buses and cars kept arriving—local people, people from New York City, many from Harlem, and some from upstate, people from as far away as New Jersey and Connecticut. The relative calm broke down abruptly as the state police forced all members of the concert defense back inside the concert grounds. As a result, late-arriving buses, many of them from Harlem, had no protection. The state police compelled the arriving buses to park across the road from the entrance and then did little to protect the occupants from harassment by the hostile crowd as they traversed the fifty yards to enter the gate. Many local policemen and even some state troopers clubbed black arrivals who dared to respond to the crowd's abuse.

By the time the concert began at 2 p.m., the state police presence had grown to two thousand. A police helicopter swooped low over the area intermittently. The audience numbered almost twenty-five thousand, a quarter of it black. Even while the harassment continued, there was a festive atmosphere of an extended-family picnic inside the concert grounds. A human wall of twenty-five hundred union guards standing shoulder to shoulder formed a protective perimeter around the entire concert area.

There were no speeches. Pianists Ray Lev and Leonid Hambro played selections from Chopin and Bach, and Pete Seeger sang folk songs solo and with a chorus. Paul performed ten numbers, beginning with "Go Down Moses" and ending with "Ol' Man River." His only spoken comments were those that introduced the songs. While he sang, the only distinguishable sound other than his voice and its rumbling echo from the surrounding hills was the distant roar of the police helicopter. The faint echoes of the hostile crowd vanished as everyone, including the police and the union guards, listened to Paul's clearly audible voice. Between numbers, the applause erupted in swelling waves. In a fitting conclusion, Paul's mighty bass voice singing the final lines of "Ol' Man River" could be heard through the roar of the helicopter as it swooped down low over the concert platform.

The horror began when the audience streamed out of the concert grounds. The piles of rocks assembled earlier at regular intervals
along extensive stretches of the highway served as an inexhaustible
supply of missiles with which roving bands of thugs continuously
bombarded the departing cars and buses. The police made no moves
to interfere, often laughing and yelling encouragement to the rock
throwers. At the section of the perpendicular access road directly in
front of the entrance, the mob had managed to get a huge boulder up
onto a utility pole from where it could be rolled down onto the roof
of a passing car. When cars stopped and bleeding occupants emerged
to plead for police help, they were clubbed and told to move on. An
hour after the concert had ended, areas along the highway were slick
with human blood.

The union security people decided that Paul's convoy should get
out early. The side windows of all the cars were rolled up and blan-
kets were placed against them from the inside to ward off flying glass.
Paul lay on the floor of the middle car with two large union guards
on top of him. As the convoy reached the entrance gate, the driver of
Paul's car barked to the guard sitting beside him, "If I'm too injured
to keep driving, I'll roll out of the car. You take over and keep driving.
Don't stop." Then, as snarling state policemen slammed their clubs
against the windshield, he fell in behind the front cars of the convoy
heading for the access road directly across the highway. The driver
of the lead car had calculated correctly that this route would get the
convoy clear of the traffic clogging the highway in both directions.

They roared across the highway and up the initial steep incline.
The lead car swerved at the last moment, narrowly avoiding the rock
that was rolled off the utility pole. The second and fifth cars peeled off
to the left and right, gunning their vehicles along the shoulders of the
road to scatter both the rock throwers and the police. With Paul's car
still in the middle, the remaining five cars accelerated up to the relatively safe area at the top of the hill while the other two cars brought
up the rear.

A few minutes later, completely in the clear, they stopped, and Paul
got up off the floor. As he stretched his legs, he turned to the others and
remarked in a contemplative tone, "How do you think the American
trade union movement will evaluate the Peekskill concert?" Everyone
cracked up with laughter, with Paul laughing the loudest.

Back at the concert grounds, many of the bus drivers had been frightened into abandoning their vehicles, and some of the buses parked outside of the concert grounds had been disabled by the mob. This left several thousand people stranded. The union guards assigned their own buses and drivers to the stranded audience members. Others were seated in departing cars that were not full. Women, children, and senior citizens received first priority.

The Harlem buses, having been stoned all the way from Peekskill south to Yonkers, finally arrived in front of the Hotel Theresa at 125th Street and Seventh Avenue. While there were many with injuries, there were, miraculously, no deaths. Paul, standing outside the hotel with William Patterson in the gathering dusk, watched in silent horror, tears streaming down his face, as dozens of shattered buses arrived filled with bleeding people—women and children as well as men. The word was out all over Harlem, and one could feel the people's anger.

Blacks outside of Harlem were angry too. Dozens of black New York City policemen vacationing at interracial Camp Unity and several black upstate summer resorts had heard on the radio that "Robeson's people" were trapped at Peekskill by the New York State Police. They loaded their shotguns and ammunition into the trunks of their cars and raced toward Peekskill, determined to see that no harm came to "Robeson's folks."

Meanwhile, the trapped men had formed ranks and marched up the hill toward the entrance, singing union songs to keep their spirits up. The state police switched on batteries of portable bright lights and charged down the hill, guns drawn. The men halted but continued to sing. The police charged into them and used their clubs, trying to split them up into small groups in order to isolate the blacks. However, the white union men kept linking arms and surrounding their black compatriots despite the clubbing they took. At last, the police gave up, and Straus negotiated an arrangement allowing the guards to drive to the nearby progressive community of Mohegan in the abandoned buses.

Back in Harlem, Paul heard his name called by a familiar voice. It was coming from the first of several cars sitting in front of the Hotel Theresa entrance. Bumpy Johnson, Paul's chess partner, and boss of bosses in Harlem's underworld, was in the front passenger seat with the car door open, his feet resting on the curb. As Paul greeted Johnson, he was startled to see men in battle fatigues in the car with a pile of weapons at their feet. Johnson said that he had heard that Paul's people were trapped at Peekskill and he was ready to go up and extricate them. All Paul had to do was give the word.

Paul, touched by Bumpy's concern but horrified by his proposal, replied that he would confer with his people. He talked with Patterson, who had just heard that the guards had negotiated their way out safely. Much relieved, he told Johnson the news. They shook hands warmly and Johnson reiterated that he was always there if Paul needed him.[8]

On September 5, Paul held a press conference in the library of the Council on African Affairs headquarters. After the crowd of reporters heard more than a dozen eyewitnesses vividly depict the events of the previous day, Paul charged the state police with aiding and abetting the attacks against the concertgoers instead of carrying out their legal duty to protect them. He called the state troopers "fascist storm troopers who will knock down and club anyone who disagrees with them." Referring to the heavily Jewish membership of the unions providing most of the concert defense force, he added with visible emotion that "we Negroes owe a great debt to the Jewish people, who stood there to defend me and all of us yesterday." Then he expressed his determination to sing wherever audiences wanted to hear him.

The white press generally criticized the violence directed against Paul and the concertgoers, but promoted the false propaganda that the Peekskill riots were deliberately provoked by communist agitators. Walter Winchell set the national tone in his radio commentary, saying, "The Reds don't want American concerts. They want to provoke Americans into rioting, so that their radio commentators can have some evidence for their ravings. And so I sincerely hope that the American Legionnaires and the other war veterans will not fall into his Moscow trap when Paul Robeson starts his nation-wide 'concert tour.'"

Liberals failed to mention the flagrant police violence or the blatant racism exhibited by the anti-Robeson demonstrators and the police alike. Mrs. Eleanor Roosevelt commented that "it seems to me quite disgraceful to allow this kind of lawlessness. I dislike everything that Paul Robeson is now saying. I still believe, however, that if he wants to give a concert, or speak his mind in public, no one should prevent him from doing so." President Truman responded to a question about Peekskill at a press conference a few days later by saying that Mrs. Roosevelt had "covered the situation perfectly and thoroughly."

New York governor Dewey accepted Westchester County district attorney Fanelli's report on the event despite its many falsehoods: "Every precaution possible was taken to insure the safety of all present. All police departments that took part should be commended for their excellent work." Dewey subsequently issued a statement in which he called the concert audience "followers of Red totalitarianism" and accused "Communist groups" of provoking the incident. Then he appointed Fanelli to head a grand jury investigation of "whether the meeting was initiated and sponsored for the purpose of deliberately inciting disorder and a breach of the peace, and whether it was a part of Communist strategy to foment racial and religious hatreds."

The Peekskill controversy raged on for months, reaching the floor of Congress in the form of a dramatic exchange between Representatives Javits of New York and Rankin of Mississippi:

Javits: The issue involved in the Peekskill riot is a much wider one, affecting respect for constitutional guarantees for minorities throughout the United States. The constitutional guarantee of freedom of speech and freedom of assemblage is best tested when its application is to a highly unpopular minority of Communists and Communist sympathizers. It reminds us also of the larger Federal anti-lynching legislation which has been permitted to languish in a shameful way.

Rankin: The American people were not in sympathy with that gang of Communists who composed that traitorous gathering. When they now undertake to investigate and persecute those ex-servicemen who made that protest, when they begin to investigate them for trying to break up that Communist meeting, the American people are with the ex-servicemen and not with that Negro Communist and that bunch of Reds.

A. Philip Randolph echoed the liberal line on behalf of the black establishment in a letter to the *New York Times*. Like Mrs. Roosevelt, he deplored the violence but asserted that the riot "was not racial" and that Paul was neither a spokesman for his people nor sufficiently engaged in the black "struggle." He also deplored "the willingness of Robeson to seize upon and even aggravate the situation."

The liberal establishment's ultimate view of the Peekskill events was expressed months later in a *New York Times* editorial in response to the Peekskill report of the Westchester County grand jury. After praising the report's "thorough and commendable job," the editorial accepted without question the colossal lie that the motives of the rioters in resisting "the Communist display of strength were anti-Communist and not anti-Negro or anti-Semitic." Then it declared, "It is a good thing to recognize the Communist tactic of trying to play upon presumptive race prejudice and to create its shadow even if its substance is absent."

The black press treated the Peekskill events in a different manner. In a representative syndicated column, James L. Hicks of the *Baltimore Afro-American* detailed the lawless conduct of the police, described his own narrow escape from clubbing at the hands of a special deputy sheriff, and vented his outrage at the brutal violence inflicted by the all-white mob on black concertgoers, who were often singled out for special punishment. The extensive photographic evidence of the consciously organized racist, lynchlike attacks that appeared widely in black media stirred an immense anger among the black masses, especially in the South. Paul became a folk hero of unprecedented stature.

Hicks ended his column with an unmistakable warning to white America: "Paul Robeson today is a 200-pound stick of dynamite swinging like a pendulum between two burning flames, and no one in America can say which flame will ignite him. The flame on the right is the American status quo. The flame on the left is a weaker, smoldering fire faithfully nursed by the Communist Party. What will happen if either one of the flames reaches out and sets fire to the dynamite? The riot at Peekskill on August 27 almost provided the answer. In this case it appears that the flame on the right came dangerously close to setting off the dynamite—the inference being that any bodily harm to Robeson will bring an explosion."[9]

Peekskill dramatically revived the issue of the Robeson family's security. Once again, Paul didn't travel without a bodyguard, and he arranged for Marilyn and me to move into a West Harlem apartment where we would be safe from racist harassment. Essie, who had been attending the Mexico City Continental Congress for Peace as Paul's representative during the period of both Peekskill riots, was now back at the Enfield house. Although she was receiving a stream of vile hate mail, she was determined not to be intimidated into moving. Cars would occasionally drive by honking their horns, but nothing serious happened, until one day a carload of hostile young white men followed her home from a shopping trip.

Essie pulled into her driveway and turned her car around so it was facing the road. She waited with the motor running. Her pursuers entered the driveway. Essie gunned her car forward at the intruders. Panicked, the driver swerved sharply onto the front lawn and back onto the main road, bouncing through the shallow roadside ditch. Essie's next-door neighbor, an avid hunter, came running out of his house with a rifle, knelt, and tracked the car with his rifle at his shoulder as it roared away from the neighborhood. The next day, several neighbors called Essie and some came over in person to pledge that they would make sure she was safe.

The local police turned down Essie's request for a gun permit, but she noticed that police cars took to patrolling near the house frequently. Nobody tried to bother her after that.[10]

On September 20, Paul walked briskly to the witness stand and took his oath as a character witness for Ben Davis in the highly publicized trial of the twelve top Communist Party leaders on antigovernment conspiracy charges. It was a high-risk move, since Hoover had been working for months to assemble enough "legally admissible" evidence of Paul's Communist Party membership to entrap him when cross examined under oath. To this end, Hoover had sent reams of intelligence information on Paul to the prosecution team.

Since prosecutor John McGohey had received no legally admissible evidence that could incriminate Paul, he decided to deny him a platform. He objected to every question put to Paul on direct examination, with the exception of two that pertained to his education. Judge Harold Medina sustained every objection and peremptorily ruled out all additional questions by the defense counsel. McGohey quickly ended Paul's testimony by declining to conduct any cross-examination. Paul walked out of the courtroom arm in arm with Ben Davis and gave interviews to the press in the lobby. Asked whether he was a member of the Communist Party, he replied that the question was "irrelevant."

Later, Paul gave an extensive interview to the *Pittsburgh Courier*. In response to a question about whether he wanted "a new kind of economic and political system in America," he replied that he wanted "any kind of system the people want," and that he did not want America to adopt a system "for which it is not ready." He added that "this country is not ready for either the socialization which was adopted in England or the system which is in operation in Russia. But it is ready for the extension of democratic principles."

The next day, he chuckled with satisfaction as he read headlines such as, "Robeson Held in Check at Trial." The government that had set out to make him disappear was now happy just to have restrained him. Moreover, since he had not been subjected to cross-examination by the government lawyers while under oath, the accusations that he was affiliated with the Communist Party had been undermined among most blacks.[11]

Paul's concert tour was successful beyond expectations. Travel security proved to be simple. At every train station or airport, he was met by a group of black redcaps or skycaps who took it upon themselves to guarantee his safety. On trains, both the Pullman porters and the dining car waiters, who were exclusively black, provided his security. Paul was immensely popular with them despite the political attacks on him by their union president, A. Philip Randolph.

The first stop was Cleveland on September 24, where a concert at Paradise Auditorium in the heart of the black community attracted a capacity audience. Two days later Paul appeared in Chicago. Since all the civic halls were closed to him, he sang at the North Side's Bakers Hall one night and the next night at the Tabernacle Baptist Church, one of the leading churches on the heavily black South Side. Both times, loudspeakers carried Paul's voice to the overflow crowds in the surrounding streets. At Tabernacle Baptist Church, A.M.E. Zion bishop William J. Walls welcomed Paul and compared him to "the noble Frederick Douglass."

In Los Angeles, right-wing columnists and organizations floated rumors of violence, and the *California Eagle*, the black newspaper sponsoring the concert, was inundated with threatening phone calls. black Los Angeles rose to Paul's defense. The NAACP Youth Council sold tickets to the concert. Alpha Phi Alpha, the leading black fraternity, in which Paul was a life member, hosted a luncheon in Paul's honor. Virtually every major black organization publicized his appearance. A predominantly black audience of fifteen thousand came to hear him on September 30 at Wrigley Field baseball park.

The National Baptist Convention, the largest organization in the United States, had just closed its annual session at the same venue a few days earlier, with President David V. Jemison's address in which he paid tribute to Paul:

> The latest technique on the part of those who would defeat us is to brand every Negro who dares speak for equality and justice as Communistic or subversive. "Be not afraid." One of the highest compliments that can come to a sincere Negro leader today is to be branded subversive. It is not Paul Robeson, the Communist, that they fear. It is Paul Robeson, the Champion of the CAUSE of black people in America and in Africa.

In Detroit, so many people came to the Forest Club that Paul sang a second concert at the Shiloh Baptist Church the same evening. The next day, he sang in the Hartford Avenue Baptist Church at the invitation of his friend, Pastor Reverend Charles Hill. There he recalled the tribulations of his father, who escaped from slavery as a teenager, and reemphasized his two main themes: racism, not communism, loomed as humankind's greatest enemy, and communists, who were both antiracist and anticolonialist, could not possibly be the enemies of black people.

Prior to Paul's arrival in Washington, D.C., seventeen local black leaders, among them prominent community figure Mary Church Terrell, distinguished sociologist E. Franklin Frazier, Congressman Adam Clayton Powell Jr., past director of the Fraternal Council of Negro Churches W. H. Jernagin, and Reverend Stephen G. Spottswood, who headed the local NAACP, issued a statement declaring that they were "united in affirming [Robeson's] inalienable right to speak and sing to all who wish to hear him" despite their sharp disagreement with his public positions on certain issues. Frazier appeared with Paul and delivered a speech in which he hailed him for "representing the Negro man in the masculine role as a fearless and independent thinker."

Paul's appearance at the Rally for Negro Freedom at Turner's Arena on October 13 attracted a capacity crowd and a heavy police presence. Police lines a block long appeared on both sides of the arena, and police guarded every corner within a six-block radius. Washington's black community, with the recent police violence at Peekskill in mind, assembled a large security force with armaments so heavy that an awed Paul later remarked, "Those guys had enough hardware to hold off the National Guard."

The Truman administration was worried about such volunteer local security forces, not least because they could be directed against local police authority as well as toward Paul's defense. After his Washington, D.C., concert, federal agencies, including the FBI, joined forces to ensure that local authorities acceded to Paul's request for a personal bodyguard of black plainclothes police personnel for the remainder of the tour. With regard to Hoover's unflagging efforts to obtain evidence of Paul's presumed Communist Party affiliations, eight years of intense and persistent efforts by the Bureau had produced no results.[12]

Paul returned from the tour greatly encouraged by the wellspring of black support that had greeted him. However, faced with the daunting problem of how to survive over the long term, he added a new recruit, Lloyd Brown, to his inner circle. A compact, light-brown-skinned writer and journalist in his mid-thirties, Lloyd was an editor of the left-wing cultural magazine *Masses and Mainstream* and had long been an admirer of Paul's artistry, cultural philosophy, and political stands. Subsidized by the party to work full-time with Paul, Lloyd filled the multiple roles of biographer, speechwriter, and personal assistant. Direct but soft-spoken, highly organized and loyal, he was a determined and independent-minded doer rather than a talker. He and Paul quickly developed a good working relationship.[13]

In the fall, Indian prime minister Jawaharlal Nehru was on an official U.S. visit to confer with President Truman. Nan Pandit, his sister and ambassador to the United States, had written Essie to arrange a secret meeting for Nehru with Paul and Essie in New York. November 6, the day after Nehru was officially scheduled to leave the country, was the agreed-upon meeting date. To Essie's consternation, Paul abruptly announced he would not meet with Nehru because Nehru had clashed with the Indian Communist Party and many communists had been killed. However, Paul refused to denounce Nehru publicly, as urged by the U.S. Communist Party.

Essie met with Nehru on her own and made excuses for Paul's absence, but Nehru did not believe her. He spent most of his last day in the United States tracking Paul down, and finally, with Essie's assistance, he reached him by telephone. When Paul heard Nehru's voice asking, "Why didn't you come," he had no escape. He responded, "Because your hands are too bloody." Nehru was so wounded by this exchange that it took eight years for him to forgive Paul.[14]

One Saturday afternoon late in December, my father stopped by our apartment to spend time with Marilyn and me. At the end of his visit, he asked me to accompany him to a meeting farther uptown. On our way there he briefed me. We were going to meet with Henry Winston, one of the top party leaders, and he wanted me as a witness. This was the extent of his briefing.

Winston greeted us jovially and ushered us into the living room without manifesting any surprise at my presence. Four second-rank party leaders were there. After some general good-natured banter, a dialogue developed between Winston and Paul about Paul's future plans. Winston leaned forward to express an idea from some of the leadership. Perhaps Paul should cease his political activity and just sing. Moreover, since his passport had not been revoked, he could travel abroad for a concert tour and function exclusively as an artist.

Paul was momentarily silent and visibly angry since this suggestion was similar to the State Department offer he had refused at great risk to himself and his family. Then he broke the silence, replying sharply that he didn't think that was a good idea. In one continuous motion, he rose from his chair, spun around, and headed for the front door with giant strides, snatching up his coat and hat on the way. I had to move fast to catch up with him. We walked down at least six flights of stairs, instead of waiting for the elevator, and traversed an entire block before my father said a word.

He asked me, "What did you make of that?"

"It seems to me," I replied, "that they would be happy to be rid of you and hope that you go abroad and stay."

He nodded, adding that he needed to make up his mind about what to do, since he had been invited to attend a session of the World Peace Council in a few months. Although his passport was still valid, he didn't think he could keep it for long. It would almost surely be revoked whenever the next international crisis arose. He added wistfully, "I'll go over there one last time, but I'll come right back."

My and Marilyn's wedding. (Left to right) Paul, Marilyn, me, Essie, and Marilyn's mother, Rae Greenberg. Marilyn's brother, Harold Graham, attended but left to secure taxis so the wedding party could escape the mob outside. New York City, June 19, 1949. *From the personal collection of Paul Robeson Jr.*

Me and Marilyn at our private wedding party at Freda Diamond's home, New York City, 1949. *From the personal collection of Paul Robeson Jr.*

Essie, circa 1950. *Courtesy CPUSA Photographs Collection, Tamiment Library, New York University.*

Greeting Benjamin J. Davis Jr. at the May Day celebration, Union Square in New York City, 1947. Daily Worker *photo. Courtesy of the Paul Robeson Foundation.*

With Clara Rockmore (right) and her sister, Nadia Reisenberg, a famous pianist and piano teacher, late 1940s. *From the personal collection of Paul Robeson Jr.*

With Sam Park[
leader of the Uni
Packinghouse Work
circa 1947. *Courtesy CPU*
Photographs Collection,
Tamiment Library, New York
University.

With a young Julian Bond (right), Atlanta, circa 1948. *Courtesy of the Paul Robeson Foundation.*

With (left to right) former vice president Henry Wallace, Albert Einstein, and Lewis L. Wallace, Princeton, New Jersey, September 1947. *From the personal collection of Paul Robeson Jr.*

With Leontyne Price, Dayton, Ohio, 1951. *From the personal collection of Paul Robeson Jr.*

On a concert tour in the Panama Canal Zone, 1947. *Courtesy of Dr. Natalia Kanem and Mandela Gregoire.*

With American Labor Party New York congressmen Vito Marcantonio (left) and Leo Isacson (right) before addressing a "Committee to Defeat the Mundt-Nixon Bill" rally, Washington, D.C., June 1948. Daily Worker *photo.*
Courtesy of the Paul Robeson Foundation.

Paul on a sound truck campaigning for the Progressive Party, 1948. Daily Worker *photo. Courtesy of the Paul Robeson Foundation.*

With longtime accompanist Lawrence Brown during an informal performance on a Scandinavian tour, Copenhagen, Denmark, 1949. *Photo by Willy Hansen. Courtesy of the Schomburg Center for Research in Black Culture/NYPL.*

Celebrating the 150th birthday of the famous Russian poet Alexander Pushkin, who was of African descent, Moscow, 1949.
From the personal collection of Paul Robeson Jr.

On stage with orchestra, Gorki Park, Moscow, 1949. *From the personal collection of Paul Robeson Jr.*

Paul (right) being greeted on his arrival in Stalingrad, accompanied by Peter Blackman (second from left), 1949. *From the personal collection of Paul Robeson Jr.*

Speaking at the Paris Peace Conference, April 1949. *From the personal collection of Paul Robeson Jr.*

With Dr. W. E. B. DuBois at the Paris Peace Conference, April 1949. *From the personal collection of Paul Robeson, Jr.*

Concertgoers driving through the mob gauntlet during the Peekskill, New York, riot, August 27, 1949. *Courtesy of Barbara Kopple Peekskill Riot Photographs Collection, Tamiment Library, New York University.*

Crowd gathered outside the Golden Gate Ballroom in Harlem to hear Paul speak at a rally protesting the first Peekskill riot, New York City, August 30, 1949. *Courtesy CPUSA Photographs Collection, Tamiment Library, New York University.*

Part of the line of security (center) at the Peekskill concert facing the anti-Robeson mob (background) and protecting concertgoers (foreground), Peekskill, New York, 1949. Daily Worker *photo. Courtesy of the Paul Robeson Foundation.*

Relaxing at Furriers Union resort, Crystal Lake, New York, 1949. *From the personal collection of Paul Robeson Jr.*

At Wo-Chi-Ca children's camp with famous lifelong Communist Party activist Mother Ella Reeve Bloor, New Jersey, 1946. *From the personal collection of Paul Robeson Jr.*

Speaking at a civil rights rally in New York City, 1949. *From the personal collection of Paul Robeson Jr.*

At Hartford Avenue Baptist Church, Detroit, 1949. *From the personal collection of Paul Robeson, Jr.*

At Peace Arch Park in Blaine, Washington—the international boundary between Canada and the United States, 1952. *From the personal collection of Paul Robeson Jr.*

INTERNATIONAL BOUNDARY

UNITED STATES

Speaking with Harlem tenants, circa 1952. *Photo by Jack Zessman. From the personal collection of Paul Robeson Jr.*

Meeting with a Harlem tenants organization, circa 1952. *Photo by Jack Zessman. From the personal collection of Paul Robeson Jr.*

Presenting "We Charge Genocide" petition to UN official, accusing the United States of genocide against black Americans, New York City, 1951. Daily Worker *photo. From the personal collection of Paul Robeson Jr.*

Me (left) with famed African American UN diplomat Dr. Ralph J. Bunche during a reception at the Soviet Union's Mission to the United Nations, New York City, 1957. *Photo by Leo Rosenthal. From the personal collection of Paul Robeson Jr.*

Freedom Tour concert program, Roxbury and Cambridge, Massachusetts, 1951. *From the personal collection of Paul Robeson Jr.*

In New York City, circa 1952. *From the personal collection of Paul Robeson Jr.*

The Robesons (Paul, center; me, foreground; Essie, far right) in a Harlem night club celebrating Paul's fifty-sixth birthday with friends, New York City, 1954. *From the personal collection of Paul Robeson Jr.*

Speaking at a Harlem church against U.S. support of the French war in Indo-China, New York City, 1954. *From the personal collection of Paul Robeson Jr.*

Comeback concert, Oakland, California, 1957. *Courtesy of the Paul Robeson Foundation.*

With Prime Minister Jawaharlal Pandit Nehru of India, New York City, 1957. *Courtesy of the Paul Robeson Foundation.*

Essie in Peking, China, 1950. *From the personal collection of Paul Robeson Jr.*

Essie with UN secretary general Dag Hammerskjöld, at UN headquarters, New York City, 1958. *From the personal collection of Paul Robeson Jr.*

Paul (right) at the christening of his first grandchild, David Paul Robeson, with me and Marilyn at Mother A.M.E. Zion Church, New York City, 1951. *Photo by Austin Hansen. From the personal collection of Paul Robeson Jr.*

1957 family portrait for a Christmas card. Clockwise from top left: Marilyn, Essie, me, David, Paul, and Susan. *From the personal collection of Paul Robeson Jr.*

Paul (front, third from right) with his elder brother Reverend Dr. Benjamin C. Robeson (back, third from right) and his sister, Marian Forsythe (back, fourth from right). Clockwise from Paul: Frances Robeson, Rev. Robeson's wife; Marian R. Liggins, Rev. Robeson's eldest daughter; Paulina Forsythe, Marian Forsythe's daughter; E. Bruce Liggins, M.D., Marian Liggins's husband; unidentified Robeson cousin; Naomi Perry Blassengil, Dr. Bruce Liggins's cousin; William A. Forsythe, M.D., Marian Forsythe's husband; Bennie R. Ryan, Rev. Robeson's youngest daughter; and Vivian R. Portee, Rev. Robeson's middle daughter. *Photo by Austin Hansen. Courtesy of Dr. Gregory R. Smith.*

Rehearsing with his
accompanist Alan Booth,
New York, 1956. *Courtesy of
Freedomways.*

Working on music theories at Jumel Terrace, New York, 1956. *From the personal collection of Paul
Robeson Jr.*

III
PAYING THE PRICE

(1950–1958)

Paul testifying before the House Un-American
Activities Committee (HUAC) accompanied
by his attorney, Milton Friedman, Washington,
D.C., 1956. *From the personal collection of Paul Robeson Jr.*

Paul and Essie with the Soviet Union's Prime
Minister Nikita S. Khrushchev (second from
left) at his vacation retreat near Yalta, Crimea,
1958. *From the personal collection of Paul Robeson Jr.*

9

STRUGGLE FOR SURVIVAL

(1950–1954)

The end of 1949 marked an intensification of the cold war between the United States and the Soviet Union. In September, the Soviet Union tested its first nuclear weapon, and the Truman administration exploited this development to stoke public fears of a Soviet military attack. Tensions increased in October when the communists led by Mao Tse-tung drove Chiang Kai-shek's U.S.-supported regime out of mainland China to the island of Taiwan. Paul defied the growing anticommunist hysteria by appearing on November 10 as the main speaker at a banquet sponsored by the National Council of Soviet-American Friendship at New York City's Waldorf-Astoria Hotel.

Celebrating the thirty-second anniversary of the Soviet Union, Paul's theme was "The Negro People and the Soviet Union." He hailed the Soviets as true friends of the people of Africa and the West Indies. He went on to say that "in America today the Negro people are the core of the struggle against war and fascism. We anti-fascists—the true lovers of American democracy—have a tremendous responsibility. If we mobilize with courage, the forces of world fascism will be defeated—in Europe, in Africa and in the United States."[1]

At the beginning of 1950, Paul concentrated on building an institutional base in Harlem. With the aid of both funding and personnel from the party he founded the monthly newspaper *Freedom*. The Council on African Affairs sold its West 23rd Street town house headquarters and leased a building on 125th Street in Harlem to house both the council and *Freedom*. Louis Burnham became the monthly's editor. Energetic, with a brilliant intellect and a talent for organizing, he had served ably as the executive secretary of the Southern Negro Youth Congress and as southern director of the Progressive Party. He assembled a staff not only to publish the newspaper but also to organize support groups in other cities and schedule concert appearances in black churches and for left-wing unions.

Since Larry Brown felt he could no longer cope with the irregularity of Paul's concerts and the security problems associated with them, Paul agreed that they would make only selective appearances together. Although no one could fully replace the incomparable Larry, Paul found a talented new accompanist who could also perform as assisting artist. Alan Booth, a compact, dark-skinned man in his mid-thirties, was a fine musician with great flexibility who quickly adapted his skills to Paul's needs. He also shared Paul's dedication to social causes and his views about the role of the artist in society. They worked well together.

Meanwhile, Hoover took a special interest in Paul's foreign contacts, maintaining a close liaison with the CIA and the Department of State. The CIA reported to him on a meeting of African political leaders at which it was stated that Paul was sending a personal letter suggesting they cooperate closely with African political bodies outside their own country. A May 15, 1950, memorandum from the New York office to Hoover transmitted Paul's handwriting specimens, obtained from the State Department's Passport Office, for placement in the Bureau's "Communist Key Figure handwriting file."

The FBI kept track of Essie with similar zeal. A February 9, 1950, memorandum reported on her departure on November 9, 1949, for Moscow as an American delegate to the Women's International Democratic Federation. It was noted that she would subsequently attend the First Conference of Asian Women in Peiping (Beijing), People's Republic of China, as part of a four-woman group of American observers.[2]

On February 24, Paul traveled to Chicago to deliver the keynote speech at the Second Annual Convention of the Progressive Party and to spend a few weeks building his base in the city's black community, in left-wing unions, and in progressive organizations. His message everywhere was one of unity in the struggle against the common enemy: the two-party cold war status quo.

In his address to the convention, Paul appealed for unity within the Progressive Party, which was in danger of fracturing over the issue of expelling communists from its membership. He said, "The road has been hard. We have all labored and sacrificed; we have all made our mistakes; but we have never been discouraged. On and on we have plodded—together, black and white, Jewish and Gentile, of different opinions about the way to full freedom; of different social backgrounds—scientists, scholars, teachers and workers; liberals, middle of the roaders, reformists, radicals—all intent upon common goals." He urged his audience to live up to their responsibility: "We can only fulfill our historic tasks if we move forward in the closest unity—a unity built on our program for a truly democratic America and a world living in brotherhood and peace."

Behind the scenes, Paul joined Henry Wallace to help craft a unity resolution to avoid a split: "The Progressive Party calls to the support of its program all those who believe whole-heartedly in it, no matter what party they belong to. We will not attempt the purge of any individual because of past or present labels."

Paul remained in Chicago for several weeks, meeting with black ministers, community leaders, and especially black trade unionists. He stayed at the home of Sam Parks, the thickset, blunt-spoken former leader of the Packinghouse Workers' predominantly black local union. Sam and Paul discussed the National Labor Conference for Negro Rights that was to be held in June in Chicago. The aim of the conference was to unify the loosely connected black caucuses in the CIO unions into a coherent national organization.

Most white union leaders resisted this growing movement among rank-and-file black workers, and a few, including Harry Bridges, the dynamic and highly respected leader of the International Longshore and Warehouse Union, were outspoken in their hostility. They condemned black caucuses as a road to dual unionism and black nationalism. However, the overwhelming majority of black trade unionists disagreed and intensified their efforts to build a national organization.

From the outset, Paul gave all-out support to Revels Cayton, Sam Parks, and other leaders of the black caucus movement. He believed, as they did, that in the near term, assimilation and/or integration of a vast majority of black Americans into the mainstream were unrealistic goals. Moreover, the acceptance of a small minority of upper- and middle-class blacks had produced only token gains for blacks as a people. Paul's open advocacy of collective Black self-determination placed him directly at odds with the mainstream black leadership, with one exception. Black labor leader A. Philip Randolph, a dedicated anticommunist and cold war advocate, agreed with Paul on the issue of black autonomy.

On March 12, during Paul's Chicago visit, Elliott Roosevelt, Eleanor Roosevelt's son, announced that Paul, speaking on behalf of the Progressive Party, would debate Harlem representative Adam Clayton Powell Jr., a prominent Democrat, and Perry Howard, black Republican National Committee member from Mississippi, on NBC's Sunday afternoon television show *Today with Mrs. Roosevelt*. The next day, NBC announced that as a result of an avalanche of protests against Paul's scheduled appearance they had canceled his participation, adding that Paul Robeson would never appear on NBC with the management's consent. Elliott Roosevelt requested that the Progressive Party select another spokesperson, but they refused, asserting their right to choose their spokesman. As a result, the program was canceled.

Mrs. Roosevelt steadfastly declined to criticize the NBC action, choosing instead to disparage Paul's political views and to question his credentials as a spokesman for blacks. The liberal establishment and its press followed suit. The *Baltimore Afro-American*, in a March 25 editorial titled "Air Not Free at NBC," supported Paul unequivocally. Paul responded at a Progressive Party meeting in Chicago's black South Side community to a cheering crowd of fifteen hundred. He denounced NBC but avoided criticizing Mrs. Roosevelt directly: "Keeping me off any program will not prevent the truth from being known. I shall continue to fight for a decent life for the Negro people and all oppressed people, and for a peaceful world in which all men can walk with full human dignity."

Refusing to take a defensive stance, Paul traveled from coast to coast and appeared at benefit concerts, union conferences, and political rallies, and he led a vigil in front of the White House in support of fair employment practices. He used his still valid passport to travel to London in May to attend a meeting of the World Peace Council, where he sang and spoke to twenty thousand people, declaring that the awakening resistance of the American working class would prevent fascism from ever coming to the United States.

Upon his return to the States, Paul delivered his message of struggle and hope to the National Labor Conference for Negro Rights in Chicago on June 10. He reminded his audience that the millions of slaves, indentured servants, and immigrants had built the wealth of America, adding that "these are the forces that have made America great and preserved our heritage. They have arisen at each moment of crisis to play the decisive role in our national affairs." He also condemned the U.S. shipment of arms "for the French imperialists to use against the brave Vietnamese patriots in the 'dirty war' in Indo-China," and defended communists as the "solid core of the struggle for freedom."

Paul called for Negro trade unionists "to increasingly assert their influence in every aspect of the life of the Negro community." On their shoulders rested the responsibility "to rally the power of the whole trade union movement, white and black, to the battle for the liberation of our people." He challenged the white trade unionists present to "fight in the ranks of labor for the full equality of your Negro brothers, for acceptance of the fact that the Negro workers have become a part of the vanguard of the whole American working class." Paul closed by asserting, "As the black worker takes his place upon the stage of history—not for a bit part, but to play his full role with dignity in the very center of the plot—a new day dawns in human affairs. This is history's challenge to you. I know that you will not fail."[3]

On June 25, 1950, the army of North Korea, a close ally of the Soviet Union, attacked pro-Western South Korea after months of political and military tension between the two countries. President Truman chose to interpret the North Korean invasion as a Soviet military challenge to the United States and pressured the United Nations Security Council into sanctioning the dispatch of U.S. troops to support the crumbling South Korean army. "Truman's War" began, and most Americans, responding to the mass media's war drums and anticommunist hysteria, rallied around the president.

Henry Wallace joined the trend, denouncing North Korea and the Soviet Union and requesting the Progressive Party leadership to follow his lead. When the executive committee, including Paul, refused, Wallace resigned from the party, taking most of its liberal wing with him. The remaining left-progressive core soldiered on against overwhelming odds. In September, Congress passed the McCarran Internal Security Act, targeting "un-Americans and subversive activities," which gave the president powers to declare a national emergency and detain "subversives" in concentration camps. Truman, to his credit, vetoed it at considerable political risk, but Congress overrode his veto. Repression of dissent was firmly established by the fall of 1950.[4]

Defying this intimidation, Paul denounced Truman's commitment of U.S. troops to South Korea in a June 28 speech delivered to a civil rights rally in Madison Square Garden. His speech referred to his 1949 Paris statement: "I have said it before and say it again, that the place for the Negro people to fight for their freedom is here at home."[5] Apparently, both the State Department and the FBI took note of his remarks. When he announced in July that he planned a return European trip in September, FBI director Hoover ordered agents from his Internal Security Division to confiscate Paul's passport. Additionally, the State Department prevailed upon the Immigration and Naturalization Service (INS) to issue a "stop notice" to prevent Paul from departing from the continental United States to destinations for which a passport was not required, such as Canada and Mexico.

FBI agents intruded on family and friends. They came to my apartment, where Paul was a frequent visitor, and to the McGhees', where he was now living, demanding the surrender of his passport. We told them that Paul was not there. Finally, Paul agreed to meet with them in the presence of Nathan Witt, a progressive attorney of the firm Witt and Cammer, and informed the agents that, on Witt's advice, he refused to surrender his passport as requested. On August 4, 1950, the State Department demanded that Paul do so. The only reason cited was that his travel abroad "would not be in the best interests of the United States." He refused.

Paul issued a strong statement through the Council on African Affairs, in which he characterized the cancellation of his passport as "another blatant example" of the Truman administration's efforts to "silence the protests of the Negro people," and pointed out that he required his passport to travel abroad to earn a living. He added George E. C. Hayes, a prominent black Washington lawyer, to his legal team, and after a fruitless August 23 meeting with State Department officials, filed a civil suit in December against the secretary of state in the U.S. District Court for the District of Columbia.

Throughout the late summer and fall of 1950, attacks on the right of dissent escalated. Madison Square Garden refused to house a Council on African Affairs rally in support of Paul. Left-progressive unions became targets of government attempts to decertify them on the grounds of suspected ties to "subversives." Any civic or fraternal organization participating in or encouraging criticism of U.S. government policies was threatened with a listing on the U.S. attorney general's roster of "subversive organizations," with attendant legal sanctions. The mayor of Boston banned the display of Paul's portrait in an exhibition of famous blacks, proclaiming he would not allow the glorification of "avowed Communists, whether white, Negro or yellow."

This assault on the traditional right of dissent was met with widespread grassroots resistance that went largely unreported by the mass media. A few days after Paul was banned from Madison Square Garden, over six thousand people showed up at a Harlem rally for him. And though the leadership of the black establishment either failed to support Paul or joined in the attacks against him, a significant portion of black public opinion became even more sympathetic.

December 1950 marked the appearance of the introductory issue of *Freedom*. Anchored by what would be Paul's regular column, titled "Here's My Story," and a feature article by W. E. B. DuBois, the journal was promoted in black communities across the nation with the energetic support of the besieged and greatly reduced left-progressive movement. A national tour by Paul on behalf of the United Freedom Fund representing *Freedom*, the Council on African Affairs, the newly formed National Negro Labor Council (a coalition of the black caucuses in the CIO and independent unions), and the Committee for the Negro in the Arts was planned for the 1951–1952 concert season.

The pressure on Paul continued to escalate. Syndicated columnist Robert Ruark commented in a January 10, 1951, column that "in the modern emergency, Mr. Robeson is as worthy of internment as any

Jap who got penned away in the last [war]." FBI director Hoover wrote, "Certainly well said" on an FBI copy of Ruark's column. The FBI intensified its surveillance of Paul and began harassing the people with whom he stayed. To relieve the pressure on the McGhees, Paul stayed occasionally with the Browns in the Bronx and took some of his meals with the Caytons. Louise Patterson found a small apartment for him on Edgecombe Avenue in Harlem, so that he would have his own private retreat.[6]

Appearing in public was now a major problem for Paul. Many venues followed Madison Square Garden's example and refused to accept events if he was on the program. In planning his 1951–1952 concert tour, the Freedom Fund was compelled to steer clear of the regular concert halls and schedule appearances in black churches and fraternal or union halls. Wherever he did appear, Paul required extensive security, but he remained undaunted, appearing at progressive cultural events, peace rallies, benefits, union conventions, and civil rights meetings. His professional career in the mainstream entertainment business had vanished, and the boycott against him was so thorough that no record store would sell his records and no radio station would play them.[7]

Attitudes were markedly different abroad, especially in Africa and Asia where the Truman administration was feverishly trying to win support for its cold war with Russia. American propaganda was continually undermined by the question, "If you're so democratic, why won't you let Paul Robeson travel?" The news of Paul's passport fight had reached many Africans and stirred their sympathies. In an extended January 9, 1951, memorandum, Roger P. Ross, the State Department's public affairs officer in Accra, capital of Gold Coast (now Ghana), suggested to the department that an article be "specially written" about Robeson for use throughout Africa.

"It should be told sympathetically," he wrote, "preferably by an American Negro devoted to his race, as the tragedy which in fact it is." Ross went on to spell out the ideological-political line that was ultimately adopted and maintained by the U.S. government and mass media. According to Ross, "There's no way the Communists score on us more easily and more effectively, out here, than on the Negro problem in general, and on the Robeson case in particular.

And, answering the latter, we go a long way toward answering the former." He recommended that the Robeson story be told simply, "in language which the most inexpert reader can grasp, yet with dignity and restraint which invites belief. It must pay genuine homage to the man's remarkable talents as an artist, must take pride in his achievements on the stage and screen and radio. Then it must grant quite candidly the racial problems in America out of which his bitterness grew. And finally it must grant an early, and perhaps still operative, zeal in Robeson to serve the cause of his people."

Ross outlined a false Robeson image: "Much more with regret than rancor, it must detail Robeson's spiritual alienation from his country and from the bulk of his own people—how he apparently in his blind bitterness, missed all the evil signs which unmistakably betray Moscow as in fact the champion of a cynical, repressive order far more loathsome and dangerous to human freedom than even the worst of Jim Crowism." Ross proposed that Paul's stance be treated as "an illness of the mind and heart which is not easily recognized, yet contagious, and thus a deadly danger."

The November 1951 issue of the NAACP's official organ, the *Crisis*, featured a lead article titled "Paul Robeson—the Lost Shepherd" by a "Robert Alan," written to the specifications outlined in the Ross memorandum. A handwritten note in the upper right corner of the first page of Ross's memorandum reads, "Action taken: air parceled article on Robeson; *The Crisis*, 11/51. Date of Action: 1/29/52." The note was initialed by Secretary of State John Foster Dulles. It appears that the NAACP, under Roy Wilkins's leadership, collaborated with the U.S. State Department to publish an anti-Robeson article for U.S. government propaganda use in Africa.

As part of the coordinated assault on Paul, an article by Walter White appeared in the February 1951 issue of *Ebony* magazine under the title "The Strange Case of Paul Robeson." White claimed that Paul had abandoned the struggle for black freedom at home to support the Soviet line abroad, and that "for some mysterious reason" he had "always harbored" a "deep resentment" and an obsessive "oversensitivity" to "racial slights." However, White added that "no honest American, white or Negro, can sit in judgment on a man like Robeson unless and until he has sacrificed time, talent, money and popularity in doing the utmost to root out the racial and economic evils which infuriate men like Robeson. It would be wise for the white world, instead of querying Negroes on their attitude toward Robeson, rather to take stock of themselves. White America is more fortunate than it deserves to be in that there are so few Robesons as far as political beliefs are concerned."

Essie replied promptly to White's piece with an article titled "The Not So Strange Case of Paul Robeson."*Ebony* refused to publish it, but the *California Eagle* printed it in full. In it she demolished White's psychological arguments and focused attention on the undeniable fact that Paul was a champion of the oppressed everywhere. Her closing was defiant: "Paul Robeson is awful big, and there he stands, like a giant oak, like a mountain—solid. I do not believe they can uproot him, or blast him down."

Black boxing champion "Sugar" Ray Robinson, just returned from a successful European tour, was recruited to make a press statement that the United States offered "opportunity for everyone, regardless of race, creed or color," and anyone who claimed otherwise was merely spouting communist propaganda disseminated by Paul. The January 25, 1951, issue of the *Pittsburgh Courier* published a letter from a reader titled "Every Cat on the Avenue Knows, Why Not 'Sugar'?" He wrote, "It was not so sweet to read the quotation attributed to you in the *Herald Tribune*, Wednesday, Jan. 3. If you were quoted correctly, you must think a miracle happened while you were in Europe. Don't let the folks use you like that, man. Every cat on the avenue knows what the man's putting down, why not you?"

April 20, 1951, marked a significant court victory for Paul: the Washington, D.C., district court refused to order Paul to surrender his passport. The State Department immediately appealed the decision, arguing in its brief:

> Even if [Robeson's] complaint had alleged, which it does not, that the passport was cancelled solely because of appellant's recognized status as a spokesman for large sections of Negro Americans, we submit that this would not amount to an abuse of discretion in view of appellant's frank admission that he has been for years extremely active politically in behalf of the independence of the colonial peoples of

Africa. Though this may be a highly laudable aim, the diplomatic embarrassment that could arise from the presence abroad of such a meddler, traveling under the protection of an American passport, is easily imaginable.

Paul used this statement to buttress his charge that the Truman administration was an inveterate supporter of Western colonialism, and the "Truman Doctrine" was a recipe for U.S. imperialism. He also submitted yet another passport application, stating that he intended to travel to Paris for an international peace conference and to London to arrange a concert tour and a production of *Othello*. The Passport Office immediately denied the application. In mid-April, a federal judge upheld the State Department and dismissed Paul's arguments for the return of his right to travel. Paul's lawyers prepared an appeal. A Provisional Committee to Restore Paul Robeson's Passport was launched. And Lloyd Brown published a widely read pamphlet titled *Lift Every Voice for Paul Robeson*, which laid out Paul's case for restoration of his constitutional right to travel.

Paul and Essie became proud grandparents on May 5 when Marilyn and I had our first child—David Paul Robeson—and nine months later the family gathered to celebrate his christening by his great-uncle, Reverend Benjamin C. Robeson, at Mother A.M.E. Zion Church.

Due to his loss of income, Paul addressed the need to reduce his expenses, which had increased significantly due to the high cost of his legal fight to regain his passport. Essie, sensing a financial crunch looming, had prepared for the inevitable sale of her cherished Enfield home. But health problems abruptly intervened, delaying the sale of the house for over a year. At fifty-five, chronic ailments that had been under control flared up, and she checked herself into the Washington, D.C., hospital affiliated with Howard University. She underwent a successful operation for circulatory problems in her legs, and a tropical disease specialist finally defeated the intestinal parasite she had picked up in Africa sixteen years earlier. She left the hospital in good condition to tackle the twin problems of selling "the Beeches" and finding a new home.

Paul's political activities continued. He became one of the prime movers of the growing resistance to the intensifying legalized repression against blacks in both the South and the North—repression that accompanied Truman's increased pandering to conservatives in the wake of his adoption of an aggressively anticommunist, pro-colonialist foreign policy.

Internationally, Paul sent a stream of letters and statements to the United Nations. To Warren Austin, chief U.S. delegate to the UN, he addressed a letter petitioning him to reconsider the World Peace Council's proposals. To Jacob Malik, the Russian chief delegate who was then chairman of the UN Security Council, he sent a statement urging the Security Council consider resolutions opposing Western colonialism and military interventions. Through Essie, he maintained his personal contact with Nehru's sister, Nan Pandit. And through Bob Rockmore he explored the possibility of Marie Seton writing a biography with his collaboration.[8]

During the summer and fall of 1951, the FBI, increasingly alarmed at Paul's successful public appearances and political organizing, intensified its harassment. His numerous passport applications—to travel to Paris, Beijing, London, Australia, Moscow—were immediately and automatically rejected without review. The Internal Revenue Service abruptly and arbitrarily disallowed Paul's tax deduction for support of his mother-in-law, who was now in a nursing home. My passport application to attend the Berlin World Youth Festival was denied on the ground that my trip "would not be in the interests of the U.S."

On October 27, 1951, Paul spoke at the historic Founding Convention of the Negro Labor Council in Cincinnati. Despite the city council's unanimous condemnation of the convention as a communist operation and a red-baiting campaign by the *Cincinnati Inquirer*, over a thousand delegates attended. They represented local councils in every major industrial center. William Hood, leader of the United Auto Workers' Ford Local 600, set the tone for the convention with a keynote address titled "Uncle Tom Is Dead!" Featured speakers Dr. W. E. B. DuBois and Harry Bridges were joined by Velma Hopkins, leader of Local 22, Food, Tobacco, Agricultural and Allied Workers Union CIO, which had organized the R.J. Reynolds Tobacco Company in Winston-Salem, North Carolina.

Paul chose to emphasize a black challenge to American imperialism, evoking an enthusiastic response from the delegates. In a typical passage he said, "And then there's the whole continent of Africa. That continent is just seething, and they look to us here in Cincinnati to stop this government from going over to Africa and trying to put the people back into a kind of serfdom and slavery when they are about to emerge."

The same day, *Collier's* magazine published its historic issue devoted entirely to "Russia's Defeat and Occupation, 1952–1960." The dramatic cover page showed an American soldier holding a bayoneted rifle and wearing a United Nations helmet, superimposed on a map of the Soviet Union. Paul believed this special issue was inspired by the Truman administration to prepare the American people for an all-out nuclear war "to end the threat of communism."

William Patterson asked Paul to join him in presenting a Civil Rights Congress petition to the United Nations in Paris accusing the U.S. government of genocide against black Americans. Paul readily agreed to participate not only in drafting the petition and presenting it but also in recruiting signatories. When he applied for a passport to travel there to present the petition, the State Department immediately denied the application. While Patterson presented the original petition in Paris, Paul presented a copy to the United Nations offices in New York.

In December 1951, Paul's spirits were lifted by an encounter one evening in Harlem's famous Red Rooster nightclub where he was hosting several friends. A group that included Don Newcombe, the first black major league pitcher and Brooklyn Dodger star, sat down at the table near Paul's. James Hicks, editor of the *Amsterdam News*, had this to say about what happened next:

> One of the young ladies in Robeson's party asked Paul to go and get an autograph. When Robeson came over to Newcombe's table—and Paul is always polite—Newcombe very loudly proclaimed, "I'm going into the Army to fight, precisely to fight people like you and all the things that you stand for. I don't want to have anything to do with you or any of your friends."

Robeson was never a man to take a confrontation lying down, so there came a moment of tension there where it was pretty obvious that what you had cooking there was a real Donnybrook coming up. But the significant thing to me was that the people in that place, and I was one of them, they rallied around Robeson. And so much so that Newcombe found himself surrounded. I remember a guy standing behind Newcombe said: "Well, man, you're a great pitcher, but ain't nothin' gonna happen to Paul, not in the Red Rooster.". . . And he showed his blade [opened his switchblade knife].[9]

When Hicks was asked at the time by a white friend, "What are we going to do with colored people like Paul Robeson?" Hicks asked what he meant by "we." The friend replied, "We Americans—you and I." Hicks replied that Paul wasn't a problem for him or for other black people and that whites would have to solve it on their own. He added that if it were left to him, he would abolish segregation and discrimination immediately, and then Paul would have to go back to singing.[10]

As the stalemated Korean War dragged on with no end in sight and the truce talks remained deadlocked, the danger of an all-out U.S. attack on China and the Soviet Union increased dramatically. President Truman's state of mind was more accurately reflected by his private diary notes than by his more moderate public statements. His January 27, 1952, entry includes the following passage:

It seems to me that the proper approach now would be an ultimatum with a ten-day expiration limit, informing Moscow that we intend to blockade the China Coast from the Korean border to Indochina, and that we intend to destroy every military base in Manchuria by means now in our control—and if there is further interference we shall eliminate any ports or cities necessary to accomplish our purposes. This means all-out war. It means that Moscow, St. Petersburg, Mukden, Vladivostok, Peking, Shanghai, Port Arthur, Darien, Odessa, Stalingrad and every manufacturing plant in China and the Soviet Union will be eliminated.[11]

Truman's "tough" stance against "the commies," amplified by the mass media, raised international tensions to a dangerous level and imposed a nationwide public mind-set that nourished fear, war fever and anticommunist witch hunts. The much-publicized Rosenberg spy case was used to exploit this state-sponsored cultural environment for the purpose of institutionalizing the quasi-fascist political climate subsequently referred to as "McCarthyism."[12]

The "McCarthy Era" lasted only a few years but had dramatic long-term consequences. The majority of Americans were so intimidated by their inculcated fear of foreign and domestic "communist" assault that they avoided even discussing "divisive" issues lest they be labeled "unpatriotic." Antiblack prejudice was given unofficial license, including open legal frame-ups of black "militants" who were automatically assumed to be "pawns of the communists." Demands for social justice were suspected of being "communist inspired." The standard FBI questionnaire designed to ferret out communists or "communist sympathizers" included an inquiry as to whether the suspect had black friends. Black politicians and establishment leaders responded by keeping a low public profile.

Paul reacted to his increasing isolation from mainstream America and the black establishment's attacks on him by securing and expanding his base in major black urban communities outside the South. But he had to overcome many obstacles on the tour sponsored by the Freedom Fund. Media-inspired prohibitions by local city councils and mayors, combined with threats of violence by right-wing organizations such as the American Legion, made it extremely difficult to obtain safe appropriate venues for his appearances anywhere but within the black community. Even there, the FBI attempted to intimidate audiences by aggressively photographing them and writing down license plate numbers of arriving cars.

Government workers were fired for attending Paul's concerts or possessing his records. My father told me he met a federal employee in Washington, D.C., who had lost his job for attending a Paul Robeson concert. At his appeal hearing, he argued that when he arrived at the concert hall, the seats were sold out and he had to leave. Although his story was corroborated by several witnesses, his appeal was unanimously rejected by the appeals board on the grounds of his self-confessed "intent to attend a Paul Robeson concert."

Nevertheless, Paul's 1951–1952 Freedom Fund tour was a modest success. His concert fees added up to $12,000, of which he contributed $8,000 to *Freedom*. Though this level of income appears to be insignificant compared to the $100,000 or more he had earned from his commercial concert tours, it represented a significant amount at the time.

Paul decided to create an independent record company as a means to reconnect with his progressive-liberal white audience, from which he had been cut off, and to reach black church audiences with an album of traditional spirituals and hymns. Because of my musical ear and knowledge of audio engineering, Paul invited me to join Lloyd Brown in setting up Othello Recording Corporation, in which I served as president and producer and Lloyd as secretary-treasurer. Our first album would be *Robeson Sings*, consisting of six Robeson favorites to be released in 78 rpm and long-play formats.

We sent out a mailing to fifty thousand readers of the left-wing *National Guardian* weekly newspaper and received a phenomenal response of five thousand mail orders at five dollars apiece. However, the production process proved to be an obstacle course. Goddard Lieberson, head of Columbia Masterworks, whose friendship with Paul dated back to the 1940s, met with us about our request to hire Columbia facilities to record and manufacture the album. Shamefacedly, he told us that his trustee board had turned down our request and reprimanded him for transmitting it.

After many other refusals, we found an independent recording studio on Manhattan's East Side and a small plant in Yonkers to manufacture the albums. When we attempted to market the albums, no commercial distributor would handle them, no stores would display them, nor would any radio station play them. The boycott of Paul Robeson was airtight.

In spite of this, thousands of Paul's records were sold by mail order, through black churches and progressive organizations. During the four years from 1952 through 1956, two more record albums were produced and close to twelve thousand were sold. Othello Recording Corporation generated nearly $60,000 in income and paid Paul $12,000 in royalties. We also recorded many high-quality masters to create an archive of Paul Robeson recordings.

Essie's life was unsettled for over a year while she was attempting to sell the Enfield house. She was also faced with the deterioration of her mother's health and visited her frequently in the Grafton, Massachusetts, nursing home until she died in the spring of 1953.

That summer, Essie sold the house, placed the family's papers and artifacts in storage, and moved to New York. For a time she lived with my family and later rented an apartment in an Upper West Side hotel. Now that she was based in New York City, Essie became an accredited United Nations correspondent for *New World Review*, a left-wing publication with a focus on the Soviet Union and Eastern Europe. She also continued lecturing and writing for black and progressive organizations.

The Canadian Mine, Mill and Smelter Workers Union invited Paul to sing a concert on February 1, 1952, in conjunction with their annual convention in Vancouver, British Columbia. However, at the State Department's request, the INS instructed its Seattle district to prevent Paul's departure from the United States at the Blaine, Washington, border crossing and also made arrangements with the Canadian Immigration Service to deny him entry.

When Paul arrived at the U.S. border crossing in Blaine on January 31, his car was stopped; he was taken to the INS office and presented with the formal order preventing him from leaving the United States. Failure to comply would result in a prison sentence of up to five years and a $5,000 fine. Although he protested the order as a violation of his constitutional rights, he complied and returned to Seattle.

The following day at a press conference held at the Marine, Cooks and Stewards union hall, Paul said, "I'm here in Seattle and not in Vancouver because I am a black American who dares to stand up and say, 'I'm as good as you are.' I'm confident the [appeals] court will rule in my favor. What else can it do? The basic question is that of free speech, and in my case I'm being deprived of my interest in concerts which are a livelihood."

Paul then spoke over a telephone connected to a public address system to a Vancouver mass meeting organized by the Canadian Mine, Mill and Smelter Workers. The Seattle Marine, Cooks and Stewards recorded the event and made it available to members of both unions. Subsequently the two unions invited Paul to Peace Arch Park in Blaine in May. The park, divided by the U.S.-Canadian border, would enable Paul to appear on a platform located on the U.S. side of the border and perform for the audience gathered on both sides.[13]

On May 18, during his Freedom Fund tour, Paul appeared at the Peace Arch and sang to forty thousand people—thirty-five thousand on the Canadian side of the border and the rest on the American side. The Canadian roads were so jammed with automobiles that thousands had to walk more than a mile to reach the site. The sponsoring unions decided on the spot to repeat the concert as an annual event. The INS, as detailed in their May 19 and May 27, 1952, memoranda, photographed the license plates of the cars that drove to the concert on the American side and filmed the audience. The results were forwarded to the FBI.

Paul's tour was made possible by local committees made up mostly of black members of left-wing unions and black church-people, supported by local white communists and progressives. He visited fourteen cities, including Seattle, San Francisco, Los Angeles, St. Louis, Minneapolis, Milwaukee, and Detroit, encountering many difficulties along the way. The mayor of San Francisco denied Paul use of the Opera House, and the Oakland City Council refused him the main city auditorium. In Seattle, Jack Kinzell, a popular radio personality and prominent supporter of Paul's concert, was fired. A black minister withdrew his church when city officials warned him it might be attacked by "vandals." The president of the University of Minnesota canceled the university's approval of a Robeson concert. In Pittsburgh, the authorities condemned the concert building, forcing the sponsors to make repairs so that the event could take place. FBI memoranda dated June 24, July 8, and July 21 describe their filming of the audiences.

The CIA, whose Operations Division had been tracking Paul's foreign travels and contacts since 1949, attempted to undermine his support within the Communist Party and its affiliated groups. A March 26, 1952, memorandum from Lyman D. Kirkpatrick, assistant CIA director, to Hoover reported that Paul was "almost ready to break with the Communist Party" and that he had declared himself "primarily a Negro nationalist and secondarily a Marxist." The memorandum went on to describe Paul as "a very independent person who will not let himself be used." It added that "the New York Negro community is reaccepting Robeson, not because they think Robeson has modified his views, but rather because they feel less need to avoid identity with Communist adherents." This assessment of Paul directly contradicted Hoover's obsessive conviction that he was merely a puppet of the Communist Party and could be isolated from the black community through external pressure.

Paul continued to function, though on a limited basis. He did not neglect his contacts abroad. In April, he sent a message to the All-India Cultural Conference, warning of the threat posed by "American Imperialism" and expressing the hope Indian leaders would "help, not hinder" the struggle of the Indian people for "full liberation." In September, he spoke at the New York–Peking Peace Meeting, condemning the U.S. role in the Korean War and expressing solidarity with the "Vietnam patriots" in their struggle against the "French colonialists."

Paul remained active as vice chairman of the Progressive Party. On the Fourth of July, he addressed the party's national convention in Chicago, stressing the peace issue as central to the upcoming presidential election. "We alone offer a chance to vote for peace, for equality of all peoples, for true security, for freedom and full human dignity," he said. On October 27, he spoke at an American Labor Party mass meeting in Madison Square Garden, where he rejected both the Republican and Democratic parties as political evils, and called for a vote for "the people's candidates of the Progressive Party, the American Labor Party and local civil rights and Peace tickets.

In October, an afternoon visit with Albert Einstein in Princeton at Einstein's invitation provided Paul with a welcome change of pace. The two recalled their previous meetings—especially backstage in Princeton when Einstein had seen Paul in *Othello*. They talked at length about the right to travel, Paul's fight for his artistic life, and scientists' responsibility to speak out against the trampling of constitutional rights. My father told me that although Einstein was in frail health, he insisted on extending the visit and was very cordial. Paul felt greatly honored.

Despite the Progressive Party's dismal performance in the November 4, 1952, elections, receiving just under two hundred thousand votes (Eisenhower won in a landslide), Paul continued his activities in support of left-wing and progressive causes. On November

19, he spoke and sang at the Rosenberg Theater Rally for Julius and Ethel Rosenberg, who had been sentenced to death after a questionable conviction on charges of atomic spying for the Soviet Union, a cause shunned by most liberals and many progressives.

Two days later, Paul delivered the keynote speech of the Second Annual Convention of the National Negro Labor Council in Cleveland. He said, "I will never forget that the ultimate freedom and the immediate progress of my people rest on the sturdy backs and unquenchable spirits of the vast mass of Negro Americans from whom all talent and achievement rise in the first place. If it were not for the stirrings and the militant struggles among these millions, a number of our so-called spokesmen with fancy jobs and appointments would never be where they are." Then he once again recalled his Paris statement:

> Now, I said more than three years ago that it would be unthinkable to me that Negro youth from the United States should go thousands of miles away to fight against their friends and on behalf of their enemies. You remember that a great howl was raised in the land. Well, I ask you again, should Negro youth take a gun in hand and join with British soldiers in shooting down the brave peoples of Kenya?
>
> I say again, the proper battle field for our youth and for all fighters for a decent life, is here; in Alabama, Mississippi, and Georgia; is here, in Cleveland, Chicago, and San Francisco; is in every city and at every whistle stop in this land where the walls of Jim Crow still stand and need somebody to tear them down.

On December 21, 1952, the Soviet newspapers announced that Paul had been awarded the Stalin Peace Prize along with six other international public figures. The award consisted of a gold medal and a cash prize of 100,000 rubles ($25,000). Paul was immediately attacked in the mainstream press as the beneficiary of a reward for anti-American activities on behalf of Soviet communism. He defiantly treated the award as a badge of honor. Speaking in Detroit's Hartford Avenue Baptist Church in April 1953, he said:

> It's a peace prize, and I'm very proud that somewhere people understood that I'm struggling for peace, and that I shall continue

to do so. I wanted to go to get the prize, but they said down in Washington that, "Mr. Robeson out of his own mouth said that he is fighting for the independence of the peoples of Africa. And that's against American foreign policy so he can't go, see?" Okay. Well, I'm going to keep on interfering with that policy, I assure you. Everybody else has gotten over to Moscow to get that reward. It's a very important one, because it's a very nice gold medal and a lot of rubles—about a hundred thousand of them which translates into twenty-five thousand American dollars. I've been refused going there, but, in a not too distant time, it looks like I'll have to get it here. Yeah, that's right.[14]

On September 23, 1953, at a ceremony in Harlem's Hotel Theresa before three hundred guests, Paul accepted the Stalin Peace Prize from Howard Fast. Dr. W. E. B. DuBois spoke of the honor bestowed upon America and the Negro people, and Paul accepted the award "in the name of the American fighters for peace."

The year 1953 was difficult for the Robesons. On July 7, Essie was subpoenaed to appear before the feared McCarthy Senate Permanent Subcommittee on Investigations of the Committee on Government Operations. Headed by Senator Joseph McCarthy, a right-wing Republican from Wisconsin, this so-called McCarthy Committee was spearheading the anticommunist witch hunt throughout the nation with its high-profile hearings.

Unfriendly witnesses were trapped in the equivalent of a kangaroo court. Under oath, they were asked whether they were or ever had been members of the Communist Party. If they answered in the affirmative, they were asked to name all the other Communist Party members they knew or had known. Refusal to become an informer meant a one-year contempt sentence, at the end of which one could be called again and asked the same question with the same result. If they replied in the negative, they would be indicted for perjury on the basis of testimony from anonymous paid informers. Refusal to answer the question, by exercising the constitutional right of free speech and association under the First Amendment, still drew an automatic contempt citation.

The only escape lay in citing the Fifth Amendment, which provides immunity against self-incrimination, as the basis for refusing to answer. However, the public, mass media, and employers treated any use of the Fifth Amendment as an implied confession of guilt. Appearing as an "unfriendly witness" and refusing to become an informant led to instant loss of employment and public pariah status, and many decent people lacked the courage to face these consequences. Consequently they informed, often falsely, on others, including family members.

Apparently, the committee's counsel, based on information provided by the FBI, believed Essie was vulnerable and would be cowed by Senator McCarthy's intimidating power as chairman. They were mistaken. Essie, ably advised by civil rights lawyer Milton Friedman, refused to answer questions on grounds of the Fifth Amendment and also the Fifteenth Amendment designed to protect the rights of Negroes. When McCarthy said the hearings had nothing to do with race, Essie replied she was still treated as a second-class citizen and pointed out that the Senate was all white. To McCarthy's assertion that the voters were responsible, Essie replied that many southern Negroes were denied the right to vote. Asked whether she was married to Paul, she said she was proud to be his wife. Responding to a question about Paul's political affiliations and opinions, she shot back, "Why don't you ask him?"

Paul was elated by Essie's performance. The mainstream press reported her testimony fairly. The progressive press and the black press were full of praise. Alice Dunnigan, in a July 7, 1953, dispatch to the Associated Negro Press, called her "a very cool, deliberate, intelligent witness" and noted that Senator McCarthy had called her "a very charming woman—an intelligent lady."

Paul's passport case was stalled after the court of appeals had ruled against him, and he had to start a new case. The local committees supporting his annual tour—the fourth since 1949—were being worn down by constant harassment. Only eleven concerts were scheduled, nine of them in large cities with major black communities. One of the brightest spots of the year came on August 16 at a repeat of the previous year's Peace Arch Park Concert at the Canadian-U.S. border. An estimated audience of twenty thousand flocked to hear Paul despite tight media censorship, and Paul declared, "There is no force on earth that will make me go backward one-thousandth part of one inch." The FBI was present again, taking down the license numbers of cars on the U.S. side.

Paul was encouraged when his November 12 concert in Philadelphia was sponsored by A.M.E. Zion's Bishop Cameron C. Alleyne at his church. Bishop Alleyne, one of the denomination's most influential bishops, joined with Bishop William Walls to convince the Board of Bishops to open the denomination's churches nationally to Paul.

During the course of 1953, Paul's British royalties from his recordings and films remained considerable, and his popularity there was high. Offers from abroad (Britain, Russia, India, the British West Indies, Canada, and Mexico) kept arriving. At home, he continued to work on his language skills in quiet solitude at the McGhees', studying Hungarian, Romanian, Polish, Czech, and Bulgarian, with an eye toward recording songs in these languages. To the delight of the grandparents, Marilyn and I had a daughter, Susan, in February 1953.[15]

The year ended with a December 1, 1953, FBI memorandum containing a "Status of Health" item quoting an unnamed informer to the effect that Paul had "a heart condition." This information was accurate. Paul's annual medical checkup had revealed a minor heart abnormality. Apparently, the FBI had tapped the phones of his physicians. Four years of harassment had taken their personal toll, and the FBI was keeping close track of Paul's physical and mental condition.[16]

Paul's living arrangements in 1954 settled into a pattern. While on concert tours with Alan Booth or on speaking trips, he stayed with friends. In New York, he moved to the parsonage at Mother Zion Church at his brother Ben's invitation. One of Ben's studies was converted into a bedroom, complete with a seven-foot bed and a spinet piano. Paul felt safe there.

Paul's infrastructure at *Freedom* newspaper provided a stable support system over three difficult years. The publication had attracted a number of talented black writers who contributed regular columns. They included Alice Childress, a popular playwright; Lorraine Hansberry, who was just beginning her writing career; John O. Killens, who in 1954 published his first, highly acclaimed novel *Youngblood*; and Beah Richards, poet and actress. There were also pieces by Alphaeus Hunton, Louis Burnham, and Paul and Essie, among others. *Freedom* was now a welcome and influential addition to the black and progressive press. However, *Freedom* and the Freedom Fund continued to operate underfunded, despite their growth, since subscription and concert ticket prices were kept low for the predominately low-income subscribers and audiences.[17]

Paul's 1954 concert tour began early with a major concert at Newark, New Jersey's Galilee Baptist Church on January 31. An overflow audience of a thousand people heard him along with assisting artist Nadyne Brewer, a rising young black opera singer. Alan Booth served as Paul's accompanist and also played several classical solo pieces. However, after three or four more successful concerts, the tour petered out. The local Freedom Fund support groups could no longer mount effective campaigns.

The main cause for this downturn was the cumulative weakness of the progressive movement after five years of relentless harassment and negative propaganda. But dissension in the Communist Party was also an important factor, since party members were still a major force in all progressive struggles. The top party leaders, who had exhausted their appeals and been jailed in 1951, returned at the beginning of 1954 after serving their prison sentences. They found the party in disarray, embroiled in factional disputes fueled by genuine differences about domestic and foreign policy.

Stalin's death in March 1953 had triggered a power struggle for succession among the Soviet leadership that sowed uncertainty throughout the world communist movement. By early 1954, Nikita Khrushchev, a populist party secretary known for his direct and practical style, had become the preeminent Soviet leader and reestablished party rule in place of Stalin's one-man rule. He instituted a series of liberalizing reforms in the Soviet system, creating political ferment throughout the world's communist circles. In the United States, the party split. One faction, led by John Gates, wanted to Americanize the party by distancing it from the Soviet Union and muting its militancy on the black and labor issues. The opposing group, led by Ben Davis and Gene Dennis, with the blessing of ailing party chairman William Foster, favored a continuation of the party's prioritization of black and labor issues and continued solidarity with a reforming Soviet Union. Paul's sympathy lay with Davis and Dennis, but he did not involve himself in the controversy.[18]

At the end of 1953, Essie convinced Paul, whose weight had ballooned to over 270 pounds, to undergo several weeks of a diet and exercise regimen at the Howard University Medical Center where she had been treated several years earlier. He shed over twenty pounds and emerged feeling and looking much better. Paul now turned to recording a growing collection of songs he and Larry had been working on. He scheduled a recording session at Nola Studios on Manhattan's East Side and invited me to attend. Relaxed and in magnificent voice, he recorded a wide cross section of his repertoire.

As a result of this session, I set up an informal system that enabled my father to record comfortably whenever he wished. I selected several venues available on short notice—a small recital hall adjacent to Carnegie Hall, Esoteric Studio on Manhattan's East Side, and the Rosens' large living room where heavy curtains kept out street sounds. I also identified three expert sound engineers who were among Paul's admirers: Tony Schwartz, an independent media expert who specialized in taping interviews and events with portable equipment of his own advanced design; Peter Bartók, son of the great Hungarian composer Béla Bartók; and David Hancock, who was also a musician. I served as a reserve recording engineer and editor when the others were not available. Either Larry or Alan Booth provided piano accompaniment, and on one impromptu occasion Judy Rosen, the Rosens' daughter and a good amateur pianist, was the accompanist.

More than 130 masters were recorded in this informal manner, providing a representative collection of Paul's work as a concert artist. He and I developed a professional producer-artist relationship, jointly selecting the final takes and critiquing the performances. I cannot remember a single instance when my father pulled rank. That must have required considerable restraint on his part, because he was both a perfectionist and impatient when it came to his artistic work. Encouraged by his recording successes, he refocused on his passport fight.

In 1952, the NAACP's Legal Defense Fund, led by attorney Thurgood Marshall, had filed the case of *Brown v. Board of Education* against segregated schools. One of the main arguments of the supporting brief was that racial segregation undermined the U.S. capacity for national survival in the context of the cold war. When in May 1954 the U.S. Supreme Court unanimously ruled in favor of the NAACP's position and struck down school segregation, the justices were strongly influenced by the Justice Department's amicus brief supporting the NAACP, which essentially echoed the Eisenhower administration's statement that racial discrimination was the "Achilles' heel" of U.S. foreign policy. These developments strengthened Paul's credibility among blacks, since he had consistently praised the Soviet Union and its allies as positive factors in the worldwide struggle against racism and colonialism.[19]

With implementation of the school desegregation ruling looming on the national agenda, Paul concluded that black issues would rise in importance and the civil rights movement would grow in strength. In this context, he intensified his calls for international support of his passport fight. The response was prompt and impressive. It included messages of support from peace groups around the world, as well as from many prominent individuals. Charles Chaplin's message from exile in England was particularly memorable: "To deny a great artist like Paul Robeson his right to give his art to the world," he said, "is to destroy the very foundation upon which our culture and civilization is built. It negates every principle of democracy and freedom and follows a path of the worst type of tyranny."

A Paul Robeson Passport Committee was formed in England and launched a "Let Paul Robeson Sing" campaign that mobilized support from several major trade unions and received major coverage in the British press. At home, the campaign to return Paul's passport was launched with a Harlem Salute to Robeson at the Renaissance Casino. The audience filled the casino and spilled over into a nearby church. The sponsors and participants included Alice Childress, Julian Mayfield, Thelonius Monk, Pete Seeger, Lorraine Hansberry, Karen Morley, Dizzie Gillespie, Charles Parker, Leon Bibb, and many other black and white progressive artists who were willing to defy the blacklist.

• • •

The FBI and the CIA launched a campaign of lies and fantasies against Paul after the failure of their intimidation campaign to isolate him from the black community. A January 12, 1954, FBI memorandum reported on an article by Cholly Knickerbocker in the *New York Journal-American*:

> Paul Robeson supposedly has finally seen the light, and would like to break with the Communist Party. The only obstacles are his wife and his Communist-trained son, who threaten to expose the fact that Robeson was a "secret courier" between the Kremlin and the Communist Party in America. File of NYO [New York office] reveals no information of dissatisfaction on part of Robeson.

The Hearst press kept the item alive until it was picked up by several black publications. When a January 28 article repeating the false rumor appeared in *Jet* magazine, Paul, having previously ignored the matter, responded decisively:

> Though I realize the difficulty truth has in overtaking the lies which abound in the public press these days, I feel I must address myself to a few of the irresponsible fantastic and absurd items which have appeared recently concerning my work, my outlook and my family. I know of no force on this earth that can make me retreat one-thousandth part of one inch from my firm, well-considered, repeatedly declared and fully openly-lived beliefs.
>
> I have shouted and shall continue to shout at the top of my voice for liberation, full emancipation—yes by 1963 (a full hundred years after the bloodstained promise) but before 1963, now, if possible. Change my mind? Gentlemen of the press, you'd better change *yours*, because what I believe in is happening![20]

Paul backed up the declaration of his beliefs with a series of public statements attacking U.S. policies abroad and at home. In the March 1954 issue of *Freedom*, he denounced American intervention in Vietnam, asking, "Shall Negro sharecroppers from Mississippi be sent to shoot down brown-skinned peasants in Vietnam to serve the interests of those who oppose Negro liberation at home and colonial freedom abroad?" On September 25, he addressed black issues in a speech, titled "Fight We Must," delivered to a meeting of the National Council of the National Negro Labor Council at Harlem's Hotel Theresa. In it he outlined an approach aimed at including the interests of the black working class and poor among the immediate goals of the nascent civil rights movements led by the black middle class. He also announced that he would make another effort to place his passport case before the federal courts.

On July 2, 1954, Paul, who was still waiting for a hearing on a previous passport application, submitted a new application for travel to accept offers for a run of *Othello* in London, and concert tours of England and Israel. The State Department denied his application, stating that he could appeal the decision if he signed an affidavit swearing that he was not a member of the Communist Party. Paul refused. Back to square one, he announced he would appeal to the U.S. Supreme Court. He engaged two new lawyers—James T. Wright, a black Washington, D.C., civil rights lawyer, and Leonard Boudin, a prominent progressive white lawyer from a New York law firm specializing in passport and immigration cases. In the meantime, Paul's only hope was intensified international pressure on his behalf.[21]

By the fall of 1954, Hoover had abandoned efforts to portray Paul as would-be "defector" from communism and revived his staple "Kremlin agent" line. Hoover directed his main attack against Paul's passport campaign, relying heavily on his media contacts with right-wing columnists. An editorial in the September 4, 1954, issue of the *Saturday Evening Post* was typical. It claimed that in Paul's passport case the issue was "the alleged right of a nominal American citizen, who at heart is a Soviet subject, to go abroad in what is practically wartime in order to help our enemy." These crude distortions were highly successful in influencing white public opinion.

When Eisenhower ended the Korean War in July 1953, Truman's crusade against communism had already lasted eight years and had converted most liberals into supporters of the cold war. It also fueled American national chauvinism and intensified the assertion of the dominant Anglo-Saxon ethnic group known as "WASPs" (white Anglo-Saxon Protestants). Paul turned to progressive ethnic groups where he was warmly welcomed, not least because he could sing and speak in their languages.

In March 1954 he spoke to readers of the *Hungarian American World*, asserting, "This America is ours!" In a November article for *Jewish Life* greeting three centuries of Jewish life and work in America, he struck a similar note: "It is good for all Americans to be reminded once again that the 'Anglo-Saxon' image of America is a false-face. Certainly no Negro can hear the declaration of the Committee for the 300th Anniversary of Jewish Settlement— 'We have always been part of America'—without reflecting that such has been our own insistent claim: 'We too are America!'" He added that "the cause of democracy, the rights of all other minorities, are inseparably linked with the liberation struggles of the Negro people."

In October, Paul and Essie appeared together at a tribute to both of them by *New World Review*. The gala banquet served as the culmination of a gradual process of reconciliation between them that had transpired over the previous four years. As an October 14 clipping from the *Daily Worker* described the event: "This time Robeson did not sing. For 20 minutes he talked of his wife, Eslanda. He described her contributions to his own development as artist and man. He told of her efforts in behalf of first-class citizenship for the Negro people and in behalf of peace and human advancement. He paid tribute to the 'magnificent heroism' of women everywhere in the struggle for progress."

Then Essie replied, "I thank you on behalf of the Robesons. Three generations of them—Paul and me, Eslanda; Pauli and our lovely Marilyn; small but rugged David Paul, and still smaller, dimpled Susan." Expressing pride in the Constitution, the Bill of Rights, and the Supreme Court decision to end segregation in our public schools, she declared that she would "never rest until these magnificent principles and decisions are put into practice for every single American citizen."

By the end of 1954, Paul and Essie decided to live together again. Paul, prevented by external security threats from moving about in his previous nomadic way, felt a need for a home base of his own. It had also reminded him of his advancing age—he was fifty-six and his singing career would probably end in the next five years. He needed to eliminate the extra expense of two households. Essie needed to end her humiliation of living separately from Paul. Living together would provide mutual support and create a better public image for both of them.

Paul conferred with Rockmore, who approved the purchase of a house. Essie found a large brownstone in Upper West Harlem, at 16 Jumel Terrace, that was in excellent condition. She negotiated a good price for it, then furnished and decorated it with Freda Diamond's help, using mostly the stored furniture and accessories from the Enfield house. Paul and Essie had revived their partnership.[22]

10

VICTORY OVER DESPAIR

(1955–1956)

The beginning of 1955 was marked by a series of events that buoyed Paul's spirits. In February, the U.S. district court overturned the denial of a passport to Otto Nathan, Albert Einstein's secretary. In the Deep South, Mississippi farmers, businessmen, and professionals who had been illegally denied loans banded together to conduct a highly publicized fightback campaign. Black resistance to segregation was rising in many areas of the country.

The cold war started to moderate. Khrushchev led a delegation to Yugoslavia in the spring of 1955 and in cordial but cautiously phrased language apologized to Yugoslav leader Tito for several years of Soviet vilification and threats. In June, Khrushchev invited Prime Minister Nehru of India to the USSR for a two-week state visit during which they laid the groundwork for friendly relations. In July, the Soviet Union signed a peace treaty with Austria and withdrew its troops from its Austrian occupation zone, announcing the intention to withdraw all Soviet troops from foreign soil upon the signing of a peace treaty with Germany. In just two years, Khrushchev had altered the grim visage of Stalin's Russia for the better.

Paul was encouraged by the changes Khrushchev was introducing to reform the Soviet political system. He chose not to discuss Stalin's crimes, which he had known about since the 1930s, and talked exclusively about Khrushchev's reforms. Even in private conversations, Paul refused to discuss or to criticize Stalin. When pressed, he did not deny the crimes but said simply that it was for the Russian people, not for outsiders, to judge Stalin. To me he expressed relief that Khrushchev, whom he called "Russia's last great peasant leader," had ended the worst of Stalin's abuses so quickly.

I had several conversations with my father about the implications for his career inherent in the vast international changes under way. He saw irony in the undeniably positive shift in U.S.-USSR relations. Civil rights and peace, the two issues that the left had virtually "owned," were now "legitimate" in the mainstream. Yet there was no letup in the pressures against the left. If anything, they were ratcheted up. The Council on African Affairs was forced to defend itself against legal action compelling it to register as a "subversive" organization, and *Freedom*'s distributors and subscribers continued to suffer FBI harassment. Both organizations were going out of business.

I gave my father a bleak assessment of Othello Recording Corporation's future. I had found employment translating Russian scientific journals into English and Lloyd Brown was back on salary at *Masses and Mainstream*, leaving only a part-time secretary on the payroll. We could continue with the recording sessions but had no resources to produce more records or to continue marketing the three albums already produced. The support system was collapsing.

My father replied that he wasn't surprised and planned to return to his primary role as an artist. He was in the process of developing a new concert format—a presentation delivered in both song and spoken word appealing to a broad cross section of music lovers. Tickets would be priced lower than for formal concerts. His idea was to pioneer in developing a new trend of independently produced folk concerts staged in halls in large cities and at universities.

Paul looked forward to uninterrupted work on this project when he and Essie moved into Jumel Terrace that summer. Meanwhile, he was working diligently at Ben's parsonage, where he rehearsed regularly with Alan Booth and studied and wrote consistently. A Soviet friend sent him a classic Russian translation of Shakespeare's plays, and he was studying *Othello* in Russian, making numerous notes in the margins. On one occasion, I found him recording Othello's soliloquies in English, German, French, and Russian. He was preparing to play the role again, conscious that, having aged since his triumph a decade earlier, he would have to create a somewhat different interpretation.

Lloyd Brown began work with Paul on a book that was to be a combined autobiography and political statement. Lloyd had traveled with Paul and cowritten all of his *Freedom* columns, making many notes and observations along the way. Their goal was to produce a short book with a message for a black constituency. They also worked on key messages abroad, including one to the historic 1955 Bandung Conference in Indonesia. Attended by twenty-nine Asian and African countries, many newly independent, the conference's aims were to promote Afro-Asian economic and cultural cooperation and to oppose colonialism and neocolonialism

In addressing the conference, Paul asserted, "The cries of dismay which the calling of this conference evoked from the rulers of our country found no echo in the hearts of my people. Nor did they reflect the feelings of other sections of America's common people who have not forgotten that our country was founded in a revolution of colonies against a foreign tyranny—a revolution proclaiming that all nations have a right to independence under a government of their own choice." He went on to say that "nearly 100 years have passed since the struggle to abolish Negro slavery was won—yet today the Negro people here are still fighting to win true freedom and equality. In hundreds of laws we are branded as inferior, set apart, humiliated. But this is the time of liberation, and soon Africa too shall rise in freedom and glory."

Harlem congressman Adam Clayton Powell Jr. spoke at a U.S. press conference in Bandung, rebutting Paul with the claim that America was making great progress in race relations and criticizing him for echoing "Communist propaganda." The Powell-Robeson exchange received wide coverage in the black press. Paul's new concert format was put to the test in the spring of 1955. In March, he sang two concerts to appreciative overflow audiences in the First Unitarian Church during a weeklong visit to Los Angeles. While the concerts were free of any interference, several threatening events marred his stay in the city. On two occasions, the right front wheel of the car belonging to his driver-bodyguard, Frank Whitley, came off after having been tampered with. Both times it was sheer good luck that Paul was not in the car and Whitley was not injured. Since the FBI files confirm that Whitley, his car, and his house were under constant surveillance, it is suspicious that the files contain no mention of the two mishaps. On a third occasion, the brakes failed on the car driven by Whitley's wife on the same day the car had been checked. The attendant at the gas station where she went to get help said the brake fluid had probably been deliberately drained.[1]

In April and May, Paul appeared at City College of New York, where he had been banned four years earlier, and at Swarthmore College in Pennsylvania. A review of the Swarthmore concert in the May 3 issue of the campus newspaper the *Swarthmore Phoenix* describes Paul's impact: "Paul Robeson sang, read from *Othello* and discussed world problems. While in his political opinions he stands in a minority in this country, the statement that he is one of America's greatest artists should go unchallenged. Mr. Robeson's beautiful bass voice with its incredible fullness and resonance was perfectly and sensitively controlled. His powerful phrasing was full of warmth and understanding. The high point of the evening was the reading of the closing speech from *Othello*." The review added:

> During his song program, Mr. Robeson gave a musically illustrated talk of some of his views on world cultures. He stated that Africa leads the world in the rhythmic development of music; the Middle East in tonal variations; the Orient in melodies, and the West in counterpoint. He felt that we have a rich world, full of different cultures, each with its own strong points, each worthy of respect and appreciation. At the same time, he has found basic similarities in music and culture among the varied peoples he has known. Peace, he concluded, has a strong cultural basis.

Just as Paul and Essie settled into their Harlem brownstone, Paul's hopes for the recovery of his passport were raised dramatically by a June 2 court of appeals ruling. The right to travel for Max Schachtman, a member of the Independent Socialist League, which was listed as subversive by the attorney general, was upheld on the ground that travel was "a national right." The ruling struck down the arbitrary right of the secretary of state to withhold passports. Paul's lawyers immediately reapplied for his passport and won a conference in Washington, D.C., on July 18, where Paul and his chief counsel, Leonard Boudin, met with Loy Henderson, undersecretary of state for administration, and Frances Knight, director of the Passport Office.

Knight informed Boudin that the State Department was still following the passport regulations even though the recent court decisions had struck them down. Although exceptions had been made, Henderson asserted there would be none for Paul. When Boudin requested an immediate reply on permission for Paul to travel in Canada, Henderson and Knight agreed to do so within a day. The next day Paul received permission for his trip to Canada, but his Canadian hosts had already received unofficial word from their government that he would not be admitted.

Instead of attempting to enter Canada, Paul sang to a large crowd at the fourth annual Peace Arch Park Concert on July 23 while once again standing on the American side of the border. He declared that soon he would he would be able to travel anywhere he wished.[2]

The State Department was determined to block all of Paul's attempts to regain his passport by locking him into an endless procedural morass that would prevent him from gaining a court hearing on the substance of his case. As for his permitted travel to Canada, State Department files obtained under the Freedom of Information Act reveal a July 23 memorandum from Vancouver to Secretary of State John Foster Dulles stating that Canadian immigration officials would deny any request from Paul to enter Canada.

A few days later, Paul's passport application was denied, noting he would still have to sign a noncommunist affidavit to gain an administrative hearing. Boudin immediately filed motions in the court of appeals. A hearing date of August 16 was set, and the State Department scrambled for viable evidence with which to rebut Boudin's motions.

Cyrus Vance, a top State Department official who later became an important figure in the Kennedy and Johnson administrations, was assigned to organize background information for the Robeson case. His contact at the Justice Department, who supplied him with the FBI information upon which the government's case relied, was Assistant Attorney General Warren E. Burger. Burger subsequently became chief justice of the Supreme Court in 1969.

That would seem to be the reason why an August 12, 1955, internal FBI memorandum reports the Bureau's refusal to permit the Justice Department to name the FBI as the source of its evidence or to use the evidence in any legal proceeding. Since the State Department had no other evidence, its strategy was to prevent Paul, by administrative procedural means, from reaching any court but the U.S. Supreme Court for an evidentiary hearing. A great deal was at stake on August 16 when the appeals court held its hearing.

Court of appeals judge Burnita S. Matthews had just ruled favorably on behalf of Clark Foreman, a former treasurer of the Progressive Party, in a similar case. However, she upheld the State Department's argument that Paul's case was different and ruled that he had not exhausted his administrative remedies, thus precluding any discussion of evidence. Paul was deeply disappointed. Boudin immediately requested an administrative hearing, which was granted for August 19, three days later. Two issues were on the agenda—the application of administrative procedures to Paul's passport request, and rescinding the original stop order, approved by President Truman, forbidding Paul from traveling outside of the continental United States to places for which a passport was not required. I joined Boudin, William Patterson, and Lloyd Brown in accompanying Paul to the hearing.

Scott McCleod, head of State Department security, met us at the entrance to the State Department building. He greeted Paul effusively, asking him for an autograph for his son, who greatly admired Paul's career at Rutgers University. Paul graciously assented, addressing McCleod's son by name and adding an inspirational phrase. The meeting was businesslike and polite. Our counterparts were Loy Henderson, undersecretary of state for administration, who acted as chairman; McCleod; Passport Office director Frances Knight and her deputy; and Leo Rover, attorney for the State Department. What transpired is summarized below from the notes I took.

Boudin and Paul requested that Paul's passport be issued for singing and acting, based on the appeals court ruling that the State Department's administrative procedures were unconstitutional. Boudin also requested that administrative procedures and their application in Paul's case be spelled out in detail. Rover replied that Paul was required to exhaust the administrative remedies first, whether they were constitutional or not. According to him, Secretary of State Dulles had the power to issue passports and draw up appropriate regulations in the interest of national security. The key administrative procedure that Paul had to satisfy was to sign a noncommunist affidavit. This procedure had been followed in almost all other cases, and was deemed necessary due to allegations in the media concerning Paul's speeches and information indicating his possible membership in the Communist Party.

Boudin rejected allegations based on newspaper articles, invoking Paul's First Amendment right to speak, and said Paul refused to sign the affidavit as a matter of constitutional principle and on the basis of court rulings in the other cases. Moreover, the Passport Office had no right to make signing the affidavit a condition for a hearing on his application. Paul said he would take the case back to court, adding that the real reason for the passport denial was his speaking out about colonial freedom and the position of the Negro in the United Sates.

In response to Boudin's request that Paul be allowed to visit Canada, Henderson promised to reply in one day, strongly implying a positive response. However, he made no commitment on all other matters.

When we emerged from the hearing, the press and television cameras were waiting. Paul stepped forward and summarized the essence of what had transpired from his point of view. "The most important questions," he said, "were about my political opinions. Here's a question of whether one who wants to sing and act can have, as a citizen, political opinions. And in attacking me they suggested that when I was abroad I spoke out against injustices to the Negro people in the United States. I certainly did. And I'm very proud to have been a part of directing world opinion to precisely that condition."

The next day, Boudin received a telegram from Frances Knight that read, "Stop order was rescinded to travel Paul Robeson to Canada." It did not rescind the ban on his travel to other places for which a U.S. passport was not required. A few days later, Paul's passport request was refused, and Boudin appealed the ruling to the court of appeals, which promptly dismissed the appeal. Paul once again had to submit a new passport application, exhaust the State Department's administrative procedures, and then begin litigating in the courts, starting with the district court and working his way up to the U.S. Supreme Court. The process could take years more.

Paul's case received wide coverage in the black press, which was virtually unanimous in criticizing the denial of his passport as racially discriminatory. J. A. Rogers, columnist for the *Pittsburgh Courier*, asked why the State Department was more afraid of Paul than of the whites to whom it issued passports. Abroad, there was widespread public criticism of the U.S. government's action against him. During a tour of Europe, Harlem congressman Adam Clayton Powell Jr. was constantly asked why Paul was denied the right to travel. At a London press conference at the U.S. embassy, he declared his belief that "everyone should be free to travel." Although Paul had lost another round in his legal fight, he had won increased support from black and international public opinion.[3]

Paul suffered two unexpected heavy blows in the fall of 1955. Essie, after keeping her condition secret from everyone, told Paul she had been diagnosed with breast cancer and was going into surgery within days for a mastectomy. Paul was shocked and deeply concerned. Although her surgery and recovery went well, the prognosis was uncertain. Essie submerged her fear, resuming her writing and her work as UN correspondent. Soon thereafter, Paul began passing blood in his urine and was diagnosed with a degenerative prostate requiring surgery. Confronted with a feeling of physical vulnerability and worried about his security in a hospital, he was gripped by fear. Having just comfortably settled into a more secure lifestyle in a stable new home, his personal world seemed on the brink of descending into chaos.

Paul refused to go to a white-run hospital outside of Harlem. He consulted with Dr. Aaron Wells, a Harlem physician who took care of Ben Robeson and his family. Wells recommended Dr. McKinley Wiles, an urologist at Sydenham Hospital in central Harlem. Against the recommendations of his regular physicians, Morris Pearlmutter and Ed Barsky, who urged the operation be performed at Beth Israel Hospital by a surgeon chosen by Barsky, Paul chose to go to Sydenham under the care of Dr. Wiles. The FBI continued their interest in Paul's health. Their "Status of Health" file on him contained detailed and accurate information on every aspect of his stay at Sydenham Hospital.

In the days immediately prior to his hospitalization, Paul was convinced he had cancer or would die in surgery. He drew up a will and bade farewell to close friends. His fears were not allayed when Dr. Wiles, a deeply religious man, knelt beside him just before he was wheeled into the operating room and offered up a prayer for the Lord to steady his hand as he operated on "this great American."[4]

Paul's surgery was successful and no cancer was found. However, he was in considerable pain and his recovery was slow. It was at least two months after his October surgery that he came to dinner at our apartment with Essie, looking and sounding more like his normal self.

The black mass movement for civil rights erupted in full force in Montgomery, Alabama, on December 5, 1955, when a crowd of several thousand gathered at the Holt Street Baptist Church to protest the arrest of Rosa Parks, who had refused to give up her seat to a white passenger. A twenty-six-year-old minister, Reverend Martin Luther King Jr., was the main speaker at the meeting, and the Montgomery bus boycott movement was launched. In the ensuing months, Paul was confronted with his isolation from the movement due to his identification with the left and the government's relentless labeling of him as a dangerous subversive. Because he did not want to jeopardize the burgeoning movement, he accepted his role as forerunner rather than direct participant. His isolation was aggravated by his inability to find a professional outlet for his singing or acting.[5]

Meanwhile, the State Department was continuing to exert pressure on local authorities to refuse Paul entry in places that required no U.S. passport. A December 8, 1955, confidential memorandum on behalf of the colonial secretary of Trinidad, British West Indies, to the American consul general in Port of Spain states that "as this Government considers that Mr. Robeson is *persona nongrata*, His Excellency has deemed the said Paul Robeson to be an undesirable visitor, and he will not therefore be permitted to land in the Colony."

In early February 1956, Paul, Alan Booth, and Lloyd Brown set off for several Canadian appearances—the first public events for Paul in four months and the first time in six years that he was permitted to travel outside the continental United States. He began with an appearance at the Mine, Mill and Smelter Workers Convention in Sudbury, Ontario, giving a brief but highly emotional speech: "A new epoch has dawned. The end of colonial exploitation is tortuously and slowly approaching. These are new days. My art is a weapon in the struggle for my people's freedom and the freedom of all people. And to that I will contribute as long as breath stirs within me."

At his main concert appearance in Toronto's Massey Hall before a capacity audience, Paul was greeted by a standing ovation. Although his singing voice was not yet fully in shape, its resonance was present and his judicious choice of repertoire helped him to sing through his fatigue near the end. He added recitations from Chilean poet Pablo Neruda's "Let the Rail Splitter Awake" and Shakespeare's *Othello* to his program. The audience loved him. The critics noted that his voice had lost some of its luster but conceded that his personal magnetism remained irresistible.[6]

Paul returned home exhausted to learn that the court of appeals had once again dismissed his passport case appeal. He would have to reapply once more and go through the maze of administrative remedies to gain yet another hearing from which he could appeal a negative reply. Boudin submitted another brief, this time appealing the decision to the U.S. Supreme Court. At the same time, buttressed by a torrent of petitions and protests from abroad, especially from England, he submitted a new passport application designed to win another hearing.

Paul found solace in his music. The Massey Hall concert in Toronto had gone so well that the sponsor, Jerome Concert Management, arranged an April–May Canadian concert tour, and Paul took to preparing eagerly and confidently for it. I bought him a high-quality home-use tape machine and a supply of recording tape so he could record his rehearsals and comments and then listen to them critically. This work refining his repertoire led him to an exploration of the structure of folk and classical music and a search for the essential links between the two. In this connection he began to focus on Johann Sebastian Bach's musical works.

My father often talked with me about his work on the theory of music. His main thesis was that all modern classical music is based on the ancient universal pentatonic (five-tone) scale that constitutes the structure of the world's folk music. The standard diatonic (seven-tone) scale is the pentatonic scale with two transitional notes added. The (Schoenberg) twelve-tone scale is the sum of the diatonic and pentatonic scales. The piano (Bach's well-tempered clavichord) is based on a seamless interweaving of two pentatonic scales—one on the black keys and one on the white keys. Paul believed that by proving those postulates in a scholarly way he would more fully understand the structure of the music he had been singing all his life.

One day in early March 1956, I went up to Jumel Terrace to brief my father on Khrushchev's "secret speech" to a closed session of the Twentieth Congress of the Communist Party of the Soviet Union, which had taken place about ten days earlier. Rumors about Khrushchev's sensational exposure of Stalin's crimes were rife, but no text had been published. Tim Buck, head of the Canadian party, had been a delegate to the congress and obtained an unofficial copy of the speech from the Polish delegation. On his return to the United States, he shared it with the top U.S. leadership and Ben Davis had summarized it for me.[7]

I found my father sitting at the piano, so immersed in playing chords and scales that he barely acknowledged my presence. I busied myself reading until he took a break and settled in an easy chair. He began the conversation by saying emphatically he would not comment on the speech to anyone so no one could quote him—he was determined to stay clear of the whole issue. I told him there was nothing in the speech we didn't know about or at least suspect, except that the scale of the repression—millions of people affected—was far greater than we had imagined. The effect on the U.S. party leadership had been traumatic. I thought many would leave the party in disillusionment, while those remaining would probably split into right and left factions.

My father's only comment was that he found it difficult to understand why a member of the U.S. party would leave because of something that happened in the Soviet Union. With that, he ended the discussion. (However, on March 9, Paul, concerned about the negative effect of Khrushchev's revelations on the U.S. Communist Party, appeared and spoke at the seventy-fifth birthday banquet for William Z. Foster, chairman of the party, to demonstrate his support. Paul's full remarks were published in the *Daily Worker* and picked up by the mainstream press. The FBI duly noted his appearance.)[8] His demeanor then changed abruptly, and he invited me to sit beside him at the piano, where he excitedly demonstrated his current musical explorations. He explained that there were two pentatonic scales on the piano—one on the black keys beginning on

F-sharp (F#-G#-A#-C#-D#) and the second beginning on C on the white keys (C-D-E-G-A). He noted that Johann Sebastian Bach's statement "Fa-Mi and Mi-Fa is all of music" is the foundation of modern music, indicating how the diatonic scale (C-D-E-F-G-A-B) is interwoven with the two pentatonic scales. The F and the B are transitional notes between the diatonic and pentatonic scales. His demonstrations on the piano accompanied his explanation.[9]

After a while, I asked what had spurred him to study music theory so extensively. He replied that the approach he was working on constituted a general theory of music that linked classical Western harmony to the universal pentatonic scales of folk music. He was intent on proving this connection in classical theoretical terms. As a practical matter, his work had significantly expanded his understanding of the harmonic structure of classical music and improved his ability to learn a variety of new songs.

Just before the start of his much-anticipated Canadian concert tour of sold-out venues, the entire tour was abruptly canceled. The Canadian government announced Paul had been denied admission because of the "Communist auspices" of his sponsorship. Despite the storm of protest that erupted in Canada, the authorities refused to change their ruling. The small opening in the walls that sealed him off from the outside world had slammed shut.

Paul received news of the cancellation just prior to his fifty-eighth birthday on April 9, so he was not in the best of spirits for his modest birthday party at our apartment. However, he put up a brave front, especially for his grandchildren, who by now were five and three. Marilyn and her mother outdid themselves with the cooking and a good time was had by all.

In response to the cancellation of his Canadian tour, Paul intensified his study of the pentatonic folk-music scale. His preoccupation was intense to the point of obsession. While there was considerable musical evidence to support his ideas, it became apparent that proving his theory to skeptics had become a means of self-validation. Over the next few weeks he tried out his theoretical ideas on anybody who would listen. Composers Marc Blitzstein and Herbert Haufrecht heard him out politely and concluded he needed psychiatric help. Dr. Aaron Wells, whom he visited for a checkup and harangued for almost an hour, believed Paul might be suffering from some form of early senility. I was able to calm him down by sitting at the piano with him as he demonstrated his "technical argument."

In mid-May, Paul became depressed. He wouldn't leave the house, spent most of his time in bed or sitting aimlessly at his desk, ate little, and slept even less. He refused to see a psychiatrist. When sleeping pills didn't help, Sam Rosen, Ed Barsky, and Morris Pearlmutter arranged for a psychiatrist—Joseph Furst—to come under the guise of an internist. Furst came the same day. Paul refused to cooperate but did accept medication that helped him sleep. His depression, however, persisted.

Suddenly everything changed. On May 22, Paul was served with a subpoena by a U.S. marshal to appear before the House Committee on Un-American Activities in Washington, D.C. The date of his scheduled appearance was one week away.

Milton Friedman, whom Paul chose to represent him at the hearing and who had represented Essie at her hearing before the McCarthy Committee, joined Dr. Pearlmutter and Dr. Wells in requesting a postponement for medical reasons, stating Paul was confined to his home due to his condition. The House committee granted a delay until June 12, hoping to cite Paul for contempt if he left his house between May 29 and June 12.[10]

Drs. Pearlmutter and Wells felt Paul was in no shape to appear and wanted to apply for a further extension, but Paul adamantly refused. On June 12, Paul, accompanied by Friedman, Bill Patterson, Lloyd Brown, Essie, and me, sat in a hearing room of the House Office Building waiting to be called as a witness. He slumped in his chair, looking desolate. Friedman appeared calm and confident; the rest of us were numb with fear.

Paul's name was called. He sat bolt upright, raised his considerable frame in one continuous motion, and strode rapidly to his witness seat. Defiant from the outset, he demanded to know who his questioners were.

Mr. Arens: I am Richard Arens.
Mr. Robeson: What is your position?
Mr. Arens: I am director of the staff. Are you appearing today in response to a subpoena served upon you by this committee?
Mr. Robeson: Oh, yes.

Mr. Arens: Now, during the course of the process in which you were applying for this passport, in July of 1954, were you requested to submit a noncommunist affidavit?

Mr. Robeson: We had a long discussion with the State Department, about just such an affidavit and I was very precise that under no conditions would I think of signing any such affidavit, that it is a complete contradiction of the rights of American citizens.

Mr. Arens: Are you now a member of the Communist Party?

Mr. Robeson: What is the Communist Party? What do you mean by that? As far as I know it is a legal party like the Republican Party and the Democratic Party. Do you mean a party of people who have sacrificed for my people, and for all Americans and workers, that they can live in dignity? Do you mean that party?

Mr. Arens: Are you now a member of the Communist Party?

Mr. Robeson: Would you like to come to the ballot box when I vote and take out the ballot and see? I stand upon the Fifth Amendment of the American Constitution.

Mr. Arens: Do you honestly apprehend that if you told this committee truthfully—

Mr. Robeson: I have no desire to consider anything. I invoke the Fifth Amendment, and it is none of your business what I would like to do, and I invoke the Fifth Amendment. And forget it.

Mr. Arens: Have you ever been known under the name of "John Thomas"?

Mr. Robeson: Oh, please, does somebody here want—are you suggesting—do you want me to be put up for perjury some place? "John Thomas"! My name is Paul Robeson, and anything I have to say, or stand for, I have said in public all over the world, and that is why I am here today.

Mr. Arens: I put it to you as a fact, and ask you to affirm or deny the fact, that your Communist Party name was "John Thomas."

Mr. Robeson: I invoke the Fifth Amendment. This is really ridiculous.

Mr. Arens: Do you know a Manning Johnson?

Mr. Robeson: Manning Johnson? I only have read in the papers that he said that Dr. Ralph Bunche was some kind of fellow [traveler], and he was dismissed from the FBI. He must be a pretty low character when he could be dismissed from that.

Mr. Arens: Have you ever been chairman of the Council on African Affairs?

Mr. Robeson: I invoke the Fifth Amendment.

Mr. Arens: Do you know Max Yergan?

Mr. Robeson: I invoke the Fifth Amendment. Why do you not have these people here to be cross-examined? Could I ask whether this is legal?

The chairman: This is legal.

Mr. Robeson: To whom am I talking?

The chairman: You are speaking to the chairman of this committee. [Representative Francis E. Walter of Pennsylvania]

Mr. Robeson: You are the author of all of the bills that are going to keep all kinds of decent people out of the country.

The chairman: No, only your kind.

Mr. Robeson: You do not want any colored people to come in?

Mr. Arens: May I ask you now, was there, to your knowledge, a communist core in the Council on African Affairs?

[Dr. Max Yergan had testified on December 17, 1948, that it became clear to him that a communist core was functioning inside the council.]

Mr. Robeson: I will take the Fifth Amendment. Could I be allowed to read from my own statement here?

Mr. Arens: Will you just tell this committee, while under oath, Mr. Robeson, the communists who participated in the preparation of that statement?

Mr. Robeson: I invoke the Fifth Amendment. I am not being tried for whether I am a communist. I am being tried for fighting for the rights of my people, who are still second-class citizens in this United States of America. My mother was born in your state, Mr. Walter, and my mother was a Quaker, and my ancestors in the time of Washington baked bread for George Washington's troops when they crossed the Delaware, and my own father was a slave. I stand here struggling for the rights of my people to be full citizens in this country. And they are not. They are not in Mississippi. And they are not in Montgomery, Alabama. And they are not in Washington. They are nowhere, and that is why I am here today. You want to shut up every Negro who has the courage to stand up and fight for the rights of his people, for the rights of workers, and I have been on many a picket line for the steelworkers too. And that is why I am here today.

The chairman: You ought to read Jackie Robinson's testimony.

Mr. Robeson: I know Jackie Robinson, and I am sure that in his heart he would take back a lot of what he said about me. I was one of the last people, Mr. Walter, to speak to Judge [Kenesaw Mountain] Landis, to see that Jackie Robinson had a chance to play baseball. Get the pictures and get the record.

Mr. Arens: Did you make a trip to Europe in 1949 and to the Soviet Union? Did you go to Paris on that trip?

Mr. Robeson: I went to Paris.

Mr. Arens: And while you were in Paris, did you tell an audience there that the American Negro would never go to war against the Soviet government?

Mr. Robeson: May I say that is slightly out of context? No part of my speech made in Paris says fifteen million American Negroes would do anything. I said it was my feeling that the American people would struggle for peace, and that has since been underscored by the president of these United States. Now, in passing, I said it was unthinkable to me that any people would take up arms, in the name of an Eastland, to go against anybody. Gentlemen, I still say that. This United States government should go down to Mississippi and protect my people. That is what should happen.

Mr. Arens: Then you did go to Moscow, on this trip?

Mr. Robeson: Oh, yes.

Mr. Arens: Did you write an article that was subsequently published in the USSR *Information Bulletin*?

Mr. Robeson: Yes.

Mr. Arens: "Moscow is very dear to me and very close to my heart. I want to emphasize that only here, in the Soviet Union, did I feel that I was a real man with a capital 'M.' And now after many years I am here again in Moscow, in the country I love more than any other."

Did you say that?

Mr. Robeson: In Russia I felt for the first time like a full human being. No color prejudice like in Mississippi, no color prejudice like in Washington. It was the first time I felt like a human being. Where I did not feel the pressure of color as I feel [it] in this committee today.

Representative Gordon H. Scherer of Ohio: Why do you not stay in Russia?

Mr. Robeson: Because my father was a slave, and my people died to build this country, and I am going to stay here, and have a part of just like you. And no fascist-minded people will drive me from it. Is that clear?

Mr. Scherer: The reason you are here is because you are promoting the communist cause in this country.

Mr. Robeson: I am here because I am opposing the neofascist cause which I see arising in these committees. You are like the Alien [and] Sedition Act, and Jefferson could be sitting here, and Frederick Douglass could be sitting here, and Eugene Debs could be here.

Mr. Arens: While you were in Moscow, did you make a speech lauding Stalin?

Mr. Robeson: I do not remember.

Mr. Arens: Have you recently changed your mind about Stalin?

Mr. Robeson: Whatever has happened to Stalin, gentlemen, is a question for the Soviet Union, and I would not argue with a representative of the people who, in building America, wasted sixty to a hundred million lives of my people, black people drawn from Africa on the plantations. You are responsible, and your forebears, for sixty million to a hundred million black people dying in the slave ships and on the plantations, and don't you ask me about anybody, please.

Mr. Arens: Now I would invite your attention, if you please, to the Daily Worker of June 29, 1949, with reference to a get-together with you and Ben Davis. Do you know Ben Davis?

Mr. Robeson: One of my dearest friends, one of the finest Americans you can imagine, born of a fine family, who went to Amherst [College] and was a great man.

Mr. Arens: Did I understand you to laud his patriotism?

Mr. Robeson: I say that he is as patriotic an American as there can be, and you gentlemen belong with the Alien and Sedition Acts, and you are the nonpatriots, and you're the un-Americans, and you ought to be ashamed of yourselves.

The chairman: Just a minute, the hearing is now adjourned.

Mr. Robeson: I should think it would be.

The chairman: I have endured all of this that I can.

Mr. Robeson: Can I read my statement?

The chairman: No, you cannot read it. The meeting is adjourned.

Mr. Robeson: I think it should be, and you should adjourn this forever, that is what I would say.

Mr. Friedman: Will the statement be accepted for the record without being read?

The chairman: No, it will not.[11]

Without a trace of despondency, or even uncertainty, Paul had answered 150 questions in the space of an hour, consulting with counsel only five times and dominating the hearing. The planned discussion of Paul's "communist problem" had been turned into a discussion of America's "race problem." Paul released his rejected statement, which linked his passport fight with the black freedom struggle, to the press as he left the hearing. The committee voted to cite Paul for contempt, but Congress refused to vote on their recommendation since he had appeared and replied to all questions in accordance with congressional rules.

The black press hailed Paul as a hero. Typically, the *Baltimore Afro-American* featured a front-page story with a large picture of him under the banner headline "What Robeson Said: 'I want protection for my people.'" An inside page carried extensive excerpts of his testimony under the title "Protect My Folk in Mississippi—Robeson." The editorial, headlined "Mr. Robeson Is Right," agreed with Paul that the committee's members "could more profitably spend their time questioning white supremacists." The *San Francisco Sun-Reporter* said that "whites hate and fear him simply because he is the conscience of the U.S. in the field of color relations." The *Charlottesville-Albemarle Tribune* of Virginia called Paul "a great artist and a deeply sympathetic human being," adding that "his own success did not blind him to the wrongs suffered by his race." Claude Barnett, director of the Associated Negro Press, wrote a letter to Paul two weeks after the hearing to tell him, "Your performance was magnificent and we felt it deserved all we could give it."

The mainstream white press emphasized the committee's contempt citation, while ignoring Paul's remarks about the race issue. Liberal commentators did the same, unanimously failing to support his right to travel despite his political opinions. Only the left-progressive press joined the black press in supporting him.[12]

Paul's spectacular and gritty performance at the hearing won him both admiration and, most important, relevance in the black community with one grand stroke. He seemed his old self—confident, focused, determined. Systematically, Paul undertook three simultaneous tasks—completion of his book with Lloyd Brown, organization of his notes on music theory into a series of articles and ultimately a monograph, and restoration of his concert career over the ensuing two years.

By October 1956, Khrushchev's speech revealing Stalin's crimes had led to political upheavals in Poland and Hungary. Military intervention by Soviet troops stationed in Poland was averted by an agreement between Khrushchev and Wladyslaw Gomulka, a popular communist leader who two years previously had been released from imprisonment on charges of "nationalism." Matters did not unfold that well in Hungary, a prewar Hitler ally that fought on the Nazi side during the war. A mass uprising led to full-scale intervention by Soviet troops, which suppressed all resistance.

The West responded with a strong condemnation of the Soviet action, but stopped short of military intervention. Extremist cold war anti-Soviet rhetoric was revived in the United States, threatening to derail the "Geneva spirit" generated by the Eisenhower-Khrushchev summit meeting of the previous year.

Suddenly, a new international crisis displaced the news about Hungary. President Nasser of Egypt seized control of the Suez Canal, and Israeli troops, backed by British and French air and naval forces, attacked Egypt in an effort to restore western control of the canal. President Eisenhower strongly denounced the invasion. However, the Soviets announced that they were sending Russian volunteers to fight the invasion alongside the Egyptians and challenged the United States to join them in sending military aid to Egypt. When Eisenhower indignantly refused, the Soviet Union appeared in the role of savior of "Third World" nations as Israeli troops and their British and French backers withdrew under the Soviet threat.

Paul commented on the Hungarian and Egyptian crises in an extensive interview in the November 17, 1956, issue of the *Baltimore Afro-American*. Regarding Hungary, he speculated that the armed revolt had been sparked by former Hungarian fascists who had returned among émigrés during the early stages of the upheaval. Adding that the same people who had attacked Egypt supplied money and arms to the Hungarian rebels, Paul denounced the Western invasion of Egypt as proof that the West still had colonial ambitions. But most of the interview was devoted to his views on the domestic scene. He criticized Eisenhower for being disengaged from the issue of civil rights and failing to support or implement the U.S. Supreme Court's desegregation decision. The black press wholeheartedly agreed with him, condemning the hypocrisy of whites' sympathy for the "freedom fighters" while remaining indifferent to the wave of violence against blacks engulfing the South.[13]

The Montgomery bus boycott movement withstood fierce and sustained attacks by the local authorities and by November was still in full force. On November 13, a U.S. Supreme Court ruling declared Alabama's state and local laws requiring segregated bus seating to be unconstitutional. The black mass movement had won. It had also sparked the introduction of a civil rights bill on the floor of Congress by a reluctant Eisenhower administration. Once again, supporters of the bill argued that its passage was critical to the ability to wage the cold war successfully.[14]

On November 5, Paul received the bad news that the U.S. Supreme Court had denied him a hearing on his passport case. His only option now was to gain another State Department hearing and fight his way back to the Supreme Court. Undaunted, he asserted his continuing friendship for the Soviet Union by attending the November 7 reception at the Soviet embassy in Washington, D.C., in honor of the thirty-ninth anniversary of the Bolshevik Revolution. On November 13, Paul braved an angry missile-throwing crowd of picketing Hungarian refugees to speak at a New York rally of the American-Soviet Friendship Association.[15]

The end of 1956 found Paul revitalized. Not a trace of his previous depressed state remained, and his determination matched his optimism. He believed the civil rights movement would continue to grow and spread, ultimately becoming unstoppable. He was equally convinced he could play an indirect role by influencing the movement with his forthcoming book and by reestablishing his career in spite of the mainstream concert establishment's boycott. His deep convictions and spiritual strength, marshaled by the direct clash with his persecutors during his testimony before the House Committee on Un-American Activities, had lifted him out of the depths of despair.

Just before Christmas, Paul received an unexpected tribute that warmed his heart. Jawaharlal Nehru, having completed a state visit to confer with President Eisenhower in mid-December, invited him and Essie to a reception in Manhattan hosted by the Indian consul general. When Nehru saw Paul in the reception line, he stepped forward, beckoning to Paul to come to the head of the line. He greeted him with a warm hug and chatted animatedly with him for a couple of minutes, then kept Paul next to him until they left the receiving group together. On Nehru's part, it was an extraordinary demonstration of friendship and respect, as well as a courageous political act.

I I

RISING FROM THE ASHES

(1957–1958)

Encouraged by his reception in black communities, Paul scheduled a series of concerts for the summer and fall of 1957 in Los
Angeles and the San Francisco Bay Area. There he could rely upon
the support of a powerful coalition of black churches, surviving left-
wing unions, and broad-based progressive organizations. His summer
appearances, after the usual spring concert season, allowed progressive producers to promote his concerts with minimal risk to their regular business. If the summer and fall concerts went well, he would be
positioned to complete his comeback during the 1958 winter-spring
concert season.

Paul's preparation for his return to the professional concert stage
included recording sessions and his usual rehearsals. Our audio engineer David Hancock, a pianist with a highly sensitive musical ear,
developed a ribbon microphone specially designed for Paul's voice,
which significantly enhanced the quality of the master recordings.
Paul achieved some of his best recordings during the first several
months of 1957, and by June he had sung his voice into top shape.
Having completed a series of published articles on music theory titled
"Thoughts about My Music," he drew upon this material for the
narration to accompany his concert songs.

Working with Lloyd Brown, Paul completed the manuscript of his
autobiography, *Here I Stand*, which presented his credo and offered
a strategic vision for the civil rights movement. He dedicated it to
Essie, expressing his "deepest gratitude" for her "help and guidance

over many years of struggle, aspiration, achievement and constant awareness of a better future for our children and grandchildren."[1]

Here I Stand describes Paul's roots in black life and in America, and sets the record straight. As he put it, "I shall try to make clear exactly what my ideas are and how I came to hold them." He added, "Let me make one thing very clear: I care nothing—less than nothing—about what the lords of the land, the Big White Folks, think of me and my ideas. I do care—and deeply—about the America of the common people that I have met across the land. Most of all I am mindful of the Negro people as I meet them in the Harlems of America."

After tracing his early life, Paul spoke of his cultural philosophy:

> It was in Britain—among the English, Scottish, Welsh and Irish people of that land—that I learned that the essential character of a nation is determined not by the upper classes, but by the common people, and that the common people of all nations are truly brothers in the great family of mankind. And even as I grew to feel more Negro in spirit, or African as I put it then, I also came to feel a sense of oneness with the white working people whom I came to know and love.

Then Paul laid out his case for entitlement to a passport in the context of the struggle for black rights:

> When I, as a Negro American, can be restricted and charged with having acted against the "best interests of the United States" by working in behalf of African liberation, some very important questions arise: What are the best interests of *Negro* Americans in this matter? Can we oppose White Supremacy in South Carolina and not oppose that same vicious system in South Africa? Yes, I have been active for African freedom for many years and I will never cease that activity no matter what the State Department or anybody else thinks about it. This is my right—as a Negro, as an American, as a man!

In discussing his controversial political stands, Paul wrote,

> My views concerning the Soviet Union and my warm feelings of friendship for the peoples of that land, and the friendly sentiments which they have often expressed toward me, have been pictured as

something quite sinister by Washington officials and other spokesmen for the dominant white group in our country. It has been
alleged that I am part of some kind of "international conspiracy."
The truth is that if the government officials had a shred of evidence
to back up that charge, you can bet your last dollar that they would
have tried their best to put me *under* the jail! But they have no such
evidence, because that charge is a lie.

He went on to say that "in 1946, at a legislative hearing in California,
I testified under oath that I was not a member of the Communist
Party, but since then I have refused to give testimony or to sign affi-
davits as to that fact." His reason was that the fundamental issue was
freedom of speech and conscience under the First Amendment to the
Constitution.

He asserted his "belief in the principles of scientific socialism"
and his "deep conviction that for all mankind a socialist society repre-
sents an advance to a higher stage of life—that it is a form of society
which is economically, socially, culturally, and ethically superior to a
system based upon production for private profit." He did not argue
his point, commenting that "the large question as to which society is
better for humanity is never settled by argument. The proof of the
pudding is in the eating."[2]

In the remainder of the book, Paul presented his ideas on the moral,
ideological, and political foundations of the civil rights movement.
What is striking is the degree to which he anticipated the struggles to
come and the strategy and tactics that proved successful in later years.
He defined the challenge facing the movement: "Freedom can be
ours, here and now; the long-sought goal of full citizenship under the
Constitution is now within our reach. We have the power to achieve that
goal: what we ourselves do will be decisive. Developments at home and
abroad have made it imperative that democratic rights be granted to the
Negro people without further delay."

He pointed out that

the granting of our demand for first-class citizenship, on a par
with all others, would not in itself put us in a position of equality.
Oppression has kept us on the bottom rungs of the ladder, and
even with the removal of all barriers we will still have a long way
to climb in order to catch up with the general standard of living.
But the equal *place* to which we aspire cannot be reached without

the equal *rights* we demand, and so the winning of those rights is not a maximum fulfillment but a minimum necessity and we cannot settle for less.

The moral support of the American majority is largely passive today, but what must be recognized—and here we see the decisive power of Negro action—is this: Wherever and whenever we, the Negro people, claim our lawful rights with all of the earnestness, dignity and determination that we can demonstrate, the moral support of the American people will become an active force on our side.

As early as 1957, Paul had put his finger on what was to become a crucial issue after the civil rights movement of the 1960s had run its course: The winning of civil rights was only the first step on the road to equal opportunity and ultimately full equality.

Paul advocated black mobilization of "the power of numbers, the power of organization, and the power of spirit." The power of numbers should be invoked to deter antiblack mob violence and to engage in coordinated mass action in support of political demands. The power of organization could be harnessed most effectively by a nonpartisan coalition of all black organizations, with a common program and a central fund. Black churches and the two million black trade union members would be the mainstays of the coalition. He invoked the power of spirit as an intangible but great force that had to be unleashed and could be identified with "the poignant beauty of all our spirituals."

In dealing with the decisive question of black leadership, Paul rejected both the subservience of many black leaders to the white "Establishment" and the concept in certain communist circles that only a "Communist Party vanguard" could lead the black liberation movement:

> The primary quality that Negro leadership must possess, as I see it, is *a single-minded dedication to their people's welfare*. Any individual Negro, like any other person, may have many varied interests in life, but for the true leader all else must be subordinated to the interests of those whom he is leading. All too often Negro leadership here has lacked the selfless passion for their people's welfare that has characterized the leaders of the colonial liberation movements.
>
> Dedication to the Negro people's welfare is one side of a coin: the other side is *independence*. Effective Negro leadership must rely upon and be responsive to no other control than the will of

their people. We have allies—important allies—among our white fellow-citizens, and we must ever seek to draw them closer to us and gain many more. But the Negro people's movement must be led by *Negroes*, not only in terms of title and position but in reality. Good advice is good no matter what the source and help is needed and appreciated from wherever it comes, but Negro action cannot be decisive if the advisers and helpers hold the guiding reins. For no matter how well-meaning other groups may be, the fact is our interests are secondary at best with them. [Emphasis in the original.]

Paul ended by invoking the dream of black freedom: "To be free—to walk the good American earth as equal citizens, to live without fear, to enjoy the fruits of our toil, to give our children every opportunity in life—that dream which we have held so long in our hearts is today the destiny that we hold in our hands."

In the meantime, Paul's campaign for his passport shifted into high gear. On January 22, 1957, Boudin requested a hearing on Paul's passport application. The State Department replied that he would have to submit a new application. When Boudin objected, the State Department delayed for a month before replying that Paul's "present travel plans" were required. Boudin sent a letter stating that Paul desired to travel to Europe on May 1 to sing and act. He also requested a hearing date and a ruling on Paul's right to travel anywhere a U.S. passport was not required.

The State Department restated its original requirement that Paul complete the administrative procedure (i.e., sign the noncommunist affidavit) before a hearing would be considered. An internal Passport Office memorandum dated May 27, 1957, provides the State Department's "analysis" of Paul's case:

> Robeson refused to furnish an affidavit with respect to present or past membership in the Communist Party. He filed a civil action to complete the issuance of a passport. The District Court held that he had failed to exhaust his administrative remedies. The Court dismissed the complaint.
>
> The Court of Appeals, in affirming the District Court's decision, commented that it would not pass upon the invalidity of a

hearing that had not been held or on the illegality of questions that had not been asked.

This ruling is a classic example of how the judicial system used procedure to subvert substance in Paul's passport case.

Boudin finally gained a hearing on May 29, which went as expected. Accompanied by Boudin and Essie, Paul endured four hours of questioning, but he held his ground, refusing to answer any questions concerning communist affiliation and asserting his constitutional rights. In a memorandum to the FBI on the same day, Robert Johnson, who chaired the hearing, wrote that he "threw the book" at Paul without eliciting any satisfactory answers. The State Department waited over two months before informing Paul on August 9 that his passport application had been rejected. However, the ban on his travel to places not requiring a U.S. passport was lifted.[3]

As Paul pursued the legal fight for his passport, support for his right to travel continued to grow abroad, especially in England. On May 26 the London Paul Robeson Committee organized a telephone broadcast via transatlantic cable to an audience of over a thousand people in St. Pancras Town Hall, and Paul sang and spoke to them from a studio in New York. The listeners included two hundred delegates representing 1.75 million Londoners. Letters from twenty-seven members of Parliament and the British Actors' Equity Association urged the U.S. government to allow Paul to travel.[4]

Among the FBI documents referring to Paul's passport case, I found an interesting June 6, 1957, memorandum that discusses an anonymous informer who appeared at the FBI's New York office. The reply to the memorandum inadvertently reveals that the informer was Noble Sissle, famous black producer-entertainer of the 1920s and 1930s.[5]

However, Paul's high standing in the black community was demonstrated unexpectedly at the annual November reception hosted by the Soviet ambassador to the United Nations. Ralph Bunche, the famed African American peacemaker for the UN, sought Paul out and greeted him warmly, chatting with him for some time.

On May 17, 1957, the third anniversary of the U.S. Supreme Court's school desegregation decision, a predominantly black audience of thirty thousand assembled at the Lincoln Memorial in

Washington, D.C., for the Prayer Pilgrimage called by Martin Luther King Jr. Serving as master of ceremonies was A. Philip Randolph, Mahalia Jackson, the "Queen of Gospel," sang, and Reverend King capped the three-hour ceremony by delivering a memorable peroration as the crowd roared in response to his repeated trumpet call: "Give us the ballot!"

Paul attended the Prayer Pilgrimage accompanied by Essie and me. He stationed himself under a large tree on the periphery of the crowd, far from the platform and the celebrities. Throughout the afternoon's program, people kept coming from everywhere—first intermittently in ones and twos, and at one point in a steady stream—to meet and greet Paul. A sizable reception line formed as they expressed their joy at seeing him, uttering a constant refrain that was some version of "We wouldn't be here but for you." They were civic leaders and ministers, ordinary people and union members, midlevel politicians and a few celebrity artists, young and old, longtime acquaintances and total strangers. At times we were close to tears. It seemed of small consequence to Paul that the proceedings taking place on the platform ignored his existence.

The power demonstrated by the pilgrimage produced an invitation to King to attend a White House meeting that helped shape the civil rights bill that was submitted to Congress that summer. Its key provision was a guarantee of strong Justice Department enforcement of both voting rights and school desegregation. Despite Democratic senator Lyndon Johnson's compromise nullifying this provision, the bill was accepted as a modest step forward.

In June, Paul traveled to Los Angeles for two sold-out concerts at the First Unitarian Church. He was in excellent voice, and in the second concert tried out the difficult "Prayer and Death" from the Mussorgsky opera *Boris Godunov* without a misstep. The enthusiastic responses of his audiences inspired him.

During his monthlong stay, Paul lived in the heart of the black community with his old friends George Sims and his wife, Frankie Lee. They connected him with a broad range of community leaders, including several ministers from the largest black churches in Los Angeles. While the mainstream press ignored Paul's presence, the black and progressive press covered his appearances, praising both his singing voice and his message. Among the latter, the *Los Angeles*

Herald-Dispatch said in an editorial, "Our people need Paul Robeson." It called him "a leader whose courage and endurance in the good fight have been tested in the fires of hell." Paul returned to California in mid-August, appearing in Los Angeles and San Francisco five times within two weeks before ten thousand people, and several more concerts were scheduled for the fall of 1957.[6]

Between his August West Coast appearances, Paul was interviewed for *Ebony*, the leading black magazine, by Carl Rowan, a black staff writer for the *Minneapolis Tribune*. The interview appeared as the lead article in *Ebony*'s October issue under the title "Has Paul Robeson Betrayed the Negro?" The extensive quotes from Paul contradicted both the title and Rowan's opening description of Paul as a "tragic figure." Among his defiant comments, Paul called on the black masses to exercise their power, asserting that "Negroes are finally more powerful than they know. Man, if we'd had 200,000 people in that prayer pilgrimage to Washington, if we'd had thousands of Negroes to swarm that Senate building while the civil rights double-talk was going on, this nonsense would be stopped. We don't have to go begging to these people. All we need to do is face this nation with a unified voice."

When Rowan asked Paul to respond to Thurgood Marshall's comment that the Negro in the United States was better off than colored people anywhere else in the world, he said, "Who's double-talking whom? Hell, 15 years ago I could have boasted that I was the most fortunate black man in the world. I had everything. But hell, man, what about my folks? What about 10 million Negroes in the South?"

Concerning his warm feeling toward the Soviet Union, Paul commented that he just couldn't help "feeling kindly toward a country that has no color prejudice, a country that restrains these Western white boys who want to wipe out all the colored people. I think the Negro should solve his problems within the American framework, and he is definitely on the way to dignity and equality."

Rowan summed up his article on the same note on which Paul ended his book: "Robeson is convinced that he will have the last laugh, for he is sure that the day will come when American Negroes will find that 'black power' holds the key to their freedom."

On October 2, Rowan appeared on the popular *Tex and Jinx* syndicated radio show to discuss his *Ebony* article on Paul. Asked about his personal view of Paul's passport case, he answered unequivocally, "I think that American citizens ought to have the right to travel freely unless we're in a condition of war and there is a very clear and present danger to the government. I disagree with [Robeson] greatly on a great many issues. But when he's talking about what's happening to Negroes, or when he's crying out for freedom of Negroes, or when he's talking about a constitutional issue like freedom to travel, I find it very difficult to disagree with him."

The *Ebony* article and its national repercussions provided Paul with priceless positive publicity only a few weeks before his concert tour began. Rowan, despite the harsh criticisms that peppered his article, had done him a great favor.

On October 5, Paul received an inspirational and symbolic send-off on his comeback concert tour. The South Wales Miners Union set up a telephone link between him in a New York studio and the traditional miners' choral festival (the Eisteddfod) in Porthcawl, Wales, via the new transatlantic cable. The emotional drama of this historic broadcast was captured on a recording:

> Hello, Paul Robeson. This is Will Paynter, president of the South Wales Miners, speaking. On behalf of the South Wales miners and all the people gathered at the Eisteddfod, I extend to you warm greetings of friendship and respect. Our people deplore the continued refusal of your government to return your passport and to allow you the right to join with us in our festival of song. We shall continue to exert what influence we can to overcome this position. We look forward to the day when we shall again shake you by the hand and hear you sing with us in these valleys of music and song.

Paul responded:

> My warmest greetings to the people of my beloved Wales, and a special hello to the miners of South Wales. It is a great privilege to be participating in this historic festival, and all the best to you as we strive toward a world where we all can live abundant, peaceful, and dignified lives.

Paul sang five songs, and the Treorchy Male Voice Choir sang back to him. Noting that there had been some progress in his passport fight, Paul promised that soon he would be in Wales. He added:

I can't tell you what it means to hear you like this—it seems as though I'm really standing there right with you. And I can see many of my old friends, and I want you to know that it is a very moving occasion. My family is here in the studio with my little grandchildren—I have a grandson and granddaughter, David and Susan, and they also send you their love. David is a good Welsh name, as you know.

Paynter bade farewell to Paul:

Thank you very much, Paul; and our best wishes to you. You know that the fervor with which we sing is no greater than the fervor with which we struggle in the cause of freedom for all peoples. And now I'm going to ask the Male Voice Choir and all this great audience to sing a song and to dedicate it to you: "We'll Keep a Welcome in the Hillsides."

As we were engulfed by the wave of affection surging from the voices of the choir, joined by those of thousands of people from the mining valleys of South Wales, there wasn't a dry eye in the New York studio.

Paul concentrated on his upcoming concerts in California, which were billed as "informal recitals." On October 18, he sang to an appreciative capacity audience at the Saints Rest Baptist Church in Oakland. He received excellent reviews in the black press, but, once again, the mainstream press made little or no mention of his appearance.

A week later Paul appeared in Sacramento at St. Paul's Baptist Church. This time there were glowing revues in the major press. The music critic of the *Sacramento Union* wrote, "Nobody can sing like Paul Robeson. He has a deep-toned resonance which he controls with clarity and ease. The delight of the audience showed that their expectations had been met, that their memories of that voice need no longer range back 10 or 20 years." Under the headline "Paul Robeson Singing Again—Great, Spiritual, Powerful," the *Sacramento Bee* praised both his performance and his choice of program:

Paul Robeson, at 59, and after 32 years on the concert stage, is still a remarkable performer—a big man, an incredibly big bass voice, a big, warm, magnetic personality. He used these attributes to good advantage last night before a capacity audience. It was an unusual program, not so much in content as in arrangement. It ranged from folk songs to opera, with Othello's final speech tossed in as an encore; it offered an initial group which was mainly religious, but within this unity it placed Bach next to Roger Quilter and a Negro spiritual alongside a Jewish chant in disregard of long standing, if perhaps unnecessary, concert tradition.[7]

The next day Paul filled in the First Unitarian Church of Los Angeles, even though he had sung there twice less than three months earlier. He flew back east in time to attend the Soviet embassy reception in Washington, D.C., on November 7 celebrating the fortieth anniversary of the Bolshevik Revolution. Surrounded by crowds of Soviet and American admirers, Paul was a recognized international celebrity, as reported by the *Pittsburgh Courier*:

> It was amazing to stand aside in the crowd at the Russian Embassy the other night and watch the hundreds of guests crowd around Paul Robeson as if he were a Grecian god. Reporters, radio commentators and TV cameramen haunted him for a statement or a picture. Other guests ganged around him just to be in the picture.[8]

In mid-November 1957, Paul received a letter from Glen Byam Shaw, general manager of the Shakespeare Memorial Theatre of Stratford-upon-Avon, England, inviting him to play the role of Gower, the storyteller in Shakespeare's *Pericles*, in a summer 1958 production. The director would be the newly famous young Tony Richardson, known for his highly successful production of John Osborne's new play *Look Back in Anger*. Paul accepted, although with some trepidation about playing an unfamiliar Shakespearean role.

His acceptance was big news in England, and as a result Paul received several major offers from British television. On December 10, as pressure on the State Department escalated, Boudin applied for a limited passport for Paul to fulfill these engagements.

On January 17, 1958, the State Department, impervious to foreign protests and Paul's professional offers, denied his passport application on the previous ground that he had failed to sign a noncommunist affidavit. Since two litigations similar to Paul's—the Walter Briehl and Rockwell Kent cases—were scheduled to be argued before the U.S. Supreme Court in April, there was no chance the State Department would fatally undermine its legal arguments by granting Paul even a limited passport. Boudin's strategy was to lay a solid foundation for filing an appeal before the Supreme Court and hope for a favorable Court ruling in June on the Briehl and Kent cases. He promptly made a request of the State Department to reverse its denial in light of new television and concert contracts that had been received by Paul.

The possibility of Paul's arrival and the subsequent State Department refusal to issue him a passport were headline news in England, resulting in significant public support there and in many other countries. Paul received a letter from world light heavyweight boxing champion Archie Moore, who wrote, "For me you have played a great part in my life. I have followed you many years and I have always believed in your fighting spirit. I am not a hero worshipper by a long shot, but there are men I admire and you are one of the few."[9]

Paul's book *Here I Stand* was published in early February 1958 by Othello Associates, the successor to Othello Recording Corporation. While there was no mention of the book in any white commercial newspaper in America, the black press reviewed it widely. The *Baltimore Afro-American* led the way with an editorial on February 22 calling it "remarkable" and announcing they would serialize several chapters in the newspaper's magazine section. Saunders Redding, a leading black journalist and author, reviewed the book in the March 15 issue. "[Robeson's] principles and convictions should find response in every heart. 'Here I Stand' is a program of action for colored Americans. It is a challenge to fulfill the American dream."[10]

The only negative review was written by Roy Wilkins in the *Crisis*, the official publication of the NAACP. He dismissed *Here I Stand* as the work of one who had forfeited any claim to leadership of blacks because of his ties to communists and the Soviet Union.

The book sold well in the black community and among white progressives. The first printing of ten thousand was sold out in six weeks and over twenty-five thousand were sold within a year. The Communist Party leadership backed the book enthusiastically, and party activists across the country distributed and sold copies. Progressive and black bookstores formed the other part of the distribution network, circumventing the hostile publishing industry. As a result, the book made a significant impact on black politics.[11]

Paul Endicott, a successful concert manager based in Garden City, Michigan, who was impressed by Paul's performances, arranged two major comeback concerts, one in Oakland in February and another at Reed College in Oregon in March, followed by a series of six in April and early May in Chicago, Milwaukee, Pittsburgh, and Detroit. The venues were large halls seating an average of over two thousand people, with fees of over a thousand dollars. Looking ahead to the fall of 1958 and beyond, Endicott predicted Paul could gross $150,000 to $200,000 for the 1959–1960 season.[12]

On February 9, Paul sang the pivotal concert of his tour at the Oakland Auditorium Theater to a capacity interracial audience. He was appearing in a civic auditorium for the first time in six years, largely through the efforts of Reverend F. D. Haynes of the Third Baptist Church, the largest black church in San Francisco. Reverend Haynes had secured the auditorium from the Oakland City Council and faced down furious right-wing protests.

Paul's performance was outstanding. Typical headlines were: "Ovation for Robeson," "Robeson Makes Triumphal Return," and "Paul Robeson—More Music Than Politics." Thomas Albright of the *San Francisco Chronicle* wrote, "Paul Robeson proved the years have done nothing to the greatest natural basso voice of the present generation. Nor have they done anything at all to one of its most magnetic stage presences." Clifford Gessler of the *Oakland Tribune* indirectly recognized Paul's loss of the upper part of his baritone range when he commented that "while it would be too much to expect the velvety smoothness of that magnificent bass voice to continue as consistently as of old, the sincere conviction, the dramatic vitality which he infuses into his songs, created the same strong impact."[13]

On March 18, Paul sang to a standing-room-only audience at Reed College, with similar success. Hilmar Grondahl, music critic of the *Oregonian*, wrote, "He is musically as fine a singer as ever, perhaps interpretively a bit ahead of those days [1946 and 1947]. His voice has shifted to a lower range. You could no longer call him a baritone, but his bass register is more opulent than ever. No doubt about it, Robeson is vital and vibrant at 60. And he still carries onto the concert platform a diction that is among the clearest."[14]

The news that Paul Robeson was singing concerts as of old had an immediate effect. Endicott received an offer for Paul amounting to $25,000 for a ten-concert tour of Canada. He felt he could bargain successfully for $40,000. Paul's April and May concerts were rapidly selling out, and the 1958 fall tour was ready to be confirmed pending his passport situation.[15]

The entertainment industry was watching. On March 15, Oscar Hammerstein II was asked by Mike Wallace in a television interview whether he knew Paul and what he thought of him. Hammerstein answered that he would "have no compunctions to work with Paul now, or to have lunch with him. His political views wouldn't bother me."

The international campaign to restore Paul's passport intensified as his sixtieth birthday approached. The British press began to criticize the U.S. ban on his travel as "foolish." A growing list of British notables, including Dames Flora Robson and Sybil Thorndyke Casson, D. N. Pritt, and Canon L. John Collins wrote tributes to Paul in anticipation of his birthday. Indira Gandhi, Nehru's daughter, wrote Essie about plans by an All-India Sponsoring Committee to celebrate Paul's birthday in India's large cities. At home, the black press publicized his passport fight and African criticism of the United States for denying his right to travel.[16]

India's plans for a government-sponsored nationwide birthday celebration caused a flurry of activity at the highest levels of the State Department. On March 4, U.S. consul general Turner sent a dispatch to Secretary of State John Foster Dulles informing him of the formation of an "influential All-India Committee, with separate committees in Delhi, Madras and Calcutta," to celebrate Paul's birthday. He also reported that the movement had the support of Krishna Menon (a top aide to Nehru) and Indira Gandhi. There followed a series of dispatches between Secretary of State Dulles and Undersecretary Christian Herter in Washington and Consul General Turner and Ambassador Ellsworth Bunker in India concerning attempts to thwart, or at least blunt, the celebrations.

The U.S. efforts began with a lobbying campaign in India to dissuade notables from joining the committee. When Nehru sent a personal message to the committee on March 18 supporting its work and extolling Paul, the State Department expressed U.S. "concern." The wording of Nehru's message was especially galling to Secretary Dulles:

> This is an occasion which deserves celebration not only because Paul Robeson is one of the greatest artists of our generation, but also because he has represented and suffered for a cause which should be dear to all of us—the cause of human dignity. The celebration of his birthday is something more than a tribute to a great individual; it is also a tribute to that cause for which he stood and suffered.

Indian ambassador Gaganyihari L. Mehta was told bluntly that Nehru's statement "will be misunderstood in the United States, could antagonize the American press and certain influential Americans, possibly including some in Congress, and, might in fact, have a damaging effect on Indo-American relations." Given the strong congressional opposition to India's latest requests for aid, the implied threat was unmistakable. However, Mehta held his ground, agreeing merely to inform his Ministry of External Affairs of the State Department's concern. Unable to budge the Indian government, Dulles ordered all U.S. diplomatic personnel in India to boycott Paul's birthday celebrations.[17]

On April 9, programs honoring Paul were held in India's major cities. A special tribute was paid to him in Parliament. A tape-recorded message from Paul was played at all of the events:

> Warmest and heartfelt greetings to the people of India. May I express my gratitude to, and profound respect for, your beloved guide and father, Jawaharlal Nehru; and may I send sincerest thanks and warmest greeting to his daughter, Mrs. Indira Gandhi, and to his whole family.
>
> You all know of my closeness to your struggle and my unbounded admiration for your vast achievements. You are building anew a great nation and continuing, as you have through so many centuries, your priceless contributions to the achievements of all humankind.
>
> Soon I hope to stand on the soil of beloved India, to sing for you—and for you to sing with me. All the best from my family. Your devoted friend, Paul Robeson.

The celebrations were covered extensively by the Indian press under headlines such as: "Symbol of Man's Aspirations for Freedom," "American Bid to Scuttle Robeson Celebration," and "Apostle of World's Poor, Oppressed." The U.S. press covered Nehru's statement and the preparations for Paul's birthday celebrations but bypassed the actual events.[18]

There were Paul Robeson birthday celebrations in twenty-seven countries around the world, coordinated by the London Paul Robeson Committee. In China, Paul's birthday was celebrated as an event of major international significance. His recordings were played on the radio for three days, the entire cultural page of China's leading news-paper was devoted to articles about him, and a three-hour tribute was held in Beijing's new Capital Theater. In the Soviet Union, a major concert tribute was held in the Hall of Columns of the House of Trade Unions, a glowing review of his book *Here I Stand* appeared in the English-language *Moscow News*, the major Soviet newspapers carried articles about him, and an arrangement was made to publish a Russian edition of *Here I Stand*.[19]

In the United States, Paul's stature continued to rise. The Actors' Equity union passed a resolution backing his passport rights at their quarterly meeting. After his friend the actor Ossie Davis introduced the resolution and many members rallied to its support, the vote was 111 to 75 despite the negative recommendation of the union presi-dent, Ralph Bellamy. The action was well covered by the media and added to Paul's growing public viability. The popular black magazine *Jet* carried an item that read, "Sign of the Times: Government lead-ers are gossiping about the trend concerning Negro leadership. Long ignored in the U.S., singer Paul Robeson and Dr. W. E. B. DuBois suddenly are enjoying popularity sprees."[20]

Maynard Solomon, the president of Vanguard Records, a well-established classical and folk label, signed Paul to make his first mainstream commercial album in ten years. Paul recorded it at the end of March in the state-of-the-art Vanguard studio in a single highly successful session. The program included a group of songs with instrumental and choral backing, imaginatively arranged by con-ductor-composer Robert DeCormier. The album, *The Essential Paul Robeson*, broke the ban on Paul in the commercial record market.[21]

Early in April, Paul traveled to Chicago to begin his six-concert spring tour. Just before departing, he received the good news that New York concert manager Art D'Lugoff, who had secured Carnegie Hall for a concert on May 9, had sold out the event in advance. Paul could now look forward to a climactic finish to his tour.

The tour, however, began with a rebuff by the most important television show in Chicago, which canceled an interview with Paul because of right-wing protests. But he received a warm welcome at Chicago's Masonic Temple, where he was embraced by the black and white-progressive communities on his birthday. Two concerts at Mandel Hall a few days later were sold out. In fine voice and buoyant mood, Paul held his audiences spellbound. One reviewer wrote that "the deep resonant tones pealed out like some magic had touched them off to resound with great appeal and warmth. It's a rare experience to hear such a voice and Robeson's is as fine as ever." Before Paul departed, his old friend Ishmael Flory, a longtime black communist and community activist, organized a public meeting for him with black community leaders at the Parkway Ballroom. Five hundred people came, including some skeptics. By the end of the encounter, very few had not become Robeson supporters.

Then it was on to concerts in Milwaukee, Pittsburgh, and Detroit and invariably enthusiastic standing-room-only audiences. The reviews were good to excellent, with some critics lamenting the lack of vocal brightness (or "glow"), and a few faulting his use of a microphone and explanations about the universality of folk music. All agreed on his undiminished personal magnetism, command of the stage, and musicianship.

In Pittsburgh, the city council denied Paul the use of Soldiers and Sailors Memorial Hall. Central Baptist Church, the largest black church in Pittsburgh, offered their premises, and an audience of two thousand gave him "a thunderous standing ovation." According to the *Pittsburgh Courier*, "It was amazing to hear this great voice again. The years have not diminished its beauty, resonance, intonation and power."[22]

After his Detroit concert on May 4, Paul looked forward to appearing at Carnegie Hall on May 9—his first major concert in New York in eleven years. Adding to the pressure was the decision to have Vanguard Recordings tape the concert.

Paul strode onstage and was greeted by a standing ovation. He gave an inspiring performance, weaving a tapestry of song and spoken word. Alan Booth's versatile accompaniment enhanced the artistry of the evening. When the concert ended with Othello's speech and the curtain calls, standing ovations, and encores followed, it was clear that Paul Robeson was back on the concert stage.

The reviews were generally positive but mixed. Harold Schonberg of the *New York Times* wrote, "As a lecturer, Mr. Robeson was superb. The most musical vocalism of all came not in the singing but in the brief 'Othello' excerpt." *Musical America*'s critic, on the other hand, reported that "never have I seen an artist, who, by his sheer personality, can hold such complete interest and attention of a public. Mr. Robeson was in full command of the evening." Irving Kolodin, in the May 24, 1958, issue of *Saturday Review*, wrote, "The voice is still potent. Robeson remains a man of magnificent vocal endowments with a highly cultivated sense of phrase and accent, a power of articulation second to none among his contemporaries."

The concert was so successful that a repeat performance was advertised for two weeks later and sold out in one week. The second concert on May 23 was just as impressive and received similarly good reviews. Paul had become the only concert artist ever to fill Carnegie Hall twice within two weeks on two different occasions—once in 1929 and now in 1958.[23]

Two weeks later, he sang a concert in Harlem's Mother A.M.E. Zion Church. He performed the first group of songs, all spirituals, with Larry Brown at the piano. In the last group, he performed a Hebridean song and a Chinese song, then compared their similarity with the tones of an African song and a southern black work song. He ended by comparing the African and Chinese languages, all to the delight of the audience.

Paul introduced his last song with a brief but moving expression of gratitude to his brother Ben and the congregation for providing him sanctuary during his years of travail. He paid a special tribute to Ben's wife, Frances, who had recently passed away. Then he sang "Jacob's Ladder," inviting the audience to join him.

Victory! On June 16, 1958, the U.S. Supreme Court, in a five-to-four decision, overturned State Department regulations denying passports to suspected communists and others of allegedly doubtful loyalty. Nine days later, the State Department announced that it was issuing Paul his passport. The eight-year struggle was over. Paul and Essie immediately booked a flight to London for July 10 and packed their bags. Invitations poured in: Glen Byam Shaw cabled a tentative offer for Paul to open the Shakespeare Theatre's centennial 1959 season with *Othello*; Chilean poet Pablo Neruda invited him to "sing for the people of Chile." The Czechs invited him to Prague, and the Russians invited him to Moscow. Essie responded to them all. She also wrote Indira Gandhi, thanking her for the strong support India had given Paul and saying that they would love to visit the country when the Indians thought it was appropriate.[24]

The day after my father's passport was restored, I went to Jumel Terrace to congratulate him, thinking he would be celebrating. I was puzzled to find him in a wistful, even somber mood. He looked at me with sadness in his eyes and said, "In my heart of hearts, I don't want to go. I've finally reclaimed a place in black life—just as the civil rights movement I dreamed about and fought to bring about all my life is coming to pass. If I go now, I'll become irrelevant."

"But Dad," I interrupted, "you can go for a few months and then come back. You can go and come, like others do." "I know, son, but I'll inevitably get caught up in the 'citizen of the world' maelstrom—I just feel it." In response to my comment that after the eight-year crusade, he had no choice, my father replied, "I know—that's why I'm going to leave. But I'm worried about getting back here."

Three years later, I would recall those words as prophetic.

Paul and Essie, Moscow, 1958. *From the personal collection of Paul Robeson Jr.*

Paul and Essie arrive in London after
regaining their passports, 1958. *From
the personal collection of Paul Robeson Jr.*

With famous Russian tenor
Ivan Kozlovskii, Sochi, Soviet
Union, 1958. *From the personal
collection of Paul Robeson Jr.*

With Russian
writer Boris
Polevoi, Moscow,
1959. *From the
personal collection of
Paul Robeson Jr.*

The Royal Shakespeare Company, 1959 season (clockwise from left): Charles Laughton, Peter Hall, Paul, Glen Byam Shaw, Harry Andrews, Dame Edith Evans, Mary Ure, Angela Baddeley, and Leslie Caron, Stratford-Upon-Avon, England, 1959. *Photo by Roger Wood. From the personal collection of Paul Robeson Jr.*

Paul with Aneurin Bevan (second from left, top row), Esssie (center, bottom row), Jenny Lee (right, bottom row), Cecil W. Smith (right), and Mr. and Mrs. Ron Jones (left). Ebbw Vale, Wales, 1958. *From the personal collection of Paul Robeson Jr.*

With workers at the Moscow Automated Gear plant after singing and speaking to them, January 1960. *Courtesy CPUSA Photographs Collection, Tamiment Library, New York University.*

Singing "Water Boy" at the Humanité Festival, Paris, 1959. *From the personal collection of Paul Robeson Jr.*

Performing at the World Youth Festival in Vienna, 1959. *From the personal collection of Paul Robeson Jr.*

Singing to construction workers
of the Building Workers Industrial
Union of Australia at the Sydney
Opera House during an Australian
tour, 1960. *Courtesy of Alfred Rankin.*

With longtime accompanist Lawrence Brown
(standing, left) and the manager of the Australian
tour, 1960. *From the personal collection of Paul Robeson, Jr.*

Paul (center) with Dizzy Gillespie and Sarah Vaughn in London, 1962. *Courtesy of the Paul Robeson Foundation.*

At the Freedomways Salute to Paul Robeson, Americana Hotel, New York City, 1965. *Photo by Beuford Smith. Courtesy of Freedomways.*

Paul (seated) celebrating his seventy-seventh birthday with cousin Gertrude Cunningham at his sister, Marian Forsythe's home, Philadelphia, 1975. *From the personal collection of Paul Robeson Jr.*

IV
JOURNEY TO JERUSALEM
(1958–1976)

Paul at Trafalgar Square peace rally in London, 1959. *From the personal collection of Paul Robeson Jr.*

Paul at Idlewild Airport upon his return to the United States, New York, 1963. *From the personal collection of Paul Robeson Jr.*

I 2

A HERO'S WELCOME

(1958–1960)

On the morning of July 11, 1958, Paul and Essie stepped off a British Overseas Airways plane onto the tarmac of London's main airport. A hero's welcome greeted them. Several hundred friends and fans were present, including Glen Byam Shaw; Tom Driberg, chairman of the Labour Party Executive; London county councilor Peggy Middleton; Cedric Belfrage, deported editor of the *National Guardian* and prime mover of the Paul Robeson Committee; and Harry Francis, assistant secretary of the Musicians' Union. A large press contingent was on hand.

The *News Chronicle*'s story, appearing under the headline "Robeson Flies in on Wings of Song," said that Paul was "welcome as a singer" and that there was "something pathetic about Mr. Dulles and the President chasing Paul Robeson's passport." The writer observed that "within 10 minutes of landing, he was singing Negro Spirituals, Scottish folk tunes, ancient African melodies and snatches of Beethoven's Ninth Symphony. It was the most remarkable press conference I have ever attended."

The *Daily Mirror* reported that when asked about his "campaign for Colored people's rights," Paul answered, "My fight for the Negro people is my whole life as a [U.S.] citizen—but I have another life and it is as a singer that I am here." The *Daily Mail* began its reportage with the headline "Robeson's Answer Is a Brotherly Song." The subhead read, "It's Better to Sing a Song of Friendship Than Talk Politics."[1]

In the first days after their arrival, Paul and Essie sorted through a large number of offers that had been winnowed down from the original avalanche by Paul's agent-manager Harold Davison. Paul signed contracts for a series of three television programs beginning in late July, a loosely scheduled radio series, a concert tour of the British Isles in the fall of 1958, and a production of *Othello* at Stratford in the spring of 1959. He also scheduled a monthlong visit to the Soviet Union for mid-August 1958.

Paul and Essie's activities over a five-week period included tea at the House of Lords hosted by Lord Stansgate and his son, Anthony Wedgewood Benn, Labour MP; lunch at the House of Commons, followed by tea with Dame Peggy Ashcroft; and lunch or dinner with high officials of the Soviet Union, China, Ghana, Poland, Czechoslovakia, India, Romania, Nigeria, and Hungary.

Paul's record fee for three half-hour television programs was $8,400. The first program was an informal concert of folk songs from many lands. Accompanied by Bruno Raikin, Paul introduced the numbers and linked their cultural traditions. The second consisted of a formal recital of spirituals with Larry at the piano, and the third was a concert of favorite popular tunes with Larry and a full orchestra.

On August 3, Paul was escorted by Aneurin Bevan, Wales's most popular politician, to the Welsh national Eisteddfod (choral festival) in Ebbw Vale, located in the heart of South Wales's mining valleys. It was an emotional reunion, as thousands of miners and their families gave Paul a thunderous welcome. Then their choirs sang to him and he spoke and sang to them.

Paul's sold-out Albert Hall concert on August 10 was another triumph. Before an audience of seventy-five hundred, he sang two groups of songs—folk songs with Bruno Raikin accompanying, and spirituals with Larry at the piano and joining Paul in several duets. After standing ovations and encores, Paul concluded with his favorite lines from "Let the Rail Splitter Awake" by the great Chilean poet Pablo Neruda.

The reviews, for the most part, were glowing. The *Times* of London reported that "his depth, richness and resonance of tone were a feast for the ear, while the genuine fervor behind it all suggested that in speech he can find just as great an outlet for his powers of expression as in song." The *Evening News* critic wrote that "Robeson stands in a class by himself."[2]

In early August, Paul gave an interview to Australian journalist Therese Denny, in which he spelled out the sharp change in the role he now chose to fulfill. Contrary to his stance from 1947 through 1955, when he had used his artistic talent as a political weapon, he now would appear as an artist whose politics were expressed as a citizen. "I have not only the right and the privilege, but the responsibility to speak out in the interests of my people," he said, adding that "this doesn't mean doing that on the concert stage."

When asked whether he regretted the suffering he endured because of his political stands, Paul replied, "I can't even use the term 'regret.' I'm very proud of any contribution I've been able to make to the struggles of my people. If you want freedom, you have to suffer sometime." When Denny asked whether he had a desire for revenge, Paul commented, "Quite the opposite. I come back as an artist, as one who loves people. I don't know where this idea came [from] that I'm bitter."[3]

Paul held court at a book signing on August 12 at Selfridges, London's largest department store, to mark the publication of the British edition of *Here I Stand* by Dobson Books Ltd. He basked in the warmth of many ordinary Londoners who came not just to buy an autographed book and meet a celebrity but to welcome their "Paul" back to England, and he responded by writing personal notes to them above his autograph. A month after his arrival, people on the street continued to welcome him back, and taxi drivers still refused to take his payment for the fare, asking him for his autograph instead.

Paul and Essie departed for Moscow on August 15 for a month-long tour sponsored by the Ministry of Culture. They received a rousing welcome. Thousands of people engulfed them at the airport, making it impossible to conduct the official welcoming ceremony. During the ride to the city, people in cars and buses called out and waved their welcome. People on the streets shouted "Friend" and "Welcome." At the hotel another large crowd greeted them, and a police escort was required to get them into the building.

The next day, Paul sang an afternoon concert in the huge Palace of Sports to an audience of eighteen thousand. He began with a moving speech in Russian, briefly thanking the Soviet people for their support and expressing his joy at being among them once more. Then he sang spirituals and folk songs, performed some of the Soviet favorites in perfect Russian, and finished with "Joe Hill" and "Ol' Man River." That evening he appeared on television in a twenty-minute interview. He spoke about his life in the United States, noting that the political situation at home had improved and the freedom struggle of his people was growing rapidly.

After a round of official events in Moscow, Paul and Essie flew to Tashkent, capital of the Soviet Central Asian republic of Uzbekistan, to another overwhelming welcome. The next day, the army had to clear the way through huge crowds to get him to a large arena, where he spoke and sang at an international film festival. Despite the oppressive heat, Paul's voice sounded especially rich and resonant as he pitched it in slightly lower keys than usual.

They flew to Sochi on the Crimean coast of the Black Sea for three days of rest and relaxation, followed by a leisurely twenty-four-hour boat trip along the coast to the famous Yalta summer resort, where they stayed for two weeks at Orianda, the luxurious government rest house. They made side trips to sightsee, conferred with the minister of culture, bathed in the Black Sea, taped several radio interviews, and filmed regularly with the film crew that accompanied them for the entire trip, headed by well-known film director Vassily Katanian.[4]

On August 31, Paul and Essie received an invitation to Premier Khrushchev's summer vacation retreat where he was entertaining the party leaders of Hungary, Romania, Poland, East Germany, and Italy, as well as some of his Soviet colleagues. Khrushchev and his wife, Nina, chatted with Paul and Essie, posed for pictures, and then watched a pickup volleyball game between two teams of guests. On the spur of the moment, Khrushchev invited the Robesons to join them at dinner.

Paul and Khrushchev had a genuine respect for each other's accomplishments and engaged in several substantive exchanges in Russian. Khrushchev recalled his visit to India, emphasizing the importance of his friendly relationship with Nehru. Paul, in turn, shared some of his experiences with Nehru and offered Khrushchev insights about the black freedom struggle. He was deeply impressed by the premier's grasp of what the Soviets called "the nationalities question," including its racial aspects. The dinner was "a tremendous affair, with speeches," Essie wrote in her diary, noting that "Paul gave an especially moving toast which evoked tears from many."[5]

The white U.S. press published the photos of Paul with Khrushchev as proof of the propaganda about Paul's role as a so-called dupe of the communists. The black press proudly published them as proof of his great international stature.

Upon returning to Moscow, Paul devoted two days to television and radio interviews, appearances at factories, and official meetings with foreign students, artists, and top officials. He and Essie spent an afternoon visiting with Frank Goode, Essie's brother, and his Russian wife and daughter, who was named Eslanda after Essie. Along with other American blacks, Frank had emigrated to the Soviet Union in the 1930s to escape racism and became a Soviet citizen. Paul granted Frank open access to his substantial Soviet royalty account so Frank and his family would never be in want.

Paul and Essie flew back to London on September 15, and Paul immediately began rehearsing with Larry for his twenty-two-date concert tour of the British Isles scheduled to begin in Blackpool on September 21 and end in Brighton on December 6, singing in Scotland, Wales, and Ireland along the way. He could do no wrong before his capacity audiences, and the reviews were consistently excellent. Pianist Bruno Raikin joined Paul and Larry on the tour as the assisting artist. In an October 1958 letter to Clara Rockmore, Paul gave major credit for his success to his British sound engineer, who had improved the feedback system, allowing him to hear himself more fully:

> This is the middle of a long concert tour. It has gone so well that I am relaxed for the first time in years in my professional work. The sound is wonderful—I stand in a bath of sound. The engineer has really solved it. Also, most importantly, I finished the third of my television appearances. It was a great success. Now I shall tape the appearances in front—so I will not have the terror-stricken feeling of being bad before millions. I shall also have a series in which I act as host.[6]

On October 12, during a break in his tour, Paul gave a recital in hallowed St. Paul's Cathedral, becoming the first layperson to read scripture from the pulpit. He was in magnificent voice throughout, beginning with his choice of the first lesson at Evensong—Micah, chapter 4: "And they shall beat their swords into plowshares, and their spears into pruning hooks. Nation shall not lift up a sword against nation, neither shall they learn war any more." Then, with Larry accompanying, he sang with a dignity and restraint that merged with the historic ambience of the cathedral. The audience of four thousand filling St. Paul's made barely a sound as they listened with rapt attention. In the vestry afterward, Paul commented that "this has been one of the great honors of my life."[7]

While Paul went back on tour, Essie found a spacious apartment at 45 Connaught Square in central London, where she settled in for the long term. In mid-November, she flew back to New York to attend the sessions of the United Nations for two weeks and to make decisions about the Jumel Terrace house. She decided not to rent it out but to keep it ready for them to "come back and forth" from London. In an interview with the black press, Essie said that Paul was keeping his New York home because his family, his people, and his roots were in the United States. She also announced that she would be the guest of the Ghanaian government at the All-African People's Conference in Accra in December, and that Paul and she had been invited to India by the Paul Robeson All-India Birthday Committee in January of the next year.[8]

The U.S. State Department was once again in a state of anxiety about Paul's planned visit to India. The department's two months of urgent memoranda and command conferences reached the highest levels of the U.S. government. The process began with a November 21, 1958, cable from the U.S. embassy in New Delhi to the U.S. Information Agency requesting that "all Agency resources be utilized to provide us with material which may be used in countering Robeson activities." The message added that the embassy was researching its files for "best copy showing Negro advancement in U.S." The exchanges on the matter were brought to a close by a January 12, 1959, memorandum from Secretary Dulles to the U.S. ambassador and consuls in which he noted that a "walkout would be extreme last resort since publicity gain for Robeson would be considerable and possibly detrimental [to] U.S. interests."

Back on tour, Paul received continued acclaim. The *Sheffield Star* of October 29, 1958, commented that "his extraordinary hold over the British public is as firm as ever. The voice is as magnificent as ever—wonderfully firm, pure, with every note dead center. It is, in fact, the unique vocal instrument of the day. Both in range and his ability to reduce the mighty organ to a breath-taking whisper without the slightest loss of tonal roundness or pitch brings back to mind no less a singer than Chaliapin." With his earning power assured, Paul set about resuming his familiar lifestyle. He engaged Joseph "Andy" Andrews, his valet and friend from the 1930s, who found him a comfortable "getaway" apartment. Paul also established a relationship with the British left through two key people—Harry Francis, assistant secretary of the Musicians' Union, and John Gollan, top leader of the British Communist Party. Having organized his professional, personal, and political life, Paul ended the year with a flourish by appearing as one of the main attractions of the London BBC Christmas broadcast, on which he sang a half-hour program accompanied by Larry.[9]

On December 29, Paul and Essie flew to the Russian capital for a two-week visit prior to their scheduled trip to India on January 12. They planned to return from India via Moscow for a week of rest before Paul reported for *Othello* rehearsals at Stratford in mid-February. The opening of the play, which would run in repertory with four other plays for a period of seven months, was set for April 7, 1959. Paul kept a copy of the script with him, constantly studying and making notes in the margins during his free time.[10]

Just as Paul and Essie were scheduled to depart to India after a busy round of Moscow appearances, their plans were abruptly shattered. Essie was hospitalized for uterine bleeding, and Paul came down with severe flulike symptoms and a bronchial infection. When he developed incapacitating dizzy spells, he was taken to the hospital as well.

Essie, diagnosed with a "precancerous condition," agreed to undergo seven weeks of gamma-ray treatments. Paul, after being treated for his flu symptoms, was still having dizzy spells, and underwent a series of tests to determine whether he had suffered "heart complications." Tests proved that his heart and circulatory system were normal and the dizzy spells ceased, although they were never adequately explained.

Essie, fearing that they were warning signs of a stroke, insisted that Paul cancel his *Othello* engagement and go into semiretirement to preserve his health. However, Paul was reluctant, feeling that he would be missing a historic opportunity. Ultimately she prevailed, and on January 20 she wrote to Glen Byam Shaw canceling his engagement.

Shaw, devastated and having tried without success to recast *Othello*, sent Paul a desperate cable two weeks later begging him to reconsider so that the season would not be "ruined." Paul would not have to report for rehearsals until March 10 instead of mid-February. Now feeling much better and slated to go to the famous Barveekha Sanatorium for a month to rest, diet, and exercise, Paul took only a day to make a firm decision. After a sharp and at times angry argument with Essie, he wired Shaw his acceptance.[11]

At Barveekha, Paul worked diligently to prepare himself, both mentally and physically, for the *Othello* run. He dieted, ice-skated, visited the gymnasium with a trainer, and went on walks. All the while, he studied the *Othello* script and worked out a way to play the role as an old warrior in his declining years, rather than a young general at his peak. By the end of his stay, having lost significant weight, he was brimming with confidence.

On March 2, he was the featured speaker at a Moscow tribute to the legacy of Sholem Aleichem, the great Jewish writer. Keenly aware of the anti-Semitic undercurrents in the Soviet Union, Paul chose his words carefully: "Sholem Aleichem belongs to all of us. How wonderful that his tender works are a natural part of the heritage of my grandchildren—a clear, living example of the closeness of my father's people and the folk of Sholem Aleichem." He sang three songs in Yiddish and ended with the anthem of the Warsaw Ghetto Uprising, likening the death struggle of the courageous Jewish partisans to the struggle of the multitudes of Soviet citizens who fought to the death against the Nazi invaders.[12]

Paul flew back to London on March 9, leaving Essie in Moscow to complete her treatments. He went directly to Stratford, accompanied by Andy, and plunged into intensive rehearsals for the initial *Othello* run of thirteen consecutive performances. He faced a daunting challenge, with less than a month's rehearsal time to adjust to an unfamiliar cast under an unorthodox director who had shaped a nontraditional production. Twenty-seven-year-old Tony Richardson's production included a fireworks display, drums beating out rock and roll, three Great Danes running across the stage, a scene acted behind a smoke screen, a ferocious combat scene with thrown swords, and the death scene on a high platform.

Paul adjusted his execution of the role to the challenges and negotiated only minor changes that would ease his physical burden. He consulted with both Sam Wanamaker (Iago) and Mary Ure (Desdemona) about how they could best interact to enhance the credibility of their characters. Paul had to do most of the adapting, since Wanamaker and Ure had each defined their roles prior to his arrival. For example, Wanamaker's Iago was more a jaunty, in-your-face villain than Ferrer's devious and malevolent character who had presented himself as a loyal professional military man. To balance this, Paul's Othello was more prone to suspicion and jealousy.

Paul found a comfortable place to live in Shottery, a village just outside of Stratford, where he rented a suite of spare rooms in a large converted farmhouse owned by Mrs. Whitfield, an old-fashioned English matriarch. She lived with her family—the unmarried oldest daughter, Mary, the middle daughter, Bunty, and her husband, Andrew Faulds (who later became a Labour member of Parliament from Stratford), and the youngest daughter, Thisbe, who was married to a young actor. Paul charmed them all and became an adopted family member.

He survived the pressure-packed opening night on April 7 with flying colors, while the production and his two costars received considerable criticism. But the play was a sensational success with the public. All performances continued to sell out. Paul's portrayal of the Moor was hailed as a triumph, and he received congratulatory messages from a celebrity list that included Lawrence Olivier, John Gielgud, and Sean O'Casey, as well as from Gerry Neale Bledsoe, an old and dear friend dating back to Paul's years at Rutgers College. Other old friends were present on opening night, including Alphaeus Hunton and Helen and Sam Rosen.

The reviews reflected a near-total validation of Paul's strategy and execution. The *Birmingham Mail* critic wrote, "We saw the *Othello* of a lifetime. The power of Mr. Robeson's performance finally left me defenseless and emotionally shattered." The *Coventry Evening Telegraph* reported that "Othello rises through Robeson to tragedy at its most moving. The triumph is mostly his." The *New York Times* published a "London Letter" headed, "Robeson's Performance in *Othello* Is Hailed by Stratford Playgoers." In it, W. A. Darlington, the leading London critic, called Paul's Othello the best he could remember seeing. The reviewer in the *Statesman* wrote that "Mr. Robeson has an effortless dignity and power, a voice like a cathedral organ, over which he has complete control, and, even when silent and tucked away in one corner, a presence that dominates everything."[13]

Paul's hard-earned accolades, including his fifteen first-night curtain calls, meant a great deal to him. At the cast party, Glen Byam Shaw raised a toast to Paul's sixty-first birthday, to which Paul responded, "This is one of the greatest nights of my life."

After the opening thirteen performances, the schedule was reduced to two or three performances a week until the end of November, with two ten-day breaks in July and August. Having triumphed on opening night, Paul remained in command of the performance throughout the initial run. In an April 18 letter to Freda Diamond, Essie reported, "The audiences have continued ecstatic. Paul gives very fine performances, magnificent often. When I got here [from Moscow], he had everything under control." In May, however, Paul injured his knee, which he had originally hurt playing professional football, and for three weeks he performed onstage fearing he wouldn't be able to finish. But with the aid of a knee brace, he managed to get through with barely a limp.

Throughout the run of *Othello*, Paul stayed in Shottery except for occasional visits to London, while Essie lived in the Connaught Square flat. When she visited Paul, she stayed at an inn across the street from the theater. On May 8, she wrote to Freda Diamond from London with news about herself, saying that she was finally getting the rest she needed after her treatments in Moscow and that the flat was shaping up. She organized several social events during Paul's visits, including dinner at the Chinese embassy with Dr. DuBois and his wife, Shirley, who had regained their passports and were visiting in London. On May 1, Paul spoke and sang at a May Day celebration in Glasgow to an audience of ten thousand in Queens Park. The theme of the celebration was opposition to South Africa's apartheid rule.[14]

In May, Paul hosted Bob and Clara Rockmore in Stratford for a few days. Their visit had meant a great deal to him, as he wrote in a June 26 letter to Clara:

> I too will always remember our meeting. Since you-all left, I feel very very hung in mid-air. This really becomes a serious human problem. My public contributions and artistic life are far from filling the most important "gap" of life with friends whom I love and cherish. It becomes a real necessity to see you and Bobby, as dear a friend as one could hope to have. So I see Toronto perhaps in December. Am pretty certain *not* to try coming all the way. Still sketchy I think. But I miss you and love you dearly. And the void is wide and deep.

He went on to write about his work:

> Feel better now I'm working at my music, and the work is hard. In two days last week, I made about two hundred pounds [$572] in radio and one thousand pounds [$2,860] on television. Hope to finish another half-dozen of each week by week. Actually have ten television jobs to complete. So helps security. Also have fabulous offer for Australia. Seems that I could send about ten thousand pounds [$28,600] clear to my American account. Also getting ready for recordings. See this intense activity for next year. Then I'll relax for good.

Despite his homesickness, Paul was deeply ambivalent about returning to the United States. Not much of a correspondent, he hadn't kept in regular touch with his closest friends back home. His older brother Ben was now a widower and nearing seventy years of age. His sister, Marian, had written him in January about the death of her husband, William, and Paul had responded with a comforting letter. And then there was the problem of how and where he would live and who would take care of his day-to-day needs. What about Essie and her fragile health? How could he maintain two households, since he wouldn't want to be confined to the Jumel Terrace house with Essie? What if Essie refused to come back with him?[15]

There were also political considerations. Although a growing thaw was developing in U.S.-Soviet relations, enhanced by the death of Secretary of State John Foster Dulles, Hoover and CIA head Allen Dulles were still in place and as hostile as ever to Paul. The FBI files on Paul reveal regular FBI communication with the CIA via the CIA's deputy director of plans, and a 1956 FBI report lists the U.S. Customs Service and George Jurasch of the Inspector's Office, Post Office Department, New York City as confidential informants, indicating that Robeson packages and mail were being opened regularly. By 1959, Hoover had succeeded in making Paul a marked man in the United States.

Paul's belief that he was also under intelligence surveillance in Britain was correct. Documents trace the FBI's direct communication with Britain's MI-5 through "Peter Clapham," otherwise identified as a "confidential source abroad," with the designation "T-32." Exchanges about how Paul Robeson should be dealt with in England took place between MI-5 and the Home Office throughout his stay. An August 1958 entry claims that Robeson "is largely under the control of the British Communist Party." A December 12, 1958, memorandum complains about his political appearances and notes that his work permit expires at the end of September. A December 22, 1958, memorandum states that "extant instructions to ports about Robeson require that he should be closely interrogated on arrival," but added that "the implementation of this requirement would give us far more trouble than it is worth."[16]

In mid-July, at my parents' invitation, Marilyn, David (age eight), Susan (age six), and I arrived in London for a five-week visit. Paul remained in Shottery, while we stayed in London for a week with Essie. She immediately organized us all, reveling in her combined roles of mother-in-law, grandmother, hostess, and tour guide, all of which she fulfilled superbly. We all went off to Stratford to visit with Paul and see him in *Othello*. Marilyn and I spent some time with Paul at the Whitfield home, where he was at ease and happy. We saw *Othello* twice. To my mind, despite the pyrotechnics and overly fast pace of the production, Paul created a subtle character, using his voice in imaginative ways.

I had lunch with him the day after I had seen the play for the second time, and he told me how he had found a way to work with his costars' portrayals of Iago and Desdemona. He based his growing suspicion on Desdemona's behavior rather than on Iago's psychological machinations. His Othello was far more dismissive and intolerant of Iago's insinuations than in the Broadway production, and he placed more dramatic emphasis on the "handkerchief scene" in which Desdemona offhandedly admits that she has misplaced his wedding gift of an exquisitely embroidered handkerchief.

My father seemed fulfilled and at peace in the Stratford environment. The townspeople loved to have him around, and he enjoyed the great respect and goodwill of his peers in the Stratford Theatre Company. I was about to ask how he had managed to establish such rapport with his famous and accomplished colleagues in spite of his complete dominance of the season when he noticed Laurence Olivier alone at a table across the room. He said, "There's Olivier; I want you to meet him. He's by far the greatest living actor in the English-speaking theater. You should see his Coriolanus—it's the most skilled theatrical performance I have ever watched."

We went over. Olivier was reading and didn't look up as we approached. When we arrived and halted a few feet away, he still didn't look up. Undisturbed, Paul said in his most gracious tones, "Laurence, sorry to barge in on you, but I'd like my son, Paul Junior, to meet you. Paul, this is Laurence Olivier." I said, "Honored to meet you, Mr. Olivier," leaned forward, and extended my hand.

Olivier ignored my presence entirely, turned his head toward Paul, and said, "Oh, hello, Paul. How've you been?" Without missing a beat, Paul chatted with him for a moment, then shook hands and left with me following close behind. More bemused than angry, I had stood silent and motionless during the encounter.

When we arrived back at our table, Paul smiled and said, "I wasn't surprised by that. Just wanted to check him out. He's one of the greatest actors of all time and I couldn't come near to matching him, but he can't stand the fact that I'm dominating this season with *Othello*."

Our conversation turned to politics. I filled him in about the situation in the United States, confirming his impression that the Communist Party was in a state of collapse. He listened with interest when I told him that the civil rights movement was rapidly expanding in the South, but in my view, despite the nullification of the "anti-subversive" laws, illegal persecution of dissent would continue as long as Hoover remained FBI director, regardless of who was president. Paul nodded, saying that he was ambivalent about returning home for this very reason.

Over dessert and coffee, I asked my father how things were between him and Essie. He shrugged and said that the season at Stratford had temporarily solved that problem. When the season was over, he planned to cope by working and traveling a great deal, and for rest and relaxation they would go to Moscow where she couldn't "organize" him. Then, after the 1960 U.S. presidential election, he'd figure out how to go home, regardless of the dangers.

A few days later, Marilyn and I left London to spend ten days at the World Youth Festival in Vienna, while Essie took care of David and Susan. She delighted in being grandmother, and they adored "Nana."

The World Youth Festival, sponsored and organized by the communist-led left but including many noncommunist groups from Asia, Africa, Latin America, and Europe, was being held for the first time in a Western pro-U.S. country—Austria. Its overarching theme was "peace and friendship." A large and diverse U.S. delegation of 400 attended under the sponsorship of two committees—one in New York, which sent 250 delegates, including Marilyn and me, the other from Chicago, which sent 150 delegates. The U.S. State Department adopted a policy of disruption against the festival.

Paul arrived during the closing days of the festival to meet with the delegates and speak at the closing rally in a large public square in Vienna. He was engulfed by hundreds of cheering, clapping African and Asian delegates, who inundated him with flowers upon his arrival at the Vienna airport. Paul responded by speaking briefly about the intensifying freedom struggle of black Americans and the links with the anti-apartheid resistance in South Africa. On August 3, he spoke and sang to a crowd of twenty-five thousand in Heroes' Square, declaring that the United States should grant full freedom to eighteen million blacks before claiming to be champion of freedom abroad, and denouncing "fascist infiltration" of U.S. foreign policy. In the charged political atmosphere, Paul's presence took on an immense symbolic meaning not lost on the U.S. government. His FBI file confirms that his visit was closely monitored by both the CIA and the State Department.[17]

On August 20, en route to Romania, Paul spent a few hours in Budapest, although it was off-limits for travel on a U.S. passport. As guest of the Institute for Cultural Relations, he visited with school-children and sang a group of songs from the stage of the open-air theater on Margaret Island. In an interview with a correspondent of the Hungarian Telegraphic Bureau, he said, "Next spring I shall spend four or five weeks giving recitals. I shall come back though my passport has been stamped 'Not Valid for Hungary.' Nor is my passport valid for the Chinese People's Republic. Still, I am here and I shall come back many more times and shall visit China too." Although Paul was not yet technically in violation of U.S. passport restrictions because he was in Budapest only in transit and not for purposes of travel, his remarks were a direct challenge to the State Department.[18]

Paul returned to London from his Romanian trip at the begin-ning of the final week of our visit, and I had several long talks with him at the Connaught Square apartment, mostly about politics and his personal life.

I asked him what he thought about the growing political tensions between the Russians and the Chinese. My father said he had become keenly aware of these "overtones" from subtle asides from the Chinese ambassador and his colleagues who thought Khrushchev's policy of peaceful coexistence with the West was too accommodating. He had decided to support the Soviet peace policy without criticizing the Chinese. Taking sides, he felt, would exacerbate the rift to the benefit of the Western right wing.

Recently, the invitations to him from China through high-level channels had become more insistent, with faint hints of distress because of his frequent visits to the Soviet Union. This pressure, he said, had played a major role in his recent public announcement to visit China. Undoubtedly he would lose his passport after such a trip, so he would wait until his passport was renewed in July 1960. Therefore, following an Australia–New Zealand tour, he planned to rest up in London and then go to Moscow. From there he would make his trips to Africa, India, and last to China—and then head for home.

I replied, half jokingly, that his wasn't exactly a simple plan, but it might work. At least making his trips from Moscow would mini-mize his vulnerability to the CIA and its British counterpart. I added that my experiences at the World Youth Festival had convinced me that the CIA was extremely active all over Europe, Africa, and Asia. Paul agreed, saying that he felt exposed to them in London but sensed his protection by the British people. He was confident of his security in the Soviet Union and the Eastern European countries.

Unexpectedly, Essie, who had been chatting with Marilyn on the other side of the living room but had overheard parts of our conversation, broke into our dialogue in a strident, angry tone with a near-tirade about how Paul was determined to go back to the United States and get himself killed, how it seemed he would never give up his other women and nomadic lifestyle to settle down like "normal" people, and how he was "addicted" to being onstage and performing even though he was probably headed for a stroke. Abruptly, close to tears, she broke off, got up, and left the room with the comment, "Oh, Paul—you're impossible!"

My father remained silent. I looked at Marilyn—she was astonished. I turned back to my father, and he said, "Well, now you know how bad it is between us." I said, "You have to come home soon." He looked at me sadly. "I know, son; I'm getting tired inside. I have to reclaim my personal life and I can't do it abroad."

The Passport Office decided to pursue Paul's visit to Hungary, requesting the American embassy in London send him two successive registered letters asking him to explain in writing his Budapest stopover. After conferring with British lawyer D. N. Pritt, he ignored both, deciding to delay his answer until he applied for his passport renewal the following July. A new round of cat and mouse had begun. Paul's approach was to continue taking controlled risks.

On September 4, he sang to an audience of fifty thousand at an outdoor festival in Meudon, France, sponsored by the French Communist Party newspaper *L'Humanité*. This time, in his brief remarks from the stage, he stuck to the theme of world peace. In an interview and article for the newspaper, he restricted himself to a discussion of his artistic life and his theory about the unity of the world's folk music.[19]

Two weeks later, the U.S. State Department was again sharply reminded of Paul's high esteem abroad. During Khrushchev's goodwill visit to the United States, he was heckled during his speech at a dinner by the New York Economic Club in the Waldorf-Astoria Hotel ball-room. In the tense atmosphere surrounding the question period, Khrushchev was asked why the Soviet Union jammed U.S. radio broadcasts to the Russian people. Khrushchev responded, "You also jam American voices," noting that "Paul Robeson, singer and actor was denied the right to go abroad. Why is that voice jammed?" He concluded that no nation should decide what another nation should read or listen to. That ended the questions.[20]

Meanwhile, Essie was pursuing her activities, writing articles and traveling. In a September 17 letter to Freda, she recounted her recent trip to East Berlin to attend the memorial service at Ravensbrück, the concentration camp for women. She was the only woman to speak at the antifascist annual meeting in the "big square in Berlin" to one hundred thousand people.

Two months later Essie became ill. In a November 14 letter to Freda, she described her current London hospitalization, which had revealed an ulcer caused by the aftereffects of her Moscow radiation treatments. "Paul is taking me home this afternoon," she wrote. "We have good help for the flat and I have arranged for secretarial help twice a week. I plan to start work on my new book and stay with it while I'm recuperating."

Two days later, Paul was back at Shottery, where he wrote Clara two letters on November 16 and 17 about his highly successful radio and television appearances and his national concert tour in February–May 1960, which he was looking forward to: "We [he and Larry] are preparing some interesting programs, and more excited about the coming events I have never been. Will use some poetry and many chants. Am working on my languages, including Hebrew. Will let you know about any definite plans for Israel." He went on to comment about his interview with Yehudi Menuhin. "He was most friendly and charming. Talked about his youth, his musical friends and mine, about music [and] its basic likeness." Referring to his work on languages, he wrote, "Have really broken down many languages for singing pur-poses and for radio and television appearances in countries when I get there: Czech, Norwegian, Chinese, modern Greek, Icelandic. Have wonderful offer from Iceland. Am getting down to Hungarian; [also] Romanian which is like Italian, though basically Latin."

On December 24 and 30, Paul wrote Clara again to update her on how he was doing after the grueling *Othello* run:

> Here I sit in Stratford in a lovely quiet spot with lovely people. Have had a wonderful rest already, both mentally and physically. I may go to Australia for 6 to 9 weeks. However, that will depend on my passport being renewed in July. In last weeks I have reached the point of rest and accomplishment. Have found finally a very simple approach to music in your terms of dominant tonic-subdominant. I'll [stay]—I hope—mostly in Britain. Am sure I'll have no difficulty with the people here. Think they are too sensible.

On January 18, Paul and Essie flew to Moscow for a three-week stay. They began with medical checkups. Paul was found to be in "very fine" health but considerably overweight. Essie was hospitalized for an evaluation of her continuing pain from the slowly healing ulcer. Unlike the London specialists, who had told her it would heal slowly by itself as no effective treatment existed, the Moscow doctors recommended extensive outpatient therapy that would keep her in Moscow for at least an extra month. She agreed.

Paul made public appearances and gave several television and radio interviews. He appeared relaxed, self-assured, and ebullient, especially when he visited the machine shop workers at the First Moscow Ball-Bearing Plant. He mingled with the workers and sang to them. In all of his interviews and public speeches, he chose to be pointedly political:

> New, favorable conditions have come about in the struggle for peace. The visit of N. S. Khrushchev to the United States and the Soviet proposals for complete disarmament are events of great historic importance. It is also undoubtedly true that the decision of the Soviet Government to again reduce its armed forces will exert great influence on the entire world.
>
> I'm very happy to be with you. And my deepest thanks to the Soviet people, their great leader, N. S. Khrushchev, and the Supreme Soviet. We will win peace.[21]

On February 7, Paul flew back to London to rehearse for his thirty-two-city concert tour with Larry. They set out well prepared, both musically and in terms of new, fresh repertoire. The result was an unbroken chain of successes and triumphs. In a March 11 letter to Clara, Paul wrote, "Now I want to sing well and joyously and relax. It would interest you that in the Soviet Union I got a very simple ear aid that does the job for me. So I can have normal amplification."

Paul's informal style and new, more varied repertoire of folk songs in many languages played well. He used notes, recited poetry, held impromptu conversations with Larry, chatted about his grand-children, introduced songs with commentary, and performed short excerpts from *Othello* with brief explanations of their context. For the first time in his career, he thoroughly enjoyed being onstage through-out an entire four-month concert tour.

In his March 11 letter to Clara, Paul also reflected on his *Othello* run: "I still can scarcely realize what a tremendous effort, and in the end achievement, the Stratford *Othello* was—a kind of summation of a life's work in the theater. Some things come to full fruition. There were times during last summer when the performances were really colossal and fully satisfying."

In May, Paul used a short break in his tour schedule to make two major appearances with sharp political overtones. On May 1, he led one of the largest May Day processions ever held in Glasgow. Later, a crowd of ten thousand people gave him an overwhelming ovation as he strode to the bandstand, where he gave a brief speech about world peace and sang a group of songs. The audience joined him in the chorus of "Loch Lomond." The next day, he appeared at the Miner's Gala in Edinburgh, where he was given an ovation as he walked through the city streets at the head of the miners' march. Then he sang to a hushed audience of twenty thousand miners.[22]

Khrushchev's successful September 1959 visit to the United States significantly reduced cold war tensions but exacerbated a tug-of-war between the State Department under Christian Herter, who was advancing Eisenhower's policy of cautious negotiation with the Soviet Union, and CIA director Allen Dulles, leader of the right-wing, pro-war faction. In May 1960, while Herter was busy prepar-ing for the June Eisenhower-Khrushchev summit meeting in Paris, for which both leaders had high hopes, Dulles was approving plans to invade Fidel Castro's Cuba and to assassinate Patrice Lumumba, leftist premier of the Congo.[23]

Dulles was also waging a secret air reconnaissance war against Russia, with hundreds of flights penetrating Soviet airspace. These included U-2 spy planes, flying above the presumed altitude range of Soviet anti-aircraft missiles, which photographed potential targets deep inside Soviet territory. Eisenhower authorized yet another flight on May 1 shortly before his Paris summit meeting with Khrushchev.

The Russians shot down the plane, which crashed in central Russia; the pilot, Gary Powers, bailed out and was captured. On the first day of the Paris summit, Khrushchev demanded an apology from Eisenhower. Eisenhower refused, and Khrushchev walked out with a dramatic flourish, calling a press conference at which he denounced U.S. foreign policy as "aggressive." This train of events ushered in the most dangerous two and a half years of the cold war, which culminated in the Cuban Missile Crisis.[24]

In this environment of clandestine war in preparation for direct military East-West conflict, Paul sensed he was in great danger abroad, as well as at home. It was true. The key people running the intelligence war against the Soviet Union were constantly informed about his activities: CIA director Allen Dulles; Deputy Director of Plans Richard Bissell, who directed the U-2 program and was now in charge of plans to overthrow Castro; and Chief of Operations Richard Helms, who was in direct charge of assassinations and had supervised the development of the MKULTRA Project.

The MKULTRA Project included drugging foreign and domestic "enemies" with a newly developed hallucinogenic drug later to be called LSD. It also incorporated the Personality Assessment System— a method for using a person's psychological profile in psychological warfare aimed at causing mental instability in a targeted victim. The third aspect of MKULTRA was called "mind depatterning" and amounted to lobotomizing the designated person in a psychiatric hospital through the combined application of electroconvulsive ("shock") treatment and large doses of soporific drugs.[25]

The CIA had accumulated a wealth of material on Paul, including hundreds of letter intercepts of both his and Essie's correspondence from abroad and letters from our children to "Grandpa Paul" and "Nana." And Max Yergan was now a CIA consultant. The CIA material that I obtained under the Freedom of Information Act totals 176 heavily redacted documents and a list of fifty-one reports, with twenty-one of the reports concentrated in the years 1959–1960.

After Paul helped Essie settle back into the Connaught Square apartment upon her delayed return from Moscow in early May 1960, he visited the American consulate in London to renew his passport well before its July expiration. Along with his application form, he submitted an affidavit stating that he had been in Budapest for three hours in transit between planes. His case was aided by the State Department having recently lifted its ban on travel to Hungary. With regard to his reported remarks about China, Paul stated that they were mistranslated by his Hungarian interpreter. He claimed to have said that he *hoped* to visit China in the future. The ball was now in the State Department's court.[26]

In June and early July, Essie slowly regained her energy despite occasional problems. In a July 7 letter to Freda, she wrote that she was feeling better: "Last week I had a bad setback, but I think and hope that it's all over now." Paul taped a second series of radio programs for future release over BBC. On June 15, he made a defiant political statement by visiting East Berlin to attend a press festival sponsored by the East German Communist Party newspaper. His timing was especially provocative, since Berlin was arguably the most sensitive European flashpoint in East-West relations.

On July 14, the U.S. State Department unexpectedly instructed the American embassy in London to renew Paul's passport. He was free now to travel anywhere except China and had no worry about the cancellation of his right to stay in Britain. He spent the next six weeks in leisurely preparation for his two-month Australian tour scheduled to begin in October. In September, he warmed up for his tour by making several sets of public appearances on the Continent—the French Communist Party's cultural festival in the Paris suburb La Courneuve, a similar festival in Brest, and a five-day tour of Hungary.[27]

The 1960 United Nations session opened in New York in mid-September to a considerable stir as Khrushchev and Castro arrived, heading their respective delegations. On September 19, Castro and his party moved into the Hotel Theresa in Harlem, and a few days later Khrushchev came uptown to visit him. A huge crowd of Harlem residents gathered outside the hotel. A big cheer went up as Castro appeared in the doorway—"Fee-dell! Fee-dell!" Khrushchev's limousine pulled up, and his U.S. security detail hesitated as they viewed the black crowd. Khrushchev took one look, got out of the car accompanied by his Russian bodyguards, and headed for Castro. Another big cheer went up, followed by the chant, "Fee-dell! Khrush-chev!" Khrushchev, beaming, reached out to shake hands along his way, shouting "Hello" in heavily accented English. He finally reached Castro. They embraced, turned and waved, and disappeared inside.[28]

The next day, I met with two of Castro's top aides at their request. They wanted to invite Paul to Cuba and asked to make arrangements through me. They proposed to route his flight to Havana via Madrid. I reminded them that Paul had gone to Spain during their civil war to sing for the Republican troops fighting Franco and was currently denouncing Franco as a fascist. Consequently, he would be at great risk in Madrid. I suggested that all arrangements should be made with Paul in London, keeping his security in mind because he was a target of Western intelligence. They understood and agreed. After the meeting, I called Ben Davis and he got word to Paul.[29]

On October 10, Paul, Essie, and Larry embarked on an eight-week concert tour of Australia and New Zealand. Upon their return, Essie summarized her impressions:

> We did a tour of 21 concerts in all, covering Brisbane in Australia, then over to New Zealand for Auckland, Wellington, Christchurch, and Dunedin; then back to Australia for Sydney, Melbourne, Adelaide and Perth. All the concerts were packed, and everywhere Paul received an extraordinarily warm welcome from the people. The public said they had been listening to Paul's records and seeing his films for some 30 years, and had been waiting and hoping that he would come out to them, but had almost given up hope that they would ever see him in person. They were immensely pleased and gratified that he had come to their country at last, and their welcome was very warm indeed—in the streets, hotels, taxis, and at concerts—everywhere men, women and children welcomed him.

Paul sang not only to concert audiences, but also to the Maoris and to the Aborigines at their own Community Centers. He also sang to the workers at the ports, especially to the longshoremen, and to Trade Union men in their Union Halls, and to the children over the radio.

Essie added that Paul gave a television interview on "a very popular program called 'Spotlight,' in which he explained what and why he thought and felt about his music and about his politics generally. It was shown in all the major cities and was said to be the best interview 'Spotlight' has ever done." Concerning their future plans, she said that they would take at least two months rest before making firm decisions.[30]

Thoroughly exhausted but having achieved all of his goals for the tour, Paul was immensely gratified. He had passed a severe test with flying colors—physically, emotionally, artistically. He had walked a fine line politically, taken some risks, and escaped unscathed. The tour was a spectacular financial success, generating close to $150,000 in fees from concert and television appearances.

Some of the highlights of Paul's tour of Australia and New Zealand—as fate would have it, the last concert tour of his career—were captured on film. Perhaps the most striking scene unfolded on the construction site of the Sydney Opera House, where Paul sang to the construction workers. After he finished singing, the men climbed down from the scaffolding, gathered around him, and presented him with a hard hat bearing his name. One of the men took off a work glove and asked Paul to sign it. The idea caught on, and the men lined up. Paul stayed until he had signed a glove for each one of them.

13

CIA AMBUSH?

(1961–1963)

At the beginning of January 1961, after a month of rest to recover from the Australian tour, Paul and Essie engaged in a round of activities in London. They visited Eastern European and African embassies, attended concerts and plays, and made an extended visit with a top aide to Kwame Nkrumah, president of Ghana. Paul followed world and U.S. events closely. The assassination of Patrice Lumumba, leftist prime minister of Congo, in mid-January, mainly as the result of a coordinated CIA plot, alerted Paul to the intense CIA activity abroad and heightened his concern about his security in London.

Richard Helms, the CIA's chief of operations, had given the green light to widespread overseas operations involving the use of the new hallucinatory drug LSD, lethal toxins, and electroconvulsive therapy (ECT) against foreign and American targets. One of Helms's teams was MKULTRA Subproject 111, headed by Professor Hans Jürgen Eysenck, the director of the psychology department of London's Maudsley Hospital. A respected medical facility, this institution nevertheless collaborated with British intelligence and served as a staging point for European and African MKULTRA operations.[1]

Paul was right to be concerned about his security. In 1964, I attended a cocktail party in New York City where a black member of the U.S. mission to the United Nations drew me aside for a private chat. To my astonishment, he identified himself as a former CIA agent at a U.S. embassy in Africa. After telling me that he had great admiration for my father's defiant courage, he informed me about an exchange that had reportedly taken place between

308

Richard Helms and CIA director Allen Dulles in the late 1950s. Helms had floated the idea of "solving the Robeson problem." Dulles advised him to set the idea aside for the time being, because the foreign repercussions would be too dire and the Agency did not want to "create a martyr." In addition, John Stockwell, former chief of the CIA's Angolan Task Force, told me in a 1980 interview that the Agency had viewed Paul as a dangerous "badman."

By early February, Paul was weighing the pros and cons of returning home. Motivated by the twin anxieties of fear for his security and longing for his friends in the United States, he decided to go to Moscow, plan his trips from there to the newly independent African nations of Ghana and Guinea, and then return home via Cuba.

Essie argued fiercely against his decision to return to the States, but Paul was quietly immovable. She said he'd get himself killed if he went home. He countered that he was also vulnerable in London. She argued that he would need to make more money in England before going home, where he would be shut out of television and radio. He replied that he'd compromise and do a few well-spaced, high-fee concerts. She raised the issue of his passport—he'd lose it if he went to China.[2]

Paul cut off their argument by asking Essie to arrange a mid-March trip to Moscow for him. Faced with the alternative of refusing, Essie wrote a letter to Mikhail Kotov, chairman of the Soviet Committee for the Defense of Peace on February 14 that tentatively outlined a highly restricted time window for a visit with narrowly defined purposes—not at all what Paul had in mind. When Paul realized this, he decided to make his own arrangements through the Soviet embassy in London.

Paul's anxiety was heightened by a telephone call Harry Francis had taken while visiting him at the Connaught Square apartment in early March. None other than Fidel Castro was calling to invite Paul to Havana. When Francis told Paul who it was, Paul signaled him emphatically to say he couldn't come to the phone just then. Since Cuba and the United States were in the midst of a crisis in which the United States was preparing for military intervention in the island nation, Paul felt he would be at risk discussing such an invitation. He was right. The same CIA personnel planning the Bay of Pigs invasion of Cuba were tracking his possible visit there.

Helen Rosen, who had visited Paul in early February and sensed his unease, decided to visit again in mid-March. Her arrival was ill-timed from Paul's point of view, for he was preoccupied with his immediate personal security and had decided not to share his travel plans with anybody until he was safely in Moscow. Scheduled to leave on March 20, he saw Helen the day prior and was noncommittal about his plans. When Helen went to lunch with Essie the next day, Essie told her the shocking news that Paul had left for Moscow that morning.[3]

Paul arrived in Moscow in a state of considerable agitation. He heaved a sigh of relief when he was met by Kotov, accompanied by a delegation from the hosting Presidium of the Supreme Soviet (the presiding committee of the Soviet parliament). His transla-tor, Irina, a tall woman in her thirties, spoke perfect English and was efficient, sensitive, and politically astute. His aide, Alexander, a personable six-footer in his late thirties who spoke considerable English, had a quiet, friendly demeanor, was well educated, and played excellent chess.[4]

For the next six days, Paul, comfortably established in a suite in the Sovietskaya Hotel, appeared all over Moscow: greeting peo-ple in the streets; visiting Patrice Lumumba Friendship University to sing to and talk with the many Third World students enrolled there; meeting with the editorial staff of the government newspaper *Izvestiya*, where he talked about folk music, jazz, peace, and black freedom in the United States; and visiting several factories where he sang to the workers and toured the plants. He gave an extensive interview in which he stated his intention to visit Ghana, Guinea, and Cuba after visiting the German Democratic Republic and Hungary. The press and eyewitnesses reported him to be constantly in an ebul-lient, energetic mood."[5]

On the evening of March 26, since he had an unusually early appointment in the morning, Paul decided to retire considerably ear-lier than was his custom.[6]

• • •

On April 4, my mother telephoned me from Moscow. Paul had suffered a heart attack and I must come right away. The Soviet embassy in Washington, D.C., was already making my travel arrangements. All she would say over the telephone was that he had made a sudden decision to go to Moscow. Stunned and distressed, I arrived two days later on a Soviet airliner.

My mother and Alexander met me at the Moscow airport. She was agitated and somber, and I suppressed my anxiety until we were settled in the backseat of the car taking us to our hotel. When I asked her what happened, she took a deep breath and replied that on the morning of March 27 Paul had been found lying on the bathroom floor in his hotel suite after having slashed his wrists. I was shocked. I didn't believe he was suicidal. Had he been drugged? Had the CIA ambushed him in the heart of Moscow to prevent him from going to Cuba?

I asked my mother how he was now. She said he was doing well physically but was paranoid and thought everybody was a spy. He adamantly refused to see her, even though she visited the hospital daily. She appeared to be still in shock. I decided to spend the next day investigating on my own and then go to the hospital with her the following day.

The next morning I met with Alexander and a vice president of the Supreme Soviet. Few details were known about what Paul had experienced since he refused to talk about it. When his translator, Irina, had left him just before dinner in the early evening of March 26, Paul was cheerfully looking forward to an uncharacteristically early engagement the following morning and stated his intention of spending a quiet evening. However, a raucous party lasting well past midnight was held in his suite, making so much noise that a number of guests complained. Irina arrived early the next morning to brief him for his appearance and found him on the bathroom floor. He was semiconscious and incoherent, but his wounds were apparently superficial and he had not lost much blood. She gave him immediate first aid and called an ambulance.

I was suspicious about the party in my father's suite because it was uncharacteristic for him to expose himself to strangers in this manner. I speculated that he had been deceived into agreeing to the party by someone claiming to be a government official. It seemed to me that in such an environment, it would have been possible to drug my father. I kept these thoughts to myself as they explained that because he hadn't requested intervention, the hotel personnel were unwilling to terminate the celebrity guest's party. The matter was not being officially investigated, they said, because Essie had requested that complete personal privacy be respected.

Aware that Paul had wanted to discuss his possible visit to Cuba, I asked whether he had requested a meeting with Foreign Ministry officials. The vice president replied that Paul had made such a request on the day of his arrival, but the meeting had not taken place. Apparently the top people were preoccupied with several critical issues, not least of which was the escalating tension between the United States and Cuba. As the meeting drew to an end, I requested that, as a member of the National Committee of the U.S. Communist Party, I would like to meet with a member of the Central Committee of the Soviet Communist Party and a member of the Central Committee's security apparatus. They agreed to arrange it.

Irina, who had accompanied Paul on all of his public appearances, came to see me later that day. She confirmed what had been said earlier, adding significant details. Paul had locked himself into the bedroom, so she had to get a key to reach him. His cuts were not deep, indicating more of a cry for help than a purposeful attempt at suicide. When he tried to speak, he was inconsistent and disoriented, mumbling about being "unworthy." Mostly he was silent. The hotel management could provide no details about the party, how it started, or who attended. However, according to Irina, Paul had not been expecting any guests that evening. She added that he had been fine all of the times she accompanied him and did not strike her as being depressed.

The next day, I accompanied my mother to the hospital. The doctors reported that Paul's wounds were healing well and his overall physical condition was good. The diagnosis was extreme anxiety accompanied by paranoia. He still refused to see Essie, but I felt he might see me. The doctors suggested I knock on his door and enter unannounced. They took us to his private room. As I started for the door, Essie fell in step with me, announcing that she was coming also. I said emphatically that I was going in alone. The doctors backed me up, and she retreated angrily.

My father was lying on his bed with his face to the wall. I said, "Hello, Dad." He turned over, looked up at me, and said in a normal voice, "Hello, Chappie, when did you get here?" I was flooded with relief that he was alive and in reasonably good condition. He didn't appear to be agitated. We hugged and I brought him news from home. He listened for the most part, asking occasional questions. After a short time, I felt there was something unreal about our conversation. There my father was—in bed in a Moscow hospital with his wrists bandaged—and we were talking as if we were sitting in the living room at the Connaught Square apartment.

However, I wanted to avoid agitating him—the doctors had advised me to be cautious—so I did not change the tenor of our conversation. After a while, my father leaned back on his pillows and stared out of the window, quietly contemplative. I asked him whether he wanted to look at some of the books on the shelf; he shrugged indifferently. I chose a book in English by Jack London about the northern wilderness and a book in Russian about an African child. Paul perused them and settled on the Jack London book. He seemed peaceful.

We were interrupted by the doctors, who indicated that it was time for me to leave. I asked my father whether he would see Essie, but he refused. "Maybe tomorrow," he called after me. I summarized our conversation for my mother and the doctors. They were surprised and pleased by Paul's change in behavior with me.

The next day—April 9—was Paul's sixty-third birthday, and when my mother and I arrived at the hospital, we found that the staff had arranged a small birthday party for him, complete with a birthday cake. We went in and sang "Happy Birthday" to him, joined by the doctor and nurse, whom he had come to trust. He responded with surprise and pleasure, so we invited more people to join us. Thus encouraged, the head doctor stepped forward and gave a congratulatory speech in Russian. He ended with a surprise reading of a birthday message to Paul from the presidium of the Supreme Soviet. To everyone's amazement, Paul made a brief reply of thanks in perfect Russian.

My mother and I talked at length that evening. We agreed to visit Paul daily, but we didn't agree on much else. She was determined not to let him return to the United States, insisting that they stay in London. I took the opposite view, reminding her that he wanted to go home. That's why he had come to Moscow.

During the ensuing days, I visited my father daily alone; a week would elapse before he agreed to see Essie. My goal was simply to engage him in conversation to the extent that I could and make him comfortable talking to me, as he was suspicious of everyone. Under the circumstances, I decided not to question him about what had happened, and he made no mention of his suicide attempt or what drove him to it. However, weeks later, while he was in Barkheeva Sanitorium, during one of our conversations, my father revealed some details about what had taken place in his suite. People at the party in his suite kept coming up to him with pleas for assistance: could he help them get a close relative released from a prison camp? The other typical request was, "Please, for the love of God, help me to emigrate from here." But my father didn't add any more and cut off our conversation about the events that had caused his panic.

I had no knowledge of a drug test performed at the hospital, but my suspicion that my father had been drugged was still strong. The opportunities for such an attempt abounded at the odd party in his suite. Furthermore, back home, the Communist Party leadership had warned us to be on the alert for drugging attempts because there had been some strange nervous breakdowns among party members.[7]

On April 12, Soviet astronaut Yuri Gagarin orbited the earth as the first person in outer space. The next day, my mother and I received tickets to the Kremlin reception celebrating this historic event. Once inside, she caught the eye of Anastas Mikoyan, a top party leader, and he immediately dispatched an aide to escort us into the official reception area. Mikoyan inquired about Paul, and we chatted for a moment before joining the reception line to pay our respects to Premier Khrushchev and his wife.

I was struck by the Krushchevs' attention to us and concern for Paul. They conveyed their warmest greetings and wishes for his speedy recovery. Then we circulated, with Essie leading the way to various high Soviet officials whom she and Paul had met on previous trips. Few spoke much English, so I served as simultaneous translator. My mother was impressive, remembering all of their names, positions, and the circumstances under which she had met them. Clearly, the Robesons continued to be held in high esteem by the Soviet government.

During my father's hospitalization, my mother and I met with his three-man medical team, headed by Dr. A. V. Snezhnevsky, the Soviet Union's chief psychiatrist. Snezhnevsky summarized the diagnosis as "paranoiac psychosis" with depressive symptoms, probably caused by acute anxiety and intensified by "arteriosclerosis." There was also some "dilation" of his heart, which had caused "hypertrophy of the left ventricle." The condition was not deemed to be serious; his recovery had been good, and he could expect to live a normal private life. However, they strongly recommended that he retire from his professional career with its attendant stress, and return home to his native United States.

I translated simultaneously for my mother and expressed my agreement with their recommendations. She asked two questions. The first was whether it would be wise for Paul to return to the United States, where he had been so severely persecuted. Snezhnevsky replied that the most important thing for Paul now was to inhabit the most familiar environment possible. He should be among his own people. Her next question startled me. If Paul suffered a serious relapse, would electroshock (electroconvulsive) treatments be appropriate? The answer came sharply and clearly from all three doctors: "Under no circumstances should this patient be subjected to such treatments." Essie noted that in the West such treatment was common in cases like Paul's. Snezhnevsky replied that while there was controversy over this issue in the West, in the Soviet Union no psychiatric hospital would administer electroconvulsive therapy to a patient in Paul's condition. His deputy added that "we would consider this to be malpractice." Snezhnevsky moved on to discuss the immediate future, recommending that Paul go to the Barveekha Sanatorium for two months and then return home to the United States. The meeting was over.

A few days later, I met with a member of the Central Committee named Mostovoi, a Khrushchev loyalist, and his associate who represented the Central Committee's Security Division. We conversed entirely in Russian, although the security person spoke English well. I asked them whether my father's blood test at the hospital had revealed any trace of drugs. They said they had been told no but could not confirm. Mostovoi explained that "another department" was handling this matter—one that "our people" did not directly control. Moreover, Paul's announcement that he was planning to visit Cuba had introduced a complication that involved the "other department," since "tension between the United States and Cuba had reached a crisis." He implied that there was also tension within the top Soviet leadership over this issue. It seemed that Paul had inadvertently stepped into the center of an intensifying cold war duel. I wondered if the "other department" performing the investigation was the KGB (Committee for State Security), which might be covering up what had happened to Paul.

Mostovoi's comments became far clearer in hindsight. Paul had arrived in Moscow just a month before the CIA launched its invasion of Cuba at the Bay of Pigs. Soviet intelligence was aware of the preparations for the invasion, and the Soviet leadership was divided on how to respond and what policy to pursue toward Cuba. Moreover, the Khrushchev loyalists did not control the KGB. Alexander Shelepin, the KGB head in 1961, had ties to the conservatives opposing the premier. I believe they guaranteed Paul's security as long as he was in the Soviet Union but apparently covered up what happened in his suite and concealed Paul's "breakdown" for the dual purpose of protecting his reputation and avoiding an embarrassment to the Soviet Union.

I saved my questions about the party in Paul's hotel suite till last. When I asked Mostovi about the party attendees who had implored my father to help free their relatives from prison camps or to help them emigrate, he replied, "These are not Soviet people." However, they assured me that my father was now completely secure and "in safe hands."

I expressed my opinion that he should travel home directly from Moscow, without going to London first. They agreed but became agitated when I expressed a desire to investigate whether my father had been drugged. For example, had any trace of drugs been found in his blood? Mostovoi leaned forward, speaking in a friendly but serious tone. "We urgently advise you to leave it alone. We can't help you in that regard, and it would be unwise for you to attempt it on your own." On this note, we parted cordially.

I decided to have a frank talk with my mother that evening. I told her what I thought. The party in his suite was arranged and imposed on him by a Western intelligence agent in the Soviet government; he was drugged and driven to suicidal paranoia. The incident was then covered up by the KGB to save him and the Soviet Union huge embarrassment. If this or a similar scenario was false, then why the lack of curiosity about what happened at the party? Why was there no investigation of how it occurred and who was there? Why did no one at the party report that he had locked himself in an inner room? Essie heard me out and then dismissed everything I said. I should calm down, she admonished. I was getting to be as paranoid as my father. In any case, the main thing was not to tell anyone about what had happened. She demanded that I pledge not to do so. I agreed.

The FBI documents I subsequently received show heightened interest in Paul's proposed trip to Cuba. An April 3, 1961 FBI memorandum to Director Hoover from the "Legal Attaché" in the U.S. embassy in Moscow mentions a letter submitted by the legal attaché on March 28, 1961, which says he is on the "alert for any indication re. travel to Cuba," and indicates he also alerted an unnamed person outside the Bureau.

An April 7, 1961, FBI memorandum, heavily redacted, speculates about Paul's death: "In view of the past exploitation of Robeson's popularity by the communists to further their aims, it is expected that the death of Robeson would be much publicized, and that his name and past history would be highlighted even more in propagandizing on behalf of the international communist movement. We will, of course, continue to follow his activities closely."[8]

On April 17, a force of Cuban exiles armed and trained by the United States invaded Cuba at the Bay of Pigs. The operation was a disaster. Of the 1,543-man invasion force, 114 were killed and 1,189 taken prisoner. The rest were being hunted down in the swamps. Both Richard Bissell and Allen Dulles were fired, and the CIA was shaken up. But Richard Helms, who oversaw MKULTRA and had targeted Paul, remained firmly in place. Paul had been immobilized just twenty-two days before the CIA's invasion of Cuba. The CIA knew he intended to visit Cuba from Moscow and it would seem likely that they would not want him there as they prepared for the invasion. All of this contributed to my belief that he had been subjected to a CIA "hit."

A few days later, my mother and I attended a festive banquet organized by our hosts in the hotel dining room. Toward the end of the evening I requested some tea. I had drunk about a third of it when I suddenly began to feel anxious. I excused myself and went up to my room.

Once there, I settled down to write a letter home and felt fine. I finished the letter and turned on the radio for the late news. As I listened to the commentator's voice, it turned into Lenin's speaking at the 1918 Congress of the Bolshevik Party. I switched to a music station, but the program appeared to change into a U.S. military broadcast describing a nuclear test in the Pacific islands. I turned off the radio and tried television. As I settled back to watch a French movie with Russian subtitles, the faces of the actors changed into those of people I knew. Switching to a news program, I experienced the same kind of changing identities on the screen. I realized I had been drugged and was hallucinating. I recalled that the waiter who had served me the tea had looked oddly out of place.

I set about systematically resisting the effects of the drug. I was able to get through the night, even managing several hours of sleep. In the morning, my anxiety level ratcheted up relentlessly. Suddenly there were loud knocks on the door and I froze in terror. I heard the concierge's key in the door and panicked. Picking up a chair, I turned toward the French doors leading to the terrace and hurled the chair through them. I started toward the terrace to escape but then whirled toward the door, which framed Essie and the concierge. I dashed past them down five flights of stairs and out into the street.

It was a sunny spring morning. I felt exhilarated and weightless. After I had walked a bit, people began to look strange to me—I saw auras ("halos") of various colors around their heads, and apparently could "see" their true character. I saw a barbershop and got a haircut, then ate at a cafeteria, standing at a counter for fear that I might have to make a quick getaway. I went back onto the street, which was now crowded because it was lunch hour. Waves of fear started to wash over me, and I decided to return to the hotel for help. It seemed that I weighed a ton.

When I arrived, a car, three hospital orderlies in white coats, and my mother were waiting for me. I surrendered to the straitjacket without resistance. The orderlies hustled me into the backseat of the car with one on either side of me and Essie in the right front seat.

When I woke up in the hospital a day later after horrendous nightmares, I was still paranoid, trusting only the nurse who was by my bedside when I opened my eyes. I gradually came to trust my doctors, but a full week elapsed before I agreed to see my mother. By the end of my first week of the standard three-week stay in cases like mine, I had determined that I was in a KGB psychiatric hospital for intelligence personnel, police detectives, and foreign Communist Party leaders.

Twice a week I was visited by a psychiatrist who routinely asked me whether my hallucinations and "fantasies" had left me, and I duly replied that I had fewer hallucinations but still held some "fantasies." He seemed satisfied with my answers, replying that I could leave as soon as I had none left. Meanwhile, I was to continue to take my medication. His message was clear: as soon as I agreed to deny what had happened to me, I was free to go. At the end of the third week, he said I could join my parents at Barveekha if I renounced all of my fantasies and passed a departure test. The test would be to summarize in a written report the editorial in the latest issue of the Communist Party's theoretical journal *Kommunist*. I did so, and two days later I was at Barveekha.[9]

My parents had preceded me to the sanatorium about ten days before. My father was, as far as I could tell, almost the same as when I had seen him in London in 1959. He circulated comfortably with the other guests, and his relationship with me followed familiar patterns. His quarters were separated from Essie's by a staff room, and she was not trying to crowd him. Outwardly there were no visible signs of tension. My relationship with my mother was acted out as if the recent events had never happened.

On my private walks with my father, we talked about many things but never mentioned his collapse. We did talk quite a bit about his future plans. Would he consider returning home directly from Moscow rather than going first to London? He said no, he would go back to London while he and Essie wound up their affairs there, and then go home to Jumel Terrace to pick up where he had left off in 1958. His determination to return home was clear.

In mid-May, Paul met with the Chinese ambassador, who had been insistent about seeing him and Essie, and I joined them along with a high-ranking member of the Russian Foreign Ministry. Paul greeted the ambassador and his aides warmly and even included the appropriate Chinese salutation.

The ambassador, after inquiring about Paul's health, extended a formal invitation to visit China and continue his recuperation there.

After some discussion, the first sign of tension arose in an exchange between the ambassador and the Soviet official. Paul intervened, saying he had decided to complete his recuperation at Barveekha. Only then would he determine whether to return home directly or travel first. And if he did travel, he would certainly visit China as he had been wishing to do for years. The ambassador was far from satisfied. The parting was pleasant, yet a touch strained. For me, the significance of the meeting lay in the evidence of Paul's continuing ability to participate in a diplomatic conversation.

While at Barveekha, I had plenty of time to ponder events. Assuming my father and I had been victims of CIA drugging, who could have been involved? However, since none of it could be verified, I resolved to keep it all to myself. Mostovoi had been right—there was nothing I could do except help my father get home. Not that I could accomplish much in that regard either, because officially I had suffered a "nervous breakdown." I flew home on June 2, after almost two months.

Soon after my return I went to see Dr. Joseph Furst, the psychiatrist who had seen Paul in 1956. He heard me out and asked a few routine questions about my previous mental health. His evaluation was noncommittal. His advice was clear. In his view, with no history of previous breakdowns, my symptoms could not have been caused by any known organic ("endogenous") condition. They were almost certainly due to a temporary chemical imbalance in the brain. That was as specific as he would get, and it was good enough for me.

On June 10, Paul was pronounced in "good condition" and discharged from Barveekha Sanatorium in Essie's custody. Over the next month, he appeared to be back to normal, rehearsing regularly with Larry and seriously contemplating a trip to Ghana. (Kwame Nkrumah had sent him letters on May 10 and June 21, 1961.) His voice, according to Essie, was "unimpaired," and he decided to pursue his previous plans for a limited career based on radio, television, and recording, with an occasional new-format concert. Less than two weeks later, however, despite this promising start, Paul relapsed into an anxiety-driven depressed state accompanied by almost total immobilization. Not one to temporize in a crisis, Essie wisely made an immediate decision to take him back to the Moscow hospital, where they arrived on July 24. On August 2, Paul was discharged, once again, to Barveekha, accompanied by Essie.[10]

On July 31, Essie wrote the Rosens that Paul was much improved. They remained skeptical. In mid-August, following attendance at a medical conference in Romania, they visited Paul and Essie in Barveekha. Essie told them that Paul had suffered a recurrence of his 1956 "breakdown" and that it was a by-product of "nervous exhaustion." According to Helen, they were "appalled" at his depressed state. In early September, the Barveekha doctors pronounced him in good condition and were ready to discharge him. On September 5, Essie wrote Marilyn and me that she and Paul were flying back to London that day.[11]

Between mid-July and mid-September, the highest levels of the U.S. government took an extraordinary interest in Paul's "health status." On July 21, 1961, the day Essie made arrangements to take him back to Moscow, an FBI memorandum was sent to Hoover by the FBI's London legal attaché concerning the combined cases of Paul Robeson, Eslanda Robeson, and Paul Robeson Jr. The entire substantive portion of the memorandum has been redacted, leaving only the statement that my case was placed on a less active list than my parents' case because I had returned to the United States. A hand-printed note under the last paragraph, signed with Hoover's initial, reads, "Info Re. Robeson's Health Status previously furnished State, CIA, AG [attorney general] & White House under 'Top Secret' classification." A September 6, 1961, FBI memorandum cites the CIA intercept of Essie's September 5, 1961, letter to Marilyn and me. Clearly, the U.S. and British intelligence agencies were closely monitoring every move my parents and I made.[12]

Within days of my parents' return from Moscow to London for the second time, Paul's anxiety level rose to an incapacitating level. Essie, in desperation, called Helen Rosen in New York for urgent help. Helen arrived in London the next day and found Paul terrified, "positively cowering" in fear. However, the option of taking an immediate flight back to Moscow appeared to be far too risky.[13]

Essie called Harold Davison, who recommended his personal physician, Dr. Philip Lebon. When Essie explained Paul's situation to Lebon over the telephone, he recommended immediate hospitalization at the top-rated Priory psychiatric hospital just a half-hour drive from Connaught Square. Essie agreed, and they managed to get Paul dressed and safely into the backseat of the five-passenger Priory car between herself and Helen. Apparently he went voluntarily and was signed into the hospital for observation without incident. Lebon recommended Dr. Brian Ackner from Maudsley Hospital as the consulting psychiatrist, and Essie, with Helen's support, accepted.[14]

Lebon's choice was questionable. Ackner, forty-two years old, was famous for his definitive work on insulin coma and on "depersonalization" in chronic depressives and was a consultant for the Maudsley Institute of Psychiatry. He was not known as an expert clinician and Paul had not been diagnosed as a chronic depressive. Both Lebon and Ackner failed to contact the Soviet doctors who had recently treated Paul on two occasions. Nor did they contact Dr. Pearlmutter, Paul's primary physician in the United States, to obtain Paul's previous medical history. Based exclusively on information provided by Essie and Helen, who appeared to believe that he was a chronic depressive, and one examination of him on September 15, they proceeded to diagnose and treat Paul.

After being refused repeatedly over a span of almost two decades, I finally obtained my father's Priory medical records in 1998 through the intervention of a friend in the United Kingdom. Much of what I subsequently describe about my father's treatment there is obtained from these documents.

A September 18, 1961, letter from Dr. Brian Ackner to Dr. Philip Lebon described Paul's history as told by Essie and Helen. In the same letter, Dr. Ackner refers to Paul as "the patient whom we visited together at his home on the 15th September." However, Essie and Helen made no mention of Lebon's and Ackner's presence at Connaught Square at the time or subsequently. Apparently, Paul was not examined until after he had voluntarily arrived at the Priory.

Then Dr. Ackner writes, "It was unsafe for [Paul] to remain at home and as he would not agree to enter hospital voluntarily, he was admitted under Section 25 of the Mental Health Act to the Priory on the same day that we saw him together." The admission form signed by Ackner and Lebon "warrants Paul's detention in a hospital for at least a limited period" and asserts that "informal admission is not appropriate in this case." This meant that he was legally in Essie's custody—only she could sign him out of the hospital.

The notes written by the admitting staff psychiatrist, Dr. O'Connor, raise even more serious questions. Paul is described as "a somewhat cyclothymic personality all during their married life—morose, depressed and elated at times." The description goes on to assert that Paul "always declined responsibility" and was "not a good interpersonal mixer on an individual basis." This distorted personal portrait reflected Essie's subjective biases.

Dr. O'Connor's provisional diagnosis was "chronic depressive state with severe delusional background with marked apprehension. Suicidal. He should benefit from E.C.T. [electroconvulsive therapy] and largactil." Ackner's September 18 letter to Lebon ends with the observation that "after a discussion with Dr. Flood, the Medical Director, it was agreed that there was a good chance that Mr. Robeson's condition would respond to E.C.T. and that there was no reason to delay the treatment." Since Paul's admission was stated as being for "observation," it is noteworthy that the decision to use ECT was made during his first examination.

The Priory records reveal that on September 15, 1961, on the same day Lebon and Ackner examined Paul, apparently for the first time, Essie signed a consent form for "a course of E.C.T." to be administered to Paul. Two days later, a course of eight such treatments was begun, and on October 26 Essie signed another consent form for a second course, which ended on January 5, 1962. Helen supported Essie's decisions.

Two other items in Dr. O'Connor's notes stood out. He listed a Dr. Kerinan as Paul's personal physician. However, Essie had called in Lebon instead, with whom Paul apparently had no prior relationship. O'Connor also listed Essie's roster of contacts and approved visitors. The contacts were Dr. Barsky, the Rosens, and Harold Davison. Bob Rockmore and I were excluded. The visitors were reduced to two—Harry Francis and Harold Davison, who were associates rather than personal friends. His friends, including Andy and Larry, were excluded, isolating Paul from much of his world.

Helen stayed for a month, living at the flat and often accompanying Essie on her daily visits to the Priory, helping carry home-cooked meals for him and keeping him company. My mother's letters to Marilyn and me stressed Paul's improvement and noted that Helen was staying with her to help and support her and Paul, but they told us nothing about Paul's electroconvulsive treatments. At the beginning of November, two weeks after Helen had returned from

London, Sam visited Paul, talked to Dr. Ackner and Dr. Flood, who was the resident psychiatrist in charge of Paul's case, and concluded that Paul was in good hands.

Paul's Priory files provide a detailed record of his treatment and progress during that first month. By October 8, after six courses of ECT and regular doses of the tranquilizer Largactil, his depression was "clearing" and he was "able to smile and laugh." Ten days later the record closed with the comment, "He is friendly, although I have no doubt that some justifiable paranoid ideation might emerge if the question of the 'color-bar' were raised; he has shown no paranoid affect towards patients or staff during his stay here."

Despite this major improvement, Paul was administered nine additional courses of ECT between October 18 and December 23, when he was permitted to go home for a trial period. Dr. Flood described Paul's ten-day Christmas "leave" as a "success," noting that "he was showing signs of interest in his music and career again. I would not say that the patient is completely well yet, as he still has to rely on quite substantial doses of Paraldehyde at night." This drug—a powerful hypnotic—was designed to treat manic-depressives who suffered from an organic depressive condition for which Paul had not been previously diagnosed. His successful treatment on two occasions in Moscow with the low-potency antipsychotic drugs Largactil and Nozinan, combined with a compatible environment, appears to contradict the diagnosis of the Priory physicians.[15]

On January 4, 1962, a week after Paul's Christmas leave had been declared a success, he was readmitted to the Priory because "he has become depressed and complains of severe insomnia." Dr. Flood noted that Paul had lost weight and recommended an antipsychotic and a powerful antidepressant (modified insulin and large doses of Tofranil), combined with an "occasional" course of ECT. He drew the conclusion that Paul was in "a severe depressive cycle occurring in the middle of a long-drawn out depressive state which has already lasted a year, and could well last another year."

By the end of January, Paul "became very depressed, with suicidal ruminations, severe anorexia, and early waking in spite of heavy sedation." Two weeks later, he had been given two courses of ECT, which resulted in "much improvement in his spontaneity, his sleep and his mood." The doctors concluded that "one has to consider Mr. Robeson as a very long-term problem, and that courses of E.C.T. would have to be given at times of his acute depressive swings." Since none of the antidepressant drugs lifted Paul's depression, they prescribed ECT as the only remedy.

His "up" periods were marked by visits to the Connaught Square flat, but he could sustain these for only three or four days at a time. There he was dependent on Essie and essentially isolated from others. This environment contrasted sharply with that of Barveekha where a community atmosphere was provided. During his visits to the flat, he expressed a strong desire to socialize, apparently enjoying the experience when given the opportunity. This desire was manifested even during the extended periods for which he was confined to the Priory.[16]

On one occasion, he asked to accompany Essie when she went to see Ella Fitzgerald perform with Coleman Hawkins's orchestra. Paul was enjoying Ella's performance when, to his surprise, she stepped forward and dedicated a song to a "fellow-artist and very great man, Paul Robeson, wherever he may be sitting." Unfazed, Paul happily signed autographs for the people seated near him. After the concert, he asked to go backstage to thank Ella. Overjoyed, Ella told him this was a big day in her life and she was happy to see him out of the hospital. Paul told her how much he enjoyed the concert and chatted with her about her music. Then Essie and Davison took him back to the Priory.

Just four days later, Paul and Essie went to the theater to see Peggy Ashcroft with John Gielgud in Anton Chekhov's *The Cherry Orchard*. Paul again went confidently backstage. Ashcroft asked all her other visitors to leave her dressing room, and she and Paul had a fairly long chat about the play, as well as Paul's Stratford *Othello*. Paul promised he would do a poetry reading with her the following year.

On another occasion, Paul apparently attended a jazz concert, since he was photographed, smiling happily and looking fairly fit, between Sarah Vaughan and Miles Davis. During the 1962 Christmas holidays, he went to hear Elizabeth Welch, his costar in the films *Song of Freedom* and *Big Fella*, sing a concert. According to Welch, he came backstage for a nostalgic reunion. She recalled an air of resigned sadness about him when I spoke with her almost twenty years later.

He wasn't nearly his "old self" but yet was "unmistakably Paul." She also remembered his strong desire to go "home to his folks."[17]

On March 1, 1962, Paul wrote a letter to his sister, Marian, saying that he felt much better. On the same day, he wrote to the Rockmores to announce he might come over soon; he had "turned the corner" and "was sure" he would be "alright from here on in." Despite Paul's demonstrated pleasure in briefly stepping into the sunlight of public recognition, Essie and the doctors did not encourage him to socialize. Essie insisted that Paul didn't want people to think he was accessible, even though he "felt fine."

The pattern of Paul's treatments, the frequency of his ECT over a period of twenty months (about ten days apart, averaged over five courses totaling fifty-four), as well as the number and variety of powerful drugs that were administered (antipsychotics, including insulin coma with doses of 10 to 50 units of insulin, antianxiety drugs, and antidepressants), alarmed me when I read the Priory records in 1998. The ECT was administered whenever Paul showed initial signs of depression, to bring him out of it, and immediately following major improvement in his behavior. The powerful anti-depressants were prescribed continuously, despite their failure, by the doctors' admission, to provide any benefit.[18]

I found this combined treatment especially troubling, because it resembled the "mind depatterning" treatment funded by the MKULTRA Project, which consisted of "intensive electroshocks, usually combined with prolonged, drug-induced sleep." The similarity is noteworthy because by early 1962 Richard Helms, the creator of the MKULTRA Project, had been elevated to the post of deputy director of plans and was in direct communication with Hoover concerning Paul's health.[19]

On April 9, Paul received greetings from around the world celebrating his sixty-fourth birthday. Messages arrived from Ghana, Russia, the Movement for Colonial Freedom, Cuba, China, Hungary, East Germany, Poland, Romania, Bulgaria, and from many individual admirers. The following day, President Nkrumah offered Paul a visiting professorship at the University of Ghana, causing a flurry of anxiety at the U.S. State Department. Secretary of State Dean Rusk approved a diplomatic effort to convince the government of Ghana that such an appointment "would have very unfavorable repercussions in the U.S." Paul declined on the basis of his health, but allowed his name to be used in connection with the university.[20]

The Priory entry on April 24 reported that Paul had suffered another "depressive relapse" and had responded well enough to "E.C.T. and Tofranil" to "return home over Easter" and remain well. However, three hypnotic antianxiety drugs—paraldehyde, Seconal, and Nembutal—were added to the Tofranil and Largactil he was already taking. By May, he had been placed on what amounted to maintenance ECT, which was destined to continue throughout the remainder of his stay, augmented by treatment with an array of powerful drugs.

Paul preserved his personality throughout his ordeal. Whenever his depression lifted, he regained his interest in the black civil rights struggle in the United States, as well as his desire to return home. And even after a total of fifty-four courses of ECT, his memory was not seriously impaired. His notes to family, the Rockmores, and the Rosens were invariably upbeat, stressing his belief in his ultimate recovery.

On May 18, Essie visited the U.S. embassy in London to renew her passport and Paul's. She was told that Paul would have to appear in person to submit his application. The following week, bolstered by a support network of friends, Paul answered all the questions asked of him and returned to the Priory in good spirits. The Rockmores, who were in London for a visit, rode in the car with Paul and Essie and contributed greatly to his improved demeanor.[21]

In mid-July, Essie received a letter from the U.S. embassy informing her that the State Department required both her and Paul to sign noncommunist affidavits in person before their passport applications would be considered. Essie went to the embassy promptly and signed an affidavit. Her statement was comprehensive and emphatic:

> Referring to the letter from the American Embassy of July 10, 1962, I hereby state categorically and without any reservations whatsoever, that I am not now, and have never been in all my life, a member of the Communist Party, United States of America, or in any other country. NEVER!

Paul, determined not to compromise his principles, refused to sign an affidavit or even to appear in person again at the embassy. Essie appealed for help to their friend John Abt, a leading lawyer for the

U.S. Communist Party, and to Ben Davis. They convinced Paul to sign because the U.S. passport battle had shifted to guaranteeing the travel rights of openly declared party members. They assured him that the entire party leadership was in agreement with them. Paul remained reluctant, but he finally agreed to sign a greatly watered-down statement on July 25:

> I, Paul Robeson, am not now a member of the Communist Party, U.S.A. and I have not been a member thereof at any time during the twelve months proceeding May 25, 1962, the date of application for a passport.[22]

More visitors were added to the visitor list in August, and Paul enjoyed them all. Essie's letters home were now full of optimism about his condition. He was staying at the flat for three and four days at a time, with Dr. Lebon, who lived nearby, monitoring his medication. According to Essie, Paul was "nearing the end of his nightmare; and in a month or two at the most, he will be really well again. He is much, much better, and has enjoyed being home." Although my mother prevented me from speaking to my father, his visitors, including the Rockmores and the Rosen family, gave me the impression that he was gradually improving, echoing Essie's optimistic reports.[23]

The doctors apparently did not agree with Essie's evaluation. While Paul was manifesting a strong, albeit uneven recovery, he continued to receive powerful antidepressant drugs in combination with ECT. On August 23, Flood wrote to Ackner that Paul had recently been given "one E.C.T.," and that he had been put on "a combination of Steladex [an amphetamine] and Parstelin without beneficial effect." As a replacement for these drugs, Flood suggested Marsalid, an even more powerful medication with dangerous side effects: "I have had further discussions with Mrs. Robeson and I think that she is quite willing to take a risk with Marsalid, but we will be discussing this with you next week." Essie referred to this in a September 1 letter to Helen's daughter Judy: "Paul has been here at home since Friday, August 24th, and goes back to the nursing home on Monday evening to begin a series of treatments, NOT E.C.T, on a new drug which is a strong antidepressant."[24]

Paul's Priory records for September and October show intensive drug therapy, including Marsalid and insulin coma treatments, and a new course of seven ECTs was begun on October 23, _1962_ Peggy Middleton, who visited him at the flat over the 1962 Christmas holidays, wrote that "this time we gossiped for almost an hour and I felt happy about it. Essie felt the break-through had been made." Paul, however, returned to the Priory four days later.[25] Claiming that continued ECT was necessary to prevent mood swings, the Priory doctors began a further course of twelve treatments on January 9, 1963, that was to last until May 16. After twenty months, Paul was still confined to the Priory.

14

A TEMPORARY REPRIEVE

(1963–1965)

In late January 1963, a friend sent me the January 6 and 13 issues of the *National Insider*, Chicago's weekly scandal tabloid. They featured a two-part article under the byline "Paul Robeson," along with the editors' claim that they had given Paul "a platform to tell the story no other paper dared print."

The piece was a total fabrication: "I was a Communist for a long time. I did it of my own free will because of certain convictions I had. And at times, I have also been a socialist and a Fascist. I am ashamed of being a Fascist, but not of being a socialist or Communist. I only regret what these philosophies led me to do." Then the counterfeit Paul Robeson belittles his artistic career, caricatures his minister father ("the loudest minister in the state of New Jersey"), and demeans black culture. The article ends with a rejection of the Soviet Union: "I reject the Soviet Union's type of Communism, and I think that if ever my people and other minorities become completely free and equal, it will happen in this country [the United States]."

This attempt to market a counterfeit Robeson was reminiscent of the State Department's 1951 plot to create the false public image of a "tragic" figure "duped" by the communists. However, this time the crudity of the effort pointed to Hoover's FBI. I showed the article to Ben Davis. We concluded that its publication probably signaled the beginning of a campaign by the FBI to discredit Paul while he was ill, vulnerable, and presumably unable to speak for himself. The story was not picked up by the U.S. press, but in early May the major French conservative newspaper *Le Figaro* reprinted the series. A response was necessary, preferably from Essie. After extensive consultation, she issued a highly effective statement that was widely reported:

> These articles are pure fabrication. They were not written by Paul Robeson. None of us have seen any indication that he has changed his political views in any way. Everybody who knows anything about Paul Robeson knows what his political views are; he has never made any secret of them and has always proudly proclaimed them. However, what did disturb us was the vicious attack on the Negro Church through the person of Paul Robeson's beloved father, the late Reverend William Drew Robeson. Anyone in his right mind would recognize this as an insult to the Negro Church. Certainly no one would really believe that Paul Robeson had written such a libel.[1]

As Ben and I talked, we agreed it was time to begin preparations for Paul to leave the Priory and come home. This was in part based on my suspicion and concern that my father was receiving ECT. Aroused by the secrecy surrounding the nature of his treatment at the Priory, I recalled my mother's query of the Soviet doctors in 1961 concerning the possibility of its use. (Although I have been describing in some detail his course of ECT and drug treatment throughout this period, I learned about it only over the ensuing years.)

A plan for Paul's departure from the Priory, arranging a convalescence stay at a combined hospital-sanatorium in a Soviet Bloc country, and, finally, his return home was necessary. The requirements of finding a new venue and a stimulating social environment in a country where he would be comfortable narrowed the choice to the German Democratic Republic. The East Germans loved Paul, he spoke German well, and their medical facilities were top-notch. Moreover, they stressed the social/environmental approach to psychiatry. The key to transferring Paul would be persuading Essie, in addition to Ed Barsky, the Rosens, and the Rockmores. Ben and I set December 1, 1963, as the tentative target date.

A January 28, 1963, letter from Essie to family and friends sounded an unusually positive note:

> On Saturday afternoon Harry Fra.ncis called at the Priory, as usual, to visit Paul in the afternoon. He took along Philip Lebon, who put us in touch with his present consultant.

So we all settled down to tea and a short chat. Philip got into music, with Paul listening very eagerly and with great interest. We were all deep into music. Paul made some comments on all this; sang some excerpts from Boris [*Boris Godunov*, the Mussorgsky opera] and some Negro spirituals to illustrate his fundamental idea: speech into music. It was thrilling to see him first really interested and enjoying himself, then participating, then contributing.

Just as I was planning to talk to Bob Rockmore about our decision to bring Paul home, he died of a sudden heart attack while on a trip to Philadelphia. Clara was devastated but responded courageously, organizing the funeral service and making sure that business matters were taken care of. The loss of Bob was a heavy blow for Paul to withstand, and Essie waited over a month to tell him. A brief February 7 letter from Essie to Clara reported that Paul was once again "in a down cycle," and that the doctors had advised a delay in telling him about Bobby. On March 19, she wrote again, saying she had just told Paul. He wrote a letter to Clara that same day:

My darling, darling Clarochka—I send you so, so much love. Just heard today about our beloved Bobby. Seems such a strange world already. Thanks to you for your courage and fortitude. And thanks for your letters. They mean a great deal. Take care of yourself—I'll do the best I can. Things are going much better here. Sleep is still difficult, but I'm used to it. In general, all goes much better. Will be spending more time at home and eventually will leave the nursing home.

Often think of the day it will be possible to start for New York and home and Clarochka. How strange it will be without Bobby. It seems so long since I was there with you all. My first stop will be to see my darling Clarochka. Let us hope that one day not too distant, I shall be fully recovered and able to help and not be a burden.

Much, much love, always. Letter or no letter, I think of you constantly. Take precious care of yourself as I know you will. Your adoring

Pavlik

Essie organized a flurry of greetings to Paul on his sixty-fifth birthday, April 9, 1963. Ironically, all the attention caused Paul to worry about whether too much would be expected of him and that demands would be made of him that he could not meet. On April 7,

Essie wrote to Helen that Paul has "been going down—not bad down, but down." She had talked at length with Ackner, who told her not to worry—it was "all part of the picture." He believed that Paul "couldn't go too far back," and that the setbacks were just temporary." Ending her letter, Essie added, "Of course, I will say nothing of this to Pauli."

At my urging, Dr. Barsky convened a meeting at his East Side Manhattan apartment in early May. I was present, along with the Rosens; Dr. Pearlmutter; Barsky's wife, Vita; Dr. Elliott Hurwitt, a Columbia University clinical professor of surgery; and his wife, Claire (Micki), a former psychiatric nurse. The Hurwitts were acquainted with Helen from the Progressive Party days.

Barsky opened the meeting with the proposition that Paul's eighteen months of treatment at the Priory had been relatively unsuccessful. The Buch Clinic in East Berlin was the medical facility that he and Dr. Pearlmutter recommended. Elliott Hurwitt, who had visited the clinic and was familiar with some of its leading personnel, strongly supported the idea. I spoke of the Soviet doctors' strong warning against treating Paul with ECT, as well as of their successful treatment based on a diagnosis rejecting the view that Paul was a chronic bipolar depressive. I also said that the Buch Clinic appeared to provide an environment similar to Barveekha, where Paul had done so well.[2]

By the middle of May, Essie, prodded by Peggy Middleton and increasingly by Harry Francis, began to express doubts about ECT and decided to have the treatments temporarily suspended. By June, Micki Hurwitt arrived in London and introduced herself to Essie with a recommendation from Ed Barsky. She won Essie's confidence in part because of her professional experience and was soon accorded official access to Paul at the Priory. Her observations were essential in convincing Essie that Paul had to be moved to the Buch Clinic.

Micki was alarmed by the smell of paraldehyde in Paul's room—a powerful drug she believed should be administered only to desperately ill patients. His medical chart listing the daily array of high-dosage drugs horrified her. She also noted a serious deterioration in Paul's physical state, indicating neglect in his care. She urged Essie to lose no time in getting Paul to East Berlin. Micki's husband arrived soon after and came to the same conclusion.[3]

The final step in Essie's conversion to the idea of moving Paul was her trip to East Berlin to visit the Buch Clinic. She was favorably impressed by the facility and the staff—especially by Dr. Alfred Katzenstein, a U.S.-trained clinical psychologist who had treated survivors of the death camps during his World War II service in the U.S. Army. Having arranged a tentative September 1 date for Paul's transfer, Essie discussed the plan with Paul. He wanted to go right away and made it clear that from Berlin he wanted to return to the United States. The wheels were set in motion for his departure.[4]

Essie booked an August 25 flight to Berlin on Polish Airways. The British press got wind of this and launched a campaign to interview Paul about his reported change of political views. Reporters placed a watch at the Connaught Square apartment and the Priory. Essie packed, and helped organize a carefully coordinated operation to get Paul onto the plane without encountering the media.

The U.S. State Department had apparently been instrumental in launching the campaign by the London press to intercept Paul before he departed. An August 22 memorandum from the U.S. Information Agency office in London to the department confirms this collaboration:

> The Agency is still interested in confirmation that Paul Robeson has soured on the Soviet Union and Marxism. A direct interview with Robeson is not suggested, but a story attributed to a reliable British newspaper would be most useful.

The memorandum was signed by Edward R. Murrow, who headed the agency at that time. On the morning of Paul's departure, the London *Sunday Telegraph* carried a lead story written to Murrow's specification.[5]

Although Paul had been recently subjected to a series of heavy drug dosages, he was calm and ready to face the ordeal of avoiding the press while departing from familiar surroundings. His transfer from the Priory was carried out with military precision and near-perfect teamwork by Harry Francis, who took care of getting Paul out of the Priory; Peggy Middleton and Diana Loesser, who handled Paul and Essie's eleven pieces of luggage; Nick Price, a young American friend of Essie's, who provided transportation for Peggy and Diana with the luggage; and Essie, who skillfully outmaneuvered the press.

On the night before departure, Middleton, Loesser, and Price deposited the luggage at Paddington Railway Station for delivery to the airport the next day. At the appointed time, Harry Francis, accompanied by several friends, drove to the Priory, escorted Paul out through the rear entrance and onto the floor of the car where he could not be seen as they passed the gathered army of reporters. Paul was calm, cooperative, and sure-footed. They headed to a wooded road for the scheduled rendezvous and Essie and Micki arrived, as planned, in Nick Price's car after eluding the reporters besieging Connaught Square. Francis's car was waiting and headed for the airport. There they were met by the director of Polish Airways, who had just steered the press to the VIP lounge. He led Paul, Essie, and Micki, who accompanied them on the flight, through the regular gate out to the first-class compartment before the reporters realized they had been tricked. A few minutes later, the plane took off, and Paul and Essie relaxed.[6]

As soon as they were in the air, Essie handed Paul the *Telegraph* article, which Paul read with interest and a sardonic smile. Later, he was approached by a pleasant young man who had been sitting a few seats away and identified himself as a reporter for the same newspaper. Essie rushed to intervene, but Paul appeared willing to speak to the man. Essie limited the reporter to two questions, which Paul answered eloquently. Asked what he thought of the previous day's *Telegraph* article, Paul replied that it was a vicious falsification, he had not in any way changed his political views, and he looked forward to his East Berlin visit. He answered a question about the situation of blacks in the United States with a comment that the recently held March on Washington, led by Reverend King, was symbolic of a "turning point for the Negro people in America." The reporter included Paul's answers accurately in his story published in the *Telegraph* on the following day.

An August 28, 1963, CIA cable to Director John A. McCone, after referring to this story, concluded that "in view of general press disclaimers on original *Sunday Telegraph* story, believe best if whole matter allowed to die a natural death. Incidentally, though [blacked out] had in the past interested itself in developing story on Robeson, they disclaim any connection with current affair." An August 30, 1963, cable from McCone to an unnamed London office stated that "having read *Telegraph* account Robeson story and subsequent reporting, Headquarters taking no action." An August 22 U.S. Information Service memo from London to Washington reports that "the Embassy's Legal Attaché says he has no evidence whatsoever that Robeson has changed his views about Communism or had a desire to recant." Paul himself had put the *National Insider* story to rest.[7]

Paul and Essie stayed at the Buch Clinic for almost four months, during which Paul made steady progress without relapses. He was immediately taken off all depression medication, and his physical debilitation was treated vigorously. At the same time, he was provided with ever-increasing opportunities for a variety of social interactions. Free of heavy sedation, following a well-regulated daily schedule, and adhering to a strict diet, he slept better and was far more alert and talkative, although he spoke slowly with an occasional stammer. Sam Rosen and Elliott Hurwitt saw him several weeks after his arrival and were impressed by his improvement.

Librium, a mild tranquilizer, was the only medication with which the German doctors treated Paul's depression, and even this drug was used only occasionally. They expressed deep dismay at the Priory doctors' subjection of Paul to ECT and powerful antidepressant drugs. Paul was diagnosed with an enlarged liver, caused by a toxic reaction to the insulin shock treatments, and a mild heart insufficiency. Dr. Katzenstein believed that the extraordinarily high number of fifty-four ECT treatments given to Paul may have caused a deterioration in brain function, even though no significant deficiencies were revealed by extensive tests. At the least, Paul's self-confidence had been undermined, exacerbating his anxiety about living up to the expectations placed on him.

Paul's social engagements and interactions steadily increased. He went out to dinner with friends, visited the Soviet-Germany House of Culture, where he chatted briefly, and spent an afternoon at the Soviet ambassador's residence, where he talked about the black freedom movement in the United States, his grandchildren, and the U.S.-Soviet ice hockey match. On the other hand, Ollie Harrington, an old Harlem friend now living in East Berlin, spent an evening with him and found him to be a gaunt, withdrawn shadow of his former self.[8]

Essie had a thorough medical examination during her stay at the Buch Clinic. Although only recently the English doctors had told her she was cancer-free, the German doctors' findings were grim; they concluded that her cancer had metastasized and was probably inoperable. Essie, who had sensed as much, asked them not to tell Paul and decided to wait until she got home to New York and could get an opinion from Dr. Barsky. She told no one about her condition.[9]

In November, Paul began to talk seriously about going home. On November 10, he wrote to his brother Ben, saying he hoped to see him soon and was continuing to do better. He did not know that Ben was dying of cancer and would live only another month. Ben died on December 1, 1963, but Paul would not be told about this bitter news for several weeks. Essie, faced with an inevitable downhill spiral in her health, was now anxious to go home to friends and family.

President Kennedy's assassination on November 22 shook Paul and caused him some temporary hesitation about returning to the United States. He didn't trust Lyndon Johnson, who was from a southern state. But in the end, the rising surge of masses of black people in support of King's civil rights crusade convinced him that his place was at home.

Two weeks later, Paul confirmed December 17 as the date of departure for London to collect some things and say good-bye to friends, before heading home to New York on December 22. The press knew his itinerary, and so did the FBI. An FBI memorandum, dated December 18, 1963, from the New York office to Hoover noted the date of Paul's arrival in New York and commented that no recommendation was being made that the press interview him. Hoover replied the next day, instructing the New York office to "determine details of subject's arrival in this country and ascertain the extent of his activities in the United States." In London, the same group that had assured his safe departure to Berlin met him and Essie at the airport and kept in close contact until they left for the United States.[10]

On the flight to New York, Paul wrote some notes about coming home. His thoughts were expressed in a surprisingly characteristic and coherent manner, given his recent travails:

> There have been many rumors over the years about me. [They] seem to have two objectives—to divide me from the Negro people and to divide me from my Socialist friends. A reporter recently said that I have arrived belatedly to join the fight for Civil Rights. I have been fighting for Civil Rights all my life.

It is a profound satisfaction, and indeed a form of medicine, to see my Negro people in motion well on their way to achieve their constitutional rights after 200 years of denial and postponement.[11]

A full press corps was on hand when the plane landed at Idlewild Airport (shortly to be renamed John F. Kennedy International Airport). Escorted by three Port Authority police officers, they made their way through the crowd of reporters and photographers under a barrage of questions. Paul stood tall, walked briskly, and turned questions aside with the comment, "I might have something to say later—not now." He did answer one question. When a reporter asked whether he was going to take part in the civil rights movement, he answered, "I've been a part of it all my life."

As I greeted my father, my heart ached when I saw, painfully etched on his face, the beating he had taken since I had left him in Moscow over two years earlier. But when he hugged me back with a deep murmur, "Hello there, Chappie," I knew that, somehow, he was still there. Though tired, he relaxed considerably as he and Essie were surrounded by family and friends. We quickly got them into a car and home to 16 Jumel Terrace.

The coverage in the mainstream press acknowledged Paul's commanding dignity. In a typical dispatch, Paul Hoffman of the *New York Post* wrote, "Tall and straight as ever, his face lean, his weight down, Paul Robeson strode ahead." However, the political tone was hostile. The *New York Times*'s front-page story said that Paul had returned as a "disillusioned native son" who was a forgotten man in his own country. The *Herald Tribune* referred to his "return after five years of a life behind the iron curtain," ignoring that most of this time had been spent in the British Isles. It falsely accused him of abandoning the civil rights struggle and returning to "jump on the bandwagon" after the main battles had been won.

J. A. Rogers, columnist for the *Pittsburgh Courier*, replied to these misrepresentations by observing that Paul's accomplishments had been "a great influence for good" on the race issue. The black press generally gave Paul's return low-key but factual coverage, reporting his illness and retirement due to a "circulatory ailment," along with his comment about being a part of the civil rights movement all his life. Except for the conservative *New York Amsterdam News*, they did not speculate about his rumored disillusionment.[12]

· · ·

When I visited my parents two days after their arrival, I found that a familiar pattern had already emerged. As in 1956 at Jumel Terrace and at Connaught Square, Paul had lapsed into a depressed state of dependency on Essie's smothering attention. However, unlike in 1956, he seemed unable to assert himself, having been mentally battered by his twenty-three-month nightmare of ECT and powerful drugs. Essie, on the other hand, was more assertive than usual in matters concerning Paul, and, giving no hint of her medical condition, also manifested her previous energy in pursuing her projects—covering the United Nations and writing an extended series of articles on current events.

I no longer trusted my mother to be in control of Paul's welfare. My unease was heightened by her seeming pretense that the events in Moscow in 1961 and our conflict over them had not occurred, and that Paul's Priory stay had not been a disaster that she concealed from me. Moreover, she acted as if the move to East Berlin had been her idea.

I went up to my father's darkened bedroom, turned on a desk lamp, and settled down to read. After keeping him silent company for about an hour, I ventured a sentence or two and got a monosyllabic response. After another hour or so, I managed to strike up a conversation. When I fell silent and nothing happened for about a half hour, I said good-bye and went downstairs to chat with my mother. I told her I would be back the next day, bringing my work so she could pursue her own at the United Nations. She agreed, reluctantly at first, but then with growing enthusiasm.

I came daily, and Paul rapidly extended his interactions. I encouraged close friends to call and come by. Soon he was willing to have me or Lloyd Brown drive him to visit his closest friends. He especially enjoyed seeing Clara, who talked with him about Russia and music, and even coaxed him to sit at the piano with her and sing a little. After that, when I played the piano at Jumel Terrace, he would occasionally sit beside me and pick out the melodies of his favorite songs. Sometimes Lloyd would spend a morning or afternoon to free me. An old friend of Paul's from the Progressive Party days, Theodora Peck, came by to see him, and he was so comfortable having her around that she often returned to spend part of a day. As in the past, my father and I took long walks while we talked about music, sports, black politics, the Soviet Union, and Khrushchev (but not what had happened to him in Moscow). And I fixed him his favorite meals.

On January 2, 1964, Dr. Elliott Hurwitt, who had seen Paul at his worst, wrote to the Berlin doctors to thank them and tell them how well Paul was doing just eleven days after his arrival home:

> Paul has improved markedly during his stay with you, for which we all send you our congratulations and thanks. Dr. Barsky, Dr. Rosen and I are indebted to you for the detailed case descriptions [of both Paul and Essie], which I am acknowledging for the three of us. The details have been turned over to Dr. Pearlmutter, a physician who had cared for Eslanda in the past, and is both highly qualified and sympathetic. Despite some bitter weather, Paul is taking outdoor walks, both with friends and alone. His appetite is good, and he is taking some interest in his surroundings.[13]

Dr. Pearlmutter, who was back in charge of Paul's medical care, was apparently committed to continuing the German doctors' successful use of mild tranquilizers. On January 5, 1964, Pearlmutter wrote to Ackner urgently requesting a report on Paul's treatment at the Priory, noting that he had already received a report from Berlin. Ackner replied on January 9, 1964, enclosing a copy of his report to the Berlin doctors. Although his report listed the powerful drugs and numerous ECTs with which Paul was treated, Pearlmutter, Barsky, and the Rosens never acknowledged that the Priory treatment had damaged him. Pearlmutter also wrote to Dr. Flood at the Priory on January 11, 1964, and received a reply similar to Dr. Ackner's, with the identical comment that "the only treatment which had any effect, albeit temporary, was E.C.T."[14]

In hindsight, it is troubling that Dr. Pearlmutter raised no questions concerning Paul's Priory treatment. Given the data in Ackner's report to Berlin, the German doctors' report to Dr. Hurwitt, and a letter from the Soviet doctors that he received in July 1964, it appears that the Priory doctors had placed Paul in an inescapable medical trap. It is my opinion that, falsely diagnosed as a shy, introverted, chronic manic-depressive, he was given ECT to temporarily jolt him out of depression, and then sedated in combination with antianxiety drugs to suppress his normal state, which was misperceived as "manic." This cycle was repeated for twenty-three months.

Later on in January, I drove my father down to Philadelphia to visit his sister, Marian, and he enjoyed the visit so much that he stayed for the weekend and then took the train home on his own. Over the next month, he visited her several times, and by the end of February she had organized a support network of friends and neighbors who came by and often invited him to their homes. He often visited Charlotte Bell, a retired music teacher and close friend and neighbor of Marian's, where he would practice his songs with her accompanying him from the music manuscripts he had brought along. As part of Marian's local community, Paul had many options for relaxed social interactions.

Gradually, Paul moved his base down to Marian's house and returned to Jumel Terrace for relatively short periods to visit with friends and work with Lloyd on messages and articles. Essie accepted this arrangement since it freed her to pursue her writing projects and lecture tours.[15]

On March 30, Essie went to see Josephine Baker in her show at Henry Miller's Theatre. Baker greeted her warmly when she went backstage after the show and asked how Paul was. The next day, Baker called Paul, chatted with him, and arranged to come and visit with him and Essie.[16]

On June 15, Pearlmutter wrote to Ackner that Paul had shown "dramatic improvement": "He now sleeps quite well, has an excellent appetite, is very communicative and quite intelligently so, and goes places and does things on his own. He looks and feels well, and has gained 32 pounds since beginning treatment in January. The results so far have exceeded my best expectations. He is again the Paul Robeson with a lively interest in life, people, and the world around him."

In early August, I accompanied my father from Philadelphia to Beth Israel Hospital in New York to visit Ben Davis, who was dying of cancer and had asked to see him. Ben was overjoyed. I stayed a while, thinking I might have to keep the conversation going, but Paul comfortably led Ben back along memory lane, sharing anecdotes and stories about his experiences with him. When I left them, they were talking about Ben's football days when he was a student at Amherst College in Massachusetts in the 1920s. When Paul emerged almost two hours later, Ben, pleasantly tired, was drifting off to sleep. During the drive back to Philadelphia, Paul told me that at one point he had sung a couple of Ben's favorite songs to him.

Ben died on August 22, and Paul came back to New York to speak at his Harlem funeral in his first public appearance since his return. He paid tribute to his dear friend and hailed his contributions to the black struggle, and the worldwide cause of peace and freedom. Afterward, when the police were unable to clear a path for Paul to his cab, he was happily engulfed in the crowd, responding to greetings and extending his hand to clasp those of well-wishers. For a moment, it was almost like old times.

Two days later, Paul released his first statement to the press, which he sent exclusively to black publications:

> While I must continue my temporary retirement from public life, I am, of course, deeply involved with the great upsurge of our people. Like all of you, my heart has been filled with admiration for the many thousands of Negro freedom fighters and their white associates who are waging the battle for civil rights throughout the country and especially in the South.
>
> For me there has also been the sorrow that I have felt on returning home and experiencing the loss of persons who for many long years were near and dear to me—my beloved older brother, the Reverend Benjamin C. Robeson, who passed away while I was gone; and my longtime colleague and coworker, Dr. W.E.B. DuBois, foremost statesman and scholar of our people, who died last year in Ghana. And now has come deep grief at the death of Ben Davis, a precious friend whose indomitable courage and dedication to the fight for freedom has always been a glowing inspiration for me.
>
> When I wrote in my book, *Here I Stand*, in 1958 that "the time is now," some people thought that perhaps my watch was fast (and maybe it was a little), but most of us seem to be running on the same time—now. The "power of Negro action," of which I then wrote, has changed from an idea to a reality that is manifesting itself throughout our land. The concept of mass militancy, of mass action, is no longer deemed "too radical" in Negro life. The idea that black Americans should see that the fight for a "Free World" begins at home—a shocking idea when expressed in Paris in 1949—no longer is challenged in our communities. The "hot summer" of struggles for equal rights has replaced the "cold war" abroad as the concern of our people.
>
> There is more—much more—that needs to be done, of course, before we can reach our goals. But if we cannot as yet sing, "Thank God Almighty, we're free at last," we surely can all sing together: "Thank God Almighty, we're *moving*!"[17]

Dr. Pearlmutter found Paul slightly "more restless" toward the end of October, perhaps because several public appearances were scheduled for November. However, in Pearlmutter's opinion, the unease was due mainly to "lack of activity." The more he sat around in the Jumel Terrace house, the more uneasy he felt. Although he had many friends in New York, an outing required significant planning and logistics.

On November 7, Paul attended the annual reception at the Soviet Mission to the United Nations celebrating the forty-seventh anniversary of the October Revolution. Khrushchev had been abruptly ousted from leadership in a bloodless political coup a month earlier and Leonid Brezhnev, heretofore a staunch Khrushchev supporter, had been installed as the new Soviet leader. Brezhnev signaled an end to Khrushchev's reforms, installing a conservative, nationalist regime, but he avoided a return to Stalinism. Paul had been disappointed, commenting wistfully in private that it might take a decade for the reforms to resume. However, he decided to refrain from any public criticism. As for the Russians, they engulfed him with warmth and affection when he turned up unannounced. Paul received a similar reception at the celebration of John Howard Lawson's seventieth birthday. Lawson, one of the most famous of the blacklisted "Hollywood Ten," had become a dean of America's left-wing culture and a strong supporter of the Communist Party USA. Paul enjoyed the event, Lawson was moved to tears by his highly personal tribute, and everyone came away feeling that their Paul was there for them.

On November 12, he spoke at the Carnegie Hall rally of the National Council for American-Soviet Friendship and was greeted by a five-minute standing ovation. Beaming, he acknowledged the greeting in his familiar, warm, dignified yet humble way and delivered a brief but carefully crafted speech designed to reassert his firm friendship for the worldwide left. He ended with the comment that "the American people are a friendly people. The Soviet people are a friendly people. The world will benefit enormously by the strengthening of friendship between our people and the people of the Soviet Union and of the Socialist World."[18]

As public appearances began to multiply, it became time to take my father back to Philadelphia. As I drove, I talked with him about his future. I sensed from our conversation that even though he knew he was not the powerful figure he had been, he still felt the need to inspire and perform on occasion despite the personal health risk. His idea was to make these appearances and then return to Marian's. With considerable anxiety, I remembered that both the Russian and German doctors had strongly advised his complete retirement from public life. My train of thought was broken by the soft, resonant sound of my father humming "Jacob's Ladder."

On January 16, 1965, Paul delivered one of the eulogies at black playwright Lorraine Hansberry's funeral, braving a blizzard to appear. Hansberry's funeral service, at Harlem's Church of the Master, was a major event to which blacks from all over the city came to celebrate and mourn one of their own cultural icons. With her epic play *A Raisin in the Sun*, Lorraine, despite her young age of thirty-four, had propelled black theater onto the mainstream stage.

Paul's eulogy was brief but personal: "It was a privilege to have known Lorraine over a span of years. I remember her fine articles for the newspaper *Freedom*, and was struck by her understanding of the world around her. She had her roots deep in her people. Her feeling and knowledge of the history of our people was remarkable in one so young. As an artist, Lorraine reflected the life and struggles of our day in her work, and leaves a precious heritage. Her soul has grown deep like rivers."

Paul delivered his text in a deep, strong voice that commanded the space around him. Though his voice was not nearly the instrument it had been just five years earlier, it still elicited the grudging praise of a hostile mainstream press. The *New York Times* called him "still compelling"; the *Herald Tribune* reported that "the words, although they were said, not sung, rolled out across the hundreds packed into Harlem's Church of the Master."[19]

The quietly welling affection of the audience for Paul was not the only sign of his continued importance to the black community. He was engulfed by well-wishers in the reception room prior to the funeral service. At one point, James McDonald, an acquaintance of mine, pulled me aside to say that Malcolm X was in the audience and wished to speak with me.

I had seen Malcolm only at a distance, when he was speaking as a loyal disciple of Elijah Muhammad. Now he was a hunted man whose house had been bombed and set on fire. Having left the Nation of Islam and denounced his former mentor, he had been declared "worthy of death" by the movement he helped build. The man I spoke to on this day is etched in my memory as one of the most impressive personages I have ever encountered.

Tall and lean, Malcolm had a penetrating gaze and a soft but authoritative baritone voice. He was in spiritual repose—vulnerable, yet without fear. He walked alone, at peace with himself. I felt I was in the presence of a man unafraid of death.

He asked to meet my father. When I replied that I would try to arrange it on the spot, Malcolm put his hand gently on my arm. "No, no," he said. "We shouldn't meet here, with the press all around. I'd like to arrange a private meeting where we can talk comfortably. I'm contemplating some things I'd like to discuss with your father." I said I understood and would be right back.

As I started to ask Paul about meeting with Malcolm, Essie agitatedly proclaimed that she wouldn't allow Malcolm X to come into the reception room and would stand in the doorway if she had to. Before I could say anything, Paul peremptorily ordered her to "be quiet," turned to me, and said, "Tell Malcolm that you will arrange for him to come and see me at Jumel Terrace." When I relayed Paul's message to Malcolm, he smiled, thanked me, and said that McDonald would be in touch with me. Alas, the meeting never took place. Over the following month, Malcolm was preoccupied with guaranteeing his family's survival. I hadn't yet heard from McDonald when Malcolm was assassinated on February 21 at the Audubon Ballroom, just a few blocks from Jumel Terrace.

Paul received several calls from black leaders after his appearance at Lorraine Hansberry's funeral. Bayard Rustin called twice, but Paul refused to return his calls. When I suggested that Rustin might be calling on Reverend King's behalf, he was adamant, citing Rustin's often-proclaimed anticommunism. Another black leader who called was James Farmer, who headed the Congress of Racial Equality. Paul agreed to see him. Farmer, who boasted of personal telephone access to President Lyndon Johnson and would later serve in the Health, Education, and Welfare Department of the Nixon administration, apparently used the visit as an exploratory mission. After engaging in some initial pleasantries, he said that he was certain, based on his inside knowledge of the Johnson administration's racial attitudes, that Paul would be welcomed back into the mainstream if he recanted his leftist political views. He merely had to "confirm his disillusionment with the Soviet Union and acknowledge the failure of Communism." The civil rights movement would then welcome him with open arms. Paul waited for Farmer to finish, then said, "Get out, and never call me again." Paul chuckled when he described to me Farmer's hasty exit. Twenty years later, Farmer published his memoir, in which he gave a self-serving fictional account of this meeting.[20]

In search of an independent, black, left-wing base similar to Freedom Associates of the previous decade, Paul settled upon *Freedomways*, a quarterly magazine founded by several former leaders of Freedom Associates in 1961, and headed by Esther Jackson. He agreed to the editors' proposal to celebrate his sixty-seventh birthday with a Salute to Paul Robeson that would also raise money for the magazine. Subtitled "A Quarterly Review of the Black Freedom Movement,"*Freedomways* had acquired a significant audience in the black and progressive intellectual communities.

Paul wrote an article for the March 1965 special issue of *Freedomways* celebrating the life of Dr. W. E. B. DuBois. The piece was comprehensive, paying tribute to DuBois's cultural and political contributions, but also providing warm personal recollections. To the delight of the editors, Paul attended the party celebrating the publication of the special issue and made an impromptu speech that ended with an a capella rendition of "Jacob's Ladder"—the first time he had sung publicly in four years.

The sponsor list for the Salute reflected the antileft political environment. The names of liberal black and white establishment leaders and celebrities were notably absent. Roy Wilkins coldly declined, saying that he was too busy with NAACP matters. White liberal television journalist David Susskind replied with the rude comment, "My only reaction is that you must be joking—and what a bad joke it is." Despite the Johnson-led Democratic landslide in the 1964 presidential election and the subsequent forward surge of the civil rights movement, the antileft political culture of the 1950s remained firmly in place as part of the "bipartisan" status quo.[21]

The Salute was a gala event at the Hotel Americana in Manhattan, where an audience of over two thousand filled the ballroom on April 22. Ossie Davis was the master of ceremonies; Morris Carnovsky, Howard Da Silva, Roscoe Lee Browne, Diana Sands, Pete Seeger,

Dizzy Gillespie, and Billy Taylor led the performing artists. James Baldwin and John Lewis, chairman of the Student Nonviolent Coordinating Committee (SNCC), were featured speakers.

Baldwin recalled, "At a time when there seemed to be no hope at all, Paul Robeson spoke out for all of us." Lewis paid tribute to "democracy's most powerful voice":

> The assassins of Freedom have been trying for many years to erase the personality of one whose broad shoulders were squared to confront them. Your presence here in this vast assemblage gives evidence to the totality of their failure. Tonight, as we salute Paul Robeson, we salute more than a man; we salute a cause.
>
> For two generations of Americans, Paul Robeson represented the entire Negro people of this country. In many ways we of SNCC are Paul Robeson's spiritual children. We too have been accused of being radicals, and of "Communist influence," and for the same reasons as Robeson.
>
> I would like to quote some of his words from his book, *Here I Stand*. These words seem prophetic: "We have the power to achieve our goal; what we, ourselves, do will be decisive. We ask for nothing that is not ours by right, and here lies the great moral power of our demand."
>
> Mr. Robeson, we hope to honor you best by performing that task.

Paul mounted the stage confidently, smiled broadly during the standing ovation, and delivered a twenty-five-minute speech that he read from a typed text with his handwritten notes on it. His ending, which was partly spontaneous, brought the house down:

> All the while that we were abroad we kept in touch with the remarkable progress of the freedom struggle here at home. The struggle for "Freedom Now" in the South and all over this land is a struggle uniting many sections of the American people, as evidenced in that great March from Selma to Montgomery, where thousands of black and white citizens of this country marched for the freedom of our people in the deep South and for a new kind of America. It is clear that large sections of the American people are feeling and accepting their responsibility for freedom and peace. It also is clear that from the Negro people has come a tremendous initiative and dynamic power in the forward thrust of our march toward freedom. It is clear that the Negro people are claiming

their rights and they are in every way determined to have those rights and nothing can turn us back!

In all of our struggles we see and feel that the part played by *music* is of extraordinary importance. How wonderful to hear these songs tonight and to hear the songs that serve to inspire, encourage, sustain and unite the thousands of participants, particularly the beautiful old songs which were a part of the Negro's long struggle during Slavery and Reconstruction. Today these old songs, sometimes with new words, serve the same high purpose as do the beautiful songs newly composed in the heat of the day. We sang in many languages in the countries we visited. We saw the unity of the struggles. There is one song that I have always said comes from struggles of the peoples; like we sang "Go Down Moses," there is another song from these great peoples that goes:

> Never say that you have reached the very end,
> When leaden skies a bitter future may portend:
> For sure the hour for which we yearn will yet arrive
> And our marching steps will thunder "We Survive!"[22]

I certainly go home knowing and feeling more and more deeply, We shall overcome, deep in my heart I do believe, We shall overcome some day.[23]

Paul was well satisfied, even inspired by the event. He felt he was "back" at a level he could cope with. I was far less optimistic, believing that it would be a mistake for him to reemerge as a public figure to any degree. Even if his physical and mental condition were equal to the task, the required support structure was no longer available and his performing skills were rusty from four years of disuse. His former inner circle of support could not be reassembled. Essie was in fragile health. The Communist Party of Eugene Dennis had given way to the party of Gus Hall and a rigidly bureaucratic regime that was intolerant of independent initiatives. It had ceased to be a reliable ally, and more likely was a source of trouble because it had become infiltrated by the FBI.

But the greatest negative factor weighing against Paul's return to public life was the current state of the civil rights movement, coupled with Paul's seven-year absence from active participation in Black life. Lewis's recognition of Paul on the SNCC's behalf was welcome, but the SNCC itself was in unstable transition.

And even though Paul had pioneered the idea of Black power in *Here I Stand*, the younger generation of black radicals was unaware of him.

I set aside my fears when Paul went back to Philadelphia a few days after the Salute and settled in quietly.

15

"NO CROSS; NO CROWN"

(1965–1976)

In early May 1965, just a few weeks after the celebration at the Americana Hotel, Marian called from Philadelphia with the news that Paul was scheduled to travel to California with Essie for two tributes. Marian was worried about whether he was up to it, but he seemed determined to go. I opposed the idea, but I couldn't dissuade him either. So I called Bill Taylor in Los Angeles and Revels Cayton in San Francisco, the cities where the tributes were to be held. Bill, whom I knew well, was the top black Communist Party leader in Los Angeles, and Revels, one of Paul's oldest and closest friends, had become an important figure in black and union circles in San Francisco. Taylor had arranged for Paul and Essie to stay at the home of Paul's friends, the Simses, in the heart of the Los Angeles black community of Watts. I was confident they would be safe and in good hands there.

San Francisco was another matter. Paul and Essie were to be hosted in an affluent white suburban community where Paul would probably not feel secure, and Revels Cayton was not involved in organizing their activities. I wanted to arrange for Revels to host them, but Essie refused to change the existing plans.

Essie reported on the Los Angeles part of the trip in a May 19 letter to the family:

> Got the red carpet treatment at the Kennedy Airport in New York, because the head Negro porter recognized Paul and went straight to the top guy and alerted him. We were met by Steve

Fritchman and Paul's familiar Negro "security" bodyguards Chuck Moseley and Homer Sadler, and I have never seen such security. I at once was taught how to use a 15 repeater rifle, and found it easy and great fun. There has been no incident of any kind whatsoever and no indication that there will be one. If there was any attempt to harm him in any way, I am convinced there would be one of the biggest riots ever recorded.

Friday rested all day until time to go to the big Church dinner in our honor, at 6 pm. At church, Steve Fritchman had arranged for a friendly reporter of the Los Angeles Times to interview Paul. At 8 pm the Program began in the church, which was packed to the doors and on the stairs, and was wonderful. I did a short speech, then Paul, and he was very good indeed, and at the end sang two songs, without accompaniment—Eriskay Love Lilt and Climbing Jacob's Ladder, and was beautiful. The voice is full, complete with overtones, and under very fine control. He heard himself, and was very much reassured.

"Certainly I hope to be back many times again here," Paul told the audience, "and, if I can sort of get down to it and work very hard, I would certainly be very proud to be able to sing some kind of song here with this choir. As I say, this is the first time I'm sort of playing around much with the singing, but I guess the voice is still around somewhere."[1]

Essie's letter continues:

Sunday, May 16. We went to Sunday morning Breakfast in the Negro Community. The house was packed, and Paul made a very brief speech, and we had a lot of conversation with questions and answers, which seemed to delight the people. At 3 pm we went along to Mt. Sinai church in the Negro section for an afternoon Meeting. [Paul] sang a song informally, and the people went wild with pleasure.

After that we went to a big home in the Negro section, where the professional Negroes had gathered to pay their respects to Paul and me. Somehow a question-answer period evolved, and someone in the audience—a woman—said her question was she would like to hear Paul sing 6 bars of "Go Down Moses." Paul laughed, hesitated, then said, O.K., I'll try. I don't know how it will come out, but I'll try. He then proceeded to sing it right through, beautifully, really beautifully, and the people went wild, and then the lady got up and said: I just wanted to prove to you that you could do it. Now Paul laughed and said: Well, you did.

Monday, May 17 we met at 3 pm with the Negro business men who have initiated a marvelous Credit Union, with a very successful practical program, and more than $100,000 funds. They told him, us, all about it, asked advice and suggestions, and Paul was fascinated and admiring. At 7:30 pm there was a meeting in a newly integrated View Park area in the Baldwin Hills area on Athenian Way, in a large and beautiful Negro home, and they had a wonderful crowd, everyone eager to shake his hand, look at him, hear him and just see him.

Tuesday, May 18. In the evening we did a meeting for the *Peoples World* newspaper at Larchmont Hall, and the place was packed. Paul just came out and made a beautiful speech, and then up and sang "Eriskay Love Lilt," "Peat Bog Soldiers" and "Water Boy," no less, with Waldemar Hille at the piano, filling in and supporting beautifully. His voice was magnificent and everyone stood and yelled.

The second week in Los Angeles was not as hectic, but every day included at least one gathering at which Paul spoke and sang one or two songs. He thrived on the appearances, and his audiences loved him. He embodied a unique symbol—a great black warrior who had challenged the foundations of the Jim Crow system and survived. Here he stood, wounded, but unbowed and still defiant.

Paul's interview with the *Los Angeles Times* appeared on May 16 with the headline "Robeson Cherishes His U.S. Heritage":

Now 66, Robeson expressed astonishment that his extended residence in England should have been considered as an embittered act of self-exile from this country. "Exile?" he said. "I went there to work, to fulfill and accept contracts. It was no different than any American actor who goes abroad to work, or the English actors who come here."

He emphasized that he considers America his home. "I expect to stay," he said, "and do whatever I can do in the civil rights struggle. Civil rights has been a part of my life. I feel like I was born with it."

Robeson denied that he left this country in bitterness or without hope for the Negro cause. "Just the opposite," he insisted. "I felt triumphant. I had won my passport. I felt that McCarthyism, all that, was a small part of America, as far as I could see. "I've had a long life here in America," he said. "Sometimes I got knocked down. And then I got up and sometimes I knocked the other guy down. But I always got up and kept going."

Robeson said he believes that the Negro will become "a full American in every sense of the word. These are much more than exciting times—they're definitive. Whatever the difficulties, I'm optimistic the human race will find a way out. It's the great responsibility of all of us Americans to understand the need of other peoples."

Robeson, powerfully built and towering well over six feet, appeared vigorous despite his recent illness, and insisted he is well. He has no singing engagements at present. "I've just been listening," he said. "But I'll be back at it soon."

My parents left for San Francisco on May 24. They were met at the airport by Mary Helen Jones, a black left-wing activist, who took them to the elegant home of Ruby Silverstone in a predominantly white section of Marin County. Paul, who had freshly arrived from the enveloping warmth and security of black Los Angeles, now felt insecure and isolated. Essie wrote that he was soon showing telltale signs of oncoming depression, "waking up day after day tired."[2]

Several days after their arrival, Essie developed severe back pain, further alarming an already distraught Paul. But instead of acting immediately to alter an untenable situation, she opted to stick it out. They attended a few public events without mishap during the first ten days of their planned three-week stay, but Paul began to sink into a withdrawn, uncommunicative state. By June 4, the day of the Salute to Paul Robeson at San Francisco's Jack Tar Hotel, they were both incapacitated and could not appear. They flew back to New York in poor condition.

Dr. Pearlmutter relieved Essie's pain somewhat with medication and immediately called in Dr. Nathan Kline, a noted psychopharmacologist, to supervise Paul's case. Kline prescribed Biphetamine as an addition to Paul's usual medication.

When I visited my parents the next day, their situation was grim. Essie, her activities severely curtailed by her symptoms, seemed dispirited and tired. Paul, his already high anxiety amplified by her visible deterioration, flatly refused to take his new pills after trying one. I called Dr. Pearlmutter, and he agreed to discontinue them. I stayed through the day, coming home with the conclusion that Paul needed to be at Marian's instead of Jumel Terrace. But his condition was too fragile for me to risk moving him, especially without the doctor's permission.

The next day I took my father to Dr. Kline's office for an examination. From the moment he saw Kline, a tall, white-haired, intense man with a flair for rhetoric, he froze, sitting passively and remaining silent. Kline made a few notes, told me that he was continuing the current medication, and said I should keep in touch with Pearlmutter.

When I asked Dr. John Rockmore, Bob's brother who was a psychiatrist, to check Dr. Kline's credentials, he replied that Kline was "essentially a researcher who has made a name for himself in administering drugs in mental hospitals." He did not think that Kline was a good choice to treat Paul.[3]

Over the following four days I spent most of my time at Jumel Terrace, arriving in the morning and staying till evening. Despite my efforts and Essie's, Paul became more anxious and depressed. It was apparent he did not want to be in the house alone with Essie. Each evening when I left, he gave an imploring look that seemed to say, "Please don't leave." On the fourth day, he urged me to stay. I called Marilyn to tell her I would be staying overnight, and slept on the living room couch. The next morning—June 10—I went home.

Several hours later, my mother called me in panic—Paul had held a pair of scissors to his chest that morning and nicked himself before she could induce him to put the scissors down. Now, in the early afternoon, he was pacing the floor in his bedroom and muttering.

Marilyn and I went up to the house immediately. When I appeared in the doorway of Paul's bedroom, he was standing in the middle of the room with a blank look. He abruptly extended his right arm, palm out, commanding me to halt. Then he slowly raised his left hand, which held a double-edged razor blade, and brought it to rest with the blade about an inch from the left side of his neck. I halted and started talking in as normal a voice as I could muster. I talked about whatever came into my mind. Paul stood quietly, without talking or moving. I kept slowly moving forward until I was within arm's length. I asked him to give me the razor blade. He handed it to me and sat down in his chair.

I called Sam Rosen, who quickly arrived with Pearlmutter and Barsky. They conferred, deciding ultimately to take Paul to Gracie Square Hospital under Dr. Kline's supervision. He was admitted under the pseudonym "Frank Robertson."

I visited my father daily. Pearlmutter's medication remained essentially unchanged; Paul improved steadily, asking for newspapers and receiving a variety of visitors, and was discharged to Jumel Terrace on July 1 after a three-week stay. The hospital records reveal that, although diagnosed as a chronic depressive with suicidal tendencies, he had been cooperative, friendly, and was speaking normally without memory impairment within three days of admission. Now in relatively good shape, he went visiting when Lloyd or I picked him up, dropped by my apartment a couple of times, and visited Clara on several occasions on his own.

Kline departed for his summer vacation, leaving Dr. Ari Kiev, his young associate, in charge of Paul's case. Kiev asked me to bring Paul in for weekly monitoring conversations. I agreed, but under the condition that I would sit in. Dr. Kiev was a stocky young man with a broad, open face and a gentle, engaging manner. My father felt comfortable with him, participating in considerable conversation. Kiev asked him about his career, expressing interest in his feeling of continuity with the civil rights movement and his current tentative involvement with his music. He replied alertly and accurately, sharing his trepidation about not being able to live up to the public's expectations. My father was melancholy during these conversations when reminded of his career.

Meanwhile, Paul was doing well at Jumel Terrace. He went out to visit reasonably often; friends came by regularly, and Essie was cheerfully active again. This situation prevailed for a month, during which I reviewed Kiev's credentials, which Dr. Rockmore had sent me along with Kline's. They were not reassuring. Kiev was described as "very young professionally with limited training," who had been "a mental health fellow in Maudsley, which is a psychiatric teaching institution in London."

Dr. Kiev's résumé confirms that in 1961–1962 he was attached to the Maudsley Institute of Psychiatry, for which Ackner served as consultant. Kiev had previously been at Harvard, Cornell Medical College, and Johns Hopkins Hospital, all of which had psychological research programs directed by contractors for the CIA's MKULTRA Project and funded by the CIA through a study group called the Society for the Investigation of Human Ecology. From Maudsley, Kiev had gone to Lackland Air Force Base in Texas, where he served from 1962 through 1964 as a captain and was attached to Wilford Hall Hospital, the site of secret MKULTRA research conducted by psychologist Frank Barron.[4]

On August 3, Essie called me from Beth Israel Hospital where she had been admitted after a return of acute pain. Paul had cared for her for a couple of days and then taken her to the hospital. When I went up to the house that evening, Paul seemed fine, but his staying at Jumel Terrace by himself seemed a bad idea. He was not acquainted with anyone in the neighborhood; there were no houses across the street because of the Jumel Mansion grounds, and the families living in the houses on either side of him were away. He was isolated on a quiet street. It augured disaster, but he couldn't decide to leave.

I called Kiev, explained the situation, and proposed to take Paul to Marian's. Kiev refused to give his approval, warning that such a move would be irresponsible. In desperation, I called Pearlmutter, and he peremptorily dismissed my proposal, saying I was acting like an overconcerned son. Paul would be fine, he said; taking some added responsibility for himself would be good.

For the next three days, I went up to the house to cook dinner for Paul, finding him cheerful and conversational each time. On the fourth day, I visited him in the morning. He was dressed in suit and tie, sitting poised on the edge of the living room couch with a cigarette in his mouth. The ashtray in front of him was partially filled with half-smoked butts. He looked up and smiled, then went back to smoking his cigarette with a contemplative expression.

Paul smoked only when he was anxious, so from the number of butts I concluded he was extremely apprehensive. And he rarely dressed in a suit and tie that early in the day unless he planned to go somewhere. It seemed he wanted to leave the house and was trying to decide where to go. I asked him whether he wanted me to drive him to Marian's house. He didn't answer. Marilyn and I didn't have room for him in our apartment, so I called Helen Rosen, who was at her summer home in Katonah, about an hour's drive upstate. She drove in right away.

Paul was glad to see her. She chatted with him for a short while and then asked him to come up to Katonah and spend a few days in the country. He smiled, went upstairs, packed a small bag, and came back down ready to go. Everything appeared fine as they drove off with Paul happily waving to me.

But the visit did not go well. In retrospect, I realized that a country home in a secluded and all-white area, a few miles from where the Peekskill assaults had occurred almost exactly sixteen years earlier, was not a place where he would feel secure.

Helen called me urgently that afternoon. She had gone for a swim in the pond at the bottom of the small hill behind the house, and Paul had come down with her. After her swim, she had been sitting on the grass beside him when he suddenly stood up, walked to the deep end of the pond, and indicated that he might descend the steps leading into the water. Helen, frightened because he was fully dressed and could not swim, managed to coax him back up to the house.

Marilyn and I drove to Katonah, where we conferred with Helen while Paul sat quietly in the living room. I called Kiev, who told me to bring him to his office. Paul agreed to go and to do whatever we thought best. Kiev talked briefly with Paul in our presence, asking him several questions, which he answered cogently without apparent anxiety. Then Kiev recommended that Paul be readmitted to Gracie Square Hospital, providing he agreed. Paul readily consented and was admitted under Kiev's care.

Visiting the hospital daily, I found my father communicative and in good condition for the first three days. On the fourth day, despite twenty-four-hour nursing care, he started to deteriorate. The Gracie Square Hospital records reveal that his daily medication, signed for by Kiev, included a high dose of the powerful antidepressant Niamid, as well as a small dose of the antipsychotic drug Phenergan, in addition to his normal medication consisting of Elavil and chloral hydrate. The previous evening, I had told my father that Essie had been operated on, and though I gave him a falsely optimistic report of her prognosis, he probably sensed the bad news—that her cancer had spread. No doubt this added greatly to the apprehension and discomfort caused by his overmedication.

On August 12, the fifth day after Paul's admission, Kiev wrote, "Continue meds as ordered above by me," and added a 5-milligram dose of the tranquilizer Valium. Later that evening, a staff physician, Dr. Schubert, gave Paul a 100-milligram dose of Benadryl—this despite the alarm registered by Paul's nurses and at least one resident concerning Paul's pronouncedly negative response to the medications. On August 13 and 14, Kiev, visiting daily, added 10 grams of Thorazine while continuing the Valium. I subsequently learned that Thorazine is toxic when combined with Valium and is normally used to restrain violent or unruly patients. Paul was at no time either violent or unruly.[5]

Each day, I found Paul in significantly worse condition. On the evening of August 15, he was rigid, incoherent, and behaving like a drug addict jerkily and slowly sliding off a park bench. His nurse was agitatedly signaling me that he had been dangerously overmedicated and that I should do something because he couldn't. I demanded to see a resident. A doctor came but provided no explanation of Paul's behavior and no promise of a review of the medication. I called Sam Rosen and implored him to come to the hospital right away because the drug treatment was going to kill Paul. Sam was sure this was an exaggeration but promised to come the next morning.

Sam called Dr. Pearlmutter, who refused to come in from his vacation, referring him to Dr. Richard Nachtigall. Dr. Nachtigall and Sam were already working on Paul when I arrived the next morning. Appalled by Paul's condition, Nachtigall discontinued the drugs, placed him on the critical list, and ordered a battery of tests while he immediately started him on intravenous fluids with antibiotics. This quick intervention by Nachtigall saved Paul's life, since the results of the tests showed him suffering from "dehydration, meningitis, pneumonia, syclonephritis [kidney trauma], drug sensitivity and phenothiozine induced rigidity."

Kline made a brief appearance two days later, and Kiev stopped coming. Pearlmutter didn't come in. Dr. Nachtigall, together with resident staff doctors, worked frantically on Paul for the next five days, but on the morning of August 22, his temperature reached 105 degrees. Nachtigall decided to transfer him to University Hospital where superior facilities would offer a better chance of survival. For the second time, Nachtigall's quick decision saved Paul's life. After an initial few days of uncertainty, he started to improve slowly and was discharged on September 9 after an eighteen-day stay.

The medical record I obtained from University Hospital reveals that his blood abnormality on admission was "secondary to drug reaction," and the summary diagnosis of his overall condition included "toxic metabolic encephalopathy probably secondary to combined drug therapy." For the first time in Paul's medical history it was noted that he "retained elements of an organic mental syndrome throughout his entire course." Apparently, the drug therapy prescribed by Drs. Kline and Kiev at Gracie Square Hospital had caused "elements" of an organic condition.[6]

When Paul came home from University Hospital, Essie had been back for a few days. Her surgery and radiation treatments had relieved the pain, and she had been remarkably upbeat during my hospital visits with her—full of plans engendered by a determination to make the best of her remaining time. Frankie Sims, my parents' recent hostess in Los Angeles, and a friend, Marie Bowden, arrived to care for them both. All went well for a month. Paul appeared to be in fairly good shape, although not back to the level prior to his stay at Gracie Square Hospital. Now would be the time to take him to Marian's.

I engaged in futile argument with Kiev and Pearlmutter, quickly reaching the familiar dead end. By October 13, Essie's discomfort had increased dramatically, raising Paul's anxiety level. Two days later, after spending most of the day with my parents, I was about to go home when Paul started pacing back and forth in the hallway leading to the front door. Deciding to stay until he went to bed that night, I went upstairs to take a bath after asking Frankie Sims to stay close to him. A bit later I heard the front door slam. I wrapped a towel around my waist and dashed to the head of the stairs—Paul was gone, and so were his coat and hat. Essie had called Frankie downstairs, causing her to momentarily disregard my instructions, and he had slipped out.

I dressed quickly and headed out to look for him. I was familiar with the route he usually took on his walks, but it was soon evident that he wasn't on his usual path. I guessed that he had fallen down the steeply sloped embankment of Highbridge Park. I hurried back to the house to get a flashlight, called in a request for a missing person bulletin to the local police precinct, and phoned Lloyd Brown to come assist me. Essie began calling friends on the chance that he might have shown up.

Lloyd and I searched for over two hours. Having met with no success, we returned to the house and told Essie the bad news. She sat silent, with a fixed blankly smiling expression. We did not know what to make of her reaction.

The next morning, an anonymous telephone call to the nearby Wadsworth Avenue police precinct reported that a man had been seen lying awake in a dense clump of bushes. The police found him quickly. When Essie, Lloyd, and I arrived at the Vanderbilt Clinic of Presbyterian Hospital, Paul was sitting on an examination table, coherent and seemingly not much the worse for wear. He had a slight laceration where he had struck his head on a rock, in addition to bruises on his right hip and ankle. Having no recollection of leaving the house, he kept asking what had happened to him.[7]

Paul was transferred to University Hospital, where again he made a slow but steady recovery over an eighteen-day stay. His head injury proved to be more serious than initial appearances—the University Hospital diagnosis, dated October 18, cites "cranial cerebral trauma, traumatic intercerebral hemorrhage." Nevertheless, when he was discharged on November 3 he had regained a stable condition. This time, Dr. Pearlmutter readily agreed when I requested his permission for Paul's transfer to Marian's house, where he would be under the care of her physician, Dr. Walter Klingensmith. When I picked Paul up, he happily agreed to drive down to Philadelphia, where he immediately relaxed. He and Marian were smiling when I departed.

Frankie Sims stayed on at Jumel Terrace to take care of Essie, who managed to go for her radiation treatments regularly and to the United Nations occasionally. Marilyn and I brought David and Susan to visit often, which was a great comfort to her. The children loved being around "Nana," who always had something of interest to offer. Only three weeks had elapsed when Pearlmutter recommended her readmission to Beth Israel Hospital. I took her there on November 23.

As I placed her suitcase on the bed in her private room, she asked me to bring her typewriter from home. Before I could reply, she collapsed in a chair with a piercing cry of fear and pain. Then she leaned forward, her face in her hands. I knelt in front of my mother, holding her and rocking her like a child as her whole body heaved with sobs. Suddenly she stopped, held up her tearstained face, and said, "I'm all right. Don't forget my typewriter." As I left, she commented that she would probably have to celebrate her seventieth birthday (on December 15) in that room. I emerged into the crisp autumn air, thankful for the opportunity to comfort my mother in that awful moment when she was forced to confront her own death.

Essie was invariably cheerful in the presence of the steady stream of friends who visited over the next three weeks. In early December, she began actively planning her birthday party and had her hair done by her favorite hairdresser. On the evening of December 12, I found her weaker than usual. When I asked the nurse on duty about her condition, she just shook her head.

I made myself comfortable in a chair next to my mother's bed as she dozed fitfully. Suddenly she awoke, looked at the clock, patted my hand, and told me peremptorily, "Go home. I'll be fine. I'll see you tomorrow." She was determined to make it to her seventieth birthday. I kissed her good night, and as I left she sank back on her pillow with a peaceful smile on her face. At about 4 a.m. the next morning, December 13, 1965, Beth Israel Hospital called to say that my mother had passed away.

Her funeral was attended by family only. Paul and Marian did not come in from Philadelphia. Her ashes were ultimately interred next to Paul's in Ferncliff Cemetery at Hartsdale, New York. When I took her death certificate to Marian's for Paul to sign, he read it and signed without comment. He never told me or anyone else what was in his mind at that moment.[8]

Paul was doing well at Marian's, but I could see that Marian, who was seventy, was under some strain. When I suggested that we try an experiment in which Paul would live with Marilyn, me, and our children at Jumel Terrace for part of the time, she agreed, and Paul didn't seem to object. In late February 1966, my family moved into the Jumel Terrace house. But we kept our apartment.

This arrangement lasted for several months. My father started out fairly well, going out to visit and enjoying visitors. We took him to the annual Student Nonviolent Coordinating Committee dinner in March, where the announcement of his presence prompted a big ovation. He was pleased with the warm welcomes he received from many notables, including Harry Belafonte, who came to our table to say hello. James Forman, the new chairman of the SNCC, extolled Paul's contribution to the civil rights movement in the keynote speech, and John Lewis came over to say that Paul had inspired the movement. However, as Paul was visibly tired and stressed by the end of the dinner, we hesitated to take him to similar events, prompting the rumor that I was making my father a recluse.

With the approach of his sixty-eighth birthday, Paul's anxiety increased measurably. I assured him that we hadn't planned a public event. Our quiet family dinner at the house, complete with a birthday cake and a small stack of birthday greetings selected from the many that had arrived unsolicited, was enjoyed by all. However, Paul had clearly begun to slide downhill. I called Marian and took him back to Philadelphia, where, once again, he improved immediately.

On my visits to Philadelphia over the next month, I still felt that having Paul as a permanent resident without any breaks was a strain on Marian, although she never complained. When I suggested that perhaps Paul could live with us for a few months every once in a while in a different, less isolated setting, she neither approved nor rejected the idea. Marilyn agreed to the new proposal and found a ten-room rent-controlled apartment on 86th Street on Manhattan's Upper West Side. The two-room suite in the rear of the apartment was ideal for Paul. She decorated it with Freda Diamond's help, and we all moved in during the first week in September. Things went well at first. The apartment building housed several progressives who admired Paul, and the neighborhood was marginally integrated; Dr. Aaron Wells, the black physician who had attended Paul in 1956, lived in a nearby brownstone. On Dr. Rockmore's recommendation, I replaced Pearlmutter with Dr. Alvin Goldfarb, a geriatric psychiatrist and internist. Paul seemed comfortable with him, responding readily to his questions.

However, by mid-October, Paul began to exhibit his familiar signs of withdrawal that marked the beginning of a decline. I took him to see Dr. Goldfarb, who agreed with my suggestion that he return to Marian's. In an October 20, 1966, letter to Dr. Rockmore, Goldfarb wrote that he believed "Mr. Robeson's condition can be controlled and that he will ultimately be responsive to therapeutic efforts. At present, residence with his sister during a 'settling' down period in which I can collect further information about him is indicated. I was not impressed by any organic component to the illness." Marian agreed that he should live permanently in Philadelphia, and when I drove him there, Paul was visibly relieved on arrival. Two weeks later, he had improved considerably.

Lee Lurie, Bob Rockmore's associate, who had taken charge of Paul's affairs after Bob's death, sent Marian a weekly stipend to cover expenses, including part-time help. Charlotte Bell, the piano teacher whom Paul had often visited during his previous stays, came over regularly to rekindle his interest in his music and to engage him in conversation. Lloyd Brown visited often, coming away with the impression that he was slowly getting better; the Rosens visited occasionally.

On my regular visits, I found Paul less anxious but more lethargic and less communicative. Sometimes he engaged in conversation with me and at times even became animated when I mentioned an event that stirred his interest, or an item from his past that triggered fond memories. But more often he didn't make the effort to communicate. However, he read the papers regularly and watched television often.[9]

Back during the early months of 1966, while Marilyn was searching for the new apartment and Paul was at Marian's, we had gone up to the Jumel Terrace house to sort through my parents' papers and personal possessions. On the ground floor, we found two rooms with several hundred stacked cartons, randomly filled with papers, photographs, programs, clippings, artifacts, phonograph records, tape recordings, and 8- and 16-millimeter film. The boxes themselves were imposing, but their contents were spectacular. Interspersed among scores of receipts reflecting the mundane minutiae of department store purchases, we discovered Paul's unpublished handwritten manuscripts, Essie's personal diaries, as well as handwritten letters from Jawaharlal Nehru, George Bernard Shaw, Eugene O'Neill, Helen Hayes, Rebecca West, Sergei Eisenstein, Emma Goldman, and many other historical figures. We soon realized that here, tucked away in frayed cardboard cartons, lay the record of my parents' lives, encapsulated in tens of thousands of items. We had come upon a historical treasure.

During the following weeks, we systematically went through the materials page by page, carton by carton. Initially we sorted them by category and decade, transferring the stacks to carefully labeled library boxes. This proved to be a slow and painstaking process, and by the time the new apartment was ready we had processed only a portion of the materials. Now that my father was permanently living at Marian's, we went back to Jumel Terrace to finish, transferring the boxes to our new apartment in preparation for putting the house up for sale. Our estimate of the total number of items exceeded fifty thousand, including over eight thousand photographs. For the next six years, we continued to work on this collection in our apartment, identifying and dating each item and filing it by category and year.

Marilyn and I marveled at how Essie, buffeted by the turmoil of her life, had found the dedication and tenacity to assemble and preserve this vast and invaluable historical record intact despite many moves between distant places. History is forever enriched by her feat.[10]

When I visited, my father would occasionally engage me on a topic that captivated his interest. He retained his disdain for the conventional civil rights leaders such as NAACP head Roy Wilkins, and felt that the militant young "black power" activists were, for the most part, well-meaning but without a coherent strategy or a sound historical outlook. "They don't seem to have a clear idea of what they're doing," he once commented. Yet I got the feeling he sympathized with them. When I commented that it was good they were out there, if only to provide a bit of leverage for the "moderates," he smiled.

Paul's respect for and admiration of Reverend King as a leader coming from the southern base of the black freedom struggle was a consistent thread that ran throughout our exchanges. He admired King's courage in publicly opposing President Johnson's Vietnam War, even while allied with Johnson on civil rights legislation. He also respected King's growth as a leader and his responsiveness to the "black masses."

I recall one unusually extended talk in which a comment I made on the urban riots of 1966 and 1967 in black communities across the nation elicited the response that he was impressed by King's organizing attempts in northern cities and his inclusion of economic demands in his program. I asked my father whether he thought King was trying to create a nationwide coalition of black organizations, which would be independent of outside control. After taking a moment to reflect, he replied that it looked that way, adding that perhaps King had read *Here I Stand*.

Paul didn't respond as readily about foreign events. On one of my visits, I asked my father what he thought about the growing split between the Soviet Union and China. He just shrugged, offering the comment that at least both of them were helping North Vietnam and backing Third World liberation movements. Another time, after the August 1968 Soviet invasion of Czechoslovakia, I said that I considered it a bad mistake. He nodded in agreement but made no comment.

In April 1968, the many greetings Paul received in tribute to his seventieth birthday gave him a lift despite his sadness engendered by the recent assassination of Reverend Martin Luther King Jr. in Memphis. Major birthday celebrations were held in Moscow and East Berlin, but the tribute that meant the most was organized by Dame Sybil Thorndyke and others in London on April 8, the eve of his birthday. Highlighted by a program of music, poetry, and dramatic readings, including appearances by Dame Peggy Ashcroft, Sir Michael Redgrave, Mary Ure, and Bruno Raikin, the event attracted tribute messages from Sir John Gielgud, Yehudi Menuhin, and Johnny Dankworth, among others. In New York, the independent FM radio station WBAI-Pacifica broadcast a two-hour *Tribute to Paul Robeson* on April 9. In a moving portrayal, the program used original tape recordings of Paul and interviews with a variety of his old personal friends from as far back as the 1920s.[11]

All was going well until August 1969, when Paul began to decline rapidly. As he became more lethargic and unresponsive, Marian called Dr. Klingensmith in desperation. Klingensmith called on two psychiatrists and a young cardiologist, Dr. Herbert Cohen, for consultation. I came down to Philadelphia to join Marian in meeting with them. The psychiatrists recommended hospitalization and electroshock treatments. I vetoed electroshock, and Marian agreed. Dr. Cohen then suggested that a pacemaker might alleviate Paul's heart-block condition, thus improving blood circulation to the brain. I approved this option with Marian's enthusiastic support. The pacemaker was inserted at University Hospital, and Paul improved dramatically. Marian, Lloyd Brown, and I all agreed that he was better than at any time since the 1965 California trip.[12]

The early 1970s passed uneventfully but pleasurably for Paul. He led a comfortable, quiet life in Philadelphia, interacting on his own terms with friends and acquaintances in the local community. His mood remained fairly even, with frequent good days and occasional excellent ones. A select group of close friends—Clara, Lloyd, and the

Rosens—visited with varying frequency. Occasionally, Freda Diamond came, as well as friends from out of town, such as Reverend Steven Fritchman from Los Angeles and Andrew Faulds on a visit from Stratford-upon-Avon in England. I visited often, occasionally bringing Marilyn and the children, whom he enjoyed. He was interested in Susan's photography and intrigued by David's football prowess, which he viewed on 8-millimeter film I had shot of David's college games for the University of Connecticut.

Once I asked my father why he wouldn't allow more of his old friends and admirers to visit him. His reply was emphatic. He refused to present himself in his present condition because he didn't believe his friends or his public would accept him as he was. He wanted to be remembered from the time when he performed and spoke publicly—"moved, sang, acted." He knew he had paved the way for those that came after him and needed no credit for it, so he had no desire to appear in person at events honoring him. Then he waved his hand, indicating that the matter was closed.

Paul was awarded many honors from both black and white institutions during the period 1970–1974, and he appointed me to accept the awards on his behalf. They included the National Urban League's 1972 Whitney Young Memorial Award in New York City's Yankee Stadium at halftime during the traditional football game between two leading black colleges; an honorary doctor of law degree in 1973 from Lincoln University, the historically black college from which Paul's father had graduated; and a 1973 honorary doctor of the arts from Rutgers University.

Two honors in 1972 gave him particular satisfaction. *Ebony*'s August special issue on the black male featured an article titled "Ten Greats of Black History," in which a panel of leading black historians named him one of the ten all-time great black figures. Calling him "one of the most multifaceted geniuses of recorded history for nearly a half-century," the panel concluded that "Paul Robeson, when his scholarship is better known, will win recognition as the finest ideologist of black nationalism since Sidney of the 1840s. His writings will also reveal him as one of the century's most perceptive commentators on the cultures of the East, West and Africa. No black man has ever given more to his people than Robeson."

The second recognition—for Paul the most important of all—came in November when he was inducted into the National

Theater Hall of Fame as a charter member, one of the first 122 to be so honored. Held at New York's Uris Theatre, now renamed the Gershwin Theatre, where the names are inscribed in gold letters on a wall above with those of subsequent inductees, the induction ceremony included Paul among the honorees selected for special tribute. He was proud to be in the company of such legends as Eugene O'Neill, John and Ethel Barrymore, Helen Hayes, W. C. Fields, Ira Gershwin, Fred Astaire, and Bert Williams, the only other black honoree, whom he had admired since his youth.

Paul's seventy-fifth birthday was celebrated on the afternoon of April 15, 1973, at Carnegie Hall by a multimedia Salute to Paul Robeson produced by Harry Belafonte with my collaboration. The program integrated appearances of artists and speakers with film, slides, and tape recordings, featuring a galaxy of stars including Sidney Poitier, Robert Ryan, Zero Mostel, Belafonte, James Earl Jones, Dizzy Gillespie, Ruby Dee, and Pete Seeger; among the speakers were Coretta King; Ramsey Clark, former attorney general in the Johnson administration; Angela Davis; and Mayor Richard Hatcher of Gary, Indiana.

The program closed dramatically with a message Paul recorded for the occasion with Lloyd Brown's assistance. Paul made a powerful impression as his voice came over the sound system—older, but firm, clear, and deep:

> Though I have not been able to be active for several years, I want you to know that I am the same Paul, dedicated as ever to the worldwide cause of humanity for freedom, peace, and brotherhood.
>
> Here at home, my heart is with the continuing struggles of my own people to achieve complete liberation from racist domination, and to gain for all Black Americans and the other minority groups not only equal rights but an equal share.
>
> In the same spirit, I salute the colonial liberation movements of Africa, Latin America, and Asia, which have gained new inspiration and understanding from the heroic example of the Vietnamese people, who have once again turned back an imperialist aggressor.
>
> Together with the partisans of peace—the peoples of the socialist countries and the progressive elements of all other countries—I rejoice that the movement for peaceful coexistence has made important gains, and that the advocates of "cold war" and "containment" have had to retreat.

Though ill health has compelled my retirement, you can be sure that in my heart I go on singing:

But I keeps laughing
Instead of crying,
I must keep fighting
Until I'm dying,
And Ol' Man River
He just keeps rolling along!

Produced by Harry Belafonte with Ralph Alswang as coproducer and the script by John Killens and Walter Bernstein, the Salute attracted a capacity audience and raised sufficient funds to establish the Paul Robeson Archives and rent a small office. In the following years, the archives began the work of preserving Paul's and Essie's papers.[13]

Tributes from all over the United States and the world poured in to the Salute. Especially notable were those from heads of state. The prime minister of India, Indira Gandhi, wrote, "The great voice that was heard with such thundering clarity still echoes wherever men and women gather to pursue the struggle for freedom and justice." Julius Nyerere, president of Tanzania, called Paul "an inspiration and an encouragement to his comrades in the struggle for justice and humanity." Michael Manley, prime minister of Jamaica, recalled Paul's 1948 visit to Jamaica when he sang a free concert for eighty thousand people. Other outstanding tributes came from Soviet ambassador to the United States Anatoly Dobrynin and black tennis star Arthur Ashe, who wrote that Paul was an inspiration to "all of us" and called his courage "rare." Ashe went on to express his regret that the Salute had not happened earlier due to "our lack of courage."

A highly significant laudatory greeting was sent directly to Paul in Philadelphia. It came from the sitting chief justice of the U.S. Supreme Court, Warren E. Burger, who recalled Paul's "magnificent" portrayal of Othello and his "continued" enjoyment of Paul's recordings. Ironically, two decades earlier, Burger, then a Justice Department attorney, had acted as liaison between the FBI and the State Department in connection with Paul's passport case.

Paul's spirits were lifted by the Salute. He was consistently better over the next two years. When Larry Brown died, Paul sent a message that was read at the Lawrence Brown Memorial Concert held in New York in February 1973. In it he recalled the musical history he and Larry had made as an inseparable team, and paid tribute to Larry's accompanying and arranging genius.

I often drove Clara to Philadelphia for visits that usually lasted several hours with much conversation in a mostly one-on-one setting. Paul talked about personal matters, his singing career, and his music.

The fall of 1974 brought the most significant indication that the black mainstream now accepted Paul. The Congressional Black Caucus honored him with its Special Award of Merit, and Tony Batten, host of the Public Broadcasting Service's program *Interface*, produced a sympathetic and accurate documentary film on Paul's life. Cornell Capa, head of the International Center for Photography, organized a sensitive exhibit at the center of vintage photographs of Paul.

My father's slow but steady improvement marked 1975. In the spring, he enjoyed a seventy-seventh birthday party with a birthday cake, attended by family and friends at Marian's house. In the fall, Lloyd, who came down frequently, interviewed him and shot some home movie footage of him.

When Harry Belafonte asked me to take him on a visit to Paul, I told him I'd ask my father. In all the time Paul had been in Philadelphia, he had not agreed to see any of the celebrities whom he had befriended. To my surprise, he agreed. Harry and I traveled to Philadelphia together by train. Paul and Harry talked alone for a short while, and then joined Marian and me at the dinner table. We chatted over the meal, with Paul mostly listening but following the conversation. As we left, Paul inscribed an original program from an early Robeson concert that Harry had brought from his collection.

On one of my visits near Thanksgiving of 1975, my father became contemplative during a lull in our conversation. He cocked his head slightly to one side in a typical pose and said evenly, "You know, son, you don't need to go to the trouble of coming to see me as often as you do. I appreciate it, but it's not necessary." When I started to reassure him, he shook his head. "I'm just putting in time, waiting to go. I would have checked myself out long ago, but for you, the grandchildren, the family, and the public. Anyway, if this is the way I'm to pay for my sins, so be it."

He rose from the sofa and, with a slightly bent back, laboriously climbed the stairs to his bedroom. As I realized the enormity of the suffering he had endured without complaint over so many years, I was overcome with grief.

My father seemed cheerful throughout the Christmas and New Year holidays. But when Marilyn and I visited in mid-January, he wasn't feeling well. Marian said he was upstairs in his bedroom napping, and probably wouldn't come down for dinner. Just as we began our meal, he descended the stairs, dressed as usual in a suit and tie. He paused on the landing, where he stood facing us with his right hand resting on the railings. He pulled himself up to his full height, smiled a beauteous smile, and said in a clear voice, "I'm going home; I'm going home over Jordan." Then he slumped and came to sit at the table.

We returned to New York that night with a deep sense of foreboding. The next morning, Marian called, greatly distraught. My father had suffered a mild stroke and been taken to University Hospital. During the next several days, he had a series of strokes, and when we visited him he was unable to respond in any way.

On the morning of January 23, 1976, I was in New York's Penn Station on my way to Philadelphia when I heard a radio bulletin that my father had passed away early that morning. He had gone "home."

I decided with Marian that Paul's funeral should be held in Mother A.M.E. Zion Church where his brother Ben had pastored and where he had been a member. He would lie in state in an open coffin at Harlem's Benta Funeral Parlor, on St. Nicholas Avenue near 141st Street. Throughout the two full days of the viewing, many hundreds came and waited in a long line to pay their respects and say farewell. Condolences streamed in from around the world. The funeral was held on the evening of January 27.

Despite a steady rainfall, Mother Zion Church was packed when its pastor, Reverend George W. McMurray, rose to officiate. After the opening hymn, "We Are Climbing Jacob's Ladder," Reverend William Howard Melish of Brooklyn's Trinity Episcopal Church delivered the scripture from the Book of Isaiah. He was followed by

Bishop J. Clinton Hoggard, presiding prelate of the Sixth Episcopal District of the A.M.E. Zion Church, who read the prayer. The cathedral choir sang "Every Time I Feel the Spirit," and soloist Delores Ivory Davis sang "Oh, When I Come to the End of My Journey."

Tributes closed the service. Expressing his admiration, Lloyd Brown said:

> How fortunate we were to have had Paul Robeson walk the earth among us! As artist and man he was a prophetic vision of how wondrously beautiful the human race may yet become. Now he belongs to the future.

Sam Rosen spoke of what Paul had meant to him and to his family:

> He never capitulated. We will never forget him. Our children will never forget him. Nor will their children nor their children's children. Because Big Paul's friendship is their most precious heritage. It has added substance to our lives and will—for as long as we're here and the need remains—never let us forget how important it is to continue to struggle.

Bishop Hoggard delivered a memorable and stirring eulogy:

> Paul would close a concert before labor unions by singing "Joe Hill" (a song about a union organizer executed for an alleged murder) and would sing the final line as a challenge—"Don't mourn for me—organize." Let me paraphrase it—"Don't mourn for me, but live for freedom's cause during this bicentennial of America, and say to any and all who may urge you to leave America that: 'because our ancestors were slaves, and our people died to build this country, we are going to stay right here and have a part of it, just like you. And no fascist-minded people will drive us from it. Is that clear?'" I bear on my body the marks of Jesus—but I also say—it's worth it! No cross; no crown!"

I spoke last:

> He never regretted the stands he took, because almost forty years ago, in 1937, he made his basic choice. He said then, "The artist must elect to fight for freedom or slavery. I have made my choice. I had no alternative."

To me, his son, he gave not only his love but also the freedom and encouragement to think my own thoughts, to follow my own inner convictions, to be my own man. To all of us he gave by example a set of standards to guide our own lives, each of us in our own way.

My father's legacy belongs also to all those who decide to follow the principles by which he lived. It belongs to his own people and to other oppressed peoples everywhere. It belongs to those of us who knew him best and to the younger generation that will experience the joy of discovering him.

I closed with lines from a poem that my son, David, had written that morning, inspired by Lebanese poet Kahlil Gibran and silently placed on my desk after he had observed me struggling to find the ending of my tribute:

I may keep memories of him
but not his essence.
For that will pour forth tomorrow.

Paul's casket was carried out to the hearse by twelve pallbearers, led by Harry Belafonte and Albert Ruben, to the recorded strains of Paul singing "Deep River." Emerging from the church, we beheld a crowd of several thousand Harlem residents who had gathered in the rain to listen to the funeral service over a loudspeaker. My last image was a little boy perched securely on his father's shoulders.[14]

Paul Robeson's ashes are interred at Ferncliff Cemetery in Hartsdale, New York. His epitaph reads:

Paul Robeson (1898–1976) "The artist must elect to fight for freedom or slavery. I have made my choice. I had no alternative."

NOTES

Materials from the Paul and Eslanda Robeson Collections are denoted (PERC).

Preface

1. *American Magazine*, May 1944 (article by Jerome Beatty).
2. From Paul Robeson's speech at Welcome Home Rally, June 19, 1949.
3. Marie Seton, *Paul Robeson* (London: Dobson Books, 1958), p. 95.

1. The Calling (1939–1940)

1. *New York Amsterdam News*, October 21, 1939.
2. Conversations with my father; Earl Robinson with Eric Gordon, *Ballad of an American: The Autobiography of Earl Robinson* (Lanham, MD: Scarecrow Press, 1998), pp. 93–95.
3. *Time*, November 20, 1939.
4. Eslanda Robeson's diary, 1939 (PERC).
5. Letter from Eslanda Robeson to Paul Robeson, June 25, 1939 (PERC).
6. For the New York reviews, see: *New York Post*, *New York Times*, *New York Herald Tribune*, *New York World-Telegram*, *New York Daily News*, and *New York Journal-American* (all January 11, 1940); *New York Amsterdam News*, January 13, 1940.
7. Leonard Lyon's column "The Lyon's Den,"*New York Post*, January 11, 1940 (portrait).
8. *Daily Worker*, New York, July 27, 1940.
9. *Boston Sunday Post*, January 14, 1940; *Chicago Defender*, April 6, 1940. Conversations with my mother and father.
10. *New York Amsterdam News*, October 21, 1939; *Evening Public Ledger*, Philadelphia, December 8, 1939; *New York World-Telegram*, February 1, 1940. Paul Robeson's unpublished 1939 notes served as the foundation of these public statements (PERC).
11. *Daily Worker*, December 12, 1939; *New York World-Telegram* and *New York Post*, February 1, 1940.
12. *Utica Observer Dispatch*, January 22, 1940; Paul Robeson's handwritten notes (PERC).

13. *Los Angeles Examiner*, May 5 and 14, 1940. Letter from Hattie McDaniel to Paul Robeson, April 22, 1940 (PERC).

14. Robinson with Gordon, *Ballad of an* American, p. 99. *Los Angeles Examiner*, July 24, 1940.

15. *Philadelphia Inquirer*, August 2, 1940.

16. *New York World-Telegram*, August 4, 1940 (Westport Country Playhouse); *Lambertville (NJ) Beacon*, August 15, 1940 (McCarter Theatre, Princeton).

17. Conversations with my father and John Hammond.

18. Conversations with my father.

19. Conversations with Clara Rockmore.

20. *Sunday Worker*, November 17, 1940; *Chicago Defender*, November 30, 1940.

21. *Buffalo (NY) Evening News*, December 5, 1940.

22. Letter from Brooks Atkinson to Paul Robeson, December 29, 1940 (PERC).

2. The Quest (1941)

1. Conversations with my father.

2. Letter from Marshall Bartholomew, Coordinator of Commercial and Cultural Relations Between the American Republics for the Council of National Defense, to Paul Robeson, January 20, 1941 (PERC); letter from Secretary of War Henry L. Stimson to Paul Robeson, October 1, 1941 (PERC).

3. Letter from Liu Liang-mo to Paul Robeson, January 5, 1941 (PERC).

4. Drafts of Mrs. Pinchot's letter to Paul Robeson and her press release, April 13, 1941; Associated Negro Press report of Mrs. Pinchot's press interview (April 13, 1941) (PERC).

5. *New York Times*, April 30, 1941.

6. Charles H. Wright, *Robeson: Labor's Forgotten Champion* (Detroit: Balamp Publishing, 1975), pp. 83, 93, 98–101.

7. Conversations with my father and mother.

8. Conversations with Robert Rockmore.

9. Conversations with my mother.

10. Conversations with my father.

11. *Dayton Herald* and *Dayton Daily News*, January 29, 1941. Margaret Webster, *Don't Put Your Daughter on the Stage* (New York: Knopf, 1972), p. 107.

12. *Sunday Worker*, October 12, 1941; *New York Amsterdam News*, October 11, 1941.

13. Letter from Ambrose Caliver to Paul Robeson, October 14, 1941 (PERC); Barbara Dianne Savage, *Broadcasting Freedom: Radio, War, and the Politics of Race, 1938–1948* (Chapel Hill: University of North Carolina Press, 1999), pp. 66–84.

14. *Ottawa Evening Citizen*, October 30, 1941; *Winnipeg Free Press*, November 5, 1941; *Vancouver News-Herald*, November 10, 1941; *Seattle Times*, November 14, 1941.

15. *Sunday Worker*, November 2, 1941; *Vancouver Sun*, November 22, 1941.

16. *San Francisco Examiner*, December 17, 1941 ("greatest bass voice"); *San Francisco Chronicle*, December 18, 1941 ("splendor"); *Sacramento Bee*, December 19, 1941 ("mellow richness, instinctive feeling").

17. Conversations with my father and mother.

18. *California State Prison at San Quentin News*, December 25, 1941.

3. Hero and Enemy (1942–1943)

1. Conversations with Freda Diamond, Robert Rockmore, my father, and my mother. The February 13 meeting is noted in my father's 1942 appointment book (PERC).

2. Philip A. Klinkner with Rogers M. Smith, *The Unsteady March:The Rise and Decline of Racial Equality in America* (Chicago: University of Chicago Press, 1999), pp. 171, 173. The "Salute to Negro Troops" was held on January 11, 1942, at New York's Cosmopolitan Opera House.

3. Klinkner and Smith, *The Unsteady March*, p. 172. Conversations with my father.

4. *Albuquerque Journal*, February 18, 1842; *Kansas City Journal*, February 18, 1942 (review); *Amsterdam New York Star-News*, February 21, 1942; *New York Sun*, February 18, 1942; *Albuquerque Tribune*, February 18, 1942 (headlines). Letter from Lucille Bluford, news editor of the *Call*, to Paul Robeson, February 21, 1942. *Pittsburgh Courier*, February 28, 1942 (Bibb column). Conversations with my father.

5. Conversations with my father (White House invitation). The mass meeting sponsored by the Council on African Affairs was held at New York's Manhattan Center. Letter from Eleanor Roosevelt to Earl Robinson, May 26, 1942 (re "Battle Hymn" broadcast on May 17, 1942).

6. *Cavalcade* (Birmingham, AL), vol. 2, no. 1 (May 1942).

7. *Daily Worker*, April 22, 1942.

8. Eleanor Roosevelt, "My Day" column, *New York World-Telegram*, April 22, 1942; *Nashville Tennessean*, April 21, 1942.

9. Margaret Webster, *Don't Put Your Daughter on the Stage* (New York: Knopf, 1972), pp. 106–107 and 109–110. Conversations with my father.

10. *Boston Post*, August 11, 1942; Paul Robeson interview in *Harvard Crimson*, August 14, 1942.

11. *Variety*, August 12, 1942.

12. *New York Times*, August 16, 1942; *Time*, August 24, 1942.

13. Note from Margaret Webster to Eslanda Robeson, undated, 1942 (PERC).

14. Conversations with my father.

15. *Boston Chronicle*, August 15, 1942; *Chicago Defender*, August 29, 1942; *Baltimore Afro-American*, August 22, 1942; *Pittsburgh Courier*, September 5, 1942; *Worker*, August 16, 1942.

16. *New York Times*, September 25, 1942, and a second, undated September article; *New York Daily News*, editorial, October 13, 1942.

17. *PM*, September 25, 1942.

18. *PM*, September 2, 1942 (Walter White); *Pittsburgh Courier*, September 12, 1942 (Clarence Muse).

19. *Pittsburgh Courier*, September 5, 1942. Conversations with my father.

20. *People's World*, September 22, 1942; *Hartford Daily Courant*, September 23, 1942; *Deseret News*, September 23, 1942; Associated Negro Press story by Wendell Green ("No More Hollywood—Robeson"; dateline Los Angeles), undated, October 1942.

21. *Amsterdam New York Star-News*, September 12, 1942 (Free India meeting, September 8, 1942); *Pilot*, September 11, 1942 (newspaper of the National Maritime Union, reporting on the Central Park rally); *Oakland Tribune*, September 20, 1942 (Moore Shipyards); *Daily Worker*, September 20, 1942 (Los Angeles Win the War rally).

22. Letter from Eslanda Robeson to Paul Robeson, September 13, 1942 (PERC).

23. Letter from Paul Robeson to Eslanda Robeson, undated, October 1942 (PERC).

24. *New Orleans Item*, October 20, 1942; *New Orleans Times-Picayune*, October 21, 1942. The complete text of Paul's speech is in PERC.

25. *Campus Mirror* (Spelman College, Atlanta), November 1942; *Atlanta University Bulletin*, December 1942.

26. *Washington Times-Herald* and *Daily Worker*, both November 8, 1942 (embassy reception and Madison Square Garden meeting). William Shirer, *The Rise and Fall of the Third Reich: A History of Nazi Germany* (New York: Simon and Schuster, 1959), pp. 925–934; Adam B. Ulam, *Stalin: The Man and His Era* (Boston: Beacon Press, 1973), pp. 574–577 (battle of Stalingrad), and p. 592 (Litvinov).

27. The vocabulary list of 858 words represented a special technique Paul had adapted for learning languages. Originally developed to teach basic English, the system uses 858 basic words that embody a conceptual scope sufficient to carry on a rudimentary dialogue on a wide range of subjects. Paul learned this basic vocabulary in many languages, including Chinese.

28. Letter and draft statement from Pearl Buck to Paul Robeson, August 28, 1942; letter from Arch Oboler, director of *The Free World Theatre*, and Robert Rossen, chairman of the Hollywood Writers' Mobilization, to Paul Robeson, December 17, 1942; Paul Robeson's draft classification card, issued August 11, 1942 (all PERC).

29. *New York Herald Tribune*, January 10, 1943; undated 1943 Columbia Concerts publicity flyer.

30. *Humboldt Times* (Eureka, California), March 10, 1943.

4. The Robeson *Othello* (1943–1945)

1. Conversations with my father.

2. My father put in a good word for me to an acquaintance who was a member of the Cornell University board of trustees.

3. *Atlanta Daily World*, June 2, 1943; *Daily Worker*, July 1, 1943 (reprint of the verbatim transcript of Dr. Benjamin Mays's citation of Paul Robeson); typewritten text of Paul Robeson's response to the citation (PERC).

4. Klinkner and Smith, *The Unsteady March*, pp. 180–181. Conversations with my father.

5. *Daily Worker*, June 28, 1943 (Watergate); *New York Times*, July 2, 1943; *PM*, July 1 and 2 (Lewisohn Stadium); *Chicago Defender*, July 24, 1943 (Great Lakes); *Chicago Defender*, July 31, 1943; *Daily Worker*, August 28, 1943 (July 24 Chicago appearance).

6. Letter from Paul Robeson to Eslanda Robeson, undated, August 1943 (PERC).

7. Conversations with my mother. Margaret Webster, *Don't Put Your Daughter on the Stage* (New York: Knopf, 1972), p. 110.

8. *Boston Herald*, September 21, 1943 (Hughes); *Boston Sunday Post*, September 26, 1943 (Norton); *Boston Daily Record*, September 22, 1943 (Gaffney). Conversations with my father; letter from Eslanda Robeson to Paul Robeson, September 20, 1943 (PERC).

9. *Evening Bulletin* (Philadelphia), October 5, 1943.

10. ". . . that big black jelly-fish . . ." as quoted by Martin Bauml Duberman from Margaret Webster's letters to her mother Dame May Whitty in Duberman, *Paul Robeson* (New York: Knopf, 1989), p. 269 Conflict over replacing Joe and Uta from conversations with Freda Diamond and my father.

11. Webster, *Don't Put Your Daughter on the Stage*, pp. 113–114.

12. Louis Kronenberger in *PM*, October 20 and 24, 1943.

13. Howard Barnes in *New York Herald Tribune*, October 20, 24, and 31, 1943.

14. Conversations with my father.

15. *Nation*, vol. 157, pp. 507–508.

16. Conversations with my father. Webster, *Don't Put Your Daughter on the Stage*, pp. 111 and 114.

17. *New York Amsterdam News*, October 30, 1943 ("big blow against intolerance"); *People's Voice*, October 23, 1943 ("great social document"); letter from Mary McLeod Bethune to Paul Robeson, November 10, 1943 (PERC); letter from William L. Dawson to Paul Robeson, November 23, 1943 (PERC).

18. *Pittsburgh Courier*, November 27, 1943 (Savoy Ballroom and Madison Square Garden); *New YorkHerald Tribune*, November 17, 1943 (Herald Tribune Forum; the full text of the speech is in the Paul Robeson Collection); *Pittsburgh Courier* and *Chicago Defender*, December 11, 1943; *Baltimore Afro-American* and *New York Times*, December 4, 1943 (baseball owners).

19. *Pittsburgh Courier*, January 15, 1944; *New York Herald Tribune*, January 7, 1944.

20. *PM*, April 17, 1944; *New York Amsterdam News*, April 22, 1944; *Daily Worker*, April 18, 1944 (birthday party); *Chicago Defender*, May 6, 1944 (Moscow). Quotations from personal greetings have been taken from the letters in PERC.

21. Conversations with my father.

22. Webster, *Don't Put Your Daughter on the Stage*, pp. 113–114.

23. *New York Times*, May 20, 1944 (Diction Award); Ed Sullivan in his column "Little Old New York," unidentified 1944 newspaper clipping.

24. *Pittsburgh Courier*, January 8, 1944 (eightieth anniversary of the Emancipation Proclamation broadcast).

25. *PM*, July 5, 1944 (Donaldson Award).

26. *Chicago Defender*, July 22, 1944; letter from John H. Johnson, editor of the *Negro Digest*, to Paul Robeson, August 31, 1944 (removal of Baltimore and Washington, D.C., from tour list); letters from Eleanor Roosevelt to Paul Robeson, June 2, 1944, and September 23, 1944 (Wyltwyck School) (PERC). Conversations with my father.

27. *Springfield (MA) Sunday Union and Republican*, January 21, 1945; *Pathfinder*, January 29, 1945. Extensive excerpts from the original recording are available on

the CD *Paul Robeson:Othello*, Pearl Plays and Poets, Pavilion Records Ltd., Sparrows Green, Wadhurst, E. Sussex, United Kingdom, LC 1836. Webster, *Don't Put Your Daughter on the Stage*, p. 117.

28. Interview with José Ferrer and Uta Hagen, *New York Herald Tribune*, May 27, 1945. Conversations with my father.

29. *Hartford Times*, September 8, 1944; *Boston Chronicle*, September 16, 1944.

30. Conversations with my father.

31. *Seattle Times*, December 26, 1944; *Sacramento Bee*, January 22, 1945.

32. Transcript of Robeson's WHK Radio broadcast (PERC); letter from Eleanor Roosevelt to Eslanda Robeson, November 6, 1944. Conversations with my father and mother.

33. *Chicago Daily Tribune*, April 11, 1945; *Chicago Daily News*, April 11, 1945; *Chicago Times*, April 11, 1945.

34. Conversations with my mother, my father, and Clara Rockmore. Letter from Uta Hagen to Eslanda Robeson, September 22, 1945 (PERC).

35. Letter from Margaret Webster to Paul Robeson, June 15, 1945 (PERC).

36. *Victoria Daily Times* (Canada), January 13, 1945. Conversations with my father.

37. *Chicago Defender*, July 7, 1945 (Negro Freedom Rally); *Baltimore Afro-American*, June 16, 1945 (Howard University commencement).

38. Joseph P. Lash, *Eleanor and Franklin:The Story of Their Relationship, based on Eleanor Roosevelt's Private Papers* (New York: W. W. Norton, 1971); Harold Evans, *The American Century* (New York: Knopf, 1998), pp. 344–349; *Chicago Defender*, June 9, 1945, and *New York Amsterdam News*, June 16, 1945 (USO tour).

39. Conversations with my father and Ben Davis; articles in the U.S. Communist Party theoretical journals the *Communist* (January, June, July, and November 1944) and *Political Affairs* (January, April, July, September, and December 1945).

40. Unidentified clippings from black newspapers.

5. Challenging the Mighty (1945–1946)

1. Paul Robeson's travel orders from the War Department, July 27, 1945; letter to Paul Robeson from Major General Frank A. Keating, commander, 102nd Infantry Division, August 20, 1945 (PERC).

2. Conversations with my father and with William Reuben, Miriam Solovieff's former husband. The letter from the soldier was dated August 21, 1945 (PERC).

3. Conversations with my father.

4. *Pittsburgh Courier*, October 27, 1945; unidentified October 1945 clipping from the black press.

5. Conversations with my father and mother.

6. *Springfield (MA) Union*, October 2, 1945.

7. *Worker*, October 28, 1945 (Ben Davis rally). Manuscript of Robeson's speech to the Central Conference of the American Rabbis (PERC).

8. *People's Voice* (New York), January 12, 1946.

9. FBI log of a telephone conversation between Max Yergan and Paul Robeson, March 21, 1946.

10. The Ishpeming concert was on April 27, 1946. Robeson's story is excerpted from the tape recording of a talk he gave at the People's Songs Conference, August 13, 1949 (PERC).

11. *Springfield Union* and *Springfield Daily Republican*, May 20, 1946.

12. Conversations with my father and mother.

13. "Eastlands, Rankins and Bilbos" refers to a Mississippi senator and two Georgia senators, respectively, who were notorious racists.

14. In addition to Paul Robeson in his capacity as chairman of the Council on African Affairs, the delegation consisted of Dr. Charlotte Hawkins Brown, Palmer Memorial Institute, Sedalia, North Carolina; Mrs. Harper Sibley, president of the United Council of Church Women; Reverend W. H. Jernagin, National Baptist Convention and president of the Federated Council of Churches; Dr. Joseph L. Johnson, Howard University School of Medicine and president of the Washington Committee of the Southern Conference of Human Welfare; Rabbi Irving Miller, American Jewish Congress; Max Yergan, president of the National Negro Congress; Dr. Metz T. P. Lochard, editor in chief of the *Chicago Defender*; and Aubrey Williams, publisher of the *Southern Farmer* and former chief of the National Youth Administration.

15. Conversations with my father. Accounts of the Crusade and of the encounter with President Truman were published in the *New York Times*, September 24, 1946; *Philadelphia Tribune*, September 24, 1946; *People's Voice*, September 28, 1946; *Chicago Defender*, September 28, 1946; and *Baltimore Afro-American*, October 5, 1946. The meeting with Truman had been arranged through John H. Sengstacke, owner and publisher of the *Chicago Defender*, who was a personal friend of Truman's.

16. International Longshore and Warehouse Union newspaper (San Francisco), October 18, 1946.

17. The complete transcript of Robeson's testimony was published in the October 18, 1946, issue of the *Westwood Hills Press*, a Northern California newspaper. I have excerpted the testimony without ellipses for readability.

18. Marie Seton, *Paul Robeson* (London: Dobson Books, 1958), pp. 168–169.

19. Conversations with my father.

6. Storm Warnings (1946–1948)

1. *Chicago Sun*, January 20, 1947; *St. Louis Globe-Democrat*, January 25, 1947; *Vancouver Sun*, February 17, 1947.

2. *St. Louis Post-Dispatch*, January 26, 1947; *New York Times*, January 27, 1947.

3. *Pittsburgh Courier*, February 1, 1947; memorandum from the St. Louis special agent in charge to FBI director Hoover, January 29, 1947.

4. *Philadelphia Inquirer*, March 16, 1947.

5. Conversations with my father and William Patterson. *PM*, April 20, 1947; *Hartford Daily Courant*, April 18, 1947; *Chicago Sun*, April 20, 1947; memorandum from the U.S. attorney general to FBI director Hoover, titled "Racial Unrest Created By Paul Robeson's Scheduled Appearance At Peoria, Illinois," May 3, 1947; letter from G. R. McSwain, special agent in charge, Chicago FBI Field Office, to FBI director Hoover, April 30, 1947. See also Marie Seton, *Paul Robeson* (London: Dobson Books Ltd., 1958), pp. 178–179.

6. *New York Herald Tribune*, April 25 and May 7, 1947; *PM*, April 29 and May 4, 1947; *Daily Worker*, April 25, 1947. See also Seton, *Paul Robeson*, pp. 180–181. The quote from Paul Robeson's speech is taken from the full transcript of a tape recording (PERC).

7. Seton, *Paul Robeson*, pp. 181–182 (Panama); *Chronicle* (Boston), June 28, 1947 (Symphony Hall); *PM*, July 20, 1947 (Lewisohn Stadium).

8. *Look* magazine, June 24, 1947 (Gallup poll); *Washington Times-Herald*, May 22, 1947 (Sokolsky column). At that time, passports had to be renewed every two years. Paul had renewed his passport on May 8, 1947, for possible travel to Panama, Cuba, and Mexico without objection from the FBI. This passport was valid for travel in the Western Hemisphere until June 1949 but did not permit travel to Europe.

9. Klinkner and Smith, *The Unsteady March*, pp. 213–215.

10. Eric Bentley, ed., *Thirty Years of Treason: Excerpts from Hearings Before the House Committee on Un-American Activities, 1938–1968* (New York: Viking Press, 1971), p. 131.

11. Curtis D. MacDougall, *Gideon's Army*, vol. 2 (New York: Marzani & Munsell, 1965), p. 284.

12. Earl Robinson with Eric A. Gordon, *Ballad of an American:The Autobiography of Earl Robinson* (Lanham, MD: Scarecrow Press, 1998), pp. 220–222.

13. The file number of this informant, who is referred to in FBI document No. 100-25857-467A of June 11, 1948, is Yergan's assigned file number, which appears in many other FBI documents. Conversations with my mother, father, Alphaeus Hunton, Doxey Wilkerson, and Ben Davis.

14. MacDougall, *Gideon's Army*, vol. 2, p. 284.

15. Jervis Anderson, *A. Philip Randolph: A Biographical Portrait* (New York: Harcourt Brace Jovanovich, 1972), pp. 276–281.

16. Conversations with my father and mother.

17. Excerpts from the transcript of Paul Robeson's tape-recorded testimony before the Senate Judiciary Committee (PERC).

18. *Daily Worker*, June 29, 1948.

19. MacDougall, *Gideon's Army*, vol. 2, pp. 530, 533, 586.

20. Conversations with my father and mother, and with Helen Rosen.

21. From the transcript of an October 29, 1948, Wallace-Robeson radio broadcast over the Mutual Broadcasting Company network (PERC).

22. MacDougall, *Gideon's Army*, vol. 3, pp. 881–882.

23. *National Guardian*, November 15, 1948.

24. Ibid., December 20, 1948.

25. Conversations with my father and with Robert Rockmore; 1948 and 1949 Central Bureau files of the FBI obtained under the Freedom of Information Act.

26. *New York Sun*, February 15, 1949 (George Sokolsky on the Metropolitan Opera Company).

7. Into the Eye of the Storm (1949)

1. From talk at "People's Songs" Conference, New York City, August 13, 1949 (transcribed from a tape recording) (PERC). Conversations with my father.

2. From a March 9, 1949, CIA memorandum referenced "WASH-9684." The document includes a summary of Robeson's extemporaneous remarks to the delegation.

3. Valentine Elliott in the June–August 1949 issue of *Makerere*, a literary magazine published in British East Africa at Makerere College.

4. Conversations with my father.

5. Robeson's speech was published in a bulletin of the Paris Peace Congress (PERC).

6. Conversations with my father. The mainstream press published a drumbeat of letters from readers attacking Robeson: "Paul Robeson's Mistake,"*New York Herald Tribune*, April 24, 1949; "Robeson Not Speaking for Great Majority of Negroes,"*Springfield (MA) Union*, April 21, 1949; "Negro Leaders Denounce Robeson,"*Birmingham Post*, April 1949, undated; "Robeson's Views Draw Criticism,"*Detroit Free Press*, May 1, 1949.

Lester Granger's column appeared in the June 25, 1949, issue of the conservative black newspaper the *New York Amsterdam News*; McKenzie's piece appeared in the June 25, 1949, issue of the *Pittsburgh Courier*.

W. E. B. DuBois released his statement supporting Paul on May 10, 1949, in Paris. The comments of Mary McLeod Bethune and Adam Clayton Powell Jr., as well as the editorials, appeared in the April 30, 1949, issues of the black press (e.g., *Chicago Defender, New York Amsterdam News, Baltimore Afro-American, Pittsburgh Courier, Philadelphia Tribune, Detroit Tribune, New York Age, Norfolk Journal and Guide*, and *Carolina Times*).

7. *Chicago Defender, Detroit Tribune*, and *Baltimore Afro-American*, all April 30, 1949.

8. Conversations with my father. Interviews with Peter Blackman, September 8 and 9, 1982.

9. Conversations with my father. Interviews with Peter Blackman and Bruno Raikin, London, September 8, 1982.

10. Conversations with my father.

11. Conversations with my father. Solomon Mikhoels's murder has been reliably documented. On pp. 261–262 of volume I of Nikita Khrushchev's memoir (*Khrushchev Remembers* [Boston: Little, Brown, 1970], there appears a reference to "the cruel punishment of Mikhoels, the greatest actor of the Yiddish theater, a man of culture." Frédéric Joliot-Curie was a leading French physicist, a member of the French Communist Party, and one of the top leaders of the World Peace Committee. Howard Fast was a leading American writer and a member of the U.S. Communist Party.

12. Paul's concert occurred at the same time that Stalin was conducting a devastating purge of the Leningrad Party organization (the "Leningrad Affair"). Virtually the entire Leningrad leadership was shot, and only Khrushchev's intervention at great risk to himself saved most of the Moscow party leadership.

13. Conversations with my father.

14. Conversations with my father and Ben Davis.

15. Conversations with my father.

16. This incident was brazenly falsified by the press. Under the subhead "Swings on Cameraman," the *Boston Evening American* (June 19, 1949) claimed that "Robeson attempted to throw a punch but was stopped by a police officer." The *Daily Compass* (June 20, 1949) reported that "Robeson stepped out, shook his fist at one [photographer], and moved a pace toward him, but was blocked by the crowd." The *Springfield Union* (June 20, 1949) repeated the *Compass* story: "Robeson stepped out of the other side of the cab, shook his fist at the photographer and tried to reach him." A photograph published in almost every newspaper, however, shows Paul wedged tightly in the backseat of the cab between Harold and Rae. From this position, it would have been difficult to get out of the cab and virtually impossible to swing at the reporter.

17. Transcription of the tape-recorded speech (PERC); also Philip S. Foner (ed.), *Paul Robeson Speaks: Writings, Speeches, Interviews, 1918–1974* (New York: Kensington Publishing, 2002), pp. 201–211.

18. For examples of the press coverage, see *New York Herald Tribune, New York Times, Daily Worker, Daily Mirror, Daily News, New York World-Telegram,* all June 20, 1949; *New York Amsterdam News, Baltimore Afro-American, New York Age, California Eagle, Chicago Defender, Norfolk Journal & Guide,* all June 25, 1949; *Cincinnati Union,* June 23, 1949; *Hartford (CT) Courant,* June 23, 1949; *Springfield (MA) Union,* June 23, 1949.

19. Transcription of the tape-recorded speech (PERC).

20. *Pittsburgh Courier,* September 17, 1949.

21. The black sponsors of the conference included: A.M.E. Zion bishop C. C. Alleyne, A.M.E. bishop R. R. Wright Jr., A.M.E. Zion bishop W. J. Walls, editor Percy Greene of Mississippi, United Public Workers executive Ewart Guinier, and American Federation of Labor executive Charles Collins. A detailed story on the conference appeared in the July 23, 1949, issue of the *New York Age.* The resolution stated, "Paul Robeson does, indeed, speak for us not only in his fight for full Negro democratic rights but also in his fight for peace."

22. Robinson's testimony appears in the *Congressional Record* and is obtainable from the U.S. Government Printing Office. The coverage of Robinson's testimony in the mainstream newspapers appeared on July 19, 1949. The black newspapers published their coverage on July 23. The cartoon and editorial criticizing Robinson prior to his appearance before HUAC appeared in the July 16, 1949, issue of the *Baltimore Afro-American.* The July 20 press conference at the Hotel Theresa was covered in the July 21, 1949, issue of the *Daily Worker* and the July 30, 1949, issues of the *New York Age,* the *Afro-American,* and the *Norfolk (VA) Journal and Guide.*

8. Peekskill, New York (1949)

1. *New York Age*, August 6, 13, 20, 1949; September 3, 17, 1949.

2. From a transcript of the tape-recorded speech (PERC).

3. Ibid.

4. Sources for the accounts in the preceding five paragraphs are Duberman, *Paul Robeson*, pp. 364–365. Conversations with my father and the Rosens.

5. Howard Fast, *Eyewitness: Peekskill U.S.A.* (pamphlet, 1950); *Violence in Peekskill* (American Civil Liberties Union report, 1949).

6. From a transcript of the tape-recorded speech (PERC).

7. Conversations with my father and Revels Cayton, who was one of the trade union guards and a member of the group that protected Paul on the platform. Leon Straus was vice president of the Fur and Leather Workers Union and an army officer in World War II.

8. Conversations with my father, Howard Fast, Revels Cayton, Leon Straus, William Patterson, and the driver of Robeson's car. I was an eyewitness to events at the concert, having arrived with Marilyn at 11 a.m. in a contingent from Camp Unity, where we worked, and having spent several hours in the outer perimeter of the defense line. Back at Camp Unity, I observed two groups of black police officers, guests at the resort, load up their cars and depart.

9. *New York Times*, October 9, 1949 (Randolph); *Baltimore Afro-American*, September 10, 1949; "Presentment of the Grand Jury of Westchester County" (1950).

10. Conversations with my mother and father.

11. The summary transcript of Paul's appearance as a witness appears in the September 22, 1949, report of a special agent to Hoover. The *Pittsburgh Courier* interview appears in the September 17, 1949, issue. *New York Herald Tribune*, September 21, 1949; *New York Amsterdam News*, September 24, 1949; *Hartford (CT) Courant*, September 21, 1949; *Baltimore Afro-American*, October 1, 1949 (headlines).

12. Conversations with my father. *Detroit News*, September 25, 1949; *California Eagle*, September 29, 1949; *New York Times*, October 9, 1949; *Daily Worker*, November 4, 1949; *A Paul Robeson Research Guide: A Selected, Annotated Bibliography*, compiled by Lenwood G. Davis (Westport, CT: Greenwood Press, 1982), p. 405; FBI Main Bureau file: Nos. 100-12304-172, 9/23/49; 100-12304-170, 10/14/49; 100-12304-178, 11/25/49. Conversations with my father and with tour organizer Louise Patterson.

13. Conversations with my father and with Lloyd Brown.

14. Letter from Nan Pandit to Eslanda Robeson, September 26, 1949 (PERC). Conversations with my father, my mother, Ben Davis, Marie Seton, and Geri Branton, a family friend in Los Angeles with whom my father shared this account.

9. Struggle for Survival (1950–1954)

1. The text of Robeson's speech is in PERC.

2. The other three women were Muriel Draper, a peace activist; Pearl Laws, a black trade union activist; and Ada Jackson, a black civil rights activist.

3. The text of Robeson's speech is in PERC.

4. See Harold Evans, *The American Century* (New York: Knopf, 1998), pp. 420–429.

5. The text of Robeson's speech is in PERC.

6. A copy of the Robert Ruark column with Hoover's handwritten note is in PERC (FBI Main Bureau File, No. 100-12304-220).

7. Conversations with my father and with Robert Sherman, longtime producer at radio station WQXR.

8. Letter from Eslanda Robeson to Nan Pandit (Vijaya Lakshmi Pandit), August 15, 1951; open letter from Paul Robeson to Warren Austin, June 12, 1951; statement by Paul Robeson, addressed to Jacob Malik, June 26, 1951; letter from London publisher Dennis Dobson to Marie Seton, with attached note from Seton to Robeson and a sample contract, June 29, 1951 (all PERC).

9. From interview of James Hicks in the documentary "The Tallest Tree in Our Forest," produced by Gil Noble, *Like It Is*, WABC-TV, 1997.

10. *Baltimore Afro-American*, December 1, 1951; *Daily Worker*, December 19, 1951.

11. *New York Times*, August 3, 1980.

12. Ethel and Julius Rosenberg, a New York left-wing couple, had been arrested and tried in 1951 on charges that in the mid-1940s they had transmitted to the Soviet Union the secret U.S. design of the plutonium trigger for an atomic bomb. They were convicted and sentenced to death on the questionable evidence of Ethel Rosenberg's brother, David Greenglass. Both Rosenbergs were executed in the electric chair on June 19, 1953.

13. INS memoranda of January 12, 17, and 18, 1952. *Vancouver Sun*, January 31, 1952; *People's Voice*, February 15, 1952.

14. The other recipients were French peace activist Yves Farge; Saifuddin Kitchloo, president of the All-India Peace Council; Elisa Branco, leader of the Brazilian Women's Federation; Johannes Becher, German Democratic Republic (East German) writer; Canadian peace advocate Reverend James Endicott; and Soviet writer Ilya Ehrenburg.

15. Paul's royalties are listed in Rockmore's income tax filings.

16. Dr. Morris Pearlmutter, an internist, was Paul's physician. He shared an office with Dr. Edward Barsky, an old personal friend of Paul's and a legendary surgeon of the Abraham Lincoln Brigade during the Spanish civil war.

17. Conversations with Louis Burnham and Alphaeus Hunton.

18. Conversations with my father and with Ben Davis.

19. Klinkner and Smith, *The Unsteady March*, pp. 234–241.

20. From Paul's press statement of March 3, 1954; from his March 13, 1954 (PERC), interview with the *Baltimore Afro-American*; and from his May 3, 1954, press statement in reply to Drew Pearson's comments on his May 2, 1954, radio program (PERC).

21. The law firm of Rabinowitz, Boudin and Standard provided me with copies of most of Leonard Boudin's legal files on the Robeson case, and I obtained numerous FBI and State Department memoranda under the Freedom of Information Act.

22. Conversations with my mother, father, and Robert Rockmore. Rockmore's law firm, Barron, Rice and Rockmore, made Paul's file available to me, complete with tax returns and financial records.

10. Victory over Despair (1955–1956)

1. Letter from Frank Whitley's wife, Helen Arstein Whitley, to Lloyd L. Brown, 1971; FBI cable from Hoover to the Los Angeles Field Office, March 11, 1955 (PERC).

2. Conversations with my father and documents in Boudin's files on my father's passport case.

3. *Pittsburgh Courier*, August 17, 1955. The *New York Amsterdam News* was the exception, criticizing Paul for not signing the noncommunist affidavit (September 10, 1955). Rover's argument in support of the State Department's case was reprinted in the August 26, 1955, issue of *U.S. News and World Report*.

4. Conversations with my father, mother, and Helen Rosen. I also researched my parents' medical records provided to me by Dr. Morris Pearlmutter.

5. Klinkner and Smith, *The Unsteady March*, pp. 242–243. Conversations with my father and mother.

6. *Telegram* (Canada) and *Toronto Daily Star*, February 13, 1955; *Tribune* (Canada), February 20, 1955.

7. The full text of Khrushchev's secret speech at the Twentieth Congress of the Communist Party of the Soviet Union is in *Khrushchev Remembers*, vol. I (Boston: Little, Brown, 1970), pp. 559–618.

8. FBI Main Bureau File, p. 6 of No. 100-12304-381.

9. Robeson had been pursuing these ideas for at least seven years, as evidenced by a letter he wrote to Clara Rockmore, May 8, 1949. He had amassed voluminous scholarly evidence to substantiate his theory of "The Universality of the Pentatonic Folk Scale." His published articles, based on his vast notes on music, include "A Universal Body of Folk Music," in Paul's autobiography *Here I Stand* (Boston: Beacon, 1988), pp. 115–117; and "The Related Sound of Music," in Foner, ed., *Paul Robeson Speaks*, pp. 436–439.

10. FBI Main Bureau file document no. 100-12304-366, dated May 31, 1956, states that a member of the HUAC staff called the FBI to ask if the Bureau could confidentially advise the committee whether Robeson left his home prior to June 12. It had occurred to the staff of the committee that "if it can be shown that Robeson engaged in any travel outside his home between May 29 and June 12, it will be possible for the Committee to cite him for contempt." However, a note, written in Hoover's hand and signed with his initial "H," reads, "I don't think we should be making investigations for the House Committee."

11. Paul's complete testimony appears along with his statement in Foner, ed., *Paul Robeson Speaks*, pp. 413–436; see also Eric Bentley, ed., *Thirty Years of Treason: Excerpts from Hearings before the House Committee on Un-American Activities 1938–1968*

(New York: Viking Press, 1971). I have edited the text of the testimony to convey the essential exchanges between Paul and the committee but have not always indicated the missing sections with ellipses.

12. *Baltimore Afro-American* and *San Francisco Sun-Reporter*, both June 23, 1956; *Charlottesville-Albemarle (VA) Tribune*, June 22, 1956. For the mainstream press, see the *New York Journal-American*, *New York Daily News*, and United Press, all June 13, 1956.

13. *Khrushchev Remembers*, vol. II (Boston: Little, Brown, 1974), pp. 196–207 (Poland); pp. 415–429 (Hungary); pp. 430–437 (Suez crisis). *Baltimore Afro-American*, November 17, 1956 (Paul's remarks about the Hungarian rebellion).

14. Taylor Branch, *Parting the Waters: America in the King Years, 1954–63* (New York: Simon and Schuster, 1988), pp. 192–194; Klinkner and Smith, *The Unsteady March*, pp. 246–248.

15. *Daily Worker* and *New York Times*, both November 6, 1956 (Supreme Court ruling).

11. Rising from the Ashes (1957–1958)

1. Robeson, *Here I Stand*.

2. The term "scientific socialism" is the one Marx used to describe his theoretical works.

3. FBI memorandum, May 29, 1957, Main Bureau File, No. 100-1234-403 (re Robert Johnson); letter from Frances Knight to Paul Robeson, Main Bureau File, No. 100-12304-417, August 9, 1957 (re passport denial and lifting of restrictions on travel where no passport was required).

4. *Manchester Guardian* (England), May 4, 1969 (letters); *Daily Worker* (England), May 29, 1957.

5. FBI Main Bureau File, No. 100-12304-405.

6. *Los Angeles Herald-Dispatch*, July 4, 1957.

7. *Sacramento Union*, October 27, 1957; *Sacramento Bee*, October 26, 1957.

8. *Pittsburgh Courier*, November 21, 1957.

9. *Daily Mirror* and *Daily Worker*, January 15, 1958 (television contracts); *Times* (London), January 16, 1958 (invitation to play Gower in *Pericles* at the Shakespeare Theatre). Headlines: *Melody Maker*, January 18, 1958 ("Paul Robeson Tour Looks Doomed!"); *Daily Mirror*, February 3, 1958 ("America should stop worrying about the words and let the world have music"); syndicated columnist Hannen Swaffer wrote his column on January 19, 1958, under the headline "Robeson, Victim of Hate."

Letter from Frances Knight, director, Passport Office to Leonard Boudin; January 17, 1958; letter from Boudin to Deputy Undersecretary of State Loy Henderson requesting reconsideration of refusal, January 31, 1958; letter from Boudin to Paul Robeson confirming meeting to review complaint to be filed, February 3, 1958 (PERC).

10. The rest of the black press followed suit: *Pittsburgh Courier*, February 22 and March 29, 1958; *Chicago Crusader*, Chicago, March 8, 1958; *Herald Dispatch*, May 8, 1958.

11. The party activity in support of Robeson's book is detailed in Robeson's FBI files. One document cites an informant who had access to the party accounting files on book sales (Main Bureau File, No. 100-1204-509, June 18, 1958).

12. Letters from Paul Endicott to Eslanda Robeson, January 25 and February 8, 1958 (PERC).

13. Headlines: *San Francisco Call-Bulletin* and *San Francisco Chronicle*, February 10, 1958; *San Francisco Chronicle*, February 5, 1958. Reviews: *San Francisco Chronicle* and *Oakland Tribune*, February 10, 1958.

14. *Oregonian*, February 19, 1958.

15. Letters from Paul Endicott to Eslanda Robeson, March 18, 19, and 29, 1958 (PERC).

16. *News Chronicle* (United Kingdom), undated March article, 1958; letter from Indira Gandhi to Eslanda Robeson, February 28, 1958 (PERC); *Baltimore Afro-American*, March 22, 1958 ("The Facts of Robeson vs. Dulles"); *New York Amsterdam News*, undated article, March 1958 ("Little Rock, Robeson Interest South Africans").

17. Dispatch from Undersecretary Herter to U.S. consul general Turner, March 12, 1958; dispatch from Ambassador Bunker to Secretary Dulles, March 18, 1958; Memorandum of Conversation (with Indian ambassador Mehta), March 21, 1958; dispatch from Secretary Dulles to U.S. consul general Turner, March 26, 1958.

18. *Amrita Bazar Patrika* (Calcutta), April 10, 1958; *Blitz News Magazine*, April 12, 1958; *Lucknow National Herald*, April 10, 1958; *Delhi Times of India*, April 10, 1958; *Bombay Free Press Journal*, April 10, 1958; *New York Times*, March 21, 1958; *Pittsburgh Courier*, March 29, 1958; *Afro-American*, March 29, 1958.

19. *National Guardian*, undated April article, 1958; *Daily Worker*, June 15, 1958; ticket to Moscow concert tribute, April 9, 1958.

20. *New York Herald Tribune*, April, 1, 1958; letter from Eslanda Robeson to Glen Byam Shaw, April 11, 1958 (Actors' Equity); *Jet*, April 17, 1958.

21. *Reporter*, April 17, 1958.

22. *Pittsburgh Courier*, April 19, 1958 (Chicago concert); April 26 and May 3, 1958 (Pittsburgh concert).

23. *New York Times*, May 10, 1958; *Musical America*, vol. 58, no. 7 (June 1958). See also: *Baltimore Afro-American*, May 17, 1958; *National Guardian*, May 19, 1958; *New York World-Telegram*, May 10, 1958; *Down Beat*, May 29, 1958; *Newsweek*, May 19, 1958.

24. *New York Times*, June 17, 1958 (Supreme Court decision); *New York Post*, June 25, 1958 (issuance of Paul's passport); cable from Glen Byam Shaw to Eslanda Robeson, June 28, 1958; letter from Pablo Neruda to Paul Robeson, undated, July 1958; letter from Eslanda Robeson to Mr. Petrzeka, June 30, 1958; letter from Eslanda Robeson to Mrs. Kislova, June 30, 1958; letter from Eslanda Robeson to Indira Gandhi, June 30, 1958 (all PERC).

12. A Hero's Welcome (1958–1960)

1. *Daily Sketch*, July 12, 1958; *News Chronicle* and *Daily Mirror*, July 12, 1958; *Daily Mail*, July 12, 1958.

2 *Times* (London) and *Evening News*, August 11, 1958.

3. The full text was transcribed from a tape recording and is in PERC.

4. Katanian became friends with the Robesons and subsequently made an excellent documentary film about Paul. I have drawn upon his 1971 memoir about the tour.

5. Conversations with my father.

6. Letter from Paul Robeson to Clara Rockmore, October 1958 (PERC).

7. October 13, 1958, manuscript by Eslanda Robeson: "Paul Robeson Sings in St. Paul's Cathedral" (PERC); *London Daily Herald* ("Robeson Triumphs at St. Paul's"); *London Daily Times, News Chronicle, Daily Mirror, Manchester Guardian*, all October 13, 1958.

8. *Baltimore Afro-American*, November 22, 1958. Essie subsequently wrote a series of articles on the Accra conference for the Associated Negro Press. She traveled to Accra with Shirley Graham DuBois, who was attending on behalf of the ninety-year-old Dr. W. E. B. DuBois and was to address the conference with a message from him.

9. *Sheffield Star* and *Times* (London), December 24, 1958.

10. The four other plays were *King Lear*, with Charles Laughton in the title role; *Coriolanus*, with Laurence Olivier as Coriolanus and Edith Evans as Volumnia; *A Midsummer Night's Dream*, produced by Peter Hall and with Laughton as Bottom; and *All's Well That Ends Well*, with Evans as the Countess. *Othello*, starring Paul, had generated the most excitement of all.

11. Letter from my mother to me and Marilyn, February 6, 1959; letter from Eslanda Robeson to Glen Byam Shaw, February 6, 1959; letter from Glen Byam Shaw to Paul and Eslanda, February 13, 1959 (PERC).

12. Robeson's remarks at the Sholem Aleichem tribute were taken from his handwritten notes (PERC).

13. *Birmingham Mail* and *Coventry Evening Telegraph*, April 8, 1959; *New York Times*, April 12, 1959; *Statesman*, April 18, 1959.

14. *Glasgow Herald*, May 2, 1959.

15. Conversations with my father.

16. The government of the United Kingdom has recently released portions of Robeson's MI-5 intelligence file to the public.

17. *New York Times*, August 5, 1959; *Baltimore Afro-American*, undated August 1959 editorial.

18. See the Hungarian newspapers *Esti Hirlap*, August 21, 1959 (interview); *Nepszabadsag*, August 22, 1959; *Sinház Muzsika*, August 28, 1959; *Nök Lapta*; August 27, 1959; *Magyar Nemzet*, August 22, 1959; *Elöre*, August 25, 1959; *Somogyi Neplap*, August 22, 1959.

19. *L'Humanité*, September 4 and 5, 1959.

20. *Baltimore Afro-American*, September 26, 1959; *New York Times*, September 19, 1959. The *Times* made no mention of Khrushchev's remarks about Robeson.

21. Letters from Essie to Marilyn and me, January 24–29, 1960 (PERC); *Trud*, January 19, 1960; *Vechernaya Moskva*, January 23, 1960; *Pravda* and *Izvestiya*, January 29, 1960 (ball-bearing plant).

22. *Scotsman*, May 2, 1960; *Bulletin* (Glasgow), May 2, 1960; *Daily Record* (Glasgow), May 2, 1960; *Evening Dispatch* (Edinburgh), May 3, 1960; *Glasgow Herald*, May 3, 1960.

23. *An Interim Report of the Select Committee to Study Governmental Operation with Respect to Intelligence Activities*, United States Senate, November 20, 1975; Thomas Powers, *The Man Who Kept the Secrets: Richard Helms and the CIA* (New York: Knopf, 1979), pp. 7, 146, 336–337, 341, 344–345, 374–375 (Lumumba); 7, 13, 35, 103, 106–107, 109, 119–122, 124, 129, 130, 132–133, 135–158, 287, 296, 336–337, 341–346.

24. Harold Evans, *The American Century* (New York: Knopf, 1998), pp. 480–481; *Khrushchev Remembers*, vol. I (Boston: Little, Brown, 1974), pp. 443–461.

25. John Marks, *The Search for the "Manchurian Candidate:" The CIA and Mind Control: The Secret History of the Behavioral Sciences* (New York: Times Books, 1979)

26. The text of Paul Robeson's affidavit is contained in document No. 100-12304-596, May 27, 1960, in Robeson's FBI Main Bureau file.

27. *L'Humanité*, September 1 and 3, 1960. Letter from Eslanda Robeson to the director of Interkoncert in Budapest, Hungary, August 14, 1960 (PERC).

28. I witnessed the panorama from a rooftop across the street.

29. FBI memorandum No. 100-12304-619, dated November 25, 1960, contains a summary of telephone conversations among Ben Davis, Lloyd Brown, and me concerning the Cuban invitation to Paul.

30. Letter from Eslanda Robeson to Mikhail Kotov, chairman of the Soviet Committee for the Defense of Peace, December 15, 1960 (PERC).

13. CIA Ambush? (1961–1963)

1. Documents released by the U.S. Senate Select Committee on Intelligence, chaired by Senator Frank Church of Idaho, in 1975; Marks, *The Search for the "Manchurian Candidate"*; Powers, *The Man Who Kept the Secrets*.

2. Conversations with my father and mother.

3. Conversations with my mother; also Duberman, *Paul Robeson*, p. 496.

4. Conversations in April 1961 with my father, my mother, and Alexander.

5. *Vechernaya Moskva*, March 21, 1961; *Izvestiya*, March 24, 1961; *Moscow News*, April 1, 1961; *Ogonyok*, no. 14 (April 1961); *Trud*, April 2, 1961. Letter from Essie to Paul, March 24, 1961. Conversations with Alexander, Irina, my mother, and my father, April 1961. Memorandum No. B03437, March 28, 1961; Memorandum No. B00232, March 31, 1961; Memorandum No. B00251, April 28, 1961 (all U.S. Department of State).

6. Conversation with Paul's translator, Irina, April 7, 1961.

7. John Marks wrote the following about LSD in his book *The Search for the "Manchurian Candidate"*: "LSD tended to intensify the subject's existing

characteristics—often to extremes. A little suspicion could grow into major paranoia, particularly in the company of people perceived as threatening" (p. 60). On p. 69 he wrote, "An LSD trip made people temporarily crazy, which meant mentally ill to the doctors." And on p. 71 a subject describes his hallucination from LSD as "a dream that never stops—with someone chasing you." My father's natural suspicions had already been amplified by years of FBI harassment.

8. FBI Main Bureau File, No. 100-12304-629. There was also a flurry of CIA activity concerning Paul about this time, as confirmed by three heavily redacted CIA documents: March 3 and 13, 1961, memoranda and an April 7, 1961, dispatch.

9. My symptoms, like my father's, matched those of a subject to whom LSD has been administered. In some cases, LSD can cause acute depression and suicide. (See Marks, *The Search for the "Manchurian Candidate,"* pp. 71, 102.) LSD and other similar hallucinogenic drugs then in use by MKULTRA cause enhancement of the subject's extrasensory perceptions, as well as an exaggeration of the sensory responses.

10. Paul's June activities in London were described in detail by Essie in a July 7, 1961 letter to me and Marilyn. Essie described Paul's relapse and the trip back to Moscow in a July 29, 1961 letter to Marilyn and me.

11. For the Rosens' impression of Paul's condition, see Duberman, *Paul Robeson*, pp. 501–502 and footnote 8, p. 743.

12. FBI Main Bureau File No. 100-12304-631 (July 21, 1961 memorandum). The September 6, 1961 memorandum is unnumbered and addressed to the Chief, Investigative Division from the Special Agent in Charge at the FBI's New York Field Office.

13. Helen Rosen's recollection of these events appears in Duberman, *Paul Robeson*, p. 502, and footnote 10, p. 743.

14. Ibid.

15. In addition to 3 drams of paraldehyde, Dr. Flood listed 3 grains of Seconal, with a repeat of 3 drams, and 3 grains of sodium amytal. According to Flood, Paul would "cut this down himself as he improves further. He is also having Parstelin tabs. 2 daily."

16. The quotations are from the February 14, 1962, entry in Paul's Priory file. Letters from Eslanda Robeson to Helen and Sam Rosen, December 4, 14, 1961; April 10, 1962. These letters were included in the copies of 244 CIA intercepts between my parents in London and Moscow and family and friends in the U.S. that I obtained under the Freedom of Information Act.

17. Letters from Eslanda Robeson to the Rosens (February 11, 19, and 26, 1962; March 1 and 5, 1962), and to Marian Forsythe (March 16, 1962). Conversation with Dame Peggy Ashcroft, 1982; conversation with Elizabeth Welch, 1982.

18. In a letter dated January 17, 1964, to Dr. Pearlmutter in New York, Dr. Ackner acknowledged that during Paul's stay at the Priory, "The only treatment which had any effect, albeit temporary, was E.C.T."

Four years prior to Dr. Ackner's use of Insulin Coma treatment on Paul, he had performed the definitive study that discredited this treatment as dangerous and ineffective. B. Ackner, A. Harris, and A. Oldham, "Insulin Treatment of Schizophrenia: A Controlled Study,"*Lancet*, no. 1 (1957), pp. 607–611; Marks, *The Search for the "Manchurian Candidate,"* p. 133.

The Priory's official listing of the drugs administered to Paul (see Summary Report, June 21, 1963) includes ten: the hypnotic antianxiety drugs Paraldehyde, Seconal, Meprobamate and Sodium Amytal; the antipsychotics Parstelin and the far milder Largactil; the antidepressants Tryptizol, Pertofrane (tricyclics) and Nardil (a monoamine oxidase inhibitor with questionable side effects), and Marsalid (a powerful antidepressant that can damage the liver if not carefully monitored).

The chronological entries in the files reveal the use of powerful drugs not acknowledged in the Summary Report: insulin (used as insulin coma treatment), Nembutal and phenobarbitone (hypnotic antianxiety drugs); Steladex (an amphetamine psychostimulant); Carbritol; and Delatestryl and testosterone (anabolic steroids).

19. Marks, *The Search for the "Manchurian Candidate,"* pp. 133, 134, 137, 223–224; K. Singer, "Psychotropic Drugs in Medical Practice,"*Bulletin of the Hong Kong Medical Association*, vol. 24 (1972).

20. FBI memorandum, April 19, 1962; Main Bureau File, No. 100-12304-453, April 17, 1962 (re: Rusk).

21. Letter from Essie to Marilyn and me, May 27, 1962. Helen Bailey, the U.S. consul, reported to the State Department that Paul "appeared to be a very frail and subdued old man" (FBI memorandum, Main Bureau File, No. 100-12304-654, May 31, 1962).

22. Conversation with my father, 1964; letters from Essie to John Abt and Ben Davis, July 13, 1962; photocopy of Paul's original July 25, 1962, noncommunist affidavit; letter from Abt to Essie and Paul, July 17, 1962.

23. Letters from Essie to the Rockmores, the Rosens, and to Marilyn and me, May 27, 1961.

24. Letter from Essie to Freda, August 25 1962; letter from Essie to Judy Ruben, September 1, 1962 (Paul's improved condition).

25. Letter from Peggy Middleton to Cedric Belfrage, January 27, 1963.

14. A Temporary Reprieve (1963–1965)

1. Essie article, "Re: Paul Robeson and Some Current Rumors," May 14, 1963 (PERC).

The FBI was aware of the *National Insider* article at a suspiciously early date. A memorandum dated January 3, 1963, from Hoover to the Chicago special agent in charge cited a December 21, 1962, letter containing a reference to an article "purportedly written by Paul Robeson concerning Robeson's breaking with the Communist Party" that had appeared "in a scandal sheet type paper called the *National Insider*." Since this paper was a weekly and the publication date of the first part of the article was January 6, 1963, the December 21, 1962, date of the FBI letter mentioned by Hoover indicates that the FBI may have had advance knowledge of the article.

The memorandum was part of Hoover's personal Counterintelligence Program file (No. 100-3-104-99) and points to the possibility that the FBI planted the story. This possibility is enhanced by similar January 7 and 15 memoranda (No. 100-3-104-121 and No. 100-3-104-?). The January 7 document references a Paul Robeson London file (No. 100-1182), and is a request of the London legal attaché by Hoover to advise the Bureau of any London articles about Paul's alleged break with communism. The January 15 reply from the legal attaché lists a London intelligence file No. 100-1666 (possibly a link with MI-5) and states that, "no information regarding Robeson's break with the Communist Party is known at this time. Sources are being alerted and the Bureau will be further advised."

2. The FBI was probably aware of our meeting and the preparations to move Paul from the Priory. Memoranda dated March 29 and April 12, 1963, are apparently concerned with the Hurwitts' 1963 travel plans, which included a vacation in England. A memorandum dated May 4, 1963, from the FBI's London legal attaché to the Bureau referred to a May 2, 1963, article in *Le Figaro*, a conservative French newspaper, that claimed that Paul had "just returned to the U.S. completely disillusioned, aged, ruined and alone."*L'Humanité*, the Communist Party newspaper, denied this story on May 3. Also on May 3, 1963, Harry Francis published a rebuttal in the *Daily Worker*.

A CIA cable, dated May 21, 1963, and addressed to CIA director John McCone, confirmed the Agency's interest in the controversy over Paul's falsely attributed "disillusionment."

3. Conversation with Micki Hurwitt, 1982. The Priory's June 21, 1963, Summary Report on Paul lists paraldehyde as a drug consistently administered to him throughout his stay.

4. Conversations with my parents, 1964; conversation with Harry Francis, 1982.

5. The August 25 *Sunday Telegraph* article added the false claim that Paul was being "abducted" to East Berlin on the Polish Airways flight.

6. Conversations with my mother; conversations with Harry Francis, 1982. Eslanda Robeson, "Kidnapped! A True Story," serialized in the *Baltimore Afro-American*, November 2, 9, and 16, 1963; *Daily Sketch* and *Daily Mirror*, August 26, 1963; *New York Daily News*, August 30, 1963.

7. CIA cables, Nos. 201-11448-309 and -310; U.S. Information Service document, No. 018373. The CIA's reference to a blacked-out source that "interested itself in developing a story on Robeson" may apply to the FBI as the sponsor of the *National Insider* series on Paul.

8. Duberman, *Paul Robeson*, pp. 516–519. Conversations with my mother; letter from Elliott Hurwitt to Essie, September 20, 1963 (PERC); letters from Essie to Helen Rosen, October 4 and 15, 1963 (CIA intercepts; see note 16, chapter 13). Report on Paul from Dr. Baumann of the Buch Clinic to Dr. Edward Barsky, December 14, 1963 (PERC).

9. Letter from Essie to the family, December 13, 1963 (PERC). Conversations with Dr. Barsky and Dr. Pearlmutter.

10. FBI Main Bureau File, No. 100-12304-691. Conversations with Harry Francis, 1982. Conversation with my father, 1964 (Kennedy).

11. From Paul Robeson's handwritten notes (PERC).

12. *New York Herald Tribune, New York Times, New YorkDaily News, New York Post,* all December 23, 1963; *New York Herald Tribune, New York Journal-American,* December 25, 1963; *New York Amsterdam News,* January 4, 1964; *Pittsburgh Courier,* January 11, 1964.

13. Dr. Hurwitt transmitted the details of Essie's medical prognosis to Dr. Pearlmutter, who had treated her previously.

14. Dr. Pearlmutter's medical notes during the months after his arrival reveal that Paul's medication consisted mainly of Librium, with occasional moderate dosages of Elavil, Cogentin, Florinef, and chloral hydrate. Of the medications other than Librium, only Elavil was prescribed consistently.

15. In late February 1964, Essie spoke at a Carnegie Hall tribute to Dr. W. E. B. DuBois, who had died in Ghana on August 27, 1963. In a final act of defiance, DuBois had joined the Communist Party USA a few months before he died. On April 23, 1964, Essie spoke at a symposium on "Marxism and Democracy," held at the Sheraton-Atlantic Hotel in New York City and sponsored by the American Institute for Marxist Studies.

16. Letter from Eslanda Robeson to Dr. Carlton Goodlett, a San Francisco friend, April 1, 1964 (PERC).

17. Paul's press release was reprinted in full in the *San Francisco Sun-Reporter,* the *New York Amsterdam News,* and the *Baltimore Afro-American* on September 5, 1964.

18. Letter from Essie to Mikhail Kotov, November 22, 1964 (PERC); *Worker,* November 16, 1964.

19. *New York Times* and *New York Herald Tribune,* both January 17, 1965.

20. James Farmer, *Lay Bare the Heart: An Autobiography of the Civil Rights Movement* (New York: Arbor House, 1985), pp. 297–298.

21. Independent black notables, such as Bishop W. J. Walls of the A.M.E. Zion Church; scholar Dr. Charles H. Wesley; columnists J. A. Rogers and P. L. Pratis; historians Lerone Bennett Jr. and Sterling Stuckey; comedian Dick Gregory; Dr. Benjamin E. Mays, president of Morehouse College; and musicians M. B. Olatunji and John W. Coltrane were among the enthusiastic sponsors. The same was true of their white counterparts, including Dr. Linus Pauling; journalists I. F. Stone and Nat Hentoff; artists Rockwell Kent and Raphael Soyer; film star Viveca Lindfors; and physicist Philip Morrison.

Letter from Roy Wilkins to Ossie Davis, April 8, 1965; letter from David Susskind to *Freedomways,* April 2, 1965.

22. The first verse of the "Song of the Warsaw Ghetto Uprising" ("Zog Nit Keynmol").

23. See *Freedomways,* vol. 5, no. 3 (Summer 1965) for Robeson's and Lewis's speeches, as well as a description of the Salute. See also the *Daily Worker,* May 2, 1965.

15. "No Cross; No Crown" (1965–1976)

1. A tape recording of Robeson's appearance at the First Unitarian Church of Los Angeles is in PERC.

2. Letter from Essie to family, May 31, 1965 (PERC). Conversations with my parents, Mary Helen Jones, and Revels Cayton.

3. Undated 1965 note from Dr. John Rockmore to me. Kline, who had developed and experimented with the powerful psychoactive drugs reserpine and Marsalid, as well as lithium, headed psychiatric research at Rockland State Hospital. He also served as an authority on behavior modification ("mind control"), as did Dr. Ackner in England.

4. Kiev's background appears in a June 1, 1997, article in the *Psychiatric Times* (vol. 14, no. 6). John Marks, *The Search for the "Manchurian Candidate,"* pp. 162, 147–149, 156, describes the MKULTRA research programs at Harvard, Cornell, and Johns Hopkins.

5. When I requested Paul's medical records from Dr. Kline and Gracie Square Hospital, Kline claimed to have lost the files, whereas the hospital refused to provide them. I contacted a member of the hospital management, one of Paul's admirers, and he managed to retrieve the records and give me a copy.

6. Dr. Kiev, in telephone conversations with Martin Duberman, said that, contrary to his usual practice, he thought the combination of Valium and Thorazine was appropriate in Paul's case. See Duberman, *Paul Robeson*, p. 758, note 39.

7. The Vanderbilt Clinic issued an inaccurate statement that Paul had been mugged, although the nature of his injuries indicated that they had been caused by a fall and the police report cited no sign of assault. Essie issued a statement saying Paul suffered from occasional loss of balance and had apparently fallen. Both statements appeared in the press (*New York Journal-American*, October 18, 1965; *New York Times*, October 19, 1965).

8. An announcement of my mother's death was placed in the *New York Times*, and the Associated Press ran an obituary under the heading, "Eslanda Robeson: Wife of Singer, Author of Books." It appeared in newspapers nationwide on December 15, 1965, and read, in part:

> Eslanda Robeson, 68, wife of Negro singer Paul Robeson and an author in her own right, died yesterday, almost exactly two years after the couple returned to this country from a five-year self-exile in Russia. [The Robesons never lived in Russia, nor were they in "self-exile."] On Dec. 22, 1963, Robeson, a longtime friend of Russia, and his wife returned to the homeland he had once labeled "an insolent, dominating America."
>
> Mrs. Robeson was the author of *African Journey*, and *Paul Robeson, Singer* [the correct title is *Paul Robeson, Negro*], a biography of her husband. She was also credited with steering him from a law career to the stage.

9. Conversations with Marian Forsythe; letters from Marian Forsythe to Lee Lurie, November 7, 1966, and April 24, 1967.

10. These materials constitute the Paul and Eslanda Robeson Collections, currently housed at the Moorland-Spingarn Research Center at Howard University in Washington, D.C. The Jumel Terrace house was sold in August 1967.

11. *Morning Star* (London), April 8, 1968.

12. Lee Lurie, in a letter dated August 27, 1969, requested that Dr. Pearlmutter send Paul's medical records to the Philadelphia doctors, who were "weighing the possibilities of shock treatment and other measures." Lurie described Paul's condition as "critical."

Conversations with Lloyd Brown; letter from Lloyd Brown to Lee Lurie, September 25, 1969.

13. A generally positive review of the Salute appeared in the *New York Times*, April 16, 1973.

14. A wide selection of condolences was published in *Paul Robeson: Tributes, Selected Writings* (New York: Paul Robeson Archives, 1976). The program for the funeral service, as well as the condolences, are in PERC.

The ten other pallbearers were Revels Cayton, Gil Green, John Killens, Joshua Lawrence, Vaughn Love, David T. Lynn Jr., Steve Nelson, Dr. John Rosen, Hope Stevens, and Douglas Turner Ward.

INDEX

Italic page numbers indicate illustrations.